MANAGEMENT AND ORGANISATION OF IRRIGATION SYSTEM

C.S. RAGHUVANSHI

ATLANTIC PUBLISHERS AND DISTRIBUTORS

Published by
ATLANTIC PUBLISHERS AND DISTRIBUTORS
B-2, Vishal Enclave, New Delhi-27
Phones 5413460, 5429987

Sales Office
4346/4C, Ansari Road, Darya Ganj,
New Delhi-110 002
Phones 3273880, 3285873
Fax 91-11-3285873

ISBN 81-7156-560-3

Typeset at
APD Computer Graphics, Delhi
Printed in India at
Fine Offset Press, Delhi-110 002

PREFACE

Every institution requires methods for decision-making, ways of coordinating activities of the undertaking, ways of communicating information and ideas, and ways for evaluating the success of an enterprise in meeting its objectives, which are the managers' concern for accomplishing organisational goals or objectives. However, the management pertains to that most unpredictable phenomenon – the human beings, which signifies the handling of people towards accomplishment of desired objectives by establishing an environment favourable to performance.

Management of industrial units, public and private undertakings and large agricultural farms is a common practice. Management is necessarily a broad one and it involves doing the job through people and that signifies 'the human/personnel side of management is extremely important'. The managerial functions of planning, organising, motivating and controlling are relevant regardless of the type of organisation or level of management with which one is concerned. But the irrigation management is hardly twenty years old which reminds us that our concern is with every level of personnel of the irrigation system. This aims at devoting with a large part of its attention to organisation. Once an organisation has been engineered, it must be staffed and continue to be staffed effectively. Thus, an organisation may either be more concerned with line of authority, channels of communication, or patterns of influence and loyalty in Irrigation Management. These elements play an important role in water distribution policies. In our country every state is free to decide its own water distribution policy according to its traditions, concepts and values about water, hence there are as many policies as the number of states. Although these policies differ in their aims and objectives, yet the management of them, has one common feature *i.e.* complete dependence on farmers for constructing a community channel called water course, for linking their holdings with public distributary. Farmers' motivation for such a venture naturally depends upon the benefits which a distribution policy can ensure for them. Of the several constraints which a water distribution policy has to face, the most important is the dichotomy of control over water of the state and the farmer, and each one has a different goal. Therefore, it is managed from different points of view. But, without effective farmers' participation to construct and maintain improved water courses, the benefits of new technology *viz.* improved seeds, fertilisers, pesticides, improved implements, processing, marketing and farm credit may not be realised. Water is not alone a critical input responsible to boost up agricultural production. For a balanced and sustained development of agricultural and rural economy, an equitable distribution of land and fertilisers, pesticides, improved varieties of seeds, and farm finance are also essential.

In an agricultural country like India, nothing can be more tragic than the fact that in some of its irrigation projects, the pace of actual utilisation of water remains far behind its planned schedule. The reasons for this can be traced to either some drawbacks in design or execution, or to the adoption of such distribution policies as fail to motivate farmers' involvement in irrigation management. Whereas the drawbacks in design or execution are somewhat remediable even at a later stage, but such distribution policies which do not motivate the farmers' involvement, are irreversible after commissioning the project. Either situation results in large scale discontentment amongst farmers causing lop-sided development, economic disparaties and social tensions in the command of a project. The low productivity of canal irrigated lands has been traditionally ascribed to poor water management in the command of the irrigation system. Above all, the poor performance of the irrigation schemes may be attributed to the fundamental weaknesses in the human processes of planning, organisation and management which cannot be overcome with any amount of investment in technological hardware.

Among others the most important factors that have been held responsible are irrigation water control and allocation, inequitable distribution of water to users, drainage systems at the micro-level, failure to level and reshape the fields, unreliable supplies of water at times and in the quantities required by the crops, operation and maintenance of the existing systems. Also the farmers' participation in irrigation management continues to be lacking.

The expansion and exploitation of the water resource is highly expensive in terms of energy costs and even then the efficiency of the developed system remains low to very low. Unfortunately in our country more attention has been given towards the development of water resources but the problem of efficient utilisation of water on the farmers' field has not received due attention. Over 30,000 crores of Rupees have been invested for developing irrigation potential of nearly 70 million hectares in the country during the last 40 years through various major, medium and minor irrigation projects. The poor performance of irrigation projects in terms of potential created and utilised in our country has witnessed highest concern in recent years at national and international levels.

The average foodgrain production under rainfed conditions is only 0.8 tonnes/ha while 2.8 tonnes per hectare under irrigated conditions against 4 to 5 tonnes/ha in most of the developed countries, which facts vouch that 70 million hectares irrigated and 105 million hectares unirrigated lands can produce 170 million tonnes and 70 million tonnes foodgrains, sugar, oil, pulses, etc. respectively through rational methods of resource allocation including improved water management and the use of improved agricultural technology, provision of necessary inputs, backed by extension services and adequate marketing facilities, which could be achieved through efficient management and organisation of irrigation systems, and interdisciplinary approach. For an efficient management of irrigation projects, management must devote a large part of its attention to its organisation. However, no sincere efforts have been made to use any of the tools of management, which is much more needed after introduction of High Yielding Varieties of seeds. This has added a new dimension to the management of public canals.

It is also estimated that the country would be requiring 230 to 240 million tonnes of foodgrains to sustain the population growth to the tune of 950 millions expected by the end of this century. To achieve the above targets it is essential to have irrigated land over 113 million hectares to meet the food, sugar, oil and fibre demand of increased population by 2000 A.D. The rapid growth in population which shows no signs of slowing down has further intensified the demand for sustenance of mankind dependent on the water resources which are already scarce.

This book addresses this crucial but neglected element in the equation of efficient irrigation management through an interdisciplinary approach particularly the management and organisation, water distribution, cropping pattern, diagnostic analysis of irrigation system, complementary inputs, land reforms, farmers' participation, pricing of water and energy, economic and financial evaluation, institutional needs for water conservation, command area development etc. This can be achieved through structuring of individuals and functions into productive relationships in an organisation.

This necessitates the need for education, training and timely refresher courses on these aspects which have to be a recurring process for equiping the irrigation engineers with the latest management technique and systematic application from the premise that irrigation management is best regarded as a socio-technical enterprise, where the human dimension interacts with the physical and technical ones. The book thus covers a series of organisational variables and human behaviour backed with critical inputs, institutional needs and services. Also an attempt is made to intersperse different disciplines to equip the readers with the knowledge of different disciplines involved in the process and it is a humble approach to highlight the role of each discipline and then productive interrelationship to the irrigation management strategy. This attempt, it is felt would not only serve the purpose of various curriculums being run by different Institutes/Universities and Colleges in the field of Irrigation Management but as for the individual study too. The subject matter of each related discipline has been given due weightage and it has been tried to be illustrative through various examples for easy grasping and practice in class lectures, tutorials and field exercises for diagnosing the problems of water and land resources system. All the physical, biological, social, economical and farmers' behavioural aspects have been duly covered and discussed for better understanding the management and organisation.

It is impossible to acknowledge the assistance of all those who have contributed to this work, but special appreciation is due to Prof. C.P. Sinha, Director NERIWALM, Tejpur, Assam and Dr. S.K. Rajput, R.S.M. (P.G.) College, Dhampur whose critical advice and support made it possible for me to complete the project. My special thanks to Prof. Brijesh Chandra, R.C. Bhatnagar, Prof. R.S. Virmani, Shri Indrajeet Singh, Dr. B.S. Rohal and Dr. R.P. Singh for their constant encouragement which gave me strength for this project. For the patience of my sons Tarun and Shailendra, and daughter-in-law Meenakshi, who eventually got quite tired of "what book", I am very appreciative. To my wife, Shashi who tirelessly helped in this project, I acknowledge a very special debt. Of course, the responsibility for what finally has been presented is entirely mine.

C.S. RAGHUVANSHI

CONTENTS

CHAPTER 1

MANAGEMENT AND ORGANISATION OF IRRIGATION SYSTEM

Introduction

Every institution requires methods for decision-making, ways of co-ordinating activities of the undertaking, ways of the success of an enterprise in meeting its objectives, which are the managers' concern for accomplishing organisational goals or objectives. Management pertains to that most unpredictable phenomenon – the human beings, which signifies the handling of people towards accomplishment of desired objectives by establishing an environment favourable to peformance.

Management[1] of industrial units, public and private unndertakings and large agriculture farms is a common practice. But irrgation management is hardly twenty years old which reminds us that our concern is with every level of the irrigation system. This goes devoting with a large part of its attention to organisation. For an efficient management of irrigation projects, the role of organisation (Irrigation Department and Farmers) – channels of communication, patterns of influence, lines of authority and loyalty, which can ensure some sort of efficiency, equity and social justice, cannot be over-emphasized. This necessitates that irrigation management must devote a large part of its attention to its organisation.

Management Defined

Management involves doing the job through people. Management, thus, must set objectives. Without objectives managemet is difficult.

---

1. "Today's manager requires multi-disciplinary skills. The traditional kind of specialisation in single areas like Marketing or Agriculture is no longer sufficient."

Clear-cut objectives can give a sense of direction to the organisation that should improve co-ordination and heighten motivation.

It is 'the administration of business concerns or public undertakings'. It is a 'technique by means of which the purposes and objectives of a particular human group are determined, clarified and effectuated'. It is getting 'things done through other people'. It is a process by which a cooperative group direct action toward common goal. It is 'the accomplishment of desired objectives by establishing an environment favourable to performance by people operating in organized groups'. It is 'the unifying and coordinating activity which confines the actions of individuals into meaningful and purposeful group endeavour'.

A comnon thread that appears in different definitions of management is the manager's concern for accomplishing organisational objectives. Management pertains to the human behaviour under a wide range of pressures and influences, some not easily subject to measurement. John D. Rockefeller states, 'I will pay more for the ability to deal with people than any other ability under the sun.'

Management is often used interchangeably with administration. For example, organisation and management have been treated as elements of administration. However, some effort has been made to distinguish organisation and management from each other. Organisation is 'the structuring of individuals and functions into productive relationships'. Management is identified as 'the direction of these individuals and functions to achieve ends previously determined.' Thus, it is clear that management is limited to the handling of people toward objectives, while administration is broad enough to include 'the organization and direction of human and material resources to achieve desired ends.'

Management is necessarily a broad subject and it involves doing the job through people. In any case, it is clear that the human or personnel side of management is extremely important. We shall define management as working with and through individuals and groups to accomplish organisations' goals. Management, thus, applies to organisations whether they are business, irrigation or even families. To be successful, these organisations require their management personnel to have interpersonal skills. The achievement of organisational objectives through leadership is management. Thus, everyone is a manager in at least certain part of his or her life whether Irrigation Engineer at top level or lower level and farmer at his farm level (Fig. 1). However, the managerial functions of planning, organising, motivating and controlling are relevant regardless of the type of organisation or level of management with which one is concerned.

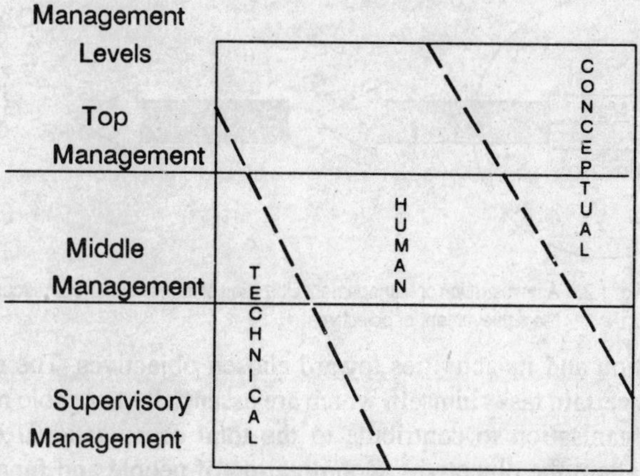

Fig. 1.1: Management Skills necessary at various levels of an organisation

Ever since people began forming groups to accomplish goals, they could not achieve as individuals, managing has been essential to assure the coordination of individual efforts. As society has come to rely, increasingly on group efforts and as many organised groups have become large, the task of managers has risen in importance. It is the task of every manager to design and maintain an environment in which people working together in groups are led to perform effectively and efficiently toward the attainment of group goals. Hence managing is essential in all organised cooperation, as well as at all levels of organisation in an enterprise. While weaknesses and difficulties may appear at any level of management, effective and perceptive management demands that all those responsible for the work of others, at all levels and in any type of enterprise, regard themselves as managers. It is in this sense that the term is used in this chapter.

Purpose

The purpose of management is to achieve certain specific ends and to maintain or improve the ability of an organisation to efficiently and effectively achieve objectives. Thus, management has a long-run orientation and most of its decisions are made with a view of the future. In fact, as a process, management is essentially the utilization of men and material resources toward specific objectives (Fig. 2).

However, the essence of management is coordination of people and functions which is because the manager directs and controls the

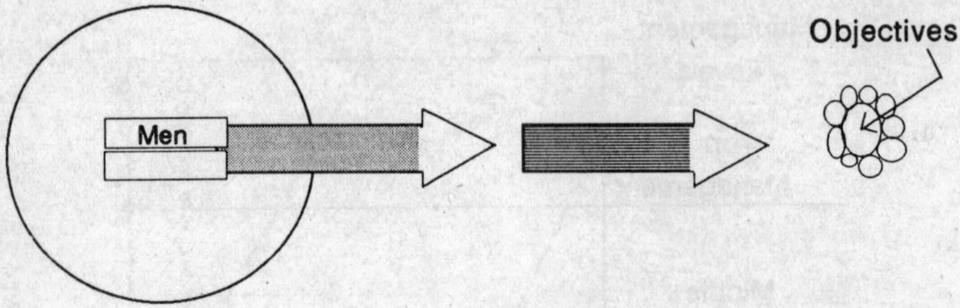

Fig. 1.2: Administration or Management Utlization of men and material resources toward the achievement of objectives.

organisation and its activities toward chosen objectives. The manager performs certain tasks himself, which are essentially to enable members of the organisation to contribute to the total organisational effort in order to attain the objectives. Coordination of people and functions is, of course, a complex process partly because people are complex individuals.

Elements of Management

Henri Fayol considered the elements of management as its functions– planning, organising, commanding, coordinating and controlling. A large part of his treatise is given to an examination of these functions and his observations are, on the whole, still valid. Fayol again and again points out that these apply not only to business but also to political, religious, philanthropic, military and other undertakings. These elements of management also apply to irrigation system to make it more effective and operate it efficiently. Since irrigation system requires management, the formulation of a theory of management is necessary to its effective teaching in the context of organisation and management of irrigation system. Once an organization has been engineered, it must be staffed, and continue to be staffed, effectively. Organisation is essentially the grouping of activities, the assignment of these activities to positions, and the grant of authority to persons occupying these positions to enable them to conduct such activities towards certain objectives. However, staffing is the process of filling the positions with the needed persons, keeping them busy and seeing to it that persons occupying the positions are able to improve or maintain their effectiveness in discharging the responsibilities of the positions.

In the context of the changing environment in which an irrigation system operates, and considering the natural complexity of handling people in group endeavours, organisation and staffing are continuing functions which must be re-examined periodically. Also, they are functions which must be dealt with, whenever possible with an eye for a balance between flexibility that would allow the viable 'tailoring' of the organisation and its movement toward desired ends, and stability that would promote organisational cohesiveness under the stresses of organisational pressures.

One does not need to strain to recognise the fact that with the advancement of civilisation, man has tended to be involved in multifaceted activities which require that he should work with other people in order to achieve certain purposes which emphasize cooperative and collective effort as distinguished from individual performance.

Organisation

Any study of management must devote a large part of its attention to organisation. In fact, organisation is concerned with channels of communication, with patterns of influence, and with lines of authority and loyality. Thus, in brief, organisation runs in terms of those elements: communication, influence, authority and loyalty. Traditionally discussions of organisation emphasize three primary types: line organisation, line-and-staff organisation and functional organisation.

Two concepts of effective organisation have developed which together comprise the theory of organisation: namely, the traditional organisation theory and the modern organisation theory. The traditional theory of organisation deals with the 'observations about the design-of-formal structure of organisation and the manner in which specialisation could be applied in the organisation process'.

Thus, under this theory, organisation is conceptually divided into three types, which are: the line organisation, the staff organisation and the functional organisation. This classification is based on the analysis of organisation as a structure of authority relationships.

Types of organisation

1. Line Organisation : The simplest type of organisation is the organisation, which is illustrated in the following Flow Chart 1.

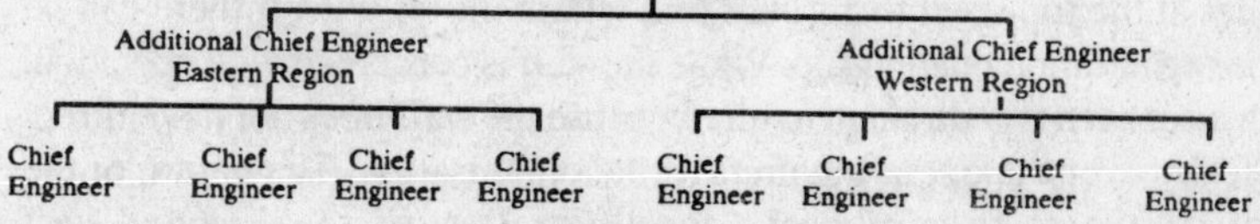

Flow Chart 1

Here the lines of authority are direct, with no advisory or auxiliary activities attached. Such an organisation is common in big states only. This form of organisation is simple, and clear-cut, but provides no room for staff specialists.

2. Line and Staff Oganisation : The line-and-staff organisation provides for advisory staff positions as given in the following Flow Chart 2. The term usually refers to those positions and departments that are of a purely advisory nature. They have the power to recommend, but have no authority to enforce their preferences on other departments.

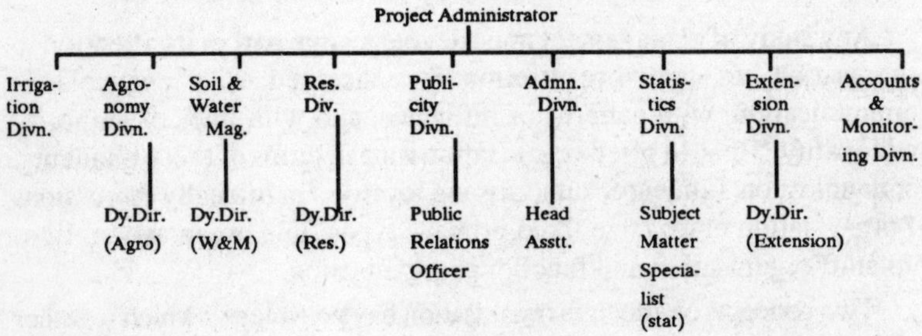

Flow Chart 2

However, the distinction between line, and line-and-staff organisation is that the line gives formal orders to next lower level, while the staff exerts its influence indirectly, through the line official superior to the particular staff official, not directly to the lower level.

The line organisation carries direct authority relationships from superior to subordinate, and each superior position has authority over position below it. The relationship is one of power and command from the top and obedience from below. It involves the main operational activities of the irrigation system. However, the staff organisation does not carry direct authority relationships between the members of the staff and those at the operating levels. Those in the staff are subordinate to the officer at the highest level and there is a direct relationship of authority from the officer at the top level to his staff and within the staff itself there can be a line organisation relationship. While the staff is concerned with operation, such a concern is indirect in nature because the staff does not have direct authority over the operating units of the organisation. The nature of the work of the staff is advisory for illustration of the line-and-staff organisations, see Flow Chart 2. The illustration shows that in an organisation like CAD's and irrigation departments, there is usually a mixture of the line and staff relationships.

The following are the advantages and disadvantages of line and line-and-staff organisations.

Line-organisation

Advantages: It is simple; there is a clear-cut division of authority and responsibility; it is stable, it makes for quick action. Discipline is easily maintained.

Disadvantages: The organisation is rigid and inflexible; there is lack of expert advice, key men loaded to the breaking point, the loss of one or two capable men may cripple the enterprise.

Line-and-staff Organisation

Advantages: It is based on planned specialisation, it brings expert knowledge to bear upon management, it provides more opportunity for advancement for able workers in that a greater variety of repsonsible jobs are available.

Disadvantages: Confusion may prevail about the relation of staff members to line positions, the staff may be ineffective for lack of authority to carry out its recommendations. Line supervisors may resent the activities of staff members feeling that the prestige and influence of line men suffer from the presence of the specialists.

A study of operating organisations reveals that few of the so called 'staff' departments are restricted to advisory or planning capacities. Within the area of their speciality, most such departments do, in fact, have some authority over lower line departments. Some staff officers are more influential than some line department heads. However, the cases of organisations following the strict theory of line-and-staff are rare.

Functional organisation as a concept 'permits a specialist in a given area to enforce his directives within a limited and clearly defined scope of authority'.

Functional Organisation

This form recognises that the specialists have authority over line officials at lower levels. However, even a 'typical' functional organisation is complex. It consists of a number of branches or divisions, each of which has staff specialists with counterparts in the central office. The organisation becomes functional when these specialists are, in part, responsible to their counterparts in higher headquarters. For example, if the Chief Engineer at Regional level is partly responsible to the over-all Irrigation Department at State level, the organisation is stressing functional lines of influence. A central line organisation almost exists alongwith functional channels, usually a branch sepcialist, or say at District level in Irrigation Department will think of himself as reporting primarily to the top line official in that district. F.W. Taylor applied the expression to a special kind of supervision at the shop level. Taylor believed that the task of the foreman should be split into a number of specialised task.

The choice among the three forms of organisaiton is, in fact, not a matter of selecting one package, but determining the right balance among the three. At one extreme is the line-organisation with no staff specialists at all, which is found to be rare. But at the other extreme is a form of functional organisation that de-emphasises the position of the line-organisation. Since there may be a tendency for the vertical functional channels to pull apart this extreme can present special difficulties of coordiantion. However, the pure line-and-staff organisation falls in-between. Thus, the typical organisation is best as a line-and-staff organisation with some measure of functional authority for certain specialists.

Informal Organisation

People have a tendency to cut across formal channels to communicate informally with other parts of the enterprise. Generally they are inclined to form small groups, whether management has planned for this or not. They are influenced by leaders who have been granted no formal authority by management. But they are motivated by group norms and social conventions not a part of their contract with their employers. In fact informal organisation is broadly defined to include not only unplanned communication and group formation, but also the customs, social norms, mores and ideals that are an important feature of such communication and such groups. Thus, informal organisation is a pervasive feature of all undertakings. The cliques of workers or managers that form at all levels are important illustrations, as are the restrictive devices which discourage employees from producing more than informally determined group quotas. This also includes the patterns of influence that some members of the organisation develop, even though these go far beyond the organisation plan Nevertheless, it is clear that informal organisation is necessary to the functioning of formal organisation.

Principles of Organisation

The traditional principles of organisation which can serve as general guidelines in the process of organising are:

1. Unity of command
2. Span of control
3. Scalar principle
4. Principle of departmentation
5. Principle of decentralisation
6. Principle of exception.

All these principles are intimately related to the basic fact that man, with his abilities and inabilities, his strengths and weaknesses, is able to do only so much. When he becomes part of a group endeavour – whether as a follower or as a leader – his upward, downward or lateral relationships with his fellow workers must be structured to maximise his contribution to the group effort.

These principles could be general guidelines and in the field of actual managerial practice, their application is a function of judgement which often must be based on a number of variables difficult to assess and predict. The behavioural sciences are responsible for an emerging theory of modern organisation which focuses attention on organisational behaviour from the standpoint of organisation as a system of human relationships. Research work in these sciences has now tended to change the traditional concepts of authority, influence, power, identification, loyalty and responsibility.

The unity of command principle requires that no member of the organisation should report to more than one man, which avoids conflicts of orders and promotes unified action. In actual practice, particularly in irrigation organisation (or in non-military organisations), the principle of the unity of command may permit some degree of deviation and allow persons down the line to receive instructions from various individuals. But the principle of span of control recognises the limitations of man as a supervisor and as a follower and it suggests the growing complexity of the superior's functions as his subordinates increase in number. However, the scalar principle which is known as the chain of command in military organisations, advocates a clear line of authority from the top to the bottom. The departmentation principle refers to the grouping of activities into specialised groups in order to facilitate staffing, direction and control, which are based on geographical location of activities, product or work process; or functional relationships. The principle of decentralisation suggests that decision-making and implementing action should be encouraged at the outer rings of the organisational circle or at the lower rungs of the organisational ladder, which helps in simplifying the work of the manager. The organisation pyramid encourages and facilitates centralisation, thus decentralisation becomes the key to effectiveness of management. The principle of exception advocates that decisions should be handled by lower managers, which seeks to make free top level managers from engagement with details and to provide them with more time for directional job's thinking and effort. Consequently, only unusual problems or extraordinary matters of information are referred to the top-level managers.

The structure of the organisation is a guide for most of the basic responsibilities of management which also provides a blueprint for the selection of people and staffing of the organisation. It provides the guide to communications among members of the organisation and a directive informing members of their expected performance or behaviour as members of the organisation. It provides a method of control over the performance of organisation members. The organisation structure is evaluated in terms of its contribution to the management task of coordinating activities for achievement of the enterprise objectives.

Structure

An organisation can be pictured in various ways to show the structure of an organisation *viz*., vertical charts, lateral organisation charts, linear charts, outline charts, 'level' organisation charts, functional charts or circular organisation charts. Organisation is essentially the allocation of activities and authority, hence the pictorial presentation of the organisation should as far as possible indicate the relationships which result from each allocation. However, no single pictorial presentation is complete by itself because the relationships are not capable of being entirely presented.

Organisations As Social Systems

We must recognise that the organistions in which most managers operate are social systems comprised of many inter-related sub-systems, only one of which is a human/social system. The focus of the human/social system is on the motivation and needs of the members of the organisation and on the leadership provided or required. The others are comprised of an administrative/structural sub-system, and information/

decision-making sub-system, and an economic/technological sub-system (Fig. 1.3).

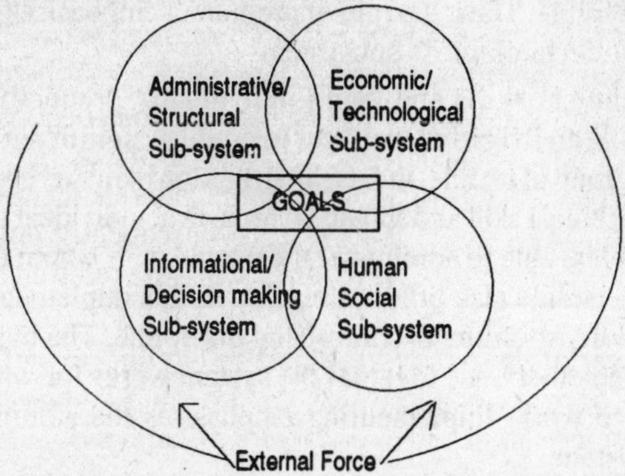

Fig. 1.3: The Interrelated sub-systems of an organization

The administrative/structural sub-system focuses on authority, structure, and responsibility within the organisaiton. 'Who does what for whom' and 'who tells whom to do what, when, and why'. But the informational/ decision-making sub-system emphasises key decisions and their informational needs to keep the system going. However, the main concern of the economic/technological sub-system is on the work to be done and the cost effectiveness of that work within the specific goals of the organisation. But it is much significant that wihtin a systems approach changes in one sub-system effect changes in other parts of the total system. If the total system, for example irrigation system, is functioning very well and is healthy, each of its sub-system is effectively interacting with one another. Therefore, an organisation in irrigation system over a sustained period of time cannot afford to over-emphasize the importance of one sub-system say technological sub-system at the cost of the others. The internal management of the organisation at the same time, cannot ignore the needs and pressures from the external environment.

Managerial Roles in a Social System

Ichak Adizes states four managerial roles which must be performed if an organisation is to run effectively. These four roles are producing, implementing, innovating, and integrating. But each of these managerial roles is related to one of the four social subsystems of an organisation (Fig. 1.3).

The role of producing assumed by the manager is expected to achieve results which is performed on account of possession of a functional knowledge of his field-like design, construction, performance evaluation, or any other discipline. Thus, the role of producing emphasises activities in the economic/technological subsystem.

Having technical skills and being individually productive do not necessarily enable an Irrigation manager to produce significant results in working with a group of people. In fact, an Irrigation manager should have more than just technical skill and should be more than individual producers. Managers should be able to administer the people with whom they work to see that these people also produce results. In this implementing role, managers schedule, coordinate, control and discipline. The managers in the role of implementers, see to it that the system works for which it has been designed to work. Implementing emphasises the administrative/ structural subsystem.

Although producing and implementing are important, yet in a changing environment managers must use their judgement. They must have the discretion to change goals and change the systems by which they are implemented. In this role managaers must be organisational entrepreneurs and innovators since, unlike administrators who are given plans to carry out and decisions to implement, entrepreneurs have to generate their own plan of action. They have to be self-starters. The innovating role, thus, emphasises the informational/decision-making subsystem.

Adizes, further states the three roles of producing, implementing and innovating in combination are insufficient for adequate managerial functioning. Therefore, for an organisation to be continuously successful, an additional role must be performed... integrating. Integrating is the process by which individual strategies are merged into a group strategy; individual risks become group risks; individual goals are harmonised into group goals; ultimately, individual entrepreneurship emerges as group entrepreneurship. The integrating role is considered to be adequately performed when a group can operate on its own with a clear direction in mind and can choose its own direction over time without depending on any one individual for a successful operation. It requires an individual who is sensitive to peoples' needs. Such an individual unifies the whole organisation behind goals and strategies. Integrating role stresses the human/social system.

Adizes contends that a certain style of mismanagement can be observed if any one of the four management roles is not performed in an organisation. Further Adizes argues, 'No one manager can manage alone'. It takes several to perform the process adequately, several people to perform roles which seem to be in conflict but really are complementary. While all the roles seem to be necessary for running an effective organisation, Adizes argues that if any one of the four roles can be truly indispensable for any executive, it is integration. If this people-part of the managerial role is not fulfilled, the entrepreneur will become a 'crisis maker', the administrator a 'bureaucrat' and the producer a 'loner'.

Motivation

Motivation is closely related to that of organisation. In organizing, interest lies in creating a structure or permitting one to grow that will encourage personnel to make full use of their skills and talents. There is a demarcation line between organisation and motivation. Organisation is concerned with relations among individuals (or positions), while motivation pays more attention to the attitudes and efforts of each individual separately.

Motivation is viewed from two angles. One that managers 'motivate' their employees or fail to do so. In this context, it implies that the concern is with how superiors influence subordinates. However, the dictionary defines a 'motive' as something within the individual which incites him to action. Basic needs of the individual result in his striving.

The nomistic theory accepts the notion of 'economic man', the man who acts only to increase his monetary rewards. Such a theory states that the higher the pay, the greater the effort. If pay is allowed to depend on effort, the effort will increase. The rewarding of 'correct behaviour' should lead to the 're-inforcement' of that behaviour. Fig. 1.4 illustrates 'greater effort not only leads to greater pay, but also the reward of greater pay stimulates greater effort'. This theory carries the following implications:

An individual incentive is more effective than a group incentive. In view of this, if an individual receives pay according to his own effort he can influence his own pay packet and will work harder. However, in a group incentive system, the whole group shares the rewards for his efforts, and the individual incentive is diluted. If some members of the group work harder and other relax, there may be strains and resentments on account of reward spread over the entire group, which is unfair.

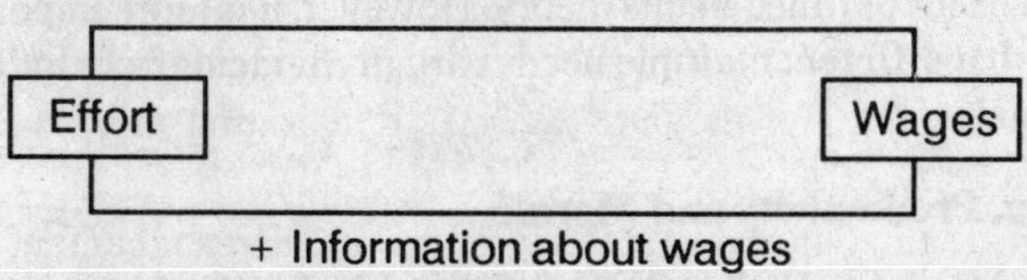

Fig. 1.4: Effort-Reward-Effort Model

The incentive is more effective, the more rapidly the wage payment reflects the added production. Bonuses at the end of the year are less effective than those at the end of the week, because the individual loses sight of rewards far off in the future.

The greater the reward for added output, the greater will be the stimulus. According to this line of reasoning, the Taylor differential piece-rate system which pays a higher piece rate for total output to workers surpassing 'standard' output, will provide an extremely high reward for reaching standard. A straight piece-rate will be more effective than a 50% bonus system, which shares the savings in wage cost resulting from higher productivity between the workers and management. The 50% bounus will be more effective than straight hourly pay.

Even the supporter of this theory would agree that management must weigh the benefits of an incentive system against its costs. Thus, differential piece rate might pay such large rewards as to increase wage costs faster than it raises output. The Taylor system is defective also as an incentive is placing too much pressure on the worker and creating too many tensions. However, some group bonus systems have produced remarkable results. But a number of profit-sharing plans have failed.

A more complete theory of *pluralistic* of motivation recognizes that individual work to fulfil a variety of needs, not one kind. These needs are: subsistence, social status, self-esteem, self-fulfilment. Monetary incentives very well fit into this framework *i.e.* pluralistic theory as the monetary rewards meet subsistence needs. Money is also a status symbol as it permits to purchase items that carry status. We could subsist on much lower levels of income but we could not properly clothe and house ourselves in a life style which would impress our fellow-beings. Several studies conducted in this context point out that employees are less concerned with the absolute level of their wages than in their relation to the wages of other workers. If workers feel pay relationships unfair, then they become discontented even though their pay may be high from the subsistence point of view. Even subsistence is a relative one which is partly socially determined. Thus, there is a very complicated interrelationship among the needs outlined in this theory. However, it is more important to recognise that different multiple needs vary in character from individual to individual.

Aspiration, Productivity and Morale

James, March and Harbert Simon constructed a model which emphasised on a psychological concept – 'level of aspiration'. Fig. 1.5 presents the aspiration level model.

The following are the main generalizations of the above:

1. The lower the individuals' satisfaction, the greater the search for alternative ways or better ways of doing the job.
2. The greater the search, the greater the expected reward, which means the more one searches for better ways of doing the job the higher his expectation of achieving higher rewards.
3. The greater the expected reward, the higher the satisfaction.
4. The higher the expected reward, the higher the level of aspiration.
5. The higher the level of aspiration, the lower the satisfaction.

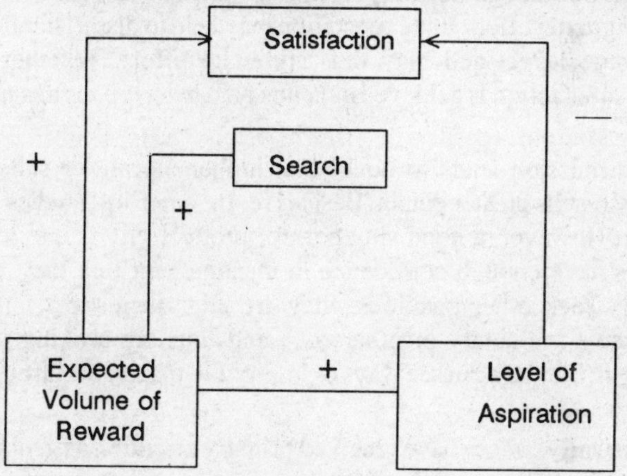

Fig. 1.5: General Model of adaptive motivated behaviour

Assuming an individual who is dissatisfied with his present, he searches for alternatives to improve the situation. For achieving this, one alternative may be to increase production in the expectation that this will increase the rewards, say the monetary rewards. Thus, the higher rewards (Fig. 1.5) lead to higher satisfaction. Simultaneously, the level of aspiration may increase which may result in that an individual having reached to this higher level, wishes to go on to greater heights. However, the increase in aspiration level lowers satisfaction. But if the level of aspiration rises almost the same rate as the expected reward, the individual will continue to be motivated by his mild dissatisfaction. If the level of aspiration does not rise while the rewards rise, the individual becomes complacent and his search activity declines. On the other hand, if the level of aspiration is much more than the possible reach of the individual, this may result frustration or even neurotic behaviour.

March and Simon conclude from this analysis that high satisfaction does not necessarily stimulate productivity. They state that motivation to produce 'stems from a present or anticipated state of discontent and a perception of a direct connection between individual production and a new state satisfaction'. From this, it appears that the March-Simon model is contradictory to the effort-reward-effort model, even if the model is broadened to include non-monetary incentives. The earlier model appears to imply that higher wages, by leading to higher satisfaction, stimulate greater effort. But according to March and Simon, dissatisfaction stimulates effort. The individual certainly expects higher satisfaction from the rewards of greater effort, this expectation may lead to dissatisfaction with present wage levels and may thus stimulate effort. Whether actual increased satisfaction is achieved depends on what happens to aspiration levels.

The discussion leads to doubt that higher morale or satisfaction necessarily results greater output. Besides recent empirical studies support this doubt. However, a good situation for productivity is one in which employees have enough confidence in management that they will not continually seek other positions; they are slightly restless with their present status (monetary or otherwise) and thus are seeking ways of improving it, but they can see ways of improving that status through their own efforts.

Historically, wages have received primary attention as a motivating force. Those who have studied wage incentives have not succeeded in separating the effects of the bonuses from the effects of other changes made at the same time. If there is an increase in output, it may well be due to the improvement in management rather than greater employee effort. It is not surprising to find that incentive systems are almost non-existence in Irrigation Systems' Management. Further, wage incentives are part of a total situation and research workers have not had success in separating the influence of wages from other factors. On the whole, incentive systems, if properly managed, are useful.

Socio-Psychological Concepts

In order to understand the socio-psychological impact in any work situation, one must understand the human behaviour and the way it influences the responses of people involved. The behaviour reflects the totality of a person, which is the composit whole of number of factors like values, attitudes, perceptions and motivation etc. Individuals do not work in isolation, they are and became part of the total system – so there is a constant interaction between the individual and the social environment around him – therefore it is essential to know the following concepts in knowing why people behave as they really do:

(i) *Values* : They are considered as standards which determine for an individual as to what is right or wrong at a given time in a society.

(ii) *Attitudes* : They are a sort of mental set, a pre-disposition, a frame of reference. In fact attitudes are the fundamental processes at systems whereby the individual orders his environment and behaviour on the basis of values. Therefore, we can say if values are the measure by which we order our social environment and attitudes are the manifestations of this order, it links these clearly to the basic assumptions of man's need for order and certainty –

(a) Values and attidues are mainly in connection with the study of man.

(b) Behaviour is shaped and maintained by its consequences.

(c) Values animate the person, they move him around his environment because they define its attractive and repelling sections.

(d) A value is a belief upon which a man acts by preferences. A value is an enduring belief.

(e) Values have two functions – standard and motivational.

(f) Values and attitudes are of central importance to the study of man.

(g) Value systems are not concerned with specific objects or persons, while attitudes are.

(h) Values are more abstract than attitudes.

(i) Values are more central in that they are more deeply enclosed in the person, perhaps part of his personality structure.

(j) One can speak of degrees of positive or negative attitudes.

It is not to eliminate values and attitudes, from the study of perceptions and motivaions, as they are also influenced by them because perception means the interpretation of experiences. It is the mental representation of the object etc. we see around.

The role of perceptions in our lives is to interpret experiences – but there is no sure way to find out how much of our interpretations can form to physical reality. It is believed that people's perceptions correspond by and large to the physical characteristics of the things they perceive. It can be said that perception is the attempt to explain how we observe the world around us. Perception is the process of gathering information. It is a highly personal process, it involves our past experiences, emotions, motivations, values, attitudes, conscious and unconscious processes as well. It is the foundation of our present and future knowledge. Besides, much of what we perceive is selective and reflects out personality characteristics as well as our social, religious and political memberships. They are also influenced by motives – as motives are energising forces – they compel a person to behave in a particular manner. In fact motives appear to be linked at least at two levels; one is the interclass dependence of motives for the function of an organism as a living entity; the other is at the situational level. Often several motives continue irrespective of their close to determine behaviour in a specific situation. So to sum up it can be said that any study concerning effect of socio-psychological factors should keep in mind the above mentioned variables.

Since the growth in agriculture is materially dependent on the increase in the production of critical inputs, *viz*., water, fertilizers, pesticides, and improved machines/implements, utilisable irrigation potential and manufacturing industries of the critical inputs have expanded tremendously during the last one and a half decade. The income of the farmers has increased due to application of irrigation and other critical inputs. The growing productivity of the rural sector due to the success of the increasing irrigation facilities and High Yielding Varieties (HYV) has changed the social values of the farmers. Their perception of their role in the social structure of society and their attitudes on problems of quality of life have remarkably changed, and this change could be an important source of motivation to them.

Social change is brought about by a number of factors *viz. technological, industrial, economic, ideological* and *religious*. No single factor has priority over all others. Some persons insist that technology is the basis of all changes in social relationships. Others are certain that the state of the industrial arts, not the same thing as technology, dominates other aspects of society. Still others maintain that the power relationships between social classes in the sense of one class owning the instruments of production are the most important. Ideological and religious factors also bring about basic modifications in status and role. Every society is a complex process of social interaction. However, with change, economic, ideological and religious overtones—all of these factors, operate in social change.

The question is what causes social change? There is no single answer. Each element in society influences every other and *vice versa*. Social change thus has no single cause. Instead, as person expresses it, there is a 'plurality' of possible origins of change. Likewise, there is no single and all embracing theory of social change.

Social change is so complex that it can be approached from a number of directions. One of these approaches is technology, which has become such an important cultural prime mover in modern society.

Oghurn says, "Technology changes society by changing our environment to which we, in turn, adapt. This change is usually in the material environment, and the adjustment we make to the changes often modifies customs and social institutions." This is the relationship between technology and social change. Technology is a cultural element, and this knowledge is part of the organised culture that is communicated from generation to generation. This cultural factor produces changes in the social environment ranging from the way men make a living, the way they rear their children and, indeed, to the number of children they will have. These adjustments involve changes in status and roles and hence are the stuff of social change.

The role of technology in social change has been the subject of considerable study. As said before, there is no single cause of social change, nor is there a single and all embracing theory of social change. Modifications in status and role may arise from religious, political or revolutionary changes, in which the role of technology is marginal. With the reservation, we may indicate the process by which technology, which is cultural instrument, gives rise to social change. In order of their occurrence the typical stages in this pattern are as follows:

1. Technological Innovations

An innovation is 'any thought, behaviour, or thing that is new because it is qualitatively different from existing forms'. An invention is a 'technological innovation, a new thing'. Technology is the application of pure science to the immediate, 'practical' ends of human beings. When the average person thinks of the changes brought about by 'science' he is usually thinking of technology and its manifold wonders. Many recent major modifications in status and role have followed innovations on the technological level, technological development is a recognized part of modern industry, and thousands of trained men are working on new applications of pure science. Changes on this level occur every day, and their combined effects upon human behaviour are literally impossible to calculate.

2. Economic Institutions

Economic institutions ordinarily feel the first impact of change from advances in technology. These institutions are the organised patterns of social relationships, existing for the production and distribution of goods and services. Comprehensive changes in economic institutions followed the series of technological and social changes known as the Industrial Revolution. The base for making a living moved the farm to the factory and from the country to the city. The size of the individual enterprise changed, as new methods of operation and financing became necessity to exploit technological innovations. In the modern world, the large corporation is an example of structural adjustment to a long series of technological changes.

The application of technological innovations to economic institutions results in the establishment of entirely new industries. The present country has seen the rise of such mass industries as the automobiles, steel, rubber, glass, petroleum, and textile industries, with chemicals, animation, and electronics, constituting even more recent industrial complexes. In a society increasingly dominated by small industries new social classes reflects the different productive functions. The big industrial unions are playing an important role in bringing about new power relations between labour and management.

3. Social Institutions

The organised patterns of relationships consisting the family, church, school, and government are next to feel the impact of social change. This is especially true of the structure of the institutions; it is less true of the concept of underlying cluster of values, which changes more slowly. Each individual plays a role in these institutions and the influences are brought to bear upon him from a number of sources. The structure of the family, for example, has undergone many important changes in recent decades because of the gainful employment of married women. With one in every four marrried women employed outside the home, the family will never be the same again. These and other changes have largely been communicated through technological innovations in industry. In the future the application of science to the cultural and biological fields will doubtless still further alter the family.

4. Social Values

The concepts on the basis of the institutions are the goals for which men strive, the ends they seek. Most of the basic values are grouped about the institutional patterns. They are deeply imbedded in the personality and remain long after the conditions that gave rise to them have disappeared. Technologies change, economic institutions follow suit, and other institutional structures undergo drastic modification but the values remain at heart. Behaviour is still defined by the values of an earlier day, and its situation, gives rise to social problems.

Leaving aside technological factors, there are cultural factors of social change as well. Cultural change is of interest to sociologists only to the extent that it produces social change. Since culture can be produced and borne only in social systems, a cultural change is a result either of the internal processes of the social system of reference or of the impact of some other social system.

REFERENCES

1. Koontz Harold and Cyril O'Donnell (1974), 'Management -- A Systems and Contingency Analysis of Managerial Functions', Sixth Edn., McGraw-Hill Kogkusha, Ltd, New Delhi.
2. James L. Douglas and Robert R. Lee (1971), 'Economics of Water Resources Planning', Tata McGraw-Hill Publishing Co. Ltd. 12/4, Asaf Ali Road, New Delhi-110002.
3. Hersey, Paul and Blanchard K. Kenneth (1982), 'Management of Organizational Behaviour : Utilizing Human Resources', Prentice-Hall of India Private Ltd., New Delhi, India.
4. Corey, G.L. 'Irrigation Water Management in India: A Farmer Involvement', Unpublished Report, 1981. The World Bank, New Delhi.
5. Pant, N. and Verma R.K. : 'Farmer's Organisation and Irrigation Management', 1983, Ashish Publishing House, New Delhi.
6. Raghuvanshi, C.S. : 'Socio-Economic Constraints in Adoption of Water Management Technology -- A Case Study of Salawa Command', Proceedings of the Seminar on Water Management Technology Transfer, May 1985, G.B. Pant University of Agriculture and Technology, Pantnagar, India.
7. Drilon, J.D. Jr. (1971), 'Introduction to Agri-Business Management', Vol. I, Asian Productivity Organization, Tokyo, Japan.

CHAPTER 2

FARMERS' PARTICIPATION IN OVERALL PLANNING AND MANAGEMENT OF IRRIGATION SYSTEM

Introduction

Water, as one of the essential resoruces in agricultural production, has several unique characteristics, especially in hill environments. Individual farmers[1] acting alone, can seldom acquire water for irrigation. Construction and maintenance of the structures to divert, convey and distribute water usually require investments beyond the capacity of a single farmer. Surface water cannot be easily stored and particularly by the individual farmer, in the way that fertiliser can be. It must be used when it is available or it is lost. Farmers generally cannot transport water economically over great distances, and the locations to which it can be conveyed are limited by the topography. In view of these facts, institutions are needed for the development and operation of irrigation systems. The form and function of these institutions vary depending on the physical, social and economic environments.

Institutions have been defined as 'complexes of norms and behaviours that persist over time by serving collectively valued purposes (Uphoff, 1984)'. Institutions regulate individuals' actions and consist of significant practices and relationships within a society. In some cases, institutions may be formalized in organizations like co-operatives, local governments,

1. Farmers-managed irrigation systems are operated and maintained collectively by groups of farmers. Management of the whole system from source of water to the fields where it is used is the responsibility of the farmers; Irrigation Systems of this type are often referred to as "community managed" systems (Coward, 1980).

or banks. For example, the institutions are land tenure systems and customary labour exchange relationships.

Institutions of both kinds contribute to production and development processes in several ways. They facilitate the aggregation of resources beyond an individual's capacity and the applicatiom of resources to the solution of problems for the benefit of many. They reduce uncertainty by the predictability of behaviour that they encourage and enforce in various spheres including the distribution of benefits from collective investments.

In this chapter institutions that have evolved to enable the collective management of water for agricultural production have been discussed. One institution is the farmers organisation itself. This organisation has been vested with legitimacy by the local community. However, another important institution is the convention of property rights in water. Both institutions, are crucial to the effective management of irrigation systems. Property rights include both the principle by which water is allocated among the farmers and the responsibilities that individuals have for maintenance of the system.

Irrigation Management Activities

Farmer-managed irrigation systems are found in diverse environments and employ a wide range of technologies to exploit different types of water sources for production of a variety of crops. All these irrigation systems, however, require that certain essential tasks be accomplished if the system is to function productively. One set of management activities focuses directly on the *water*. Water must be *acquired, allocated, distributed*, and, if there is excess, it must be *drained.*[2] A second set of management activities deals with the physical structures for controlling the water. These structures must be *operated* and *maintained.*[3] A final set of activities

2. "Water allocation" and "distribution" are often used interchangeably in the irrigation literature to describe the delivery of water. However, they sometimes refer to different activities. Water allocation is the assignment of entitlement to water from a system, both identifying the fields and farmers with access to water from the system and the amount and timing of the water to be delivered to each. Water distribution refers to the physical delivery of water to the fields and may or may not conform to the water allocation.

3. The structures must also be designed and constructed, but these are not usually considered to be management activities. The design and construction of the physical structures certainly have implications for the management of a system, however, not all types of management practices are possible with every design, and both the design and quality of the construction may limit the effective management of a system.

focuses on the organization which manages the water and structures and includes *decision-making, resource mobilization, communication* and *conflict management* (Uphoff, 1986). Fig. 2.1 depicts these three sets of irrigation management activities as a three-dimensional matrix.

There is interaction among the activities of the three sets; for example, the organization must *decide* how to *operate* the structures to *distribute* the water. Not all activities are equally important in each environment, and the farmers' irrigation management institutions will reflect the relative importance of activities in a particular location. In the context of the hills of U.P., Himachal Pradesh, J & K and Nepal, *resource mobilization* to *maintain* the system for *water acquisition* is the primary activity which influences the structure of many of the farmer irrigation organizations. In addition, the institutions of property rights in water and the principle by which water is *allocated* have important implications for the efficiency and equity of the farmer-managed irrigation systems in Nepal and other hill states.

In spite of numerous advantages of groundwater over surface water, legal control of groundwater could not be effective due to local socio-political environment in the country. The lack of technical knowledge[4] of

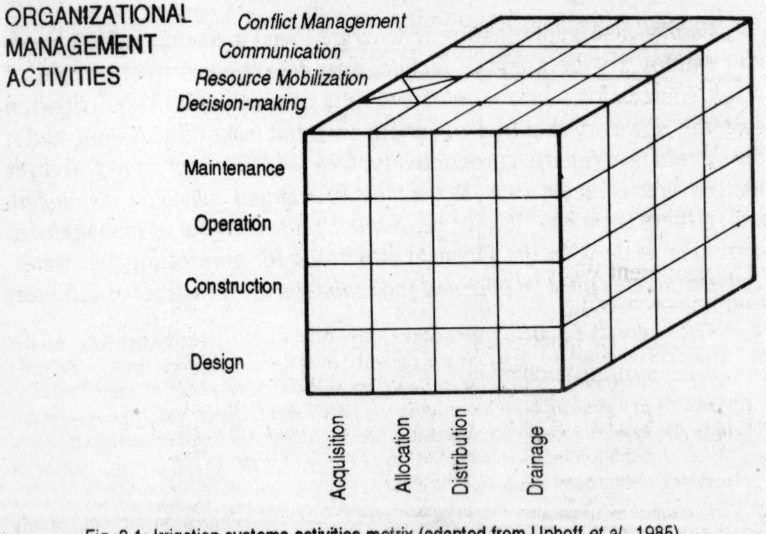

Fig. 2.1: Irrigation systems activities matrix (adapted from Uphoff *et al.*, 1985)

4. Alfred Marshall writes: Knowledge is the most powerful engine of production, it enables us to subdue nature and satisfy our wants (Shultz, 1981).

the farmers and inefficient functioning of farmers' organisations/associations are partly responsible for poor management of the system. The outlet of the irrigation system constitutes the interface between the State Irrigation Department and the farmers. But above the outlet, operation and maintenance is the responsibility of the department whereas below outlet, operation and maintenance of the irrigation system is the responsibility of the farmers. The farmers, by and large, are simple, poor and brought up in a very localised environmental conditions. Moreover, the farmers' cultivation techniques are based on the self reliance for generation and for sustenance of their family. The farmers' sense of responsibility for his family does not allow him to take any risk, therefore, he works in a very water-tight compartment. Unfortunately, in case of inflow irrigation projects, the decision-making process is highly centralised. Even at the outlet, common level starting with the position of outlets, alignment of field channels, low levelling standards and specifications, water delivery system and timing etc. are all decided by the Government agencies. The Government agencies on the other hand are generally not aware of the growing needs of the farmers-end-user, beneficiaries and thus remain in dark about emerging problems of the farmers while taking decisions about water delivery system. Consequently, while utilising the water, the farmers feel themselves as users of the facilities rather than 'Beneficiaries'. Hence, participation of beneficiaries is essential in all the irrigation projects whose ultimate objective is to increase agriculture production which is achieved by the farmers only. The decisions on use of agricultural inputs – one of them being water – are taken by the farmers[5] and to imporve upon their ability to take good decision and understand benefits arising out of them, it is crucial to have close participation of the beneficiaries in the irrigation projects. There are two important areas where participation of farmers is very significant for efficient water use *viz*., (i) On-Farm Development Works, and (ii) Distribution of Irrigation Water below the outlet command.

Irrigation Management is an inter-disciplinary system process with built-in learning mechanism to improve system performance by adjusting physical, technological and institutional inputs to achieve the desired levels of output (Seckler and Nobe, 1983). Irrigation projects are, however,

---

5. The farmers blame the Irrigation Engineers, for unequal distribution of water, poor maintenance of channels, faulty design & outlets, poor quality construction of channels, irregualr & untimely running of canals and so forth (Fig. 2.2).

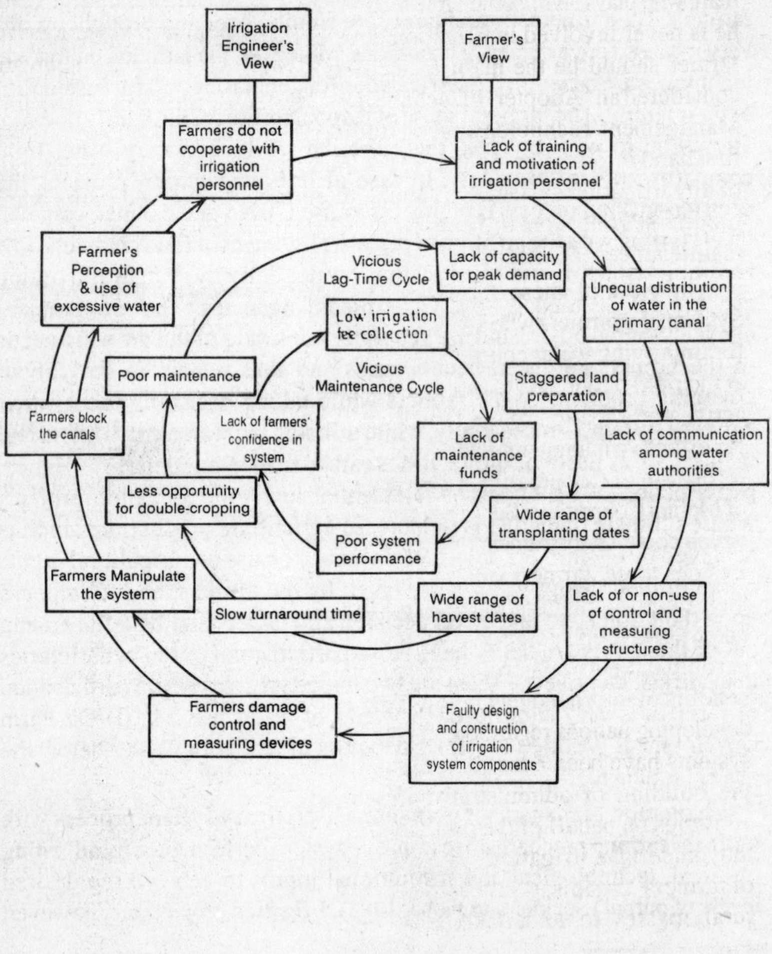

Fig 2.2 Vicious Circle of Blame Responsibe for Inefficient Irrigation Performance

organised and managed solely by the engineers[6] and supported by other disciplines/Government agencies belonging to other disciplines with a significant contribution which are agronomy, soil science, agricultural economics, extension, human behaviour (*i.e.* sociology) etc. The past experience shows that the farmer, the end-user, *i.e.* beneficiary, is the key man, who plays an important role in irrigation management, but unfortunately, he is never involved in irrigation development programmes. In fact, the farmer should be the main focus of attention (Fig. 2.2). He should be considered an 'Adopter' of technology in respect of adoption of Irrigation Management Technology, who is the target group and is a good source of first hand information right from the investigation to the opertional stage of any irrigation system. He should, therefore, be involved in the whole process starting from project planning to implementation, operation and maintenance, and management of the system.

In view of these facts, for effective Management of Irrigation System, the farmers who are the beneficiaries need to be actively involved for improving water courses and control over water quantity and timings at the field outlet. It is in this context that the need and significance of the active participation of the farmers in overall planning and management for effective management of the system are discussed. This necessitates formation of Cooperative Societies/Farmers' Association on the pattern of Mohini Cooperative Society in Gujarat and Pani Panchayats in Maharashtra which could be instrumental for efficient use of created irrigation potential. Besides these, farmers values, perception and attitudes which determine their decision-making process in irrigation water management are also taken into consideration. Without effective farmers' organisations participation to construct and maintain improved water courses, the benefits of improved technology may not be achieved. Experience of the developing nations regardless of cultural and social bonds is that irrigation systems have been constructed, maintained and improved only through the building of administrative organisations capable of undertaking activities on behalf of the participating farmers. For such organisations, they undertake irrigation system building and improvement. Formation of farmers' organisations could also serve the purpose of mobilisation of rural masses to undertake local developmental works in irrigation

6. Irrigation engineers work according to their own norms, experience and technical knowledge prevalent practices in the department. The Irrigation engineers blame the farmers for: farmers do not cooperate, farmers use excessive water, block the canal, damage gates and outlets, do not repair and maintain the water courses, use political pressure and so forth.

management in lieu of already overloaded governmental bureaucrats attempting to undertake this mammoth effort.

On-Farm Development Works

The 'On-Farm Development[7] (OFD) means construction of field channels, field drains, land levelling and shaping, construction of farm roads and village approach roads, consolidation of holdings and re-alignment of fields/plots boundaries. Since most of these are community works, farmers participation in overall planning and management of irrigation system is an imperative necessity. Corey (1981) has very rightly emphasised ....'that the field channel construction, operation and maintenance, on-farm improvements and general management of the irrigation water conveyance system below the outlet can be accomplished better with direct involvement of the beneficiaries.

Distribution of Water

Water distribution and especially practices of distribution among the farmers are crucial in management of water for increased agricultural production. The present water distribution practices in most cases do not provide equal opportunity or assured supply of water. If the beneficiaries are involved and persuaded to participate in the planning of the operation and rotation of the system, this will improve the performance of the irrigation system. Hence, farmers should be involved in micro-planning and execution of programmes in order to generate confidence in government agencies and to overcome conflicts.

Experiments through various approaches adopted for farmers participation have revealed encouraging water management practices. The important approaches are : (i) Formation of irrigation cooperative societies, (ii) Water users Associations or *chak samitis*.

Organising Farmers

For improving water courses and achieving control over water quantity and timing at the field outlet, farmers need to be organised into effective units facilitating their cooperation. The failure of most of the earlier programmes in our country has revealed the inadequacy of

---

7. The 'On-Farm' engineering-design of water courses, land levelling and water application has not been given a serious thought and therefore, the irrigation efficiency is very low in almost all parts of the country.

programmes which purports to undertake development for farmers without their meaningful programme of participation.[8]

To support this contention, views of Professor Wilson, Professor Carl Taylor, Professor Oscar Levis, Professor Opler and his team, Professor S.C. Dube, Professor Mandelbaum and many others are worth quoting who evaluated the nature of the achievements of the Community Development Programme (including improvement of the irrigation) in India and the role of the rural people and concluded that .... "Local Self Help Village Group will mobilize natural and human resources for local improvements of all kinds and all technical changes of Govt." For this initiative of people in both formulating and executing the programmes, reliance upon group work techniques and active participation of people[9] (in this case *i.e.* irrigation development) in all the stages of implementation should be forthcoming. Without effective farmers' participation to construct and maintain improved water courses the benefits of new technology *viz*., improved seeds, fertilisers, pesticides, improved implements, processing and agricultural credit are lost.

Farmers' Involvement – Crux of the Problem

The involvement of farmers can be affected at any stage of the project. At the investigation stage they could supply important local information such as highest flood levels in the past years, the existing irrigation facilities and practices, acceptability to the proposed changes etc. In the process of adoption of irrigation management practices, it is the farmer who gives us the vital information regarding the system operation and the major constraints. This helps a lot in problem identification process. However, in subsequent stages of management, practices like finding out solutions, assessment of solutions and implementation etc. are necessary. The success of the problem largely depends upon whether the water users have been taken into confidence.

8. Farmer participation means farmer playing an active role in decision-making regarding planning, implementing, operating, maintaining and evaluating projects and programmes designing to improve the productivity, equity and effectiveness of irrigation projects.

9. "Engineering is not the fundamental problem underlying irrigation development in the LDC's. Engineering principles are known and can be adapted, but the major problem, however, is to discover ways to utilise farmer clients more efficiently in operation and maintenance & development programmes which will create rural transformation. Rural transformation essentially requires changes in farmers behaviour, motivations & expectations..."

The farmer himself normally takes the major management decisions like:

– A Production inputs (including application of irrigation water).
– A Operation and maintenance.
– Adoption of technology for improving farming systems.

Any project which is designed to increase agriculture production, must improve the ability of the farmers to take these decisions. But, without the active participation of farmers, it would not be possible for them to understand the activities and the anticipated benefits likely to be received by them.

What is meant by *participation* ? Why do farmers participate and not participate in programmes ?: and how could they be motivated to participate are some of the questions that are addressed here. In the succeeding discussion light is thrown on these and other related questions drawing upon the experience with a few selected programmes in India.

The Concept of Participation

Participation in common parlance, is used to mean 'act or fact of partaking' or 'sharing in'. According to Banki (1981), participation means 'a dynamic group process in which all members of a work group contribute, share or are influenced by the interchange of ideas and activities toward problem solving or 'decision-making'. Uphoff, Cohen and Goldsmith (1979) consider it meaningful to study participation in terms of (a) what is involved in participative behaviour; (b) who participates; (c) how participation occurs; and (d) the contexts in terms of project characteristics and task environment which influence participative conduct. But here the term is used to mean the act of partaking (by farmers) in all stages of irrigation management programmes right from designing of various structures through monitoring and evaluation of their performance. Such a participation requires, among other things, that the target group of farmers voluntarily spend their time, energy, and money on the programme and adopt the recommended measures and practices, and repair and maintain them in good condition on a sustained basis (Fig. 2.3).

There is no universally acceptable measure or index of people's participation that could be used to evaluate irrigation system programmes in terms of people's participation. One could use as a crude measure of participation proportions of the target group of people who participated

Fig. 2.3: Members of a Work Group participating in Paddy Plantation

in various stages of a programme and who adopted various recommended measures and practices expanding their time and money on a sustained basis.

The experience of a few selected farmers managed irrigation systems and, soil and water conservation programmes in India can be cited to draw lessons of that experience. Among them, the important ones are:

1. Mohini Cooperative Irrigation Society (Gujarat State).
2. The Sukhomajri (Haryana State).
3. The Ralegan Sidhi (Maharashtra State).
4. The Participative and Integrated Development of Watersheds (PIDOW) (Karnataka State).
5. The Aga Khan Rural Support Programme (AKRSPI) (Gujarat State).
6. Krishna Theera Raitha Sangh (KTRS) (Karnataka State).

A review of the experience of a few selected programmes in India, are given in order to synthesise the lessons into some semblance of a theory of people's participation in overall management of irrigation system.

A growing literature which examines farmer-managed irrigation systems in a number of countries and a variety of ecological environment studies from the Philippines (Lewis, 1971; Siy, 1982), Indonesia (Geertz, 1980), Thailand (Tan-Kim-Yong 1983), Sri Lanka (Leach, 1961), and Peru (Mitchell, 1976) have described a variety of irrigation systems managed by farmer groups.

MOHINI COOPERATIVE IRRIGATION SOCIETY

Formation of Mohini Water Cooperative Society

Kakrapar is the largest completed irrigation project of Gujarat. Its canal system draws water from the weir constructed at Kakrapar village across river Tapi in South Gujarat which provides irrigation facilities to about two lakhs hectares of land. The multipurpose Ukai Reservoir was constructed subsequently in the year 1972 across the same river Tapi at about 32 kms upstream of Kakrapar weir.

Farmers in the tail areas in certain pockets of Kakrapar system were feeling that the water deliveries are not received with a degree of assurance and the supplies received are not shared proportionately among beneficiaries within subminor and outlet command. In tail end areas the fluctuations were generally experienced and internal conflicts among the beneficiaries were experienced. As a solution, the farmers of subminors 3L, 4L, and 5L and two direct outlets at R.D. 11.6 and 16.4 were persuaded and encouraged to form a water cooperative society for internal water distribution. As a result Mohini Water Coopeartive Society was registered in September 1978 at Mohini – a village located about 25 kms from Surat city, under the State Cooperative Societies Act of 1961. The farmers are progressive and they grow sugarcane crop which has a ready market in the nearby Chalthan Cooperative Sugar Mill. Good leadership is available in the persons like Shri Bhikhubhai Patel and his colleagues. The village has successfully participated in the cooperative activities in the Choaryasi Taluka which started functioning in the month of March, 1979 with the headquarters at village Mohini of Choaryasi Taluka of Surat District. It was assigned a gross command area of about 525 hectares getting irrigation facility through four water courses *viz*. 3L, 4L and 5L and IR and two direct outlets of Bhestan Minor of the Kakrapar canal system. The corresponding culturable command Area assigned to Mohini Water Cooperative Society is about 487 ha. The details of command area village-wise and canal-wise are furnished in Table 1.

TABLE 1

MOHINI WATER COOPERATIVE SOCIETY

Canal-wise and Village-wise Command Area

Canal-wise				Village-wise			
Sr. No.	Canal	G.C.A. in ha	C.C.A. in ha	Sr. No.	Village	G.C.A. in ha	C.C.A. in ha
1.	3L water course Ex. Bhestan Minor	89.13	79.05	1.	Kharbhasi	37.81	37.79
2.	4L water course ex. Bhestan Minor	201.94	176.83	2.	Mohini	343.63	305.94
3.	a. 5L w/c ex. Bhestan Minor.			3.	Goja	11.65	11.65
	b. 5.5L. 5LA w/c ex. Bhestan Minor	161.08	158.71	4.	Gangva	54.49	54.49
4.	a. Direct outlets ex. Bhestn Minor Rd.	17.15	17.15	5.	Khamb haasla	33.50	30.50
				6.	Deladva	48.94	46.94
	b. D.O. @ Rd. ex. Bhestan Mr.	11.52	11.52				
5.	IR w/c ex. Bhestan Minor.	44.20	44.20				
		525.02	487.31			525.02	487.31

To encourage the society, the Govt. had agreed to bear the losses in the first three years. Govt. has improved the canal and constructed new structures. Govt. gave grant of Rs. 26,000.00 per year for two years and supplies water on volumetric basis at the rate of 25 paise per 10000 litres but in turn the Society charge from the members on crop area basis.

Cropping Pattern

Mohini command falls in zones IIA of Kakrapar command with an estimated CCA of 1,00,000 ha.

This considerable divergence makes travesty of the designed cropping pattern. What is worse that such a divergence is observed in all the areas covered under zone IIA? Apparently, there is a wide gap in what the concerned experts from the Govt. department think necessary and what the farmers have practised.

In fairness to experts, it may be noted that though no ground level data are collected to validate the assumption, there has been a steady rise in the ground water levels, which over a period would result in water logging and salinity. Perhaps the designed cropping pattern has the underlying assumption that loading of less water intensive crop would help to control the situation. Alternatively, the question could be posed; taking into account the farmer's preferences for water intensive crops, it is necessary to control the excess water through control of delivery. However, ground water data need to be collected and analysed.

The present cropping pattern and designed cropping pattern are presented in Table 2. There is need to educate the farmers on water application methods and the long term impact of excessive water use on the soils.

Growth of Mohini Water Cooperative Society

Mohini Water Cooperative Society was registered in Sept. 1978 under the State Cooperative Societies Act, 1961, which started functioning in March 1979.

Before handing over the management to the Cooperative Society the (1) sections of the subminors/water courses were made good; (2) additional outlets were constructed to limit the C.C.A. to 8 ha per outlet; (3) lining was provided to vulnerable portions of water courses; and (4) necessary extensions etc. were carried out to subminors/water courses to provide smooth and systematic functioning for the water cooperatives.

In its first year of formation *i.e.* in 1978-79, the Mohini Water Cooperative Society started its activities with 145 share holders and share capital of Rs. 7,900. During this year distribution network of canal was renovated and all preliminary procedures were set up for smooth interaction with local officers of Govt. for all matters. Thus, the responsibility of water distribution levy and collection of water charges, and operating and maintaining the canal system within the area assigned to Mohini Water Cooperative Society were completely taken over from the Govt. Mohini Water Cooperative Society earned a profit of about Rs. 17,000 on account of its efficient management.

During next year the share capital and share holder gradually increased and now-a-days, the members of the society are 218 and share capital has also increased to the extent of Rs. 12,300.00. Due to efficient management, energetic leadership and assurance of water to each farmer, the Mohini Water Cooperative Society earned a good

TABLE 2

MOHINI WATER COOPERATIVE SOCIETY C.C.A. (487.31 ha)

Comparison of Present Cropping Pattern (Irrigation) with Designed Cropping Pattern

Sr No.	Crop	% as per designed cropping pattern		% as per present irrigation		Diff. % (+) or (-) between (3 & 5)
		%	Area (ha)	%	Area (ha)	
1	2	3	4	5	6	7
1.	Kharif paddy	15	73.09	11.8	41.00	(–) 3.2
2.	Kharif vegetables	12	58.47	3.2	4.10	(+) 10.8
3.	Rabi Jowar	13	63.35	-	-	(+) 13.0
4.	Wheat	10	48.73	-	-	(+) 10.0
5.	Vegetables	15	73.09	-	-	(+) 15.0
6.	Sugarcane	18	87.72	79.0	286.32	(-) 63.0
7.	Other parennials	8	38.98	1.9	0.67	(+) 6.1
8.	Cotton	2	9.75	-	-	(+) 2.0
9.	Hot weather vegetables	7	34.13	-	-	(+) 7.0
10.	Other crops	-	-	4.1	14.28	(–) 1.5
Total		100	487.31	100	347.37	

profit during these years. The details of loss and profit are shown in Tables 3 & 5.

The area irrigated before and after formation of Mohini Water Cooperative Society in command area on 3L, 4L and 5L water courses of Bhestan minor is also shown in Table 4.

The society has purchased one tractor and other equipments to help its share holders in carrying out various farm operations expeditiously and with least cost. Besides, the society also collected a large amount of past dues of Govt. from its members. A concession for advance payment system has also been introduced.

The society has organised an educational tour of its members not only in Gujarat but to other States also. The society organized their educational tour to agricultural university at Navasari, Mahi and Panam project and Amul dairy at Anand in Kheda district in Gujarat State and Kota of Rajasthan State, Maharashtra and Madhya Pradesh etc. The society made tremendous alround impact and its name and fame have spread

TABLE 3
Irrigation Water Management and Assessment

Year	Season	Area irrigated in Hect.	Water consumed in million litres	Amount charged by the Department to society @Re. 0.25 per 10,000 litres	20% L.F. cess	Total (5+6)	Amount charged by society from irrigators (as per prevailing Govt. rates)	Profits or loss to the society (8—7)
1	2	3	4	5	6	7	8	9
1979-80	Kharif	172.36	722.47	18061.75	3612.35	21674.10	24654.91	2980.81
	Rabi.	241.56	528.45	13211.35	2642.27	15853.62	52290.45	36536.83
	Hot	225.76	1879.21	46980.30	9396.18	56376.48	67192.13	10815.65
		649.68	3130.14	78253.40	15650.80	93904.20	144237.49	50333.29
1980-81	Kharif	300.93	2189.67	54741.92	10948.36	65690.28	37301.33	(-)28389.05
	Rabi	282.69	1120.33	28008.33	5601.66	65632.82	32025.83	
	Hot	275.77	1889.41	47235.34	9447.07	56682.41	82895.13	26212.72
		859.39	5199.42	119985.59	25997.09	155982.68	185832.18	29849.50
1981-82	Kharif	282.00	952.35	23808.89	4761.79	28579.68	50981.80	22441.12
	Rabi	278.83	1889.95	49748.80	9949.76	59798.82	20868.99	61670.37
	Hot	283.32	1214.42	30360.57	6072.11	36432.68	95491.29	59058.61
		844.15	4156.73	103918.32	29783.66	124701.98	267342.08	142640.10
1982-83	Kharif	285.41	1685.16	421128.93	8425.78	50554.71	51896.54	1313.83
	Rabi	288.10	1509.47	37736.81	7547.36	45284.17	96832.41	51518.25
	Hot	285.08	2072.87	51831.71	30364.33	62186.04	113617.95	51431.91
		558.59	5267.50	131687.45	36337.47	158024.92	262346.91	104321.99
1983-84	Kharif	236.79	464.89	11622.34	7324.47	13946.41	33146.76	19200.35
	Rabi	320.86	2210.88	55272.40	11054.48	66326.88	95932.72	29605.84
	Hot	236.33	2733.60	68339.98	13668.00	82007.98	97737.13	15729.15
		793.98	5409.37	135234.72	32046.95	12281.29	226816.61	64535.34
1984-85	Kharif	311.48	1890.73	7268.27	9453.64	56721.91	52721.38	(-)4000.53
	Rabi	228.91	2171.80	34294.96	10858.95	65153.95	101988.03	36934.08
	Hot	305.00	2938.31	73457.92	14691.58	88149.50	123101.60	34952.10
		845.39	7000.84	155021.15	35004.21	210035.36	277811.01	67785.65
1985-86	Kharif	341.88	2997.115	74927.85	14985.57	88913.42	61873.27	(-)28030.56
	Rabi	330.00	1803.064	45076.61	9015.31	54091.93	107353.95	53283.62
	Hot	307.18	2803.326	70083.15	14016.63	84099.78	132645.16	48545.83
		979.06	7603.505	192086.61	35017.50	228105.13	302874.42	73769.29
1986-87	Kharif	354.20	2811.25	70281.26	14056.26	84337.52	66477.74	(-)78859.78
	Rabi	346.70	1936.09	48404.91	9680.97	58085.88	11162.93	53537.05
	Hot	301.88	2934.15	81734.97	16347.00	98081.90	121853.55	23771.58
		1002.78	7681.49	200421.14	40084.23	240505.37	299954.22	99448.85
1987-88	Kharif	349.39	2377.68	59442.13	11888.43	71330.56	-	-
	Rabi	341.43	1737.95	43448.81	2689.76	52138.57	-	-
	Hot	314.00	3045.06	76126.52	15225.30	91351.82	-	-
		1004.82	7160.69	179017.46	35803.49	214820.95	-	-
1988-89		-	6099.96	-	-	-	-	-

not only in the state but also in the entire irrigation sector of the country at large.

In terms of the financial performance (Table 6), the society recorded a distinct success. No losses were sustained in any year and the society started paying dividends from the second year onward. It has been classified in 'A' category by the auditors of the Cooperative Deptt. The society has also built a reserve fund of Rs. 17,012.85 and has about Rs. 1.742 lakhs in different types of funds earmarked for specific purposes upto the year 1986-87.

As a result of this spectacular success, Govt. did not bear any losses. However, it may be seen that the grant for administrative expenses for the first year took about four years to materialise. What is more important is that Govt. realised the full water charges. In rest of the area of the State the arrears were mounting.

Society's responsibility is only for the water distribution beyond the measuring device points. The maintenance of the subminors is still a Govt. responsibility but maintenance of the field channels below the outlets is the responsibility of the concerned farmers and no liability to the society is involved. The society is willing to take over the maintenance of the subminors but there is a divergence of views between the department and the society on some minor details on handing over this function to the society.

The society is responsible for payment of water charges. Hitherto, these have been paid fully, though not necessarily within the stipulated time, as there are delays in the recoveries at the farmer's end.

Society has its own rules for conflict resolutions and has awarded fines for misuse of water. Such cases have been quite few. But it is gratifying to note that society's decisions have been gracefully accepted.

The society is housed in a new building, costs of which were entirely borne by the Govt. It is interesting to note that the wide publicity accorded to the successful first ever surface irrigation cooperative society led to the visits of dignitaries, officials, scholars and cultivators from outside areas. The society had no office premises to receive the ever-increasing flow of guests. Therefore, the society approached the Govt. for building the premises. The construction of about 1800 sq. ft. carpet area involved an expenditure of slightly over Rs. one lakh. However, the society pays nominal rent per month. The provision of this facility at Govt. cost has been a boon to the Society.

TABLE 4

Area Irrigated Before and after formation of Mohini Water Cooperative Society in the Command Area of 3L, 4L and 5L Water Courses of Bhestan Minor

Year	Season			
	Hot	Kharif	Rabi	Total
1	2	3	4	5
Before Formation of Society				
1976-77	100	122	124	346
1977-78	140	147	154	441
1978-79	134	163	139	436
Total	374	432	417	1223
Average of three years	124.6	144	139	407.6
After Formation of Society				
1979-80	225.76	172.73	241.56	640.05
1980-81	275.77	300.93	282.69	859.39
1981-82	278.83	282.00	283.32	844.15
1982-83	285.08	285.41	288.10	858.59
1983-84	236.33	236.79	320.86	793.98
1984-85	305.00	311.48	228.91	845.39
1985-86	307.18	330.00	341.88	979.06
1986-87	301.88	346.70	354.20	1002.78
1987-88	314.00	349.39	341.43	1004.82

Performance of Mohini Water Cooperative Society

The main reasons attributed to the success of Mohini Water Cooperative Society are:

(1) The Society is successful mainly on account of the leadership provided. Since the farmers were dissatisfied with the Departmental management but realised that the situation can be improved if they took over the management.

(2) Society performed very well as the sugarcane is grown in larger proportion of command, under the present water rate structure. If the cropping pattern is diversified, it may not be successful.

(3) The success of society depends on the efficiency of physical network of sub-minor, outlet and their capacities, provision of measuring device etc. The expenditure incurred by the

Department in remodelling the Mohini system could not be ascertained.

(4) The relatively abundant water supplies have helped the society to minimise the conflicts. Such a situation may not prevail in other areas. The reason why Mohini farmers came closer *i.e.* together is that these supplies were not required over the seasons, under the departmental management.

(5) Due to measured supply to the cooperative society, the members are naturally inspired to affect most economical use of water and avoid wastage for profit to the society and to themselves.

(6) Labour for planting, harvesting and transport of sugarcane to sugar factories is managed by the sugar factory and hence the work load and worry is comparatively low for the members for sugarcane crop which has 81% developed in this society.

(7) Society is helping the members by providing the facility of tractor and other equipments which speed up the field operation economically.

(8) Basically the members are progressive and have the added advantage of being near to Chalthon Sugar factory, National Highway and Surat city.

(9) Increase in irrigation area in phases and efficient management by the society has kept up the tempo of cooperation and self-reliance for ultimate gains in the member's pocket.

(10) No doubt, the society has been a success. But this is due to situational reasons. The objectives of water use efficiency and equitable water distribution have not been attained. Whatever equity is there, is due to the relative abundance of water. But the society is in ideal position to implement technical improvements and place it on sound footing, provided the technical guidance on agronomic practices are available.

Organisation and Management of the Society

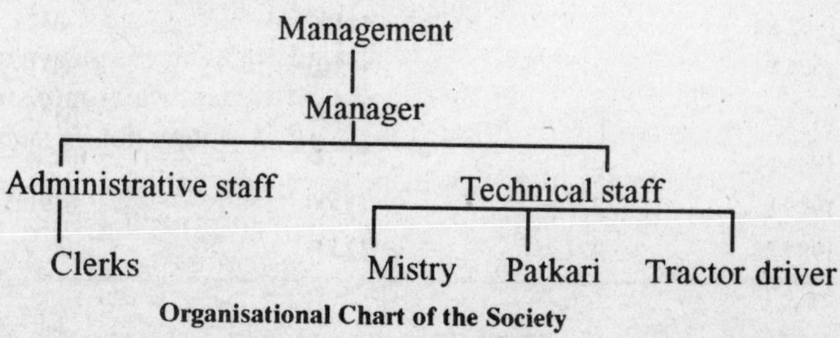

Organisational Chart of the Society

State Govt. had provided for the first three years one manager, one mistry and two clerks for functioning of the society. However, the State Govt. has sanctioned the staff for the society as one manager, one mistry, two clerks and one patkari. Thus, the society has engaged one manager, one clerk, three patkari and one tractor driver for smooth working of supply of water and management of the society. Apart from processing of the applications, the society maintains a daily record of water released cropwise, and farmwise and area irrigated. A consolidated report on daily utilisation is sent to the deptt. on a fortnightly basis. The staff is well paid, in view of the salary scales in the area.

Although relatively water use is better than the other areas, yet it is considered to be ideal. As envisaged there are four subminors with a total C.C.A. of 487.31 ha in the command area.

The management gives the whole programme to the irrigators so that the farmers can know the day and time and accordingly they can make their own planning to use water and other farm activities. Canal howkidars move in their own area and they watch whether the water received by the irrigator is according to turn and irrigators are not wasting water and take water. Discipline is maintained in receiving water.

As per the policy of the Govt. the farmers have to demand water in each season by submitting their application in prescribed form. The

TABLE 5

The growth of membership, share capital and profit

Year	Member	Share capital Rs.	Net profit in Rs.
1978-79	145	7900	17000
1979-80	161	9000	3000
1980-81	181	10000	6373
1981-82	187	10300	10403
1982-83	203	11100	7331
1983-84	212	11550	9651
1984-85	216	11800	8445
1985-86	217	11800	10836
1986-87	227	12300	6191
1987-88	227	12300	-

farmers have not to apply individually for demanding water from Govt. but they have to approach society only. Similarly, they are not required to approach the Govt. for paying water charges individually to Govt. but water charges are paid to Govt. directly by society. It means that all the irrigators are not required to approach Govt. all the times. Since such activities are undertaken by the society, farmers save their valuable time and energy. Hence, farmers are free to concentrate on their farming activities more and more. Whenever there is any dispute among the farmers, the manager and the president of the society settle the case. If there is any technical problem, then, it is solved by Department.

TABLE 6

Outstanding Achievements of Society

Year	Area irrigated in ha (sum of all sources)	Water consumed million litres	Water bill of State Govt. in Rs.	Amount charged by MWCS to its members in Rs.
1979-80	630	3130	93904	144237
1980-81	860	5199	155982	185832
1981-82	830	4156	133900	267342
1982-83	855	5267	158024	262346
1983-84	794	5409	162281	229109
1984-85	845	7000	210025	277540
1985-86	989	7600	228105	301875
1986-87	1002	7680	240505	299954
1987-88	1004.82	7160	214820	-

During the Kharif season, subminors operate as required depending on the rainfall received. Normally, there are three rotations in the seasons. In Rabi and hot weather seasons, the number of rotations are normally 4 and 5 respectively.

The Union Ministry of Water Resources is undertaking an ambitious scheme under which farmers themselves would organise cooperative societies for management of irrigation water. During the Eighth Plan period emphasis would be to organise more such cooperatives, so that distribution of water could efficiently and equitably be done and the collection of cess would be transferred to the cooperatives on a bigger scale. There were only 15 Cooperative Irrigation Societies during the Seventh Plan period in the country. These cooperatives are being drawn up on the model of the successful ones being run in the DINDORI sub-division of the Nasik District of Maharashtra where the tribals have organised cooperatives with membership going up to even 200 farmers. In fact the Maharashtra Government has decided to pay back to these cooperatives 15% of their revenue from irrigation cess in order to meet the administrative costs of running the organisations.

THE SUKHOMAJRI

Sukhomajri is a small village of about 538 people, mostly Gujars which is a well-known model of micro-watershed development (Chopra *et al*, 1988). The village is situated in the lower ranges of the Shivaliks in Haryana. The Sukhomajri project was launched in 1979. Roughly half of the total land in the village is owned privately by individual farmers and the other half is common property land. The major portion of the catchment is owned by the Forest Department. The project focused on harvesting and recycling of rain water. In Sukhomajri, a total area of 4,085 ha was treated at a total cost of Rs. 78.32 lakh or an average cost of Rs. 1,917 per ha. About 61 per cent of the total cost was accounted for by skilled and unskilled labour. A Water Users' Society was set up in 1982 to ensure equal distribution of irrigation water and forest produce among the villagers and thereby to enlist their participation in the project. The landless also had a right to water who could sell their share of water to others. The right to membership of the Society and to water was contingent on the observance of stall-feeding. The project was financially viable with an internal rate of return of about 19 per cent and B-C ratio of 2.06 at 12 per cent discount rate (Chopra *et. al*, 1988). The project resulted in a significant increase in crop and milk yield rates and production, reduction in the number of cows and goats, increase in the number of buffaloes, increased availability of water, and higher incomes. Funds for implementing the project were provided by the Haryana State Government (Forest Deptt.), Indian Council of Agricultural Research and the Ford Foundation. However, the technical guidance was provided by the staff of the Central Soil and Water Conservation, Research and Training Institute, Chandigarh.

The Sukhomajri experience (Anonymous, 1984) shows that exhortations for participation and cooperation do not work, especially if they are aimed at people who live on the margin of subsistence. The poor cannot stop grazing their animals in highly degraded and over-grazed common pool lands for the sake of their conservative views when their lives depend on the animals. Only with increased productivity of crops and increased milk yields resulting from supplemental irrigation which were made possible by the reservoirs constructed under the project and assurance of equal share of every village household in the reservoir water. These benefits were instrumental to the villagers which made them ready to invest in soil and water conservation measures and to participate in the programme whole-heartedly. Conclusively, if farmers needs are well taken care of, then people participation becomes much easier.

THE RALEGAN SIDDHI

Ralegan Siddhi is another well-known model of micro-watershed development (Patil, 1988). Ralegan Siddhi is a village of about 2100 people in the drought-prone Parnal Tehsil of Ahmednagar district, in Maharashtra state. The village receives scanty rainfall of only 250-300 mm annually. Hence, the highest priority in the project was given to water conservation. The project covered four watersheds with a total geographical area of about 892 ha. The total expenditure incurred on the project was Rs. 112.75 lakh of which Rs. 52.75 lakh was granted by the Maharashtra Government, Rs. 47 lakh was borrowed from banks, Rs. 11 lakh contributed by villagers through *Shramdan* (donation of labour) and the remaining two lakhs were contributed by other sources. However, the per ha cost of the project was Rs. 11,482 which included cost of a hostel building (Rs. 16 lakhs) and a veterinary hospital (Rs. 1 lakh). The project had a positive impact on crop, milk yield and production, fodder production, employment, and incomes. It was observed that after the implementation of the project, no villager went out of the village in search of work as they used to do before implementation of the project.

A series of check dams and bunds constructed under the project resulted in increased availability of ground water. This facilitated sinking of community wells. Water from these wells supplied at a moderate rate enabled the farmers to grow two or three crops every year including fruits and vegetables which are now even exported to Dubai. This was mainly due to active participation of the villagers. The villagers participated whole-heartedly in the project and contributed through *Shramdan* labour valued at Rs. 11 lakh. All the soil and water conservation structures were built through community action. The villagers have completely stopped grazing their animals on common property lands and have switched to stall-feeding which has become possible as a result of increased grass production from the common property land after stoppage of grazing. They have planted more than two lakh trees mostly on common property lands including hill slopes. This has prevented soil erosion besides providing a variety of products such as fuel wood, fodder, fruits, etc. The major force behind this transformation has been Padma Shri Anna Hazare who after retirement from the Indian Army in 1975 returned to his native village Ralegan Siddhi and started the village reconstruction and development work. This has very evidently demonstrated that village leadership is a significant factor to reckon with which can help in rural reconstruction. To enlist people's participation in this work, Padma Shri Anna Hazare organised the villagers into an association called Tarun Mandal (Youth Association). For ensuring equitable distribution of water, *Pani Puravatha Mandals* (Water Supply Associations) were established. Thus, the Ralegan Siddhi experience shows that the rural people under the guidance and leadership of good, enlightened and honest persons could achieve a lot through their own resources. The model could be replicated in other villages in India given proper leadership.

THE PARTICIPATIVE AND INTEGRATED DEVELOPMENT OF WATERSHEDS (PIDOW)

Karnataka's District Watershed Development Programme (DWDP) is well known for its innovative three-tier organisation structure, state-wide coverage and laudable achievements. However, inadequate people's participation has been a major weakness of the programme (Singh, 1988). To remove the weakness and to develop practicable and replicable methods for enlisting people's participation. the Government of Karnataka in collaboration with Mysore Resettlement and Development Agency, a non-governmental organisation and the Swiss Development Co-operation, launched a Participative and Integrated Development of Watersheds Project in Gulbarga district. The project has been managed successfully and community action/participation focusing on watershed management has been developed, and applied for replicability. The project staff has successfully organised people in seven selected mini-watersheds into small homogeneous associations. All the project activities are planned, executed, monitored and followed up by these associations. The associations work in close collaboration with local institutions like Mandal Panchayats, Co-operative Societies, etc. Each member of every association voluntarily and regularly saves some money every month and pools the savings to a common fund of the association out of which loans are granted to the needy members of the association. Each association has framed its own rules and regulations for utilizing its common fund and the resources of its mini-watershed. Each association meets regularly two to three times every month in order to review the progress of its activities, identify problems and bottlenecks in implementation and determine what remedial actions will be taken by whom and when. These activities in fact are quite similar to the one used in the HASD project in Northern Thailand where a seven-step problem-solving procedure was used to involve the watershed community in the decision-making process (Hoare, 1986). The villagers are motivated and trained by the project staff and technical experts from outside, in construction of various soil and water conservation structures so as to eventually do away with the contractors who presently do the project work for Government of Karnataka and take away a sizeable chunk of the funds earmarked for the project. By the end of 1989, 70 per cent of the soil and water conservation structures established in the seven mini-watersheds taken up under the project were repaired and maintained in good condition by the people themselves and 70 per cent of the farmers had accepted the recommended measures and practices (Swiss Development Co-Operation, undated).

The project experience shows that a non-governmental organisation could do a better job of enlisting people's participation in soil and water conservation programmes than a government agency. As a first step in the process of enlisting people's participation, the project staff organised the people into small homogeneous groups/associations around income generating activities, motivated them to save and use the savings for productive purposes. Finally, they motivated and trained the people to design, construct, repair and maintain various soil and water conservation structures on their own private lands as well as on the common property lands.

THE AGA KHAN RURAL SUPPORT PROGRAMME (AKRSPI)

The Aga Khan Rural Support Programme, a non-governmental organisation based in Ahmedabad (Gujarat), is engaged in rural development work with their soil and water conservation programme in three districts of Gujarat namely, Junagadh, Surendranagar and Bharuch, which shows that farmers participate in soil and water conservation programmes when the expected benefits from participation are higher than the expected costs of participation and when the role of an external agency is confined, as it was in the case of AKRSP(I), to organising and helping them identify their problems, and determine their priorities and empowering them to resolve the problems identified. This approach to rural development was translated by the AKRSP(I) into concrete action by organising people into viable and self-sustaining organisations at the grass-roots level that enabled people to build up a capacity to identify and solve their problems, to have access to resources, and services available from various governmental and non-governmental agencies engaged in rural development. AKRSP(I)'s soil and water conservation programme was initiated in early 1988. By Dec. 1989, the programme was taken up in 21 villages with 302 farmers in the three districts and 454 ha of land belonging mostly to poor and small farmers was treated [AKRSP(I) Brochure, 1989].

In the AKRSP(I)'s soil and water conservation programmes, the major role is of the Extension Volunteers (EVs) and the participating farmers. However, the EVs are selected by the farmers from amongst themselves. They are trained by the AKRSP(I) and after training they attend most of the work including contacting, educating, training, motivating, and helping the farmers. They survey the farmers' fields and prepare maps and layouts of various conservation structures. They are paid for their services by the beneficiaries at the rate of Rs. 10 per acre of land treated and an equal amount is paid by the AKRSP(I). This system of service-linked payment by the beneficiaries is rather an innovation. There is a built-in incentive in the system for the EVs to provide maximum possible service to their clientele, *i.e.*, farmers. Besides, there are many other advantages of the AKRSP(I)'s approach, which is people-centred, flexible, and decentralised *vis-a-vis* the conventional approach which is paternalistic, rigid, and centralised. Unlike government personnel, EVs are easily accessible to farmers as they come from the farmers' village/area. They are accountable to farmers. Thus, the AKRSP(I)'s approach is most cost-effecitve. The average cost of land treatment over the period January, 1988 to December, 1989 was Rs. 150 per ha which was the lowest achieved till then under any soil and water conservation programmes in India. But incremental net returns due to the programme in 1988 were Rs. 219 per ha (AKRSP(I), 1989). A positive point of this approach is that all the field level activities are handled by the EVs with a minimal involvement of the AKRSP(I)'s staff. The AKRSP(I)'s staff involved in the programme at each of three district centres consists of one subject matter specialist designated as Programme Organiser (Watershed Development) and one surveyor. Another important feature of the AKRSP(I)'s approach is that each participating farmer contributes in the form of labour to the extent of 50 per cent of the total labour cost of the works done on his land: the remaining 50 per cent is contributed by the AKRSP(I). But the cost of equipment and instruments is wholly met by the AKRSP(I). Each participating farmer is motivated to save some money (15 to 20 per cent) out of the wages paid to him by AKRSP(I) (50 per cent of total cost) and these savings of all the participants are pooled by the Gram Vikas Mandali (GVM) or some other association of the farmers promoted by the AKRSP(I) which are used as a collateral for securing bank loans to the members of the Mandali for purchase of improved seeds, fertilizers and other inputs.

However, each EV prepares, every year before the monsoon sets in, a simple one-page operational plan for each participating farmer in his village/area. The plan covers such details as the kind of conservation structures to be constructed, quantum of work to be done (area to be covered), rate of payment, amount payable to the farmer, total savings to be made by the farmer, service fee payable to the EV, kind and quantity of inputs needed, etc. The plan is signed by the EV, and the farmer, and scrutinized by a supervisory staff of the AKRSP(I). The plan document also serves as a voucher for the farmer to claim payment of the AKRSP(I)'s contribution. The payment is made to the farmer only after the quantity and quality of the works done in his fields(s) are verified by the Chairman, the Secretary, and two of the members of the GVM concerned. While making payment to the farmer, the AKRSP (I) deducts from the total amount payable, the amount that the farmer has agreed to save and the service fee payable to the EV. The EV can later claim from the AKRSP(I) the service fees due to him. There are no middlemen and contractors in the programme and hence there are no leakages of funds which is a very common feature of governmental soil and water conservation programmes in India.

Nevertheless the weakness of the AKRSP(I)'s approach is that it does not provide for treatment of degraded common property lands as a result of which farmers are deprived of the positive side effects of treatment of public lands in their watershed. Since in most watersheds, common property lands occupy most of their upper reaches and hence contribute a major share of total runoff and soil loss, their protection through appropriate treatments is necessary to harvest runoff, prevent gully formation in private lands in the lower reaches of the watershed and to augment availability of ground water through percolation. The AKRSP(I) staff are well aware of this lacuna but do not know how to take care of common property lands in their watersheds given indifferent attitude and diagonally opposite approach of the concerned government agencies. On the whole, the AKRSP(I)'s approach has been most successful in India so far as the enlisting people's participation in soil and water conservation programmes is concerned. It is easily replicable wherever there is willingness and patience to develop local human resources and allow them to share both the responsibilities and the resources.

KRISHNA THEERA RAITHA SANGH (KTRS)

The farmers of 27 villages in Jamkhandi taluk of Bijapur, Karnataka, have constructed a barrage without any outside help which is 8 metre high and 480 metre wide on the Krishna river near Chikapadasalagi village. It is a unique effort, the first of its kind in the country which has been designed, financed and built up by the farmers themselves without any help from the government or any other agencies. Built at a cost of Rs. 1.2 crore, the barrage will irrigate over 26,000 acres of agricultural land in Bijapur and Belgaum districts. The construction of the barrage (Fig. 2.4) has also solved the drinking water problems of neighbouring villages and Jamkhandi town whose population is roughly 3.12 lakh. The direct beneficiaries of this unique venture are 64,000 farmers. Mr Nyama Gowda Patil is the driving force behind this stupendous task.

The farmers had collected Rs. 50 lakh on their own to complete the project which the government was reluctant to take up. Before construction of the barrage the villagers used to build a temporary barrage with sand bags, but the sand bag structures each costing between Rs. 50,000 to Rs. 80,000 helped only till January every year. After that, the river ran dry and in the month of March and April, the crops languished.

Fig. 2.4: A View of The Barrage.

Mr. Ashok Thughal, local Engineer, quit his lucrative job and gave the leadership. The project report submitted by the farmers to the government in 1985 envisaged that an 8 metre high dam could store 2.8 TMC ft. of water in the dry months which was enough to irrigate 26,000 acres of land alongside a 42 km. stretch of the river. It was clearly mentioned in the project report that Rs. 1.3 crore would be raised for the project if every beneficiary invested Rs. 500 per acre per horse power of pumping capacity and that small and marginal farmers would contribute to the project in the form of '*Shramdan*'. Mr. Thughal reported that according to their estimate, the project could benefit the farmers by Rs. 2.00 crore annually which means that the entire cost of the project would be recovered in just one year.

The farmers formed the Krishna Theera Raitha Sangh (KTRS) headed by the local MLA, Mr. Bubu Reddy Tughal which mounted pressure on the government. The then Chief Minister, Mr. R.K. Hegde advised the farmers to raise Rs. 15 lakh on their own. The government of Karnataka had put forward a host of conditions – that the entire project cost should be borne by the beneficiaries *i.e.* farmers. The barrage will be handed over to the government for maintenance after completion and the farmers should also bear the maintenance cost and so on. The farmers agreed to all these conditions.

The State Public Works Department (PWD) estimated the cost of the construction of Rs. 1.3 crore. But the farmers' association worked out its construction cost of Rs. 93.56 lakh only. However, the Hegde Government in mid-1987 permitted Sangh for constructing the project and the project work started with the initial capital of Rs. 20 lakh. But it may be realised that more than money, it was sheer enthusiasm on the part of the farmers that provided the impetus. These were the feelings of a prominent farmer Mr. Sidhu Gowda. Besides the beneficiary farmers, several organisations and scores of bank employees, school and college teachers, students and auto-rickshaw drivers helped in this noble cause. Some others helped with implements and transport. Moreover, a Central Government Sponsored agency 'Council for Advancement of Peoples Action and Rural Technology (CAPART)' offered a loan of Rs. 60.00 lakh for the project but the farmers secured only Rs. 28.00 lakh. Keeping in view the farmers' efforts the Veerendra Patil Government also sanctioned Rs. 23.00 lakh for the completion of the project.

The cheerful farmers, after sweating in the scorching heat for years amidst the rumbles of stone-crushers and cement mixers, are waiting to enjoy prosperity in the coming days.

Theory of People's Participation

As defined earlier, participation in fact implies adoption of recommended measures and practices on a sustained basis and partaking in all other activities such as meetings, visits, training courses etc., related to the programme. It is well known from a simplistic version of the decision making theory under risk and uncertainty that a rational farmer would undertake an activity if the expected returns from it markedly exceed its expected costs and the optimum level of adoption is attained when expected marginal returns from adoption are equal to expected marginal cost of adoption. There are many factors that affect expected returns and costs such as expected yields, expected prices, risk aversion, certainty or lack of it about availability of inputs, assurance or lack of it that the expected returns will in fact accrue to the producer etc. Since these factors vary from individual to individual, extent of adoption also varies from farmer to farmer. A logical conclusion of this theory is that anything that increases expected returns or reduces expected costs will increase participaion. In brief, if the farmers' need is well recognised, there would be no hesitation on the part of the farmers to participate.

A theory of participative behaviour (the theory of margin) which is very different from the above-mentioned theory has been propounded by McClusky (1970:25-32). McClusky defines margin as a 'function of the relationship of load to the power'. Load is defined as the 'self- and social demands by a person to maintain a minimum level of autonomy' and power signifies as 'resources such as abilities, possessions, position, allies, etc. which a person can command in coping with the load'. From this characterisation of load and power, Lupanga (1988) derives a hypothesis to explain the lack of people's participation in development activities in the Third World. The hypothesis is that the majority of rural people in most of the Third World have heavy load and little power to cope there-in and hence they are too preoccupied with mere survival to participate meaningfully in development activities. In other words, the higher the margin between load and power, the lesser the participation in development activities. If the hypothesis is true, a logical conclusion can be drawn that efforts to mobilise such marginal masses to participate in development activities must, of necessity, include reduction of load or the raising of their power or both.

Although the above mentioned hypothesis could explain lack of people's participation in development activities, yet it cannot explain why the same people who do not participate in some development activities, participate in some other development activities. There are many instances of poor people in developing countries adopting some technologies or participating in some programmes and rejecting some other technologies or not participating in some other programmes. Hence, a clear conclusion must be some technology-specific or programme-specific factors that affect people's participation. In brief these factors are none other than expected returns and expected costs, project characteristics, and task environment.

Hence, the theory of decision-making under risk and uncertainty can adequately explain why the farmers participate in some programmes and do not participate in some other programmes. For example, in Sukhomajri, the farmers did not participate in the beginning because there was a lot of uncertainty about the quantum of returns. There was no assurance that the promised returns would in fact accrue to them and the expected costs in terms of benefits that were to be foregone by not grazing their animals in common property lands were high. But, afterwards, when a Water Users' Society was established in the village and equal distribution of reservoir water was assured by the Society, and when the farmers themselves saw marked increase in crop yields and milk yield, they came forward and participated in the project. The project involvement helped in increasing the expected returns and reducing the expected costs. Similarly, in all the other cases reviewed and analysed, the project interventions were aimed at either enhancing the expected returns or reducing the expected costs or both directly and/or indirectly.

The lessons may be drawn from the success stories of the model cases discussed above and can safely be concluded that the farmers' participation in overall management of irrigation system is an imperative necessity.

Farmers can be involved in irrigation projects in different ways and at different stages, such as:

1. In identifying major problems/constraints.
2. In developing solutions.
3. In planning activities for implementation and improvements.
4. In providing time, labour, finances and other resources in implementing a project.
5. In the successful operation and maintenance of improved systems through their cooperation.

Under certain conditions, although it is assumed that there is an involvement of farmers but because of the following reasons the involvement is not effective and it adversely affects the system performance:

1. Manipulating farmers for political purposes.
2. Involving only the elite farmers.
3. Involving farmers to make a project look good for a short-while.
4. Involving farmers by issuing orders or dictating terms to them.
5. Using tricks to gain farmers' cooperation.
6. Involving farmers only to please the external agencies.
7. By giving an impression that farmers have been involved but actually they have nothing to do with the process.

Farmers are generally not prepared to take any action of risk and, therefore, they hesitate to participate actively in the Irrigation Development Programme. However, farmers' active participation can be secured if adequate water supply at the right time and right quantity are assured to them. Unfortunately, in the country, formation of Farmers' Voluntary Organisations do not have any legal support and consequently farmers' active participation is lacking. Nevertheless, farmers' participation can not be secured even with the legal support unless farmers are convinced that their participation in the Irrigation Development Programme, will benefit them.

Possibilities of Forming Alternative Organisations

Some of the most important factors responsible for poor management of irrigation systems, under-utilisation of created potential and inefficient irrigation, are the inefficient functioning of farmers' organisations and the non-involvement of the farmers (*i.e.* beneficiaries) in the planning, construction and management of the irrigation systems. However, the success of the farmers organisations depends on the effective leadership and dedicated efforts of the involved persons.[10]

Keeping in view the existing system values, and perception of the farmers, there appears two possibilities of forming alternative organisations of the farmers, which are as follows:

Cooperative Irrigation Societies

Cooperative is desirable on account of its highly educative influence.

---

10. Dr. Theodore Shultz states: "The most important economic resource for India's irrigation development may not be financial capital for new schemes but the acquired abilities of people to do the job .... their knowledge, skills and professional commitment."

On this point, one cannot do better than to quote the Cooperative Planning Committee :

> "No influence is so important in the economic education[11] of farmers as their own efforts in cooperative.... The very attempt on the part of the farmers to solve their problems teaches them basic economic truths. ... Cooperatives also serve an important function in supplying information on the many factors which affect the economic status of farmers."

Although cooperatives are much desirable on account of their significant educative influence and anticipated improvement in the economic status of farmers, yet their performance in the country has been very discouraging. The past experience in the country is that barring a few cases like Mohini Irrigation Cooperative Society, Gujarat, cooperatives have sown seeds of dissatisfaction. Therefore, on the basis of the performance of the cooperatives together with the growth, we are led to believe that cooperative irrigation societies, if formed, would not be different from other cooperatives in respect of their performance and service to the farmers. Hence efforts should be made to persuade the farmers for the formation of cooperative societies and associations on the pattern of Mohini Cooperative Society in Gujarat and Pani Panchayats in Maharashtra.

Studies conducted in different parts of the country revealed that the important factors responsible for poor management of irrigation system and under-utilisation of water are Lack of Effective Functioning of Organisation of the Users. It has been the mere creation of infrastructure of irrigation which is not enough, but its proper utilisation is most important for which farmers should be involved in planning and operation of system. This also helps in building credibility between the farmers and the Government agency, and also play a vital role in the following:

(i) *Ownership Feeling*: Formation of irrigation Panchayats and their active participation in irrigation management will create a feeling of oneness with the system and ensure direct involvement besides helping in proper and efficient maintenance of the

---

11. Association of literacy with technical knowledge scores is more readily understood. A literate farmer with higher education levels has more ready access to knowledge about climate, soil moisture, intake, conveyance, regulation, measurement and application of right quantity of water at right time etc. through newspapers, posters, extension bulletin and personal contacts with irrigation engineers and other irrigation management experts.

system. Care of structure, canal, minor distributaries, water courses, outlets etc. will also be taken by the members.

(ii) *Helps in Saving Time and Money*: Local organisation can assist in construction and maintenance of system specially below the outlet, render help in acquiring the land for construction of water courses, field channels etc. They can also provide local labour, material and other resources for its construction and thus, it will save the time and government money also.

(iii) *Local Experience*: Local people are the best persons to advise about the topography, soil type, pattern of rainfall, location of outlet, social problems, etc. This knowledge will be useful in planning, designing of water-courses, outlets, field channels, etc.

(iv) *Conflicts Resolution*: Panchayat can settle all the conflicts at the local level concerning the allocation and distribution of water, maintenance of water-courses, field channels and supervision of structures which frequently occur in the villages.

(v) *Water Distribution* : The local Water Users' Associations can play an important role in water distribution and allocation of water amongst the users below the outlets. Generally, the water is distributed by the Government officials among the beneficiaries but in some of the disputes, members of Panchayat in consultation with concerned officials, will settle the disputes. It can also make rotational water supply programme effective after consulting the users and irrigation department personnel and programme shall be binding on all the beneficiaries.

Water Users' Association

Unfortunately, in our country, more attention has been paid for the development of irrigation resources but the problem of optimum use of water and its scientific management on the farmers field has not received due attention. Much too often the social and economic aspects of water use have been overlooked. Mere creation of the utilisable potential and infrastructural facilities is not enough. The farmers' active involvement in irrigation development programmes can be ensured by a participatory and community-based approach for which an appropriate organisation can be three-tier system of an elected 'Water Users' Association'. This pyramid can serve the farmers' community with :(i) at the lowest level a 'Chak Samiti' which can be constituted from the farmers within the chak or the outlet command and (ii) secondary level can constitute a sub-project committee formed of the representatives of the outlet committees in a distribution system. In this three-tier system on the tertiary level, the farmers' association can represent the farmers at the highest position in the project development. This could be named as 'Project Policy Decision Committee' (for details see Chapter 7).

The Irrigation Panchayats can play a vital role in water allocation system, maintenance and conflict management.

Level of Panchayats Formation

In most of the States, Irrigation Panchayats are formed at a village level, but as the Irrigation Department is maintaining the system upto outlet level, beneficiaries need to be organised below the outlet level for construction and maintenance of the system and distribution of water. Hence, Panchayats can be formed at outlet level which can serve about 40 hectares. This may involve about 20 farmers (average holding of 2 hectares). These Panchayats can take up the work of construction and maintenance of the water-courses, field channels, drainage and also ensure proper distribution of water among the farmers.

The second level Panchayats can be at the minor or village level which will have member of each 'Chak Level'. These Panchayats will collect the revenue, resolve disputes and help in allocation of water at 'Chak Level'. They will also maintain the liaison with officials.

The members of the Panchayats may be elected by the users and some may be nominated by concerned officials. One or two representatives from Irrigation Department and Agriculture Department, may be nominated to assist the members of Panchayat. Further, these Panchayats can settle all the conflicts at the local level concerning to the allocation and distribution of water and supervision of structures.

Constraints

For smooth functioning of the Irrigation Panchayats, some constraints are experienced which are as follows:

1. Poorly maintained system.
2. Government policies.
3. Inadequate water supply.
4. Personal interest.
5. Very few active members.
6. Interference of local politics.

If these constraints are overcome and Panchayats are encouraged, motivated and powers to the organisation and workers are provided and they are revitalised, it would go a long way in the attainment of high operational efficiency which will improve the irrigation water management efficiency in its real sense.

Participatory Management

Participatory management has been instrumental in major impact on industrial organisations through drastic improvements in workers productivity, quality control and job satisfaction. An administrative structure is maintained for implementing activities and decisions of the organisation, but workers participate at all levels in the management's decision-making process. Similarly, farmers involvement in the management of irrigation project is essential for project's success. However, a more effective management made for irrigation project is participatory management. It is assumed that the responsibility for the delivery, application, use and drainage, water control on the farm is that of the farmer. Farm water-control is simple because the flows involved are small, and, therefore, their control is simple. This is probably the only logical explanation that a farmer has the technical capacity to design, construct, operate and maintain the water delivery, water application, water use and water removal components of a farm water control system. But the matter of faulty control of water on farm is in reality a complicated process, very important and highly technical endeavour for which the best management procedures and best design approaches are not known by all. An engineer who realises this immediately, that the responsibility of water control on the farm is that of the farmer. Work at the farm level with farmers produces an awareness by the engineers of the importance of productivity at the farm level to the success of irrigation projects. Productivity is essential if the returns to investment are to occur. This realisation may also be concluded that it is important for the engineers to work with the farmers to attempt to help them in order to solve the major problems of water control on the farm for effective irrigation project management.

Engineers need to consider seriously the participatory management (Fig. 2.5) for irrigation. Farmers and engineers need to work together for better water management and to solve key problems in irrigation system operation. If it is done, dramatic improvement can be achieved in irrigation leading to overall development. To conclude, ''blaming either

engineers or farmers will hardly help in mitigating the hardships being faced by the marginal and small farmers in the country."

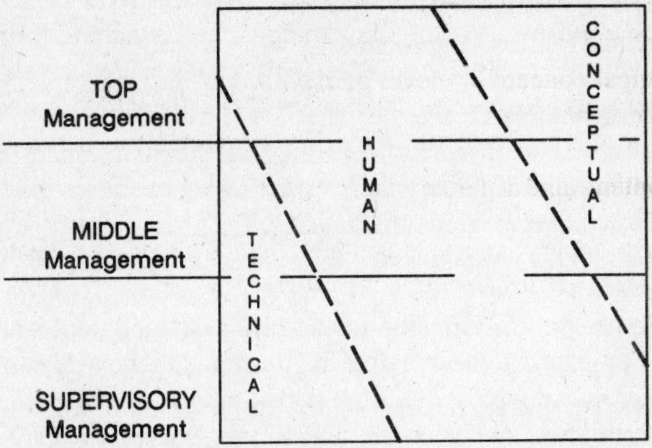

Fig. 2.5: Management skills necessary at various levels of an organization

Motivation and Aspiration

Motivation is closely related to that of organisation (Fig. 2.6). In view of this fact, it implies that the concern is with how superiors influence subordinates. Unfortunately, neither the top officials in State tubewells

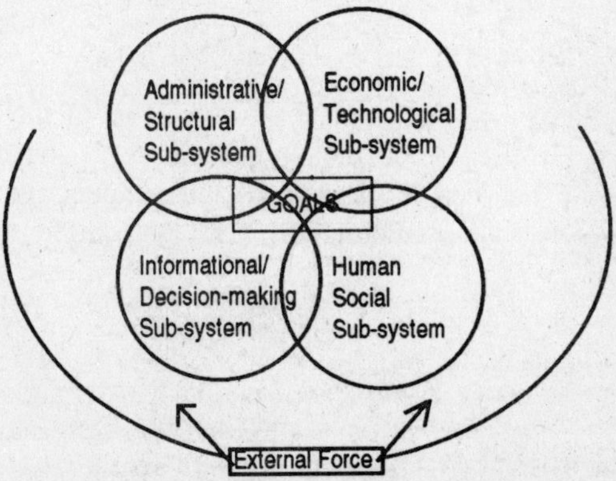

Fig. 2.6 : The Interrelated sub-systems of an organization

organisation functioning, nor local leadership could motivate the farmers. A more complete theory of pluralistic of motivation recognises that individuals work to fulfil a variety of needs *viz*. subsistence, social status, self-esteem, self-fulfilment, which have never been fulfilled, even partially and thus caused resentment among the beneficiaries.

James, March and Herbert Simon constructed a model which emphasized on a psychological concept – "level of aspiration" and conclude from this analysis that high satisfaction does not necessarily stimulate productivity. They state that motivation to produce "stems from a present or anticipated state of discontent and a perception of a direct connection between individual production and a new satisfaction". But, it is not surprising to find that incentive systems are almost non-existence in organisations like surface water development and management, which could be due to passive role of people getting benefits from surface water.

Farmers involvement in decision-making for development and management, is a necessity for the effective improvement of the irrigation systems. To achieve this objective, there are two possibilities of forming alternative organisations of the beneficiaries *i.e.* farmers, which can be either Cooperative Irrigation Societies or Water Users' Association/ Chak Samities. In view of the existing system and performance of the cooperatives in our country, one is led to believe that Cooperative Irrigation Societies, if formed, may not work well, and hence it is better that only the formation of the Water Users' Association/Chak Samities would induce the desired farmers' involvement in overall development and management of groundwater and surface irrigation.

REFERENCES

1. Corey, G.L. Irrigation : Water Management in India: A Farmer Involvement, Unpublished Report, 1981, The World Bank, New Delhi.

   Pant, N. and Verma R.K. : Farmers' Organisation and Irrigation Management, 1983, Ashish Publishing House, New Delhi.

2. Raghuvanshi, C.S. : Socio-Economic Constraints in Adoption of Water Management Technology: A Case Study of Salawa Command, Proceedings of the Seminar on Water Management Technology Transfer, May 1985, G.B. Pant Univeristy of Agriculture and Technology, Pantnagar, India.

3. Patil, R.G., S.D. Suryavanshi, and P.M. Kapase, 1980 : An Investigation into the Socio-Economic Conditions in Ghod Irrigation Project Area, Maharashtra.

4. Proceedings of the Seminar on Farmers' Participation in Irrigation Management (A Critical Consideration), Jan. 1986, Jaipur, organised by IMTI, Kota (Rajasthan).

5. Proceedings of the Seminar on Farmers' Involvement in Irrigated Agriculture (An Interdisciplinary Seminar), Sept. 1986. WALMI, Bhopal.

CHAPTER 3

WATER DISTRIBUTION SYSTEM AND POLICIES

The problem of irrigation management is of increasing concern everywhere in the world and more so in India where huge investments have been made for conserving, and controlling more water for greater agricultural production. Even before an understanding of the management systems, it is important to understand how a system actually performs.

DISTRIBUTION NETWORK

Irrigation involves management of water resources to provide water for use by crops which is not available from precipitation. Equity in distribution and adequate, assured and timely supply of water are the essential characteritics of a good project management. For water transport and its equitable distribution, a water conveyance network from the water control structure and upto the fields is needed. It consists of the following components (Fig. 3.1).

Main Canal: It is the principal channel of a distribution system off-taking from primary source of water *i.e.* a river or a reservoir or tail reach of a feeder.

Branch Canal : It is a canal receiving its supply from the main canal and acting as a feeder for distributaries. Direct outlets are also provided for areas along the canal.

Distributary: It is a channel receiving its supply from the branch canal. It supplies water to minors and water courses.

Minor : It is the smallest channel in the system receiving its supply from distributary canal, and providing direct irrigation through outlets.

Outlet: Point of final distribution of water to an area called command area of the outlet. Water course takes-off-from this point.

Watercourse: It is a channel taking-off from a branch canal, distributary or a minor from which fields are directly irrigated.

Tail Escape: It is an escape at the end of distribution system intended to convey the surplus or unused water to a natural drain, depression or other suitable place.

Above the outlet, maintenance of the canal system alongwith efficient operation has to be ensured for adequate, assured and timely supply of water to the outlets. Below the outlet, a complete and functional network of field channels (water courses) in the outlet command area with suitable number of conveyance control, grade control, distribution control and application control structures is necessary.

Generally, the main-canal runs continuously subject to availability of water except for a closure of 2 to 3 weeks a year, required for repair and maintenance and depends upon the cropping pattern prevalent. Branch, distributary and minor canals may or may not run continuously throughout a crop season depending upon the necessity to strike a balance between water supply and demand.

METHODS OF WATER DISTRIBUTION

Rotational Distribution

Rotational distribution is practised by rotating the supply of water to different areas. Under this method, there are generally three practices. Rotational water delivery is also known as 'WARABANDI' or 'OSRABANDI', wherein 'WARA' means turn and 'BANDI' means fixation. Thus, 'Warabandi' means fixation of turn for irrigating the crop/ field.

The 'Warabandi' is a system of water distribution and management. It is designed such that every farmer is entitled to receive a pre-determined amount of water in proportion to his holding. He tailors his cropping pattern according to this water allocation. The three practices are :

Rotation by section in the branch or distributary canal : The main canal carries a continuous flow while the water is rotated by the section in the branch or distrisbutary canal.

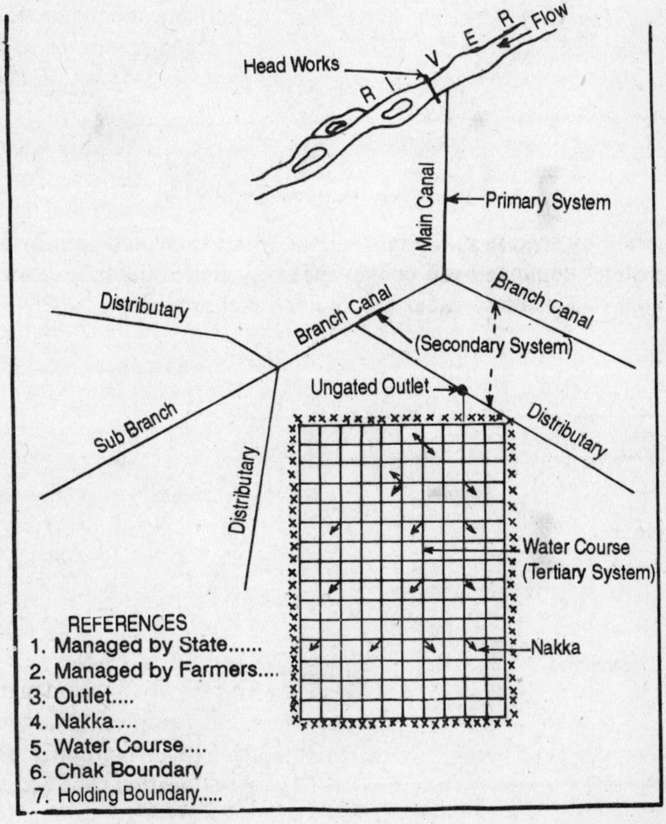

Fig. 3.1: Typical Distribution System

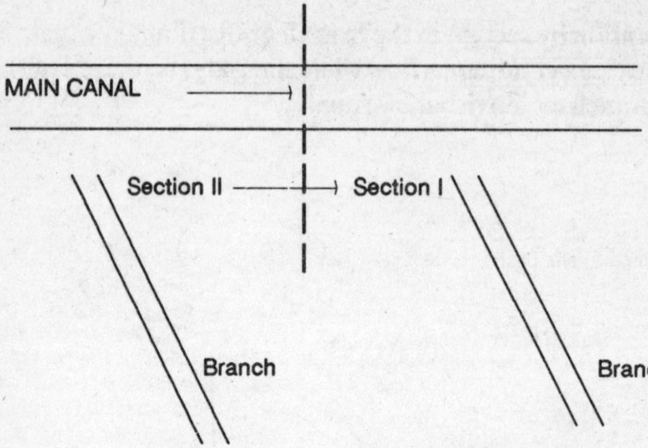

Fig. 3.2: Rotation by Section in Main Canal

Rotation by section in the farm ditch: Water is rotated among the farms in outlet command and conveyance of water in the main canal, branch canal distributary canal and minor canal are continuous.

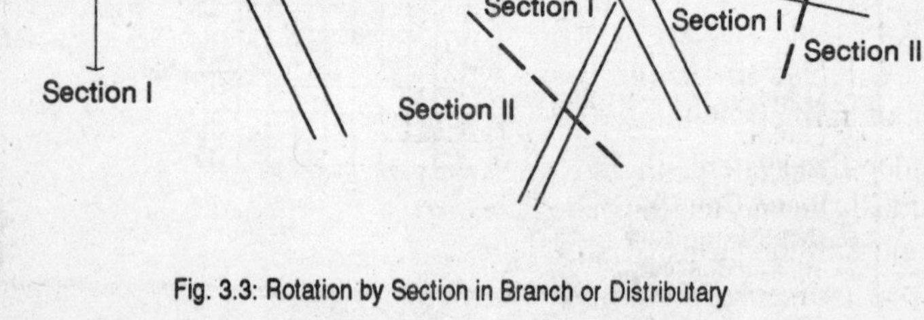

Fig. 3.3: Rotation by Section in Branch or Distributary

Water is delivered to farmers by turn according to a pre-determined schedule specifying day, time and duration of supply in proportion to farmer's area in an outlet command.

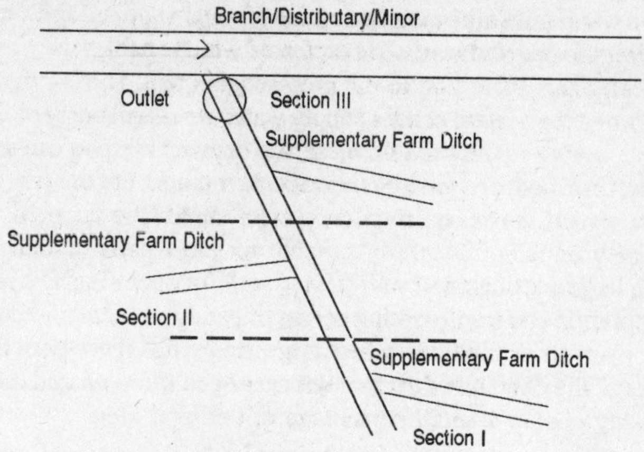

Fig. 3.4: Rotation by Section in Farm Ditch

Simultaneous Distribution

To large concentrated cropped areas such as those held by trusts or sugar factories or corporations, delivery of water can be done continuously instead of by rotation where the farmers are few and the water supply is abundant (as in the rainy season). The simultaneous delivery method can be used efficiently if proper drainage at the farm level is ensured. Water so supplied on a continuous basis can then be re-distributed to different fields according to the soil and condition of crop. Operation of the canal under continuous flow is simpler. Investment in the irrigation system is also less because of fewer water control structures and measuring devices. This method is not suitable when the size of holding is small and irrigation water is to be supplied to a large number of farmers within an outlet command.

Under the system, though each farmer can receive his supplies continuously he may use his share of water intermittently according to the requirement of the crops. The channel should, therefore, have a number of escapes to dispose of surplus water in the channels when the demand for water is less than anticipated.

Distribution on Demand

The method allows a farmer to have supply of water according to his needs but limited to the capacity of the conveyance system.

When water rates are based on volume of water supplied and the cost of water is high, demand method is preferred which enables use of water economically and according to the crop requirement. During the peak demand, when the system cannot supply water simultaneously to all the farmers according to their requirement, the demand method can still be adopted but in a modified form by introducing rotation. For the rest of the irrigation season, however, rotation system should be adopted. The demand method is not generally suitable for most parts of India as it requires a large contingent of well trained staff for operation. During the land preparation and transplanting period of paddy, demand method has an edge over other methods when large flows for short periods are required and the demand of each outlet cannot be foreseen and the area under paddy is only a small percentage of the total area.

The irrigation in-charge should use his wise judgement on what scheme of water distribution to adopt. Judgement should be based on available water supply, rotational areas, cropping pattern, crop water requirements and existing facilities of the system.

ROTATIONAL DELIVERY SYSTEM

Rotational delivery system can be defined as a system of equitable water distribution by turns according to a pre-determined schedule specifying the day, time and duration of supply to each farmer in proportion to his area in an outlet command. The rotational delivery system results in the following improvements :

- The discipline and economy in use of water.
- The reduction in wastage of water and additional coverage under irrigation.
- The farmer's awareness of his legitimate share of water.
- The farmer's keenness to receive it timely and his understanding of the significance of proper land development and water application.
- The pre-planning of cropping operation and arrangement of inputs.
- Minimizing the water disputes.
- Upward shift in agriculture production.

Rotational Water Delivery System in India

It is a simple traditional way of ensuring discipline in utilization of irrigation water from surface irrigation projects. Warabandi has long been practised in Punjab, Haryana, Western Uttar Pradesh and district Ganga-nagar in Rajasthan for decades. The Northern India Canal and Drainage Act, 1873 confers the right of distribution of water on the beneficiaries. However, when the cultivators fail to agree on a mutual settlement, they can apply individually or collectively to the Executive Engineer for enforcement of Warabandi under this Act which lays down the rules for its enforcement. In these areas, allocation of fixed period each week for application of water is calculated on the basis of area of farm irrespective of crops grown.

In Maharashtra, the water distribution system is 'shejpali' and in Karnataka and Gujarat the system of distribution of water is also rotational but the period of allocation of water is based on cropped area sanctioned for irrigation. However, there are many irrigation systems in India where warabandi has not been followed effectively resulting in inefficient irrigation water use. For example, irrigation system in Chambal basin suffered from the following major problems in the absence of warabandi:

(i) Water did not reach tail end of minors. Some of the fields in tail end never received water.
(ii) Irrigation was available at full supply level (FSL) only in head reach. Farmers resorted to their own methods for raising FSL by placing obstructions in minor.
(iii) Installation of unauthorized pipes by farmers to draw larger flow.
(iv) Unauthorized outlets on minors.
(v) Wastage of surplus water in borrow pits along the minor.

DESIGN CONSIDERATIONS OF ROTATION PLANNING

There cannot be an uniform design specification of warabandi for all the irrigation projects as soil and agro-climatic conditions vary from one irrigation project to another. A complete warabandi design may, however, involve the following considerations :

Water Allowance

Calculation of water allowance and duty of canal water based on the seasonal or the peak monthly or fortnightly water requirements for crops sanctioned for irrigation is given as follows.

It should be noted that the required water allowance does not exceed the designed value of water allowance based on actual conveyance capacity.

Example : Sanctioned crops for irrigation in the command of a minor are wheat, potato, tobacco, oil-seeds and vegetables and seasonal water requirements and the cropping pattern are given in the following table.

TABLE 1

The Crop Pattern and the Water Requirement Per Hectare

Crop	Area (Per cent)	Seasonal Water requirement (mm)	Requirement per hectare (m^3)
Wheat	50	450	2250
Potato	20	525	1050
Tobacco	10	525	525
Oil-seeds	10	375	375
Vegetables	10	600	600
			4800

The flow required per hectare : For an average length of crop season of 120 days, the farm ditch efficiency of 80 per cent and the field application efficiency of 85 per cent, the flow requirement at the outlet works out to :

$$\frac{(4800\ m^3) \times (1000\ \text{litres})}{(120\ \text{days}) \times (24\ \text{hours}) \times (3600\ \text{seconds}) \times (0.80 \times 0.85)}$$

$= 0.68$ litres/sec./ha.

i.e. 0.68 litre/sec. flow at the outlet is sufficient to irrigate 1 hectare.

'Bharai' and 'Jharai' are the filling time and depletion time respectively. However, Chusai Factor suggested by Malhotra, S.P. takes into account seepage losses, while working out 'Flow Time'.

Duty of Canal Water : Since one cumec equals 1000 litres/sec. a continuous flow of 1 cumec can irrigate 1000/0.68 or 1471 ha.

Changes may have to be made in the cropping pattern (allocation of crops for irrigation) in such a way that flow requirement (litre/sec/ha) does not exceed the permissible water allowance based on actual conveyance efficiencies.

The water allowance (l/s/ha) will be the highest at the head of the main canal and lowest at the outlet because of conveyance losses in the system *e.g.* if water allowance at outlet is 0.68 l/s/ha and conveyance efficiency at outlet is 80% the water allowance at the main canal head will be 0.85 l/s/ha. This means that if at the outlet water is released continuously at 0.68 l/sec. per hectare of irrigated land, the farmer will receive supplies at 0.68 litre/sec.

For a stream size of 30 l/s area irrigated in a rotation schedule will thus be 44 hectares. If the outlets are run in a rotation schedule of 7 days such that water is delivered continuously for 7 days and the system is closed for another 7 days. The area that can be irrigated during the rotation schedule of 14 days will be 2.2 hectares.

Stream Size

The stream size is the rate at which water is delivered at the outlet. The stream size should be such that can be easily handled by farmers, keeping in view the size of their holdings, the crops grown and the soil characteristics. In case of sandy soils in flat areas, higher discharge (upto 70 litres/sec) can be handled but on heavy soils with low infiltration rates and rolling topography, smaller discharge should be preferred. The appropriate stream size is, however, likely to be in the range of 20 litres/sec to 40 litres/sec. The field channels in the outlet command should have adequate capacity to carry peak-period water demand for designed interval of irrigation inclusive of the conveyance losses.

Volume of water supplied to a farmer can be assessed by the stream size and period of water supply. If stream size and period of supply are fixed, the supply of water will not match the varying demand of water in crop season. Varying water demand can be matched by changing the stream size or period of supply. For convenience of operation stream size is kept fixed.

Depth of Water Application and Rotation Period

The rotation period is the time interval between the irrigations. The rotation period depends upon the depth of water applied and the daily consumptive use for the crops grown. Different crops require water at different intervals. Crops like wheat require a fortnightly and tobacco even a tri-weekly water application. If soils are shallow and highly pervious, less depth of water at frequent intervals (2 days to 3-1/2 days) needs to be applied.

The rotation period should also base on the crops most sensitive to moisture stress (as more than one crop is raised in outlet commands) and the period of highest consumptive use (as the consumptive requirements vary with stage of growth). For operation and regulation convenience it is desirable if the interval of irrigation is kept a week (days are easier to remember than dates) or its multiple.

The following formulae can be used to determine depth of water available on each application :

$$W = \frac{QIT}{A}(1-L)$$

where, W : Water depth of one irrigation (metre) (It usually varies from 5 cm to 10 cm)

Q : Outlet discharge in cumecs.

A : Area irrigated, m^2.

I : Interval (frequency) of irrigation or the rotation period in days, usually a week or its multiple.

T : Time of irrigation per day (seconds)

L : Conveyance loss in farm distribution in decimal.

Formulation of Time Schedule

Allocation of volume of water to each farmer is in proportion to his farm area in an outlet command. Water availability per unit area of the outlet command per rotation is called unit-time.

$$\text{Unit-time} = \frac{\text{Time of irrigation water availability per rotation}}{\text{Command area}}$$

For Example weekly rotation time of irrigation water availability is 24 x 7 = 168 hrs.

For two week rotation it will be 24 x 14 = 336 hrs. and a weekly rotation with irrigation scheduled only during the day (12 hrs.) will mean 84 hrs. of water availability.

Basic time allocated (hrs.) to a farmer for irrigation

= Unit time (hr/ha) x farm area (ha)

Conveyance Loss and Travel Time

The loss of water during conveyance as also the travel time (or transport time) are directly proportional to the length of channel to be traversed by water before reaching to a farmer's field.

The basic time allocated to a farmer as computed above is modified so as to compensate for conveyance loss (in terms of time) and travel time upto their fields.

Time Schedule

A time schedule indicating day and time from beginning to end of irrigation to each farmer is then worked out.

EXAMPLE

An example of design detail of rotational delivery planning is given as follows:

Design Details of Rotational Delivery

Data : Sree Ram Sagar Project, Andhra Pradesh

Minor : SDR 6/D36

Outlet command name : DPI

Outlet command area : 13.38 ha (33.05 acres)

Number of farmers in outlet command: 37

Duty of Water : 1 cumec for 1425 hectares (1 cusec/100 acre)

Soils : 60% soil is red

Course to medium course

Light textured

Sandy Loam

Shallow and very erodable

Infiltration rate: 7.5 to 10.0 cm/hr.

40% soil is black soil

Clay loam

calcarious

Medium deep

Crops grown : Maize, Jowar, Greengram, Groundnut

Each farmer pays water charge of Rs. 50/ha irrespective of crop grown.

Interval of irrigation (rotation period) is kept as one week based on trials conducted for different crops grown and soils encountered.

TABLE 2

Time of Irrigation : day irrigation (14 hrs.)

Farmer groups :

Zone	No. of farmers	Area in acres for each group	
I	7	5.15	
II	12	8.57	
III	12	9.56	
IV	6	9.78	
Total	37	33.05	(13.38 ha)

Calculation of travel time and conveyance losses :

Slope	Vel. of flow	Conveyance loss
1:1000	1 ft./sec.	15%
1:500	1.5 ft./sec.	10%

Calculations are shown in Table 3. Each column is briefly explained below.

PROCEDURE :

Column 1 and 2 : Groups of farmers are formed within the outlet command area having 6 to 10 farmers after discussion with the farmers. In this example four groups of farmers are formed.

Column 3: Area belonging to each farmer is recorded. If one farmer holds more than one plot at different location, then each plot is dealt with separately.

Column 4: Length of field channel from upper distribution box to the distribution box connected to farmer's plot is recorded.

Column 5: The travel time from one box to another is a common loss to all farmers in command area. Hence, cumulative length of field channels upto distribution box connected to farmer's plot are recorded.

Column 6: Slope of the field channels shown in column 4 are recorded.

Column 7: For making computation easier, lengths of field

channels having different slopes are adjusted as if these were having same slope. Length of field channel with original slope of 1:1000 is equivalent to adjusted length which is 1.5 times longer *e.g.* 290 ft. with 1:1000 slope is equivalent to 1.5 x 290 or 435 ft with 1:500 slope because travel time loss per unit length is 1.5 times higher when slope is 1:500 as compared to that when slope is 1:1000.

Column 8: Time of irrigation water availability for day irrigation (14 hrs./day) and weekly rotation is 14 x 7 *i.e.* 98 hrs. Hence, unit time is (98). Command area or 98/33.05 *i.e.* 2.965 hrs. per acre. Basic time is unit time x farm area.

Column 9: (Column 4)/Velocity of flow – Velocity of flow in field channel with slope 1:1000 is assumed to be 1 ft per second. Velocity of flow in field channel with slope 1:500 is 1.5 ft. per second.

Column 10: Transmission loss is 10 per cent for a slope of 1:500 and a channel length of 1000 ft.

Column 11 : Transmission loss in terms of time is (basic time) x (Column 10)/100.

Column 12 : (Column 8) + (Column 11) gives the sum total of Column 12 which is 106.57 hrs.

Column 13 Sum total of column 12 exceeds (available irrigation time – travel time loss) *i.e.* (98-0.9) hrs. or 97.1 hrs.

Column 14 : (Column 13) + (Column 9).

WATER SUPPLY DISTRIBUTION SYSTEM

Following principal methods are in use for the supply and control of irrigation water to the cultivators :

1. In the states of U.P., Punjab and Haryana under the North India Canal and Drainage Act of 1873, the Irrigation Department has some control over the water courses and the distribution of water among the cultivators is done under the system known as Osrabandi/ Warabandi. The supply of water is made on the unit culturable command and the irrigators are free to use water with their own desired cropping pattern. Thus, the Irrigation Department has no control on the type of crops to be grown by the farmers, the location and extent of area.

TABLE 3

A Hypothetical case for Calculation of Time Schedules for Introduction of Warabandi under Pipe P1 of a hypothetical area

Group No.	Name of the farmer	Area in Acres	Length of F.Cs from previous wet D.B. in feet		Slopes of F.Cs from previous D.B.I.	Adjusted length for calculation in feet	Basic time allocated in hours	Transport time in hours	Total transmission losses in %	Total mission losses in hours	Total time required if compensated in hours	Adjusted time per plot in hours	Final time per plot considering 14 hours per day				Timeschedule
			Individual	Cumulative									in hrs.	hrs. min.	hrs. min.	hrs. min	
1	2	3	4	5	6	7	8	9	10	11	12	13	14	15	16		
I (1)	A	0.45	290	290	1000	435	1.33	0.08	4.35	0.06	1.39	1.27	1.35	1.20	5-00AM	6-20 AM	Monday
(2)	B	0.30	-	290	1000	435	0.88		4.35	0.04	0.92	0.84	0.84	0.50	6-20	7-10	Monday
(3)	C	0.87	100	390	500	535	2.57	0.02	5.35	0.14	2.71	2.47	2.49	2.30	7-10	9-40	Monday
(4)	D	1.00	150	540	500	685	2.96	0.03	6.85	0.22	3.18	2.90	2.93	2.55	9-40	12-35	Monday
(5)	E	0.50	250	790	500	935	1.48	0.05	9.35	0.15	1.63	1.48	1.53	1.30	12-35	14-05	Monday
(6)	F	0.50	125	915	500	1060	1.48	0.02	10.60	0.17	1.65	1.50	1.52	1.30	14-05	15-35	Monday
(7)	G	1.52	100	1015	500	1160	4.49	0.02	11.60	0.59	5.08	4.63	4.65	4.40	15-35	20-15	Monday
Group Total		5.15					15.19	0.22		1.31	16.56	15.09	15.31				
II. (1)	H	0.37	—	—	—	—	1.09	—	—	—	1.09	0.99	0.99	1.00	5.00	6.00	Tuesday
(2)	I	0.90	200	200	500	200	2.66	0.04	2.00	0.05	2.71	2.47	2.51	2.30	6.00	8.30	Tuesday
(3)	J	0.65	150	350	500	350	1.92	0.03	3.50	0.07	1.99	1.81	1.84	1.50	8-30	10-20	Tuesday
(4)	K	0.82	—	350	500	350	2.42	—	3.50	0.09	2.51	2.29	2.29	2.15	10-20	12-35	Tuesday
(5)	L	0.60	100	450	500	450	1.77	0.02	4.50	0.08	1.85	1.68	1.70	1.40	12-35	14-15	Tuesday
(6)	M	0.60	100	550	500	550	1.77	0.02	5.50	0.10	1.87	1.70	1.72	1.45	14-15	16-00	Tuesday
(7)	N	0.50	—	550	500	550	1.48	—	5.50	0.09	1.57	1.43	1.43	1.25	16-00	17-25	Tuesday
(8)	O	0.50	100	650	500	650	1.48	0.02	6.50	0.10	1.58	1.44	1.46	1.30	17-25	18-55	Tuesday
(9)	P	0.63	70	720	500	720	1.86	0.01	7.20	0.14	2.00	1.82	1.83	1.50	5-00	6-50	Wednesday
(10)	Q	1.00	—	720	500	720	2.96	—	7.20	0.23	3.19	2.91	2.91	2.55	6-50	9-45	Wednesday
(11)	R	1.00	60	780	500	780	2.96	0.01	7.80	0.25	3.21	2.92	2.93	2.55	9-45	12-40	Wednesday
(12)	S	1.00	120	900	500	900	2.96	0.02	9.00	0.29	3.25	2.96	2.98	3.00	12-40	15-40	Wednesday
Group Total		8.57					25.33	0.17		1.49	26.82	24.42	24.59				

III.	(1)	a	0.40	260	610	500	610	1.88	0.05	6.10	0.08	1.26	1.15	1.20	1.10	15-40	16-50	Wednesday
	(2)	b	0.42	90	700	500	700	1.24	0.02	7.00	0.09	1.33	1.21	1.25	1.15	16-50	18-05	Wednesday
	(3)	c	0.70	160	869	500	860	2.07	0.03	8.00	0.11	2.26	2.06	2.09	2.05	18-05	20-10	Wednesday
	(4)	d	0.45	120	1980	500	1980	1.33	0.02	9.80	0.14	1.47	1.434	1.36	1.20	5-00	6-20	Thursday
	(5)	e	1.00	120	1100	500	1100	2.96	0.02	11.00	0.36	3.32	3.02	3.04	3.00	6-20	9-20	Thursday
	(6)	f	0.18	230	840	500	840	0.53	0.04	8.40	0.05	0.58	0.53	0.57	0.35	9-20	9-55	Thursday
	(7)	g	0.52	–	840	500	850	1.53	–	8.40	0.14	1.67	1.52	1.52	1.30	9-55	11-25	Thursday
	(8)	h	0.60	190	1030	500	1030	1.77	0.04	10.30	0.20	1.97	1.79	1.83	1.50	11-25	13-15	Thursday
	(9)	i	0.77	–	1030	500	1030	2.27	–	10.70	0.26	2.52	2.31	2.31	2.20	13-15	15-35	Thursday
	(10)	j	0.52	180	1210	500	1210	1.53	0.03	12.10	0.21	1.74	1.58	1.61	1.40	15-35	17-15	Thursday
	(11)	k	1.00	150	1360	500	1360	2.96	0.03	13.60	0.46	3.42	3.12	3.15	3.10	17-15	20-25	Thursday
	(12)	l	3.10	200	1230	500	1230	9.17	0.04	12.30	1.29	10.46	9.53	9.57	9.35	5-00	14-35	Friday
Group Total			9.56					28.54	0.32		3.47	32.01	29.16	29.48				
IV.	(1)	m	2.00	–	–	–	–	5.82	–	–	–	5.92	5.39	5.39	5.25	14-35	20-00	Friday
	(2)	n	3.10	250	250	1000	370	9.17	0.05	3.75	0.36	9.53	8.68	8.73	8.45	5-00	13-45	Saturday
	(3)	o	0.55	400	650	100	975	9.62	0.07	9.75	0.17	1.79	1.63	1.70	1.40	13-45	15-25	Saturday
	(4)	p	1.40	100	950	500	1075	4.14	0.02	10.75	0.50	4.64	4.23	4.25	4.15	1-25	19-40	Saturday
	(5)	q	1.15	175	925	500	1250	3.40	0.03	12.50	0.48	3.88	3.53	3.56	3.35	5-00	8-35	Sunday
	(6)	r	1.58	130	1055	500	1380	4.69	0.02	13.80	0.75	5.42	4.97	4.99	5.00	8-35	13-35	Sunday
Group Total			1.78					28.94	0.19		2.26	31.18	28.43	28.62				
Grand Total			33.05					98.00	0.90		8.59	106.57	97.10	98.00				

2. In the states of Maharashtra and Gujarat the cultivators are required to construct and maintain the water courses. The system adopted is known as Shejpali system of water supply. The Irrigation Department has control over the water and the crops grown. Farmers use block systems. Type of crops and area to be irrigated are fixed before hand, but the cultivator is free to rotate the land area on which crops are grown during any season. Department is responsible to supply water even to the fields till their maturity *i.e.* crops maturity.
3. In the states of Andhra Pradesh, Tamil Nadu and Karnataka the Irrigation Department has very little control over the water supply beyond the outlet. The supply is based on the concept of localisation of areas for wet and dry crops under which the location of the land and the crops grown are fixed.
4. In the states like Orissa, West Bengal and Bihar, West Bengal Irrigation Act of 1976 is applicable. The Department has little control over the supply and construction of water courses beyond the outlets.

In fact, better results can be obtained if a common and uniform system of supply of water to the farmers and control with regard to the type of crops grown, the extent of the areas is adopted. Since, these systems have been practised for quite a long time and have a historical background, a sudden radical change may not be readily possible. It is, however, desirable that the Irrigation Department which supplies water upto outlet, should have control beyond outlet also. This could, perhaps be done within the framework of the existing set-up.

Shejpali System of Water Supply

Shejpali system is evolved on the Deccan canals as a result of irrigation of over a century. Topography in this region is hilly. In this system canals are designed just to cater for the area, proposed in the approved crop-pattern. This system is the product of the last 60 years experience on the Deccan Canal System. Topography and the conventions of taking particular types of crops are the factors in getting this system established successfully on the Deccan Canals in particular and in Maharashtra as a whole.

Irrigation Department is responsible for supplying adequate quantity of water till the maturity of crops. Requirement of water for every rotation, sub-division-wise is calculated and distributed among the sub-divisions by the Executive Engineer in charge of the Management Division. After the quota for each sub-division is fixed, it is further distributed among the various sections considering the sanctioned demands, duly normally obtained in each section based on the Karia registers. The Sectional Officer incharge of the section further divides the quota of one rotation among the various Canal Inspectors incharge of Irrigation Distributary-wise and outlet-wise.

Requirement of water at the outlet head is calculated on the basis of the value of AIDC as six. It is considered that 4 hours would be sufficient to consider one cusec of flow to irrigate one acre of sanctioned crop. On each outlet the Canal Inspector incharge prepares a list of sanction holders, their sanctions in terms of acreage and thus, it is calculated the total quantum of water in terms of day-cusecs for each outlet. On the basis of 4 hours requirements for one acre, he calculates the total for which a particular outlet is required to run. On this basis he gives the date and the time to the sanction holders. At a particular pre-determined place in his beats he convenes a meeting of the sanction holders and gives them the date and time for which the water will be supplied during the rotation. This time table is known as 'Pali-Patrak' and is prepared for each outlet by the Canal Inspector with the approval of the Section Officer incharge of the Section. This system of preparation of 'Pali-Patrak' and supplying water according to the pre-determined date and time is known as 'Shejpali System' of irrigation.

This system is practiced on the old established canal for years together and has proved to be successful. The irrigators have understood this system and they take water according to the rotations. In Maharashtra, as yet irrigation has not been made compulsory and it is optional. If in any particular rotation, the irrigator could not get water, the Department supplies him water by running the particular outlet for some time more.

Warabandi System of Irrigation in the North

North Indian states like, U.P., Haryana and Punjab are governed by the 'North India Canal and Drainage Act of 1873'. The main features of the Act are given as below :

(i) Water right goes with the land.

(ii) Irrigation officers should generally interfere as little as possible in the internal distribution of water on water courses. When disputes arise they should persuade the parties to settle it mutually, if not, the case may be referred to the Panchayat.

(iii) Outlet chaks are finalised from the map of 1 ft. contour intervals. Discharge beyond 2 cusecs is always avoided in an outlet. A chak area should be as far as possible wholly in one village to avoid disputes among the farmers. Final boundaries of outlets are fixed in consultations with cultivators under section 20 of the Canal Act and the position so fixed should be able to command the whole area.

(iv) The duration of supply to each holding under an outlet is fixed earlier on the understanding that each cultivator will be entitled to duration of supply in proportion to the area of his entire holding in the chak.

(v) A farmer is always entitled to get his supply on the particular time and day of the week. There should be no deviation of this. However, the disadvanctage of this system is that it affords no relief from turn occurring at night. Of course, this bottleneck can be solved if the timings are altered amicably.

The sanctioned Warabandi should be accompanied by a copy of Shajon on which the water course, the established off-take, the nakkas and the boundaries of the units are shown.

(vi) The system does not provide any incentives to the cultivators for economical use of water. They go on applying water to their fields even if the crop requirement is nil. This results in wastage of water and tends to increase water logging of culturable area. A considerable quantity of water is lost due to seepage in the water course as the Irrigation Engineer or the farmer himself does not take any responsibility. The irrigator or who takes initiative of spreading the water over a greater area in a bid to optimal use of water has to pay relatively higher water rates, a penalty for his initiative and judicious use of water to increase the output from his land and agriculture production of the country as a whole. The careless irrigators on the other hand enjoy the advantages of paying less water charges as compared to volume of water utilised by them.

Principles of Warabandi System

The cardinal principle underlying the Warabandi System of irrigation management is that the available water, whatever its quantum, is allocated to farmers in equal proportion to their Culcurable Command Area (CCA) in order to meet their total demand. This principle imposes water scarcity conditions in the system and leads to the adoption of more efficient practices by farmers. Economically, this should result in higher average production per unit of the available water and socially, warabandi stands for equitable distribution of water to the largest number of farmers in the command. Thus, in Warabandi system a farmer handles his water budget and he is free to determine/decide his own cropping pattern so long as he can manage to remain within the constraints of the water-right allocated to his holding. However, in a lean year, the hardship is shared by all which is not confined to the tail-enders or to those who are otherwise less influential.

The main components of the Warabandi System are discussed as follows:

(i) Water Allocation

Each unit of CCA is allocated a certain rate of flow of water known as Water Allowance. Its value is often a compromise between demand and supply. The carrying capacity of distributaries and water-courses is designed on the basis of this allowance. Also the outlets of water-courses are constructed so that all of them draw their authorised share of water from the distributary concurrently.

The ratio which the operating period of a distributary bears to the total period of the crop is called its Capacity Factor, which is again a compromise between demand and supply. For example in case of Bhakra Canal System the designed mean Capacity Factors for Kharif and Rabi are 0.8 and 0.72 respectively which means that during these seasons, each distributary may receive full water for about 144 and 129 days respectively *i.e.* for about 273 days in a year.

The 'Duty of Water' (area irrigated per unit of water made available) is, however, not used in Warabandi system which is replaced by three terms *i.e.* Water Allowance, Capacity Factor and Intensity of Irrigation. They cover designing, operating and monitoring the system. The mathematical relationship between Duty and other variables is shown below:

$$\begin{array}{c}\text{Duty of unit of} \\ \text{Water in hectares}\end{array} = \frac{\text{100 hectares}}{\begin{array}{c}\text{Water Allowance} \\ \text{for 100 hectares}\end{array}} \times \begin{array}{c}\text{Intansity of} \\ \text{Irrigation (per cent)}\end{array}$$

(ii) Distribution Infrastructure

In the Warabandi system, the water from the source (Fig. 1), which may be a river or a reservoir, is carried by a main canal. The main canal feeds two or more branch canals which operate by rotation and may or may not run on full supply. This constitutes the primary distribution system which runs throughout the irrigation season with varying supply. However, the secondary distribution system consists of the Branch canals which supply water to a large number of distributaries. These must run at full supply by rotation. The tertiary distributary system consists of the distributaries which supply water to water courses through ungated, fixed discharge outlets. Water courses run at full supply when the distributary is running full and its water is allocated to farmers by a time roster.

(iii) Management of Warabandi System

In this system the distribution of water is a two-tier operation and each is managed by a separate agency *i.e.* state and the farmers. In the upper tier, it is managed by the state and all distributaries, and consequently water courses are always operated with full discharges, which reduces the running time. Consequently the conveyance losses in distributaries are minimum. However, the distributaries are operated in eight-day periods, but the number of such eight-day period depends upon availability and crop water requirements.

The second tier of distribution exists in the distribution of water coming out of an outlet and flowing into a water course, which is managed by farmers. Further, the distribution of this water is done on a seven-day rotation basis under an approved roster. This divides 168 hours (*i.e.* seven days) in the ratio of the CCA of different holdings. The outlets have no gates and the eight-day period for the running of a distributary ensures a minimum of seven-days running for each water course. But the eighth day is required for filling the distributary. The system is designed and managed in such an integrated manner that it is enough to control the distributary at its head in order to monitor the performance of its several water courses only.

Each farmer's right to share water in a water course is guaranteed by law. But the state has nothing to do for administering water courses, and the farmers manage on their own under overall legal control. There is no provision in this system to compensate any individual farmer who may fail to receive his share of water because there is no unallotted time. Fortunately, this model of running a distributary and its water courses involve human control only at the distributary head leaving the outlet at the water course head automatic. Hence, the absence of human control at the water course head makes distribution fool-proof to a great extent. Further, decentralised management below the outlet minimises administrative costs. The farmers depend on their own experience. Each farmer contributes labour and money to the common cause of repair and maintenance to their water course. Despite the success of the Warabandi system, absorption losses in water courses below the outlet continue to be nearly 25 per cent of the supply at its head. The losses increase towards the tail reaches of a water course.

WATER DISTRIBUTION POLICIES

In an agricultural country like India, it is very unfortunate that in some of its irrigation projects, the pace of actual utilisation of water remains much behind its planned schedule. The reasons for the same can be either some drawbacks in design or execution, or the adoption of such distribution policies as fail to motivate farmers for involvement in irrigation management. Whereas the design or execution are somewhat remediable even at a later stage, the latter are irreversible once the project has been commissioned, which leads to several problems and the principal one being, that farmers, particularly the tail-enders are not able to get their due share of water from a public canal. The same is either misappropriated by head-reach or allowed to run waste. Either situation results in large scale discontentment amongst farmers causing lop-sided development, economic disparities and social tensions in the command of a project. For the sustained development of a project, the role of a distribution policy which can ensure some sort of equity and social justice, cannot be over-emphasized.

Present Policies

In our country every state is free to decide its own distribution policy according to its traditions, concepts and values about water, and therefore, there are as many policies as the number of states. Although these policies differ in their aims and objectives, yet the management of all of them, has one common feature *i.e.* complete dependence on farmers for constructing a community channel called water course for linking their holdings with public distributary. Farmers' motivation for such a venture naturally depends upon the benefits which a distribution policy can ensure for them. Hence, the size of an average holding being small, a number of them have to be clubbed together to form a viable unit for consuming the minimum water that can be let into a water course. The delicate aspect of its further distribution has perforce to be left to farmers themselves which leads to conflicts and as a rule, it is the lower ones which suffer. They retaliate by with-holding their contribution towards the community water course particularly maintenance without which no water can reach them and such a vicious circle cannot but upset the designed performance of a project.

In actual practice the combined share of some 20 to 80 farmers is delivered to them at a point called an outlet in a distributary, which is generally within 2 kilometres of the farthest holding. It is not believable that farmers can be indifferent to a precious input like water if only they are sure of getting their share. Their sensitiveness to equitable distribution is certainly believable. The farmers may tolerate shortage arising out of a drought as that is a natural calamity but they cannot compromise with when it arises out of a man made policy. Hence no distribution policy can afford to ignore this factor if it is to exist.

The present water distribution policies lack proper documentation and their aims and objectives remain undefined. Their broad features have been only passed down verbally by one generation of managers to the next. The circumstances leading to their birth are not known and their relevance to the present socio-economic conditions have never been reviewed. For all practical purposes they have existed in isolation without any mutual interaction. Their performance has never been monitored and the vital information as to who gets, what, when and with what results, is poor. Also there has been no fruitful research with a view to streamline them. These have never been exposed to any criticism by agronomists, water management economists and sociologists. They have never been involved to provide a comprehensive coverage to any of the problems facing them. Besides there is no sincere effort to make use of any of the modern tools of management like computers. Whatever little research has been done is of isolated nature and for want of any apex body, has remained uncoordinated.

The introduction of the high yielding varieties of crops has added a new dimension to the management of public canals. They require water not only in higher doses but also more frequently and more on time. Public canal systems have their constraints both in quantity as well as of time and are generally not able to meet the increasing demands therein. This necessitates to several debatable issues. What is the optimum in a particular case? Should a public canal be operated for maximum yields for a smaller number of farmers or for smaller yields for a larger number of them ? Which policy can ensure greater efficiency *i.e.* overall production per unit of the available water? To what extent can the equity and social justice be translated into actual practice? Should farmers have the freedom to take decisions about cropping pattern or should the state enforce the same and why? As no reliable data are available, these issues cannot be sorted out. However, an expert opinion for or against them is, therefore, based on his judgement only.

Of the several constraints which a water distribution policy has to face, the most important is the dichotomy of control over water of the state and the farmer. Whereas the state manages it from the point of view of the collective good of the farming community, the individual farmer who is the actual user of it does so entirely in self interest and the goals of the two may not always coincide, thus subjecting the water to divergent pulls. A distribution policy has to face the difficult task of striking some sort of balance.

Possible Approaches

There can be two possible approaches for fixing a farmer's right of water from a public canal. It can be related to either the 'demand' of crops allowed to be sown or the size of his holding irrespective of the crops. The former approach appears to be more sensible from the point of view of crop yields. But it has one serious practical difficulty, when the available supply of water falls short of demand, which happens quite often. It becomes difficult to apply a cut based on equity as this runs against the basic approach. The field experience shows that whenever any such effort is made, head reach farmers somehow manage to draw their full share leaving the tail-enders to bear the whole brunt of shortage.

(i) Demand-based Policies

Delivery of water to each farmer according to his demand can be considered as an ideal for an irrigation policy which would be possible only where the supplies are in abundance and holdings are so big as to have an independent outlet from a public distributary. To achieve this ideal in some of the states where the prevailing conditions are just the opposite, it renders the distribution fairly complex as the resultant one is neither equitable nor based on any form of social justice. This disadvantage has far outweighed any advantage which this policy may otherwise have. But the experience in some of the western and sourthern states is disheartening as each one of them has a history of sick irrigation projects whose slow rate of development has become a matter of serious concern to their planners. When the demand of an individual farmer is to be met, the need for devising any sophisticated or precise method for delivering only an accurately measured quantity of water to him is not felt. Unfortunately crude methods are considered to be good enough. Here, water is let into farmers' water course with the help of gated outlets which have to be adjusted manually to suit the-day-to-day requirements. This practice is bound to serious error and corruption which invariably works against the interest of lower farmers. Hence it renders a distributary unable to run full supply at any time and thus concurrently feed all its water courses – a practice which is most desirable for better control and for reducing the running period and consequently seepage losses and water logging to the minimum.

Besides this, farmers being the decision-maker to decide the need based on their cropping pattern and adequacy of an irrigation they have a tendency for over irrigation with a perception, 'more water, more production', and thus they have no incentive for economising the use of water. Consequently, several wasteful practices have crept into this system. In some states, water courses are not constructed and field to field irrigation is resorted to. Also, no irrigation is done at night and thus nearly one-fourth of canal water is allowed to go waste. All this recoils on the rights of the tail-enders as no project is designed for such wastages. The loss involved is not only of valuable water but also of canal capacity and as a consequence the latter has to be made good by running the distributaries with part discharges for extra periods to feed the tail portions. This requires greater number of control points. All this means still greater losses, further reduction of efficiency and more of water-logging. Farmers do not feel like exploiting ground-water and thus eliminating or minimizing the water-logging.

Equitable distribution of water is a difficult task even ordinarily but this is rendered more so on account of an inherent drawback of irrigation projects. Their head reaches are generally fit to receive water much earlier than their tail-end and often, this lag extends over a decade or so. During this period some surplus water is always available at the source and to avoid its wastage, it is temporarily allocated to head reach farmers. Head reach farmers start consuming it by raising such crops which are otherwise prohibited and for them there is no provision in the project. Over a short period, they acquire enough of prosperity and political power which renders the withdrawal of this temporarily allocated water, difficult.

These farmers must plead that according to the doctrine of prior appropriation, they should continue to get what has once been allocated to them. If the distribution policy is also demand-based, such a withdrawal becomes difficult and this lays the foundation for the lopsided development of a project.

(ii) Holding-based Policies

In the case of these policies, water is made available to all farmers in proportion to their holdings for meeting the requirement of a notional cropping pattern and not the actual one. It is not obligatory for farmers to stick to it and they are free to use their share in any manner they deem fit. They are also free to supplement the same from other sources like well and tubewells. For example, Warabandi systems of North-Western States is of this type.

This policy originated towards the close of the last century when big canal taking-off directly from rivers were first introduced in the Indo-Gangetic plains. The main philosophy behind it was to spread the benefits of canals rather thinly so as to provide protection against famines to as large farmers *i.e.* large areas as possible. It was initially conceived for protective irrigation but later on when more water became available, it was found to be equally good for productive *i.e.* intensive irrigation. The policy has a distinguishing feature which aims at social justice to all farmers by providing them with equitable water, irrespective of the geographic location of their holdings. The farmers, thus have always felt motivated to extend their cooperation for the construction of community water courses which in a way has no need for having an agency like Command Area Development Authority for this purpose. This policy is equally good for all types of crops including the High Yielding Varieties which is quite evident from the recent green revolution in the North-Western States. In spite of its drawbacks, it has gained popularity, and now several other states wish to switch over to it in preference to their own.

In Warabandi, every farmer gets the same volume of water in each of his turns, and the total volume received by him in a crop season can be ascertained by knowing the number of times his distributary has run. This information can be utilised for devising a simple method for assessment of water charges, which would prove a proxy for the volumetric method of assessment. One such method known as WARIMETRIC was introduced in Haryana in 1976 on experimental basis. It has since been extended to an area of 20,000 ha, which has tremendous scope for simplifying the current assessment procedure which is tedious and time consuming. This can be considered to be an added advantage of the Warabandi system.

The Present Crisis

Some of the policies governing a farmer's right of water from a public canal have failed to deliver goods, which is evident from the persistent gap between the irrigation potential created and being utilised. However, various remedies have been tried from time to time without any success.

In the early sixties it was felt that the inability of farmers to construct and maintain long watercourses was the root cause of the problem. With a view to lighten their burden, the Government decided to reduce the length of these water courses by extending public canal upto 5-8 hectares blocks, against the previous limit of 40 hectares or so. In spite of this relief, there was no improvement and change in the attitude of the lower farmers towards the construction of water courses. It was not realised then that such a lack of motivation could also be due to the distribution policies being unattractive. Therefore, in the early seventies, it was realised that this step alone was not enough and many more were needed. Accordingly, it was decided to provide a package of other related facilities besides water courses for water supply. For this, over 60 Command Area Development Authorities were set up. This was a unique effort ever made in the history of irrigation management in this country. Despite all of this, there was no break-through. However, the diagnosis lacked scientific study, therefore, the remedy applied was not adequate. Whatever else the Command Area Development Authorities may have done, they did not go into the question of distribution policies. Being powerful and multidisciplinary organisations, CADA has a unique opportunity for conducting research on this aspect of water management. They alone could have helped in locating the sensitive or popular components of different policies. The CADA deliberately or otherwise, seemed to have preferred to follow the path of least resistance by adhering to the old ones. Thus, the great hopes linked with this effort did not materialise.

Warabandi did not show spectacular results till the green revolution became visible. The belief, that it has a greater acceptability by the farmers gained ground gradually and accordingly the Govt. of India provided a sizeable amount of money in the Sixth Five Year Plan for enabling the sick projects to switch over to this policy. Several states started pilot experiments on this but their modality has left much to be desired. Also no State has thought of evolving measured quantities of water to farmers in proportion to the size of their holdings or inducing them for night or round the clock irrigation. The gated outlets, which are only a crude device for measuring water and their operation is prone to error and corruption but these, have been allowed to continue as before. At the best it is an exercise in supplying unmeasured quantities of water as before but in some sequential order. This may be good which is not enough and is certainly far away from Warabandi. The result has been, that none of the states is in a take-off stage, even after 20 years of experimentation. A correct approach appears to have failed for want of proper implementation.

Development of an irrigation project has its own significance and equitable distribution of water is its most important single propellant. After a long course of trial and error, lasting over two decades, a clearer picture of the complexities of the problems has emerged.

Traditionally, there has been a strong linkage between land and water. Whereas land policies have undergone a change but with a limited success and efforts have been made to make them more socialistic by enacting Land Ceilings Acts, but not much has been done for water. As the gap between its supply and demand is increasing, day by day, the question of rationing it from public canals in some form or the other assumes greater importance and shall have to be faced sooner or later. Unlike land, its availability is not a fixed factor as it varies from year to year and from season to season. Its distribution is a recurring and continuous process and hence the need for evolving fool-proof policies for its equitable distribution, is of much consequence. A definite tilt towards policies like Warabandi which encompasses rationing, equity and social justice, is visible. This may provide an answer to the current crisis.

REFERENCES

1. Proceedings of the Workshop on "Water Distribution Practices" July, 1982, IWRS, WRDTC, University of Roorkee, U.P.
2. Manual on "Warabandi in Irrigation Projects", Government of India, Ministry of Irrigation, New Delhi, April 1982.
3. S.P. Malhotra, "The Warabandi and its Infrastructure", Central Board of Irrigation and Power, Publication No. 157, New Delhi, 1982.
4. Manual on "Irrigation Water Management", Government of India, Ministry of Agriculture and Irrigation, Department of Agriculture, Krishi Bhavan, New Delhi, March 1979.

5. Kathpalia G.N., "Rotational System of Canal Supplies and Warabandi in India, Water Management Synthesis Project", WMS Report 6 of United States Agency for International Development. Agricultural & Irrigation Engineering, Utah State University, Logan, Utah 84322 (USA).
6. *Water Management Journal*, Vol. 1, No. 1, July 1991, published by Water Management Forum, The Institution of Engineers (India), Gujarat State Centre, Ahmedabad.
7. Proceedings of the Seminar on "Planning Operation of Irrigation Networks," May 1987, Jaipur, IWRS, WRDTC, Roorkee University.
8. Pant Niranjan (1984), "Producivity and Equity in Irrigation System", Edited, Ashish Publishing House, 8/81, Punjabi Bagh, New Delhi.
9. Bhargava, B.S. "Minor Irrigation Development Administration", Ashish Publishing House, Punjabi Bagh, New Delhi.

CHAPTER 4

CROPPING PATTERN AND CROP PLANNING

Cropping pattern means the proportion of area under different crops at a point of time. A change in cropping pattern means a change in the proportion under different crops. In actual field conditions the cropping pattern means both time and space sequence of crops. In Northern India, there are two distinct crop seasons, Kharif (July to October), and Rabi (November to March). Crops grown between March and June are known as Zaid. The land may be occupied by one crop during one season (mono cropping), or, in the sequence of cropping it is likely that only one crop is grown year after year on the same plot/area, which is known to be mono-culture. If two crops (double cropping) or more crops are grown in succession within a year, it is called multiple cropping. Of late, the trend is even towards more than two crops (multiple-cropping) in a year. If cereal after cereal is grown in multiple cropping, it is also mono-culture. Cropping pattern plays a vital role in determining the level of agricultural production, which in turn reflects on the agricultural economy of an area. A radial orientation of the cropping pattern may be affected on account of changes in agrarian policy, improvements in technology, availability of agricultural inputs etc.

In any locality, the prevalent cropping systems are the cumulative results of past and present decisions by individuals, communities or governments and their agencies. These decisions are usually based on experience, tradition, expected profits, personal preferences and resources, social and political pressure and so on. It is also affected by soils, climate, irrigation facilities available, farmers requirement of food and fodder, market facilities and prevailing prices etc. The availability of labour and capital also influence the cropping pattern to a greater extent. In addition to these factors, one has to take into account the maintenance of soil fertility and probable uncertainties and risks of crop failures due to failures of rains, occurrence of pests and diseases, unpredicatable fall in prices of commodities etc. For an individual farmer, the selection and combination of crops from his point of view, is therefore, of much significance in farming. The following points need to be kept in view for planning the cropping pattern.

- Which of the crops, now remaining on the list, are most profitable (or yield most food in a subsistence agriculture). In what combination and at what level of input application would they make the best use of local land, climate and input resources in the short term and long term situations bearing in mind the degree of food and income security required by the individual farmer and the community.
- What crops with the present pest and disease control methods are ecologically practicable. Interactions occur among the ecologically practicable crops, and the chosen crops and must be combined in a special way (rotations) in the farming system.

The existing cropping pattern in different regions may be more or less traditional, established on several years' experience in farming, after considering the suitability of crops to be grown. However, it is observed that the rigidity in traditional cropping pattern is slowly breaking down partly by the onset of the green revolution. For a farmer, it signifies even cropping scheme and crop intensity best suited to his farm, which is decided from a broad outlook adaptable to agro-climatic conditions and soil region for irrigated and unirrigated conditions.

In the cropping programme one decides how the limited land area of the farm will be used, the decision to be made is partly one of land use and partly one of rotation of crops. Besides, in case of land use, it must be remembered that land is only one of resources used in farm production.

The cropping pattern is the identification of the most efficient crops of the area under different soil and climatic conditions. The cropping pattern showing the area devoted to different crops, is of great significance in revealing the demand patterns to which it responds, as also many other economic and social factors that have been in operation, over time in the past. Labour, management and capital such as machinery, seed, fertiliser and irrigation are also used in producing crops. Soil and crop yields are important in determining which crop to produce. But at the same time, the amount of labour and capital required, prices and crop yields in relation to these resources are important, alongwith soil, in determining the returns.

Since not one resource *i.e.* soil but several other resources are required for producing crops, it is better to look upon the problem as one of deciding the most profitable cropping programme, rather than the narrower aspect of 'land use'.

Cropping Pattern Zones

Crop planning for any area should be based on a defined homogenous region or for a well defined purpose. There may be various physical, climatological and agronomic criteria which may be a basic consideration to group the different zones/areas. For example, climatic index and soil groups may be considered for defining/demarcating different zones. These two factors influence the soil moisturre regime expressed as

$$\text{Moisture index} = \frac{\text{P–PET}}{\text{PET}} \times 100$$

where,

PET = Potential evapotranspiration, and

P = Precipitation.

Moisture index can present different regions which can be further sub-divided into two to three isothermic belts which if superimposed on the important soil groups provides different CROPPING PATTERN ZONES. In Kharif season the soil moisture variation becomes dominant feature whereas in Rabi season the condition is just reverse *i.e.* moisture regime does not very too much but temperature variation becomes prominent, which influences crop growth. If soil depth is not much, irrigation becomes essential during Rabi season. Krishanan and Singh have worked out 14 major soil types of different zones and sub-zones, which are based on mean temperature (maximum and minimum) by drawing isoclines on the soil map of India. This has provided 8 zones (1 to 8) in terms of moisture. However, these may rise to 60 sub-zones, if combined with 5 temperature classes (ABCDE) and soil types.

The rotation of crops may be of any lengths, but owing to the limited number of crops usually absolute advantage is given prime consideration. There are many benefits, both direct and indirect, to be obtained from a good rotation, *i.e.* to control weeds, insects, diseases etc. which usually help in increasing crop production.

In Northern parts of India the farmers have generally responded to the 'New Technology' resulting in change in cropping pattern. Farming as a business is taking roots. There is, however, still much to be done, towards better farm planning and higher yields.

Besides, moisture index another parameter used is Thermal index based on potential evapotranspiration. However, to determine the cropping pattern for any area it is essential to ascertain whether the proposed crops would suit soils and climate. To understand this it is necessary to work out the productivity efficiency of various crops by calculating the relative average yield index and relative spread index of the crop. These are expressed as given below:

$$\text{Relative yield index} = \frac{\text{Mean yield for the crop in the area}}{\text{Mean yield of the state or country}} \times 100$$

$$\text{Relative spread index} = \frac{\text{Area of the crop expressed as percentage of the total cultivated area in the zone}}{\text{Area of the crop expressed as percentage of total cultivated area in the state/country}}$$

These indices can be grouped , based on average relative yield below 90%, relative spread below 90% and dividing the area under every crop into different zones.

Crop Rotation

Growing of definite crops in a definite period and area in such a way (sequence) that an optimum production is obtained without deteriorating the soil fertility is known as crop rotation.

Factors Affecting Crop Patterns and Rotations

The rotational grouping of crops over a time based on cropping zones is a complicated exercise since it is influenced by many considerations like:

(1) Agro-climatic conditions.

(2) Soil properties.

(3) Existing agricultural and irrigation practices

(4) Surface and sub-surface drainage characteristics.

(5) Socio-economic conditions of the population which in turn dictate, the farmer's choice, expertise, preferences and political

(Govt. policies) influences for adoption of crop pattern and rotations.

(6) Infra-structure, training facilities and agricultural demonstration.

(7) Availability of agricultural inputs such as water, fertilizer, seed, and machinery etc.

(8) Demand for various crops.

(9) Marketing facilities and distances.

(10) Labour availability.

CROP PLANNING

Kharif (rainy season), Rabi (winter season) and Zaid (summer season) are the three crop seasons which fall between the periods June to Oct., October to mid-April and mid-April to mid-June respectively. The area under Kharif and Rabi crops are generally more than Zaid crops which are being grown on a limited scale and that too in specific situations and or locations. In case a particular crop/crops dominate the cropped area, the pattern is termed as dominated cropping area, the pattern is termed as dominated cropping pattern by that (these) crop/crops. For example, sugarcane and wheat crops dominate the cropped area in Western U.P., therefore the cropping pattern of Western U.P. is considered as sugarcane-wheat based/dominated cropped pattern. Similarly the cropping pattern of Chambal Command (Rajasthan) area is a paddy-wheat dominated/ based cropping pattern. The following example presents the cropping pattern plan (Table 1).

TABLE 1

Cropping Pattern (Cultivable Area – 1000 hectares)

Name of Crops	Cropped area(ha)			Percentage to cultivable area (cropping pattern)		
Kharif	I	UI	T	I	UI	T
Paddy	300	–	300	30	–	30
Jowar	100	50	150	10	5	15
Soyabean and Others	50	50	100	5	5	10
Total	450	100	550	45	10	55

Note: I : indicates irrigated area

UI : indicates unirrigated area

T : indicates total area

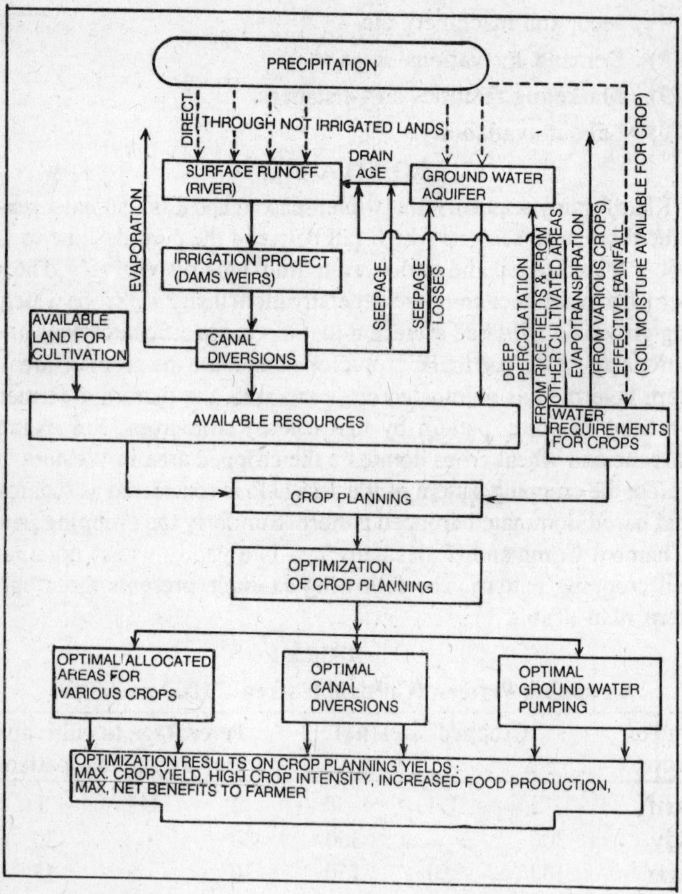

Fig 4.1: Schematic Diagram of Crop Planning

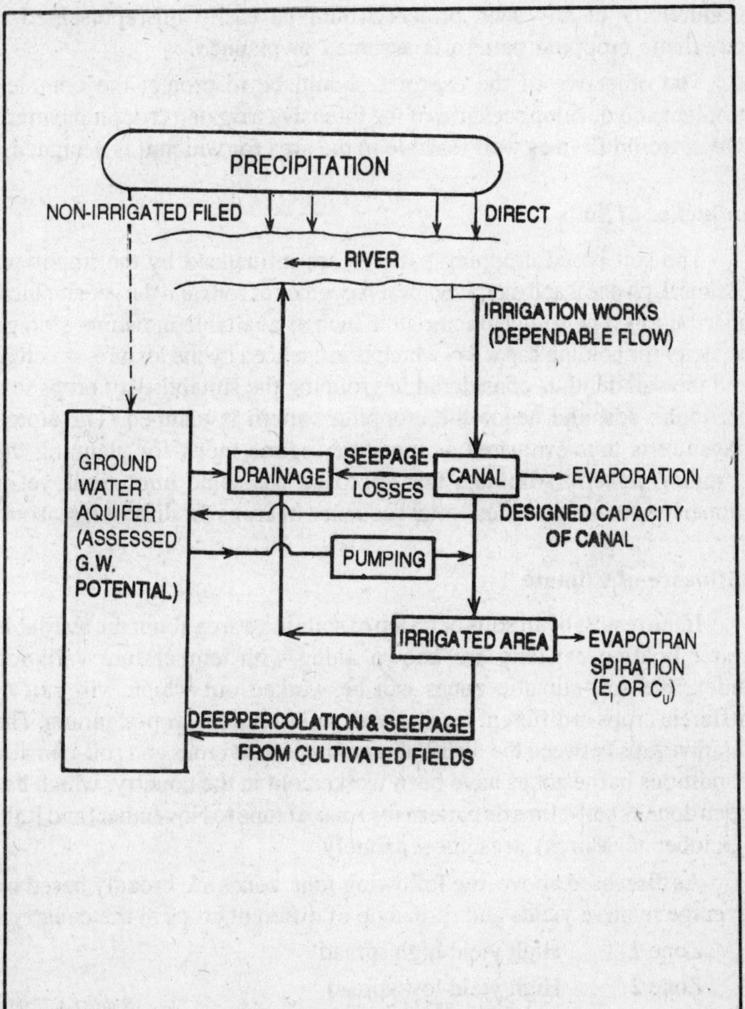

Fig. 4.2: Schematic Diagram of Crop Planning Model

Thus, for crop planning which is a continuous process the above considerations are kept in mind which makes it quite complex (Figs. 4.1and 4.2). This is particularly true in situations where the irrigation water is made available recently or when the quantity of water is increased sufficiently from insufficient or if it is protective supply conditions in the project. The productivity of any such project would be easily misrepresented if unrealistic cropping pattern is assumed or planned.

The objective of the exercise should be to project the complex problem and develop scenario of the intensive irrigated cropping pattern which would fit in as well feasible in the area for which it is designed.

Influence of Soils

The soil based cropping patterns are influenced by the important chemical, physical and morphological properties of soils and the geographical distribution. The soil characteristics such as available moisture, storage capacity (or holding capacity) which is influenced by the texture, structure and the soil depth is considered in grouping the suitability of crops to a particular soil and hence the cropping pattern is planned. The stored moisture is thus evaluated as moisture regime index for planning the cropping pattern. Although this approach has some limitations yet if properly planned provides better sequence of crops for different seasons.

Influence of Climate

If the results of all soils or group of soils in an area about the available water holding capacity are known along with temperature variation index, the soil-climatic zones can be worked out which will suit to different crops in different seasons and can be used for crop-planning. The relationships between the distribution of important crops and soil-climatic conditions in the zones have been worked out in the country, which has been done as soil-climatic pattern for Kharif (June to November) and Rabi (October to March) seasons separately.

As discussed above the following four zones are broadly based on average relative yields and spread up of different crops in the country:

Zone 1 High yield high spread

Zone 2 High yield low spread

Zone 3 Low yield high spread

Zone 4 Low yield low spread

The zone I can be considered as the most efficient and zone 4 the most inefficient zone for production. The details of these for the country as a whole in respect of all crops are available with the Directorate of Economics and Statistics, and Ministry of Food and Agriculture, Govt. of India.

During the Kharif season, temperature variations are narrowed down to such an extent that rice crop is grown in different parts of the country extending from Kashmir valley in the north to Kerala and Tamilnadu state in the extreme south. Thus, moisture distribution is an important factor in the Kharif season.

In Rabi season moisture becomes limiting factor because potential evapotranspiration (PET) exceeds precipitation (P) as seen from moisture index equation.

There are four important considerations in planning the cropping patterns, which are:

(i) Soil and water conservation practices/irrigation availability

(ii) Water budget of the soil

(iii) Suitable crop varieties

(iv) Use of inputs particularly fertilizers.

From the foregoing facts it may be seen that a particular area or areas can be conveniently grouped into different but suitable crop zones as worked out for the whole country which can be super-imposed on soil and climatic zones. The important crop zones of India are :

1. Rice crop complex zone
2. Wheat crop complex zone
3. Cotton crop complex zone
4. Jowar and groundnut crops complex zone
5. Bajra and gram crops complex zone
6. Sugarcane crop complex zone
7. Jute crop complex zone
8. Maize crop complex zone
9. Plantation crop complex zone.

These crops are grown in different pockets of the states. In the wheat crop complex zone, maize-wheat, or paddy-wheat and bajra-wheat are intensive crop rotations. Cotton and gram are also two other most efficient cash crops. In fact, wheat and cotton zones intermingle in North India.

The rice zone is mainly in the south and also a part of it produces cotton, jowar and groundnut. The most efficient sugarcane zones also lies in this belt, but jute zone is very limited which (jute) can be produced with supplemental irrigation alongwith other important crops like potato, paddy, groundnut. The Jowar-groundnut crop complex zone covers most of the black cotton and red soil area which is largely unirrigated. The maize crop complex zone represents the area along the hill regions of Northern India as well as Udaipur region in Rajasthan and parts of Bihar.

Besides, the technique of demarcating soil-climatic zones other approaches in planning cropping pattern are as follows:

1. Based on main soil types and total annual rainfall (Jethamalani, S.C. and Choubey, S.D.).
2. Based on rainfall, temperature and wet or non-wet area (Johl, S.S.)
3. Based on soil, rainfall, predominant cropping, natural vegetation, hypsometrical situation (Sahasrapuddhe, K.R.).

This discussion leads to the idea of crop planning by which efforts should be made to put each piece of land to its superior most use today or for some years till the new technology forces changes in the prevailing planning. With the development of alternative crops which are more efficient than the existing ones being available, a new cropping pattern may emerge. In fact the search for new crops needs to be more vigorous, such that more efficient cropping patterns are introduced. It is possible if the short duration fertilizer responsive and high yielding varieties are evolved which may help the farmer to increase the productivity and intensity of cropping resulting an increase in the production per unit area per unit time.

The possibility of inter-cropping in between the rows of a standing crop is now under progress but much more efforts are needed. This practice will also enable the farmer to sow the subsequent crops in rotation without waiting for the land to be free from the previous crop. The various possibilities which have either been tried or may be tried are:

1. Wheat in the furrows of potatoes.
2. Legume fodder (Berseem, Senji, Lucerne, Gram) in the standing crop of cotton.
3. Grain legumes such as urd, moong and soyabean in maize crop.
4. Red gram, moth or moong in jowar.
5. Groundnut in cotton.
6. Rape seed or mustard in wheat.
7. Groundnut in castor or tapioca.

Any cropping sequence being used should be based on the following criteria:

(a) It should not accentuate certain diseases as a result of a fixed continuous rotation.

(b) It should not form a drain on some specific plant nutrients from a particular depth in the soil.

(c) It should build up the fertility of the soil.

(d) It should result in high returns to the farmer without exhaustion of the soil.

(e) It should generate employment to farmer's family and income all the year round and ensure best utilisation of his farm resources particularly irrigation water, fertilizer, pesticides, machinery and power.

Farm management principles need to be taken care of.

Some new planting techniques can be tried, such as transplanting of Rice from the nursery can be done to save time. Thus, even a third crop of Zaid Rabi can be grown in rotation with wheat without affecting the yield of any crop in rotation. This means that more attention needs to be given to the geometry of the crop cultivation to ensure best utilisation of soil, water and fertilizer.

Forage crops and vegetables can be used for raising a catch crop in between routine Kharif and Rabi crops. For instance after wheat, maize-cowpea fodder, jowar fodder, onion, tobacco, moong (green gram) are some of the common catch crops which fit in well in rotation.

Similarly in summer, mixed cropping with a quick growing of tall crops producing shade and a short spreading crop acting as a canopy will be very profitable for making the best use of sun's energy and efficient use of soil moisture or irrigation water. Thus, combinations like maize-urd, jowar and moong, tur and moong, castor and groundnut are generally tried.

Engineering, Power and Energy Aspects of Cropping Patterns

The multiple cropping involves the basic problem of development of farm implements and machineries for different operations which should be useful, in energy saving and workable with relatively less power requirements. The type of implements required for an area depends upon the crops being grown, cultural practices, soil and power available. For example if paddy is a major crop, workable puddlers should be developed and for seed bed preparation of the crops mould board plough such as victory plough or burmese plough (melur plough) be used. For green manuring trampler is needed. For dry land crops disc-harrow or a three tyre cultivator would be necessary for ploughing. In low rainfall areas with light textured soils, the blade harrow needs to be planned to destroy weeds so that moisture may be retained in the soil as the surface mulch is not disturbed.

The modified design of bund maker, channel maker and, power tillers, power sprayers, dusters, fertilizer seed drills. seed treater devices, threshers, harvesters, shellers, processing machines, transplanters, field shapers etc. need to be fabricated, tested and implemented. This means according to the farmer, needs either new implements should be fabricated or modified. One has to be continuously thought upon to facilitate the farmer in his profession so that accordingly he may have better choice of selection of crop or cropping pattern which may be more remunerative to him.

The development of easily handling and economical field equipments would help in all agricultural practices for maximising production through improved labour efficiency and timeliness of each operation.

The working in this direction would also decrease the time lag between the irrigation potential created and utilised.

Farmer's Choice of Cropping Pattern

It is established that the crop selection in any season is the farmer's prerogative. In a democratic country it is not possible to enforce cropping patterns. In case some scientifically based and field tested cropping pattern is to be popularised, it can be done through advice, suggestions, farmers' education and demonstration to the farmer showing better cropping pattern. The most important factors which can bring about changes in the cropping patterns are the economic factors and advanced technology. Farmer in his choice of selecting cropping pattern is guided largely by his socio-economic conditions and to some extent by other factors. Most of the farmers being poor and having small holdings grow only those crops which just serve their family requirement. In such conditions the monetary considerations are not involved in choice of crops. But farmers with large holdings and considerable marketable surplus or with alternate sources of income and also if one can withstand the price fluctuation in various marketable commodities, can think in terms of economic objectives.

This human behaviour concerning the choice of crops from among the alternatives available to a farmer has also been tried to evaluate as a model by many researchers. The basis of the model is to perceive water as the most important variable and assuming other inputs at optimum level.

Cropping Intensity

The total cropped area in a given period of time (season/year) when expressed in terms of percentage to culturable/cultivable area is termed as cropping intensity for that period *i.e.* season or year. For example the following data showing cropping pattern gives the cropped area in Kharif, Rabi and Zaid as 550, 700 and 100 hectares respectively and the cultivable area 1000 hectares. From the given data the cropping intensity may be calculated as under:

(a) Cropping intensity for Kharif season $\frac{550}{1000} \times 100 = 55\%$

(b) Cropping intensity for Rabi season $\frac{700}{1000} \times 100 = 70\%$

(c) Cropping intensity for Zaid season $\frac{100}{1000} \times 100 = 10\%$

(d) Cropping intensity for the year $\frac{(550+700+100)}{1000} = 135\%$

The factors which affect the cropping pattern are also responsible to govern the cropping intensity. Out of these factors, assured irrigation is the foremost important.

Irrigation Intensity

The cropped area which receive irrigation in a given period of time (season/year) when expressed in terms of percentage to culturable/ cultivable area is termed as irrigation intensity. The data given as under furnish the irrigated area in Kharif, Rabi and Zaid as 450, 500 and 100 hectares respectively. From the given data irrigation intensity may be calculated as under:

(a) Irrigation intensity for Kharif season $\frac{450}{1000} \times 100 = 45\%$

(b) Irrigation intensity for Rabi season $\frac{500}{1000} \times 100 = 50\%$

(c) Irrigation intensity for Zaid season $\frac{100}{1000} \times 100 = 10\%$

(d) Irrigation intensity for the year $\frac{(450 + 700 + 100)}{1000} \times 100 = 135\%$

Note: Culturable area = 1000 hectare.

Water Production Functions

Amongst the various inputs water is considered to be very important. Studies have been conducted with this consideration for economic analysis of crop production. The introduction of the concept of water production function has added a dimension in crop planning strategy. The basic concept of the production function is that the yield of any crop will increase non-linearly with the amount of water supplied in the crop season.

This depth of water applied to the crop producing maximum yield is referred to as the "Saturation depth". Beyond "Saturation depth" the yield reduces with added amounts of water. Hence to the Saturation depth, the choice domain of total irrigation depth is infinite with respect to crop yields according to the production function (Fig. 4.3).

The water is usually available in short supply, hence now there is a thinking in the mind of planners, is it possible to curtail the water supply to some crops? *i.e.* even less than their total water requirements which may not greatly affect the growth and production.

Crop Planning Model

The objective of formulation of model is to develop the scenario for agricultural production. The model is developed for future crop plan that is economically feasible and socially acceptable. The approach may be the full exploitation of the irrigation potential and crop yields on the basis of known techniques of high yielding varieties or those reported under national production competition trials.

Mathematical Model

The model of crop planning may be designed to attain the maximum efficiency (*i.e.* annual net benefit), keeping in view the resources and sociological limitations. The costs and benefits are very much influenced by the designed model. Thus, if the costs and benefits are to be defined on national level planning it takes into account social-benefit cost while if farmers's behaviour model is to be worked out it would be related to the individual profits to the farmers.

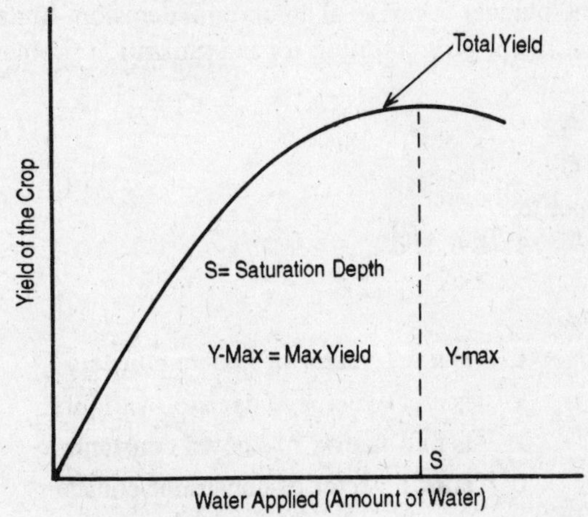

Fig. 4.3: Showing Water-Production Relationship

The general model taking into account farmers behaviour as suggested by Pomareda, Carlos (1978) and tried on Gomti-Kalyani Doab by Water Resources Development Training Centre Roorkee (1981) and Madhuresh Chandra (1990-91) are reproduced here : The main objective of the study by Madhuresh Chandra was to examine the existing cropping pattern and to suggest the optimum cropping pattern (a rational cropping pattern both feasible and profitable for Salawa Command, Distt. Meerut, U.P.). Application of modern technique of system analysis and use of Linear Programming Model and the computer were made. Determination of water requirement of various crops (that were being grown), identification of surface and ground water resources, input and output for the crops were worked out. The analysis considered different alternative crop intensities to decide on the optimum level.

On the decision-making for future cropping pattern for an area, the simplest approach is to project existing local requirement with the increasing population, especially for food crops. This could be correct for the situation where the change of staple food or the migration of population is not much. On nearly the same condition either socio-economic, physical or biological, an area which on supplemental irrigation could make itself comparison with the other area is intensively irrigated. These approaches might claim as extrapolation.

The development of the mathematical programming model in general, and the linear programming model in particular, makes it possible for the planner to arrive at an optimal decision. In its simplest form, a typical linear programming for maximization problem can be written as:

$Z_x = C' .x$

Subject to;

$Ax \leq b$, and

$x \geq o$

where

C'	is a n.1 vector of known constant
x	is a n.1 vector of decision variable
A	is m.n matrix of known constants
b	is m.1 vector of constraint constant.

Now, for $j = 1, 2, 3, \ldots\ldots n$, and
$i = 1, 2, 3, \ldots\ldots m$

The above formulation can be written as

$$\text{maximize } Z_x = \sum_{j=1}^{n} C_j \; x_j \qquad (1)$$

$$\text{subject to} \quad \sum_{i=1}^{m} \quad \sum_{j=1}^{n} a_{ij} X_j \leq bi \qquad (2)$$

$$X_j \geq 0 \qquad (3)$$

If all the coefficients in the model (Cj, aij and bi) are known constant and a linear function, the problem pertains to linear programming under certainty or deterministic. The development of the model in the determination of optimal cropping pattern for this problem with reference to Hall and Dracup (1975) can be stated as

$$V = \max \sum_{j=1}^{n} V_{jk} \; Y_{jk} \; X_{jk}$$

subject to constraints on the land area and water:

$$\sum_{i=1}^{m} A_{ijk} \; X_{jk} \leq X_k$$

$$\sum_{i=1}^{m} \sum_{j=1}^{n} W_{ijk} \; X_{jk} < W_i$$

where,

j = identity for particular crop
i = time taken
k = type of soil
Y_{jk} = crop yield per unit area, crop j on soil k
W_{ijk} = water requirement in the ith period of jth crop on kth soil
A_{ijk} = a coefficient = 1, if crop jk requires occupancy of land in time period i, and A_{ijk} = O, if it does not
V_{jk} = Values net of differential costs of unit product of the crop jk
X_k = land available of soil, type k.

In reality, the coefficient (C_j, a_{ij} and b_i) in equation (1) and (2) above are often neither known nor constant. Linear programming models are usually formulated to select some future course of action. Therefore, the coefficent used should be based on a prediction of future condition. The available information might be inadequate to make a precise determination of the appropriate value of the coefficients. Furthermore, these coefficients might actually be random variables, each with underlying probability for the value that it will take on when the decision is implemented.

A particular approach of stochastic linear programming to a risky situation (where some or all the model parameters C_j, a_{ij} and b_i are random

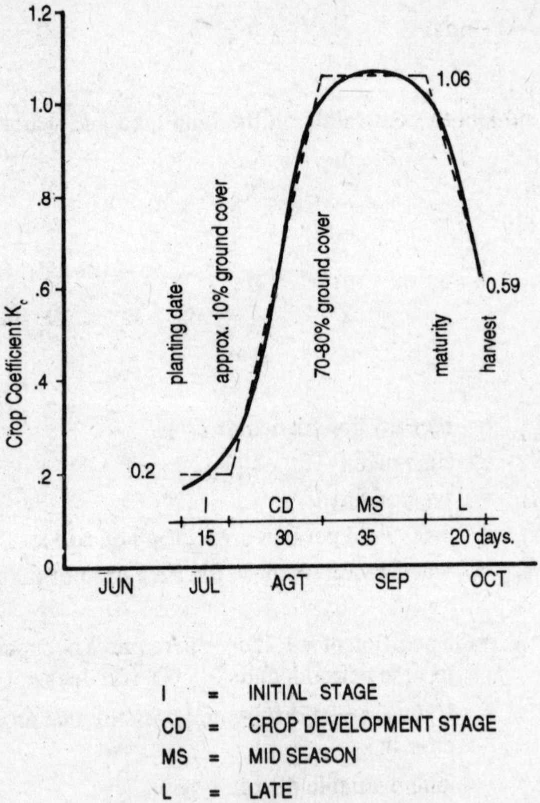

I = INITIAL STAGE
CD = CROP DEVELOPMENT STAGE
MS = MID SEASON
L = LATE

Fig. 4.4: Crop Coefficient Curve of Maize

variable) lead to the state that the size of the problem could become too large and hence computationally difficult.

Some concepts used in calculating crop water requirements are discussed as under:

Percolation Loss P

It is the downward movement of water below the root zone through saturated or nearly saturated soil in response to the force of gravity. Percolation occurs when water is under pressure. The percolation loss for paddy in an area may be considered to be about 6.1 mm/day after transplantation.

Net Irrigation Requirement, NIR

The net irrigation requirement is the depth of irrigation water,

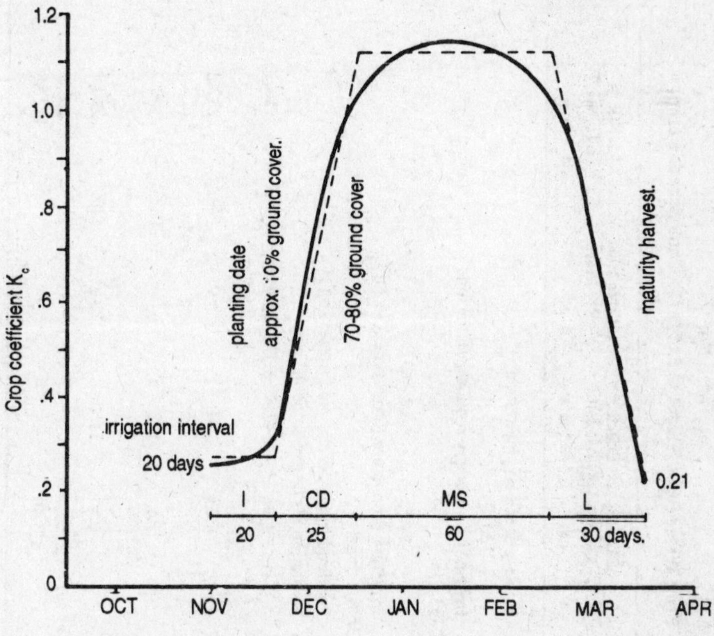

I = INITIAL STAGE
CD = CROP DEVELOPMENT STAGE
MS = MID SEASON
L = LATE

Fig. 4.5: Crop Coefficient Curve of Wheat

exclusive of precipitation, carry-over soil moisture or groundwater contribution or other gains of soil moisture, that is required consumptively for crop production. Neglecting the later part and considering the

TABLE No. 2

Crop Water Requirement of Paddy (Medium duration crop)

Dates	Duration Days	ETO mm/day	Kc	ET crop =KcxETo mm	Effective Rainfall Re* mm	Percolation P** losses	NIR = ETc—Re+P mm	FIR= NIR/0.6 mm	GIR= FIR/0.7 mm
				Nursery seed bed preparation			30		
June 16-30	15	8.1	1.1	133.7	33.4			58.4	83.4
				Irrigation for nursery requirement in June					
		1/20 x (133.7 -33.4)=						5.0	
July 1-10	10	6.5	1.1	71.5	56.8				
				Irrigation for nursery Requirement in July					
		1/20 x(71.5- 56.8) =						0.7	
				Puddling irrigation and land prepration prepration for transplantation			175	553	790
July 11-31	21	6.5	1.08	147.4	119.4	128.1	156.1		
Aug 1-31	31	5.5	1.05	179	155.9	189.1	212.2	353.7	505.2
Sept. 1-30	30	5.6	1.0	168	51	183.0	300	500.0	714.3
Oct. 1-23	23	5.3	0.95	115.8	9.3	140.3	240.8	411.3	587.6
	130			815.40			1125.8	1876.4	2680.5

* 75 mm net depth of application are adopted

** Perlocation losses of 6.1 mm/day are considered after transplantation.

Table 3

Crop Water Requirement of Paddy (Medium duration crop)

Dates	Duration Days	ETO mm/day	Kc	ET crop =KcxETo mm	Effective Rainfall Re* mm	Percolation P** losses	NIR = ETc--Re+P mm	FIR= NIR/0.6 mm	GIR= FIR/0.7 mm
				Nursery seed bed preparation			30		
June 16-30	15	8.1	1.1	133.7	33.4	58.4	83.4		
				Irrigation for nursery requirement in June					
		1/20 x (133.7 -33.4)=					5.0		
July 1-10	10	6.5	1.1	71.5	56.5				
				Irrigation for nursery Requirement in July					
		1/20 x(71.5- 56.8) =						0.7	
				Puddling irrigation and land prepration prepration for transplantation			175	553.0	790
July 11-31	21	6.5	1.08	147.4	119.4	128.1	156.1		
Aug 1-31	31	5.5	1.05	179	155.9	189.1	212.2	353.7	505.2
Sept. 1-30	30	5.6	1.0	168	51	183.0	300	500.0	714.3
Oct. 1-23	13	5.3	0.95	65.5	5.2	79.3	139.8	232.3	332.6
	120		765.1				1018.6	1697.8	2425.5

* 75 mm net depth of application are adopted

** Perlocation losses of 6.1 mm/day are considered after transplantation.

TABLE 4

Crop Water Requirement of Paddy (Medium duration crop)

Dates	Duration Days	ETO mm/day	Kc	ET crop =KcxETo mm	Effective Rainfall Re* mm	Percolation P losses	NIR = ETc–Re+P mm	FIR = NIR/0.6	GIR = FIR/0.7
(i) Dwarf Variety			Land	Prepration			50		
Nov. 16-30	15	3.8	0.27	15.4	0	-	15.4	109.0	155.7
Dec. 1-31	31	2.7	0.65	54.4	0	-	54.4	90.7	129.5
Jan. 1-31	31	2.7	1.12	93.7	0	-	93.7	156.2	223.1
Feb. 1-28	28	4.5	1.10	138.6	11.0	-	127.3	212.2	303.1
Mar. 1-31	31	6	0.60	111.6	17.9	-	93.7	156.2	233.1
	136			413.7			434.5	724.3	1044.5
(ii) Tall Variety				Land	Prepration				
Oct. 22-31	10	5.3	0.25	13.3	3.1	-	10.2	100.3	143.3
Nov. 1-30	30	3.8	0.40	45.6	0	-	45.6	76	108.6
Dec. 1-31	31	2.7	1.04	87.0	0	-	87.0	145	207.1
Jan. 1-31	31	2.7	1.11	92.9	0	-	92.9	154.8	221.2
Feb. 1-28	28	4.5	0.85	107.1	10.6	-	96.5	160.8	229.8
Mar. 1-10	10	6	0.35	21.0	5.2	-	15.8	26.3	37.6
	140			366.9			398	663.2	947.6

*75 mm net depth of application are adopted.

TABLE 5

Calculation of Crop Water requirements of Maize

Dates	Duration Days	ETO mm/day	Kc	ET crop =KcxETo mm	Effective Rainfall Re* mm	Percolation P losses	NIR = ETc–Re+P mm	FIR = NIR/0.6	GIR = FIR/0.7
July 7-31	25	6.5	0.24	39	62.8	-	0	0	0
Aug. 1-31	31	5.5	0.75	127.8	135	-	0	0	0
Sept. 1-30	30	5.6	1.05	176.4	51.2	-	125.2	208.7	298.1
Oct. 1-14	14	5.3	0.77	57.1	5.4	-	51.7	86.2	123.1
	100			400.3			176.9	294.9	421.2

*75 mm net depth of application are adopted.

percolation losses (P) the net irrigation requirement may be worked out:

$$NIR = ET_{crop} - R_e + P, \text{ and}$$
$$NIR = \text{zero, if } Re \geq ET_{crop} + P$$

Field Irrigation Requirement (FIR) and Gross Irrigation Requirement (GIR)

The field irrigation requirement and the gross irrigation requiremenare calculated by dividing the net irrigation requirement by field application efficiency, and the field irrigation requirement by conveyance efficiency respectively.

Formulation of the Model

The primary requirement of a Linear Programming Model is that the objective function and each constraint equation must be linear. A linear programming model was developed as deterministic model based on selected variables and using research work already done in the area. The objective of the study was to select the cropping pattern which could economically be feasible, socially acceptable and meet the goal of self reliance.

Objective Function

The model considered a planning period of one year, since no crop had crop period more than one year. Therefore, the objective function was to maximize the annual net benefit or net income. It was assumed that the price for the input and product were same for the entire command area.

For sixteen major crops considered here, the objective function took the form :

$$\max.\ Z = C_1X_1 + C_2X_2 + \dots + C_{16}X_{16}$$

or in general form it can be written as

$$\max\ Z = \sum_{j=1}^{16} C_j X_j$$

where,

Z = Net annual benefits obtained from the crop during one year period in Rs.

C_j = Net benefit or net income of jth crop in Rs/ha, and j = 1,2,...., 16, value C_j is presented (for crops)

X_j = Area devoted to jth crop in hectare.

Constraints

Water Availability Constraints

Twelve constraints were specified such that the amount of irrigation water required for all the crops in each month must be less than or equal to the sum of the canal discharge (surface flow) plus the groundwater. The availability of groundwater was specified over the year. To maximize the returns achieved, no groundwater constraint was put in any month. However, it was necessary to impose an additional groundwater constraint specifying that the sum of utilization of groundwater in any year should be less than or equal to total estimated safe withdrawal of groundwater in one year. The total safe withdrawal of water in one year was taken as 1850 ha.m. The groundwater constratint represented the small scale lift irrigation, which reflected in terms of net returns of crops.

By putting groundwater to be pumped in any month as decision variable the constraints can be written as:

$$W_{1,1}X_1 + W_{1,2}X_2 + \dots + W_{1,16}X_{16} - G_1 \le I_1$$

---- ---- ---- ----

---- ---- ---- ----

$$W_{12,1} X_1 + W_{12,2} X_{16} + ... + W_{12,16} X_{16} - G_{16} \leq I_{12}$$

and an additional constraint:

$$G_1 + G_2 + G_3 + ... + G_{12} \leq G$$

In general form it can be written as

$$\sum_{j=1}^{16} W_{ij} X_j - G_i \leq I_i$$

$$\sum_{i=1}^{12} G_i \leq G$$

where,

W_{ij} = water requirement of crop jth in ith month in ha. m.
X_j = area devoted to jth crop in hectare
G_i = groundwater pumped in ith month in hectare metre
I_i = surface water (canal) available in ith month in ha. m.
G = total safe withdrawal of groundwater in a year in ha. m.

The subscript i stands for month = 1, 2, ...12.
j stands for crops = 1, 2, ...16.

Since, the water requirements of crops were specified at diversion point, the total groundwater available annually was taken as 2466.7 ha-m.

Land Constraints

These constraints specified that the total cropped area in any month or season should not exceed the total land available for irrigation or culturable command area, *i.e.* 16520 ha. It can be seen that the notation in calender of cultivation was one or fraction. This was not of any use for writing land availability constraint, since land use coefficient should be presented by a 0-1 variable. Hence, this was done by dividing the year into a number of seasons (N), each season being less than or equal to a month. To avoid redundancy, the land constraints were presented by 23 constraints. The constraints can be written as:

$$L_{1,1} X_1 + L_{1,2} X_2 + ... + L_{1,16} X_{16} \leq A$$

---- ---- -----

---- ---- -----

$$L_{23,1} X_1 + L_{23,2} X_2 + ... + L_{23,16} X_{16} \leq A$$

In general it can be written as

$$\sum_{j=1}^{16} L_{NJ} X_j \leq A$$

where,

L_{NJ} = Land use coefficient for jth crop in Nth season has value one or zero; if jth crop is grown in Nth season and 0 otherwise.

N = number of season, N = 1,....,23

A = total culturable command area.

Crop Constraints

In the light of self sufficiency in food production, it was necessary to impose a maximum or minimum limit area devoted to certain crops. The consideration was local requirement, marketability, land capability, topography etc.

In general form, it can be written as:

$$X_j \leq \text{ or } \geq A_j$$

where, A_j = limit area devoted to jth crop.

Inference

Keeping in view the constraints, food-grains requirement of the local population, full utilisation of ground and surface water and the land resource, net returns and crop intensities, etc. the study revealed that no trial/run met all the requirements of the optimum allocation of the resources. Thus, there had been a conflicting resolution in each trial or run *i.e.* if one met the food requirement, it did not meet the requirement of full utilisation of ground water and surface water or the maximisation of the net returns and crop intensities. For example, trial/run one resulted that only urd (Kharif) and peas (Rabi) entered in the solution and other important foodgrains did not find the place including the sugarcane which was the cash Crop in the Salawa Command. Sugarcane was the main cash crop which covered the maximum area in the existing cropping pattern. Similarly, in the last run *i.e.*, No. 4 which met the full utilization of water resources (*i.e.*, ground water and surface water) covered almost all important cash crops but did not meet the requirement of the local area, which in view of the local requirement and the full utilisation of the resource, did not show the feasibility. Hence, the existing cropping pattern in the command based on the trial and error adopted by the farmers in the command appeared to be most appropriate and profitable which was rather based on traditional conditions. The Researcher, therefore, suggested that there did not exist any possibility of improving the existing cropping pattern which in all probability meets all conditions.

However, the overall results of the computer run showed that no feasible solution could exist.

Study on GOMTI-KALYANI DOAB (Eastern U.P.)

Maximize:

$$Z = \{\sum_{i=1}^{m} X_{it} Y_{max}, i - \sum_{i=1}^{m} \sum_{K=1}^{s} X_{ik} \Delta Y_{ik}\} P_i -$$

$$\sum_{i=1}^{m} \sum_{j=1}^{m} Q_{ij} X_{it} C_j - \{\sum_{i=1}^{m} \sum_{t=1}^{1} b_{it} X_{it} - \sum_{t=1}^{1} \sum_{I=1}^{m}$$

$$\sum_{K=1}^{s} Y_{ik} \Delta b_{ikt}\} PW \qquad \text{Equation (i)}$$

Subject to:

$$\sum_{i=1}^{m} X_{iT} - \sum_{i=1}^{m} \sum_{K=1}^{s} X_{ik} \Delta b_{ikt} \leq WRT \qquad \text{Equation (ii)}$$

$$\sum_{i=1}^{m} Q_{ij} X_{iT} \leq IP_j \qquad \text{Equation (iii)}$$

$$\sum_{i=1} Q_{ij} X_{iT} \leq A_{Tj} \qquad \text{Equation (iv)}$$

$X_{iT}, X_{iK}, K = 1$ S are positive

where;

X_{iT} = Total area under ith crop irrigated at saturation level in hectares.

X_{ik} = area under ith crop at kth level of irrigation in hectares.

P_i = Selling price of ith produce in Rupees/quintal.

Q_{ij} = Quantity of jth input (excluding water) per hectare of ith crop.

C_j = Unit price of jth input.

b_{it} = water requirement of ith crop in t^{th} season at saturation level.

Pw = Unit cost of irrigation water in Rupees/hectare meter.

I_{pj} = Total availability of the jth input over a year.

a_{it} = O-1 variable, equal to zero if the ith crop is grown in t^{th} season, zero otherwise.

At = total area available for cultivation in t^{th} season.

$Y_{max,i}$ = yield per hectare of ith crop irrigated at saturation depth.

ΔY_{ik} = decreament in yield per hectare of ith crop at Kth level of irrigation.

Δb_{ikt} = decreament in the supply of water to ith crop at Kth level of irrigation compared to saturation level for that crop in the tth season.

The sub-scripts :

i = stands for ith crop

t = stands for t^{th} season

K = stands for Kth level of irrigation

m = total number of crop activities

S = total number of irrigation levels for any crop

1 = number of seasons in a year.

n = total number of inputs for any crop excluding water.

This model provides an opportunity to predict the maximum net benefits from various crop growth conditions etc. (activities) as influenced by different levels of watering. As usual benefit values represent the money realised after selling the produce while cost is total expenditure incurred on all inputs including water cost.

The model representing equations (i), (ii), (iii) and (iv) can be defined as below:

The equation (ii) represent water constraint condition which means that the amount of irrigation water supplied in any season must be less than or equal to the quantity of water available for irrigation in that season.

The equation (iii) denotes the influence of other inputs as limitation already explained above for water in equation (ii). The equation (iii) thus shows the limitation of land, which means that the total irrigated area (ICA) must be less than or equal to total culturable command Area (C.C.A.) available for cropping in a given season.

Implicit in the above formulation is the existence of production function of the form

$$Y_i = f\ (Q_1, Q_2 \ldots\ldots Q_n) \quad \ldots\ldots \text{Eqn. (V).}$$

where Y_i represents the yield of ith crop per unit area and $Q_1, Q_2 \ldots\ldots Q_n$ are the resources including water that go into the production of the ith crop.

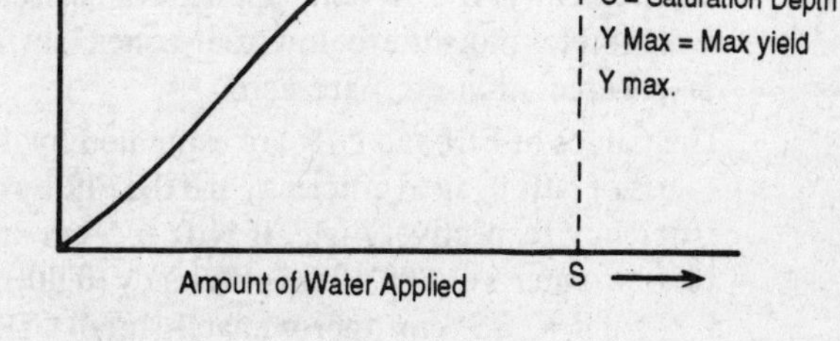

Fig. 4.5

If all inputs are held at a constant level, and only the water is variable, the one dimensional production w.r.t. water would be as given in Fig. 4.6. The saturation depth of water (S) and different levels of irrigation are also indicated.

In the model equations given above all explanatory variables and parameters are present except one *i.e.* b_{it} which is water requirement of ith and t^{th} season. The water requirement may be found by any standard method such as modified penman method or evaporimeter. The b_{it} is determined by the following procedural steps.

Step I : Determine weighed monthly consumptive use coefficients with the help of the crop growing period, mid-month and maximum crop factor and assuming probable time range between planting and harvesting distributed over the respective periods.

Step II : Compute the consumptive use in depth units by either penmen method or multiplying crop factor by readings of pan evaporimeter for different periods.

Step III : Calculate preplanting water requirements (*i.e.* for land preparation etc.) and find out gross water/irrigation requirement (GIR) by sum total of the preplanting requirement and consumptive use as per Step II.

Step IV : In case the sum total (GIR) of water requirement is more than the effective rainfall, the net irrigation requirement (NIR) would be the difference between consumptive need and effective rainfall otherwise equal to zero. The gross irrigation requirement (GIR) is equal to field irrigation requirement (FIR) if field application losses (seepage, leakage etc. moisture below root-zones, surface runoff, deep percolation etc.) are zero.

Step V : The values of FIR and GIR are estimated by dividing the values of NIR by field efficiency and the FIR by conveyance efficiency respectively [*e.g.* if NIR = 5 cm and losses = 20% of water i.e. 80% field efficiency (0.80), then FIR = 5 x 1/0.8 = 6.3 cm approximately and GIR = FIR + conveyance losses *i.e.* GIR = 6.3 x 1/0.8 = 8 cm approximately.

Alternative Formulation

In the above method, the water requirement corresponding to maximum production of crop has been considered as datum. However, for a particular level of irrigation water other than datum, the calculations can be made for that quantity of water which corresponds to the respective yield and water cost and adjustments are made accordingly. The same adjustment can be made for other constraints or limitations.

However, water requirement factor b_{it} can also be determined by considering any one crop which is being irrigated with different levels of irrigation as an independent function of growth (activity). This assumption has been mathematically expressed as under:

$$\text{Max } Z = \sum_{i=1}^{m} X_i Y_i P_i - \sum_{i=1}^{m} \sum_{j=1}^{n} Q_{ij} X_i C_j - \sum_{i=1}^{m} \sum_{t=1}^{1} b_{it} X_1 Pw \qquad \text{Eqn (6)}$$

Subject to:

$$\sum_{i=1}^{m} b_{it} X_i = WR_t \qquad \text{Eqn. (7)}$$

$$\sum_{i=1}^{m} a_{it} X_i \le A_t \qquad \text{Eqn. (8)}$$

— = O

$$\sum_{i=1}^{m} Q_{ij} X_i \le IP_j \qquad \text{Eqn. (9)}$$

$$X_1 \le O, \; i = 1,2, \ldots\ldots m \qquad \text{Eqn. (10)}$$

Variables have the same meaning as given before. The b_{it} at different level of irrigation may be computed as a linear proportion of the total season water at saturation depth.

Simplification

There can be further simplification if it is taken for granted that (i) except water input all the remaining inputs are easily available, (ii) water is to be applied to any crop at its saturation depth and that charges of water supply per hectare are fixed for every crop (*i.e.* charges are not based on the quantity of water supplied which would vary (the charges) as per unit rate used), (iii) farmer uses only the required quantity of water.

With these simplifications of assumptions, the model can be expressed as:

Max $Z = \Sigma_i X_i Y_i V_{i,}$ where V_i = net benefit per unit yield of ith crop net of all cost including water Eqn.(11)

S.T., $b_{it} X_i \leq WR_t$ Eqn.(12)

$a_{it} X \leq A_t$ Eqn.(13)

Production Function

The functional relationships between the crop yields and water in respect of major crops of the area can be developed. WRDTC, Roorkee University (1981) has developed a Quadratic functional (equation) approach of the production function for any crop.

Assumptions

The production function equation can be expressed as :

(i) $Y = a + bx + cx^2$ .....

(ii) The values of constant a, b, c were taken from the observed maximum yield of any crop at different agricultural stations in the country with the assumption that full evapotranspiration requirement of the crop was met and hence maximum yield of crop. The yields of non-irrigated fields were also recorded.

(iii) when the yield is considered to be maximum being taken after fully meeting the water requirements or evapotranspiration of the crop in question, then

$$\frac{dy}{dx} = O$$

From the above three conditions, the values of constants a, b, c in Quadratic equation were worked out in the following way *i.e.* when

x = full evapotranspiration depth

$Y = y_{max}$

when x = O

$Y = y_{max}$

when x = full evapotranspiration depth

$$\frac{dy}{dx} = O$$

With these assumptions graph between water applied (mm/ha) and yield (quintal per ha) for rice, wheat, sugarcane and gram were drawn each of which represent a water production function. However, these production functions are not very accurate because these cannot be used to work out the economics of irrigation at any level of irrigation except at full requirement or saturation depth. This is because the net benefits were calculated by considering the fixed water charges per unit area for a particular crop. In fact, if the actual water charges (based on meter measurement) for the quantity of water used at each irrigation could be worked out (if facility available) the economics of each irrigation and for the entire season will provide more accurate picture of the situation.

The data in respect of existing crop pattern, crop calender, crop water requirements of each crop, benefit calculation of crops per ha for each crop, net benefit and benefit per unit of water for various crops etc. should be compiled for tabulating the results and interpretation of programming model. The computer programme can be run for the calculation of various informations including cropping pattern required for the project area.

REFERENCES

1. Chandra, S., Sinha, C.P., and Mohan, J. (1979), 'Study of Changes in Water Balance of Gomti Kalyani Interbasin due to Sarda Sahayak Waters', Proc. International Symposium on Specific Aspects of Hydrological Computations for Water Projects, Leningrad, USSR.
2. Geophysical Survey Division I, Ramsagar Mishra Nagar, Lucknow (1980), 'Technical Feasibility of Ground Water Development in Blocks of Barabanki District'.
3. Lakshminarayana, V., and Rajagopalan S.P. (1977), 'Optimal Cropping Pattern for Basin in India', Jl. Irrigation and Drainage Divison, ASCE, March Issue.
4. 'Revised Project Report, Sarda Sahayak Pariyojana' (1976), Irrigation Department, Uttar Pradesh.
5. Sinha C.P. and Charyulu, P.G. (1980), 'Optimal Crop Planning for Gomti Kalyani Doab', Proc. International Symposium on Water Resources System, Roorkee.
6. Smith, D.V. (1973), 'System Analysis and Irrigation Planning', Jl. Irrigation and Drainage Division, ASCE, March Issue.
7. 'Statistical Report' (1977), Statistical Office, Barabanki, Planning Department, Uttar Pradesh.

8. Zope, M.Y. (1979), 'Assessment of Water Resources in Gomti Kalyani Doab', unpublished M.E. (WRD) Dissertation submitted to University of Roorkee.
9. Changkakoti, A.K. (1985), "Multi-objective Crop Planning for Garufella Watershed (Assam)", unpublished M.E. (Hydrology) dissertation, University of Roorkee, Roorkee.
10. Kirman (1983), "Cropping Pattern Studies of Salawa Command", Technical Report (Published), WRDTC, University of Roorkee, Roorkee.
11. Reuss, J.O. (1980), "Matching Cropping Systems to Water Supply Using an Integrative Model", Water Management Technical Report, No. 62, Colorado State University, Fort Collins, Colorado, U.S.A.
12. Sharma, Abhimanu (1982), "Shifting Trend in Cropping Pattern of Salawa Distributary", unpublished M.E. Dissertation, WRDTC, University of Roorkee, Roorkee.

CHAPTER 5

DIAGNOSTIC ANALYSIS : A TOOL FOR IRRIGATION MANAGEMENT

Irrigation water control and allocation, inequitable distribution of water to users, and operation and maintenance of existing systems are some of the major problems of our irrigation systems. Hence, there is a need for a systematic approach like Diagnositc Analysis or concept for analysis of an improvement in an existing system, which now appears to be a growing concensus among irrigation management professionals. With this idea a critical review of Diagnostic Analysis approach for irrigation management is done to have the knowledge of the systems problems including their magnitude, causes and effects. Solutions then can be developed to improve the system.

INTRODUCTION

With a fifth of the world's irrigated area, India has second largest area under irrigation. Water being a limited resource its efficient use is the basic to the survival of the ever increasing population of India. In spite of the spectacular progress achieved in increasing the irrigation potential through the completion of several irrigation projects, we are unable to utilize the irrigation water properly to its proposed potential.

Until recently, irrigation development was strictly a civil engineering domain of capturing water from the rivers by dams and reservoirs and conveying it to agricultural lands by major and minor canals. Therefore the major emphasis was only the water delivery. However, there was little

---

1. An interdisciplinary system process with built-in learning mechanisms to improve system performance by adjusting physical, technological and institutional inputs to achieve the desired levels of outputs (Secklar and Nobe, 1983).

concern for on-farm water management[1] problems. Design factors have usually been unrealistic because they ignored indirect costs, social and environmental impact, careful assessment of technologies, and an analysis of possible direct and indirect externalities[2] involved.

Some of the major problems of our irrigation systems are: irrigation water control and allocation, inequitable distribution of water to users, and operation and maintenance of existing systems. In view of these facts, there is a need for a systematic approach by adopting Diagnostic Analysis of an improvement in a system, which is now growing concensus among irrigation management professionals. With this idea, a critical review of Diagnostic Analysis approach for irrigation management is done to have the knowledge of the systems problems including their magnitude, causes and effects. Solutions are then developed to improve the systems Flow Chart.

The concept of Diagnostic Analysis was first reported by Lowdermilk *et. al.* in 1983. The rationale for the Diagnostic Analysis model, being built into new projects and utilized for the improvement of existing projects is based upon long observation and experience which indicates that many, if not most, irrigation and agricultural personnel do not fully understand how irrigation system works in practice at farm level. This is because such personnel often have not perceived the system from the farmers' perspective. Few developing countries today can field an experienced inter-disciplinary team of social, biological and physical scientists and professionals in order to make a careful diagnostic analysis of system operational characteristics relative to system design standards.

The farm management[3] focuses on the Diagnostic Analysis process at the farm level and does not, however, ignore the importance of the main irrigation system providing water supplies. Specially, it views the total system in terms of both the farmer decision-making and the local irrigation authorities who are involved in day-to-day system delivery operations. The productive end of the system (on-farm water use) is used as a barometer of how well the total system is operating in terms of

---

2. In view of the existence of externalities in canal irrigation project, neither private individuals nor enterpreneurs undertake such projects and hence canal projects are public sector undertakings and government ownership is one of the most effective means of internalising the externalities.

3. Chandler (1979) stated that the differences of rice yields in the Philippines (less than 2 tons/ha.), Taiwan (4 to 5 tons/ha.) & South Korea (6 tons/ha.) is attributed to irrigation management. Farm management in fact encompasses irrigation management as a sub-system of the total farm management system.

providing predictable supplies of water. Problems are diagnosed at the farm level first and the causes are investigated at each control point up to the entire system. The characteristics that Diagnostic Analysis incorporates are a system perspective, an inter-disciplinary approach, and an active involvement of the farmer.

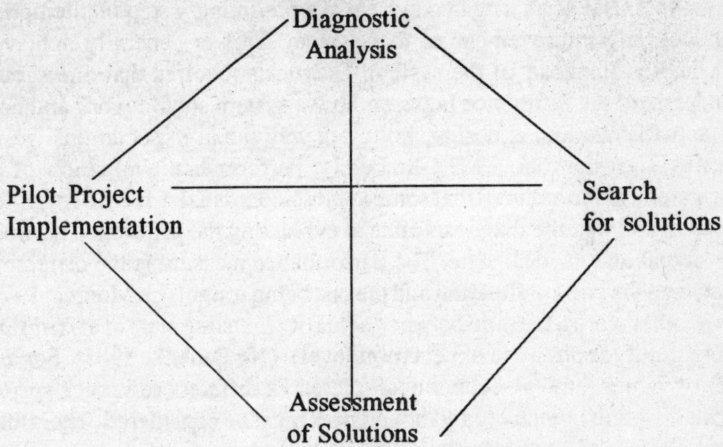

Flow Chart 1: A Research Process Improving Irrigation systems.

Key Concepts	*Essential Components*
1. System Approach	1. Client Involvement
2. Interdisciplinary Research	2. Communication
3. On-Farm Client Focus	3. Team Collaboration
4. Host-Country Involvement	4. Training
5. Management Oriented	5. Institutional Building
6. Action Research	6. Monitoring and Evaluation

A functional tool for irrigation systems (whether tank irrigated systems or other types of systems) is meant to assess the performance of an irrigated system, carry out a proper diagnosis and provide a relevant diagnostic. Here, three key concepts (*i.e.* terminology namely performance, diagnosis and diagnostic) have been used, which are defined as follows:

1. Performance: manner or quality of functioning

2. Diagnosis : thorough analysis of facts and problems in order to gain an understanding of the system, which process leads to the diagnostic.
3. Diagnostic: conclusion of the diagnosis; opinion reached after the analysis.

Appraisal of an irrigated system is a preliminary step in attempting to seek any improvement of that system. This is generally achieved through a diagnosis of the system. Diagnosis requires that one should understand the difference between how a system should work and how it actually works *i.e.* design, policy or individual expectations *versus* reality (Lowdermilk, 1983). Sincerely, performance evaluation of an irrigated system assumes that some ideal standards exist for the irrigation system and that the diagnosis aims at evaluating the difference between its actual and its ideal state. The performance measure is the difference between the present situation and the one being sought (Le Moigne, 1977) or in other words, the ratio between actuality (existing state of affairs) and potentiality (normative expectation level) (Ng Pohkok, 1985). For any set of values (ethical, economical interest) a different reference system with different objectives and boundaries must be considered. Therefore, any diagnosis is intrinsically linked with a set of expectations (the ideal reference state of the system) on which the diagnostic process is based.

Diagnosis identifies the performance of the system, its problems and their causes according to the formally chosen reference: each reference will result in a different diagnosis and the choice of the reference will be subjective. Analysis of a situation provides a picture, an understanding based upon facts and mechanisms. However, it requires technical data mechanisms, facts and rules that remain true in any chosen reference state. Because of the bias inherent in a diagnosis there is an imperative necessity to select what informations are required to make an efficient diagnosis. The characteristic of good experts' strategy is 'that they only ask for what is required (no excess information query and yet all necessary information to produce a relevant and accurate diagnosis') (Pollock, 1985).

Basic Technical Knowledge

All the basic knowledge concerned with the irrigated system can broadly be categorised into four domains, which are interlinked fields. These four technical domains are:

Civil Engineering covers meteorological data, hydrology, water resources, water storage, hydraulics and irrigation structures, aquifers, hydrological balance, losses and discharge, distribution in the channels (water storage and distribution).

Agronomy is concerned with the cropping pattern, soil conditions, water scheduling, inputs use including labour, agronomic considerations, needs and requirements, crop water requirements, irrigation practices etc.

Agricultural Economics. This includes farm management decisions, costs and returns, market conditions, farm credit, project investment and viability, institutional services, farm performance.

Social Structure covers social and organisation, availability, equity and dependability, political tensions, leadership, attitude and behaviour, values and perception, tradition, kinship and factionalism, laws and rules related to land and water, taxation and irrigation management.

At any step of the diagnostic process, the progress within each module starts from the synthesis of the knowledge obtained in each field, and in the course of the assessment process, the investigation will shift from one field to the other according to the requirements of the reasoning process. However, human factors account for much of the management of an irrigation system. Generally collection of information regarding human factors is biased and the value of a piece of information given by a respondent depends on his/her perception of the person collecting the information. The answers are often not only qualitative but also subjective.

DIAGNOSTIC ANALYSIS DEFINED

Diagnostic analysis is an orderly method of examining a system and identifying its values and its constraints.

Diagnostic analysis, therefore, can be defined as an interdisciplinary approach which involves farmers in the examination of an operating irrigation system* with its interrelated components. The Diagnostic analysis is an orderly approach of examining a system and identifying its value and its constraints. Flow Chart 2 shows the primary activities of a Diagnostic Analysis which are in sequence as follows: (1) Preliminary objectives, (2) Reconnaissance, (3) Revised objectives, (4) Detailed studies, (5) Interdisciplinary analysis and synthesis, and (6) Report writing. These steps, though presented as separate often overlap or occur simultaneously.

---

* Corey (1982): "No one seems to be observing, analysing, keeping track of, thinking, or worrying, about the irrigation system as a whole."

DIAGNOSTIC ANALYSIS

PRELIMINARY OBJECTIVES

RECONNAISSANCE

(a) Background Information

(b) Preliminary Field Surveys

REVISED OBJECTIVES AND PLANS

DETAILED STUDIES

INTERDISCIPLINARY ANALYSIS & SYNTHESIS

REPORT WRITING

(a) Disciplinary

(b) Interdisciplinary

Flow Chart 2 : The Six Steps of Diagnostic Analysis

Preliminary Objectives

The preliminary objectives of the Diagnostic Analysis are (1) The understanding of the irrigation system as it actually operates, recognizing its strength as well as its constraints, (2) The identification of the major physical, biological, economical, and organisational constraints to an irrigation system which limits agricultural production, and (3) The listing of these constraints in an order of priority based on stated criteria so as to assist the development and assessment of possible solutions.

Before field visits, the objectives of Diagnostic Analysis, methodology to carry out Diagnostic Analysis, the importance of reconnaissance and the objectives of reconnaissance are discussed.

Reconnaissance

The reconnaissance is the initial examination or survey of an irrigation system. The reconnaissance is used to examine quickly the entire system as it operates and looking for its positive or negative aspects. In fact intelligent observation is a basic tool of reconnaissance. The aim of the reconnaissance is not the accumulation of unmanageable amounts of data, but rather the systematic selection of data within the limits to the interdisciplinary team task. The reconnaissance study, has seven steps which are : (1) Objectives, (2) Allocation of responsibility, (3) Information collection, (4) Development of work plans and methods, (5) Data collection, (6) Analysis and synthesis and, (7) Team report writing. In doing so, those constraints that most limit the viability and effectiveness of an irrigation system will emerge.

Revised Objectives and Plans

The third activity phase of the Diagnostic Analysis is the on-going revision of the team's objectives and plans. On the basis of the reconnaissance and the team hypothesis, objectives will be more specific. Therefore, revised planning is imperative in the light of the revised objectives.

Detailed Studies

Detailed studies of Diagnostic Analysis have five activity steps and they include : (1) objectives, (2) Allocation of responsibility, formal field studies, (3) Data analysis, and (4) Disciplinary report writing. The entire period of detailed studies consists of field investigations and data analysis. The inter-disciplinary team continues to function collectively although there may be a disciplinary focus within the team activity.

To carry out detailed Diagnostic Analysis, the irrigation system is grouped into four sub-systems. However, the basic objectives of detailed Diagnostic Analysis of main sub-system, on-farm sub-system, cropping sub-system and socio-economic sub-system are–

Objectives of the main sub-system :

(i) To check the discharge releases passing through distributaries,

(ii) To evaluate seepage losses,

(iii) To determine coefficient of discharge of the outlets, and

(iv) To determine the conveyance efficiency.

Objectives of the on-farm sub-system :

(i) To understand the constraints in alignment sections, grades and pucca structures on water courses,

(ii) To understand the constraints imposed on farmers by existing operating procedures, and

(iii) To understand the organisational set-up below outlet.

Objectives of the cropping sub-system :

(i) To study the existing soil and crop conditions, and

(ii) To identify the major problems of crops and soils and their effects on yield potential of the existing cropping system.

Objectives of the socio-economic sub-system :

(i) To study the social and organisational aspects of water availability, equity and dependability to identify the cause of problems,

(ii) To identify levels and use of institutional services to farmers.

(iii) To evaluate farmers level of understanding the irrigation system, and

(iv) To study the levels of resource allocation, yield, net income and costs, and returns of inputs.

Inter-disciplinary analysis and Synthesis

Taking the whole system apart, the team examines the separate components of the system and then synthesizes the results so that the exact causes of the constraints now can be substantiated by the detailed studies.

Report Writing

Normally two types of reports need be prepared : (i) a disciplinary report, and (ii) an interdisciplinary report. The disciplinary reports from the detailed studies will serve as the draft manuscript for the final disciplinary summation of the irrigatin system. Like the disciplinary report, the inter-disciplinary report itself should illustrate the systems perspective of the interdisciplinary approach, and an active involvement of the farmers. The report then should not reflect simply parallel views of the system, for that is a multidisciplinary approach. Rather, as a result of the synthesis process the interdisciplinary report presents, the irrigation system and the teams findings about it in such a manner so as to reflect the mutually interdependent components, the teams collective understanding of how it is functioning, and thus the proposed recommendations.

Once the knowledge of the systems problems including their magnitude and causes are gained solutions then can be developed to improve the system on this knowledge *i.e.* feedback knowledge.

The concept of Diagnostic Analysis is rather new to India. From the Diagnostic Analysis studies carried out during recent past for various irrigation projects in the State of Gujarat, Madhya Pradesh, Rajasthan and Uttar Pradesh, it is evident that Diagnostic Analysis approach can be applied successfully to any of our irrigation project to understand for better irrigation management.[4] Also the loss of valuable water due to poor management and inequitable distribution of water to users can be minimized.

Many performance indicators may be used for sustaining assessment which usually focus on a particular aspect:

1. The irrigation system (focused on hydraulic and hydrologic aspects).
2. The irrigated agricultural system (crop yields expressed as ratio per hectare, per unit of water).
3. The irrigated economic system (economic returns, benefit-cost analysis....)
4. The socio-political system (labour, equity, living standard and quality ....).

---

4. Early at IRRI (1982) stated that Management represents the most indigenous portion of the whole technology in the process of operation of an irrigation system. The management has a very unique quality in any culture. Hence, the management methods generally should be specified based on cultural procurements on known or predictable behaviour patterns as the predecessor to the structural component decision.

5. The ecological system (focused on long term trends, irreversible changes and degradations of climate, vegetal cover, water resources and animal species balance).

However, a brief review of the indicators commonly used for performance evaluation are given as under:

PERFORMANCE INDICATORS

1. Irrigation System Indicators

The working group on irrigation efficiency formed by ICID in 1974 has collected the following irrigation indicators (Bos, 1985):

(i) *Conveyance efficiency*: Efficiency of canal and conduit networks from the reservoir, river diversion or pumping station to the off-takes of the distribution system:

Ec = \f(Vd + V2, Vo + V1)

Where, Vo = volume diverted or pumped from the water source (m^3)

Vd = volume delivered to the distribution system (m^3)

V1 = inflow from other sources (m^3)

V2 = non-irrigation deliveries from conveyance system (m^3)

(ii) *Distribution efficiency:* Efficiency of distribution of canal and conduits supplying water from the conveyance network to individual fields.

Ed = \f(Vf + V3, Vd)

Where, Vf = volume of water supplied to the field (m^3)

V3 = non-irrigation deliveries from distribution system (m^3)

Vd = volume delivered to the distribution system (m^3)

(iii) *Field application efficiency:*

Ea = \f(Vm, Vf)

Vm = volume of irrigation water needed and made available for evaporatranspiration. we–Pe,

Where, we = crop water requirement in mm. This is the total depth of water required, during a specific time period (rainfall and/or irrigation), when soil water is maintained so that it does not limit plant growth.

Pe = effective rainfall.

(iv) *Tertiary unit efficiency:* combined efficiency of the water distribution system and water irrigation process:

$$Eu = \frac{Vm + V3}{Vd}$$

(v) Overall efficiency:

$$Ep = \frac{Vm + V3 + V2}{Vo + V1}$$

First of all, indicators should be capable of providing realistic criteria; in other words, they must be simple enough to make comparisons possible between different systems (no ambiguity on the entities to be measured and feasibility of the measures). The indicators mentioned above satisfy these requirements.

The precision of the indicators depends on the constituting parameters which vary thoroughly according to the type of device being used and the location of the sites. Therefore it seems hazardous to work on the values taken by these indicators without considering their confidence intervals.

The conveyance efficiency (Ec) gives a global value, which will not give a true account of the variation of this ratio as a function of

– the discharge ahead,

– the total length of canal or gross area irrigated,

– local defaults of the conveyance system,...

The availability of such information Ec(L)=f(Q,L), where L is the distance between the point in which one is computing efficiency and the head of the distribution system, would be very helpful in building an adequate diagnosis and improvement of the system.

The distribution efficiency is a good indicator though it may result in a wrong value due to water stealing.

As regards the field application efficiency, the indicator seems far less adequate although theoretically convenient, it is far less practicable.

To measure water application to each field as well as soil water content before every application, requires a very intense measuring organisation. Besides, consumptive use and good meteorological data are seldom available in most of the sites. The accuracy of such an indicator is bound to be poor or at least not quite relevant. As a matter of fact, the soil root zone available for water storage increases with the development of the culture and, moreover, great spatial variations occur within one field. But the consumptive use scheduled per month, seems a very rough proxy.

The next two efficiencies are second order efficiencies, cumulating all the drawbacks of the first order efficiencies and are not very informative. They give only a rough estimate; yet they are the sole parameter used for evaluation by the decision-makers.

2. Agricultural System Indicators

(i) Application efficiency at field level.

Ea = \f(Vm, Vf)

The target application efficiency as expressed above is always below 100% since leaching or deep percolation is compulsory in some cases to maintain an acceptable salt balance and suitable aeration in the root zone. It is not correct to say that this volume of water is not necessary for crop production. The water requirements for a crop are distinct from the consumptive use of a plant.

(ii) Irrigation efficiency (IE):

IE = \f(Vc, Vd)

Where,

Vd = volume delivered, and Vc = volume beneficially used, is a theoretical parameter which is difficult to evaluate since the benefits may be of various types. Since one has to cope with non-uniformity of water application, the following indicators are suggested:

(iii) Uniformity coefficient:

Ud = \f(\f{V1,4),V}

Where;

\f(V1,4) is the volume of water infiltrated in the lower quarter of the field.

V is the average volume received in any quarter of the field.

Such a ratio is relevant for furrow or basin irrigation.

(iv) Christiansen's uniformity coefficient, Ucc is expressed by:

Ucc = 1–\[f(\S\DO(1,Σn)lyi-ȳl,(n.ȳ))]

Where,

yi is the depth of absorbed water representative of the one nth of the irrigated field,

ȳ is the mean of the absorbed water in n fields.

(v) field application efficiency is defined by the ICID, taking account of variability as follows:

Ea, target = \f[Vm,(Vm+s.Tp)]

Where,

Vm = volume of water required to maintain the soil moisture above the minimum level for the crop.

s = standard deviation of the depths of water applied to the field at the observed grid points

Tp = the value that is exceeded by a random variable, normally distributed with 0 mean and unit standard deviation, with the probability p.

This new target value allows an increased mean field application, reducing thus the under-irrigated part of the field. p is the accepted threshold value. The assumption of normal distribution of water may not be representative especially under heterogeneous conditions.

Three other parameters are commonly being used to characterise field application (Gideon Peri & Al, 1979):

(vi) Delivery efficiency at the field level:

Vd = volume delivered to the distribution system (m^3)

Ed = \f 9Vum Vd)

Where,

Vi = volume of infiltrated water

Vd = volume of delivered water.

This ratio gives a measure of the losses due to other factors than run off, *i.e.* wind drift, tail water reuse system, evaporation, etc.

(vii) Deep percolation efficiency: This parameter is a measure of the water loss to deep percolation:

Ep = \f(Vsr, Vi)

Where,

Vsr = volume of water stored in the root zone water storage.

It is very difficult to obtain measures of the percolation losses, and practically this parameter is rarely made use of.

(viii) Storage efficiency is the fraction of available root zone water storage (at the time of irrigation) that is filled by irrigation. It gives a measure of the adequacy of the irrigation.

Es = \f(Vsr, Vs)

Where,

Vs is the available root zone water storage.

These indicators are still insufficient; they are based on external knowledge assumed to describe properly the developing process of the crops; but the only real estimate of the irrigation efficiency is the yield of a crop.

(ix) The [Yield/Evapotranspiration] (ICID) and [Yield/water supply] are defined as:

Rye = \f(y_i-yr, ETi-ETr)

Ryw = \f(yi-yr, Wf)

Where,

yi = mass of marketable crop produced with irrigation

yr = mass of marketable crop that could be produced without irrigation

ETi = mass of water evapotranspired by the irrigation crop

ETr = mass of water that would be evapotranspired by the same crop if not irrigated

Wf = water delivered to the field.

These parameters are built with assumed values on what might be the situation without irrigation. Gross assumptions of these values are being done knowingly to influence opinions or sometime unknowingly.

The marketable crop, if measured by its sole mass or dry matter mass does not allow differences between main crop produce and byproducts. The introduction of costs and prices will account for it.

After adding certain amount of water, the additional yield due to incremental dose of water will decrease, resulting in the reduction of overall yield per unit of water. Moreover some crops give higher yields with less water. The following parameters give measures allowing meaningful comparisons:

- Yield per unit of ha
- Yield per unit of water
- Water use efficiency:

net WUE = \f[crop production (kg), evapotranspiration from planting to harvest].

The comparison of mass harvested for different crops is very poor: fodder, oil seed, sugarcane, cereals, pulses, even two varieties of the same crop do not provide the same type of matter. High opportunity cost, or a particular strategy (individual or public) may justify going for less efficient crops.

The quality of the crop itself may be decreased by irrigation: some varieties of ragi, when irrigated give a less nutritious grain.

Besides water use efficiency (WUE) is not a complete indicator, for example, millet has a very good water efficiency, but only one crop can be grown round the year, whereas rice water use efficiency is low but the short duration of rice allows 2 to 3 crops a year in the same plot.

All these parameters consider water scarcity conditions but even under such conditions, one may find in the same location excess water conditions and as such there is no specific detector of such a situation, neither measures of the attempts to cope with it. The ratios per unit of water are a step towards it.

The timing adequacy of irrigation is another aspect barely approached by most authors:

(x) the interval ratio and the depth ratio are defined respectively as:

INR = \f(RI,AI) and DAR = \f(RD,AD)

Where:

RI = recommended intervals between irrigations
AI = actual interval between irrigation
RD = recommended depth of application
AD = actual depth of application.

Evaluation of these parameters is based on two irrigation scheduling parameters:

- The time of irrigation,
- The irrigation requirements, which depends on the crop stage, and the soil type.

The delivery of water for the crop development is characterised by:

- its adequacy, whether the amount meets the requirements,
- its timeliness, whether the delivery occurs whenever is required.

– its reliability, if amounts are delivered when expected and needed, it contributes to reliability, but since these aspects are changing ones, they are quite difficult to assess.

(xi) Water availability index. WAI (Wijayaratna, 1985):

This index is computed to analyse the water inputs, taking into account both amount and timing; 5 different ranges of water supply are differentiated and given a different weight:

X_1 a>severe shortage of water (soil cracking)
X_2 b>moderate shortage (soil dry)
X_3 c>saturated conditions (soil wet)
X_4 d>standing water
X_5 e>flowing water.

WAI is calculated adding the number of days in each category weighted with X_1, X_2, X_3, X_4 and X_5 etc.

This is done first for all the cropping season, and then only for the critical periods, according to the phenologic stage of the culture. This index can be calculated for the fields, the channels or the whole irrigated area.

However, it is quite difficult to find relevant indicators to measure some correlative negative effects of irrigation, in the agricultural system for example, its effect on weeds and pests is well known, but not quantified.

3. Economic Indicators

(i) The first well-known indicator, is the yield-water-cost ratio:

$$R_{yc} = \backslash f\{C_i - C_{r,}(C_f)\}$$

Where,

C_i = value of crop under irrigation

C_r = value of crop (and by-products) that could be produced without irrigation

C_f = cost of applied irrigation water, including amortisation, labour and supplementary production costs (ICID).

Very often when an economic evaluation is made, the actual state of the irrigation system is considered as the result of a previous project characterised by some investments (dam, channels, etc...) and the objective is to estimate the returns on investments, the ability of the system to self-funding its maintenance cost, paying back the initial investments (whether it is decapitalising or not) and the income it provides to each and every farmer. The charges and net product per hectare, per volume of water or per volume of harvest are broadly used as indicators, though the type of assessment they bring is very rough without consideration of the production context. The present situation may also be analysed in connection with future planned investments on projects. Under such conditions benefit -cost ratio is computed and net returns are estimated. Benefits and costs to farmers, to the project authority, to the state and to the national economy are computed, the expected income level, water rates, and rate of internal return (actualisation rate for which the actualised benefit equals zero) allow the planners to make a comparison between various projects; the internal rate of return is very commonly used. But none of these well known indicators, give a cost utility analysis which tends to assess non-quantifiable consequences (satisfaction) as well as indirect impact (externalities).

The reduction of risk is a very important prospect of many projects but its economic impact is very difficult to estimate and often the costs for such estimation is very high; the financial criterion computes the variation of the cash capacity of the project. However, certain other indicators like present worth are frequently used.

4. Social Criteria

The employment generated or maintained by an irrigation system may contribute to social stability and social welfare. Thus, the social welfare and equity are two main parameters that most of the projects pretend to increase for the sake of humanitarian principles.

(i) ratio similar to the equity ratio is computed as follows:

Re = \f[$V_{1/3\ TAIL}$, $V_{1/3\ HEAD}$]

Where,

$V_{1/3\ TAIL}$ = volume delivered at one-third tail end part of the irrigated area

$V_{1/3\ HEAD}$ = volume delivered in one-third head part of the irrigated area

(ii) Relative equity ratio (P.S. RAO, 1988):

RER = \f(Supply at the head, Supply at the tail) = \f(\fpercentage of total volume of water, percentage of total area at the head), [\f(percentage of total volume of water, percentage of total area at the tail)]. The subsequent definition of tail and head is given as:

Head: All the offtakes in the conveyance and distribution system which are supplied with a volume of irrigation water more than their due share which are proportional to their cultivable area. These areas are over-supplied.

Tail: All the offtakes that receives less than their due share of water. They are undersupplied.

In most of the projects while summarising the benefits expected or achieved, a mixture of qualitative social benefit is converted to financial units and added to economic benefits which provide the evaluation assessment with a definitely positive figure in majority cases supposed to summarise the benefits expected or achieved by this project.

Differential benefits among the various socio-professional categories are evaluated through relevant criteria but not one definite specific index has yet been found. It seems that till now, no real indicator exists. The sociological analysis is made through a description of situations, which makes comparison or absolute assessment quite difficult.

The cost of equity is seldom low and no method could possibly maximise simultaneously the social equity, the profit for every individual, and the profit of the irrigated system as a whole. Often the scale of economy and gravity consideration [the most efficient way of using water is said to be using it as much as possible in the upper reaches so that excess water (run off, seepage, collector waters....) might be used again] bring elements against the consideration of equity.

Besides this equity may be looked upon by various criteria; some institutions consider equal volume of water delivered per hectare; some consider equal volume per individual, and some others consider the volume just below the sluices, some in the field itself.

Qualitative parameters that reduce duration of work, better predictability lessening the risk factor or the stress on the farmers' mind contribute to improved relations between farmers and the respect of rules, though they are difficult to assess.

Proper indicators to objectively assess social parameters of irrigated system are important; otherwise personal opinions of the people in charge of the performance evaluation assessment are bound to interfere with the evaluation itself.

6. Environmental Aspects

It would do little to quote the real importance of some global and ecological factors; of these the following indicators are frequently used: whether to assess the rate of collection of water at the watershed level (available water storage/area), and the impact of irrigation works on ecological system:

- % of runoff
- Biomass production/ha
- Water logging problems.

Often irrigation planners and environmentalists oppose these schemes as their objectives are competing ones and not of complementary nature. Mnay of these schemes are based upon the principle of transferring water from one location to another, concentration of the rainfall in the tank at the bottom of one watershed or even translocation of water resources from one watershed to another one which is bound to produce a modification in the balance of the ecosystem and induce ecological imbalance.

Moreover, excessive irrigation may result in salinisation of upper layers in the soils, depletion of the soil productivity and, in the long term, loss of land for crop production.

According to the objectives of performance assessment, adequate criteria must be selected among the traditional ones. If they are not suitable, other indicators need to be worked out to suit particular conditions or objectives. Thus, the final criteria of selection depends on the particular focus of the study, on the level of analysis (the field, the farming system, the tertiary channel, the watershed, the village, the district....), the precision is required, as well as the time, funds and technical means available. The optimal indicators may have to be abandoned for lack of adequate time or funds. In such a situation, assumptions will have to be made, which will downgrade the accuracy of the performance assessment and quality of the expert diagnosis.

In a Rapid Rural Appraisal, a thorough analysis of systems using methodologies which aim at multidisciplinary assessment is tried.

'Because a number of factors – physical, social and economic–influence each other, they are of equal importance to the engineer, agronomist, economist and sociologist.'

In the study of the social organisational system it is advised to study the pattern of social relations and the organisational arrangement necessary to manage the water. A sociologist needs to study how the physical irrigation technology is linked with the social organisation of irrigation. Both formal and informal patterns of behaviour have to be analysed (organisations, cooperatives, implicit rules, penalties, rewards and values). Farmers behaviour needs to be studied and their impact on productivity or water efficiency needs to be analysed. This method consists in dividing the farmers social environment into situations and actions–situations comprise particular settings (physical and social environment) of the farmer, the culture (thinking, feeling and behaviour) of the area, and the social structures and processes (influences tending to change the social conditions) surrounding the farmer – actions are the actual results and decision of the farmer.

To conclude it is emphasized that no absolute indicators exist. A correct way of assessing performance evaluation should start with the hierarchial specification of the objectives. Based upon these priorities, the most adequate indicators could be applied and the boundaries of the irrigated system defined.

REFERENCES

1. Chandler, R.F. (1979). Rice in Tropics : A Guide to the Development of National Progress, West View Press, Boulder, Colorado.
2. Early, A.C. (1982). Collaborative Irrigation System Management Research Results from the Upper Pampanga Integrated Irrigation Systems. Proceedings of the Seminar on Irrigation Water Management Development, Manila, Philippines.
3. Lowdermilk, M.K. (1984). Professional Development Needs for Improved Irrigation Management. Proceedings of the Seminar on Education and Training in Water Management, Vadodara, India.
4. Lowdermilk, M.K. and M. Svendsen (1983). Issues in Third World Development. West View Press, Boulder, Colorado.
5. Lowdermilk, M.K., W. Clyma, L.K. Dunn, M.T. Haider, W.R. Latios, L.J. Nelson, D.K. Sunada, C.A. Poduore, and T.H. Podmore (1983). Diagnostic Analysis of Irrigation Systems, C.S.U., Fort Collins, Colorado.
6. Seckler, D. and K.E. Nobe (1983). The Critical Role of Management. Factor in Developing Countries. Proceedings of the Seminar at the International School of Economic Development, C.S.U. Fort Collins, Colorado.

CHAPTER 6

COMMAND AREA DEVELOPMENT–FUNCTIONS AND ORGANISATION

Introduction

The low productivity of canal irrigated lands has been traditionally ascribed to poor water management in command areas. Among the more important factors that have been held responsible are inadequacies in water delivery and drainage systems at the micro level, the failure to level and reshape all the fields situated within the command of an individual outlet in conformity with the demands of flow irrigation and, above all, unreliable supplies of water at times and in the quantities required by the crops. Although these deficiencies are sought to be removed by the Command Area Development, yet this has still to get-off the ground.

Since the beginning of planning in the country, a massive programme of irrigation development has been taken up. Several large dams and canals have been constructed. But the main emphasis has been on construction and the utilisation has been lost sight of. Consequently there has been a large gap between irrigation potential created and utilised. The Command Area Development Programme (CADP) was initiated in December 1974 as centrally sponsored scheme with matching contribution from the states and with the objective of faster utilisation of created potential and optium agricultural production from irrigated land as a follow-up of the recommendations of the Irrigation Commission (1972) and the Committee of Ministers (1972), Planning Commission and the Ministry of Agriculture with the State Governments. The basic idea underlying the Command Area Development Programme was to reduce the lag in utilisation of the created irrigation potential and improvement in productivity of crops per unit of area and also per unit of water from irrigated commands since massive investments were made in construction of gigantic irrigation projects. But the utilisation and productivity of these projects were considerably lower than what was envisaged during their formulation.

Objectives

The programme envisages execution of 'on-farm development works'. Warabandi or rotational system of water distribution is undertaken with a view to ensuring equitable and timely supply of irrigation water. Adaptive trails are also encouraged for establishing a suitable cropping pattern with appropriate soil and water management practices. However, one of the main objectives under CAD Programme is to raise irrigation utilization to the level of created potential. The main features and functions of the Command Area Development Programme in the Irrigation Projects are:

Functions –

1. Modernisation and efficient operation of the irrigation system as well as development of main drainage system.
2. Construction of field channels and field drains.
3. Land shaping and land levelling alongwith consolidation of holdings.
4. Lining of field channels/water courses.
5. Exploitation of ground water, installation of tubewells etc.
6. Adoption and enforcement of a suitable cropping pattern.
7. Enforcement of an appropriate rostering system on irrigation.
8. Making timely and adequate supply of inputs like fertilisers, pesticides, improved seeds, credit etc.
9. Strengthening of existing extension training.

Thus, the efficiency of the irrigation hardware to deliver water all over the command area and the enforcement of a well conceived and developed water policy are the primary functions, which actually control the utilisation at farm level. Besides, certain other programmes such as construction of roads, setting up of processing and marketing facilities are also important components of the CAD Programmes.

It was felt that a broad area development authority which can orchastrate all the activities conducive to improvement of utilisation and productivity of irrigation projects needs to be promoted. These activities included the irrigation, agriculture, credit, co-operatives etc.

In brief, the functions which should exclusively be carried out by CADA and the ones for which CADA would act as a coordinating and monitoring agency should be clearly spelt out. Based on such functions one can then come out with proper organisational structure of CADA. However, it must be kept in mind that completion of 'on-farm development (OFD) works' is just not the end of CADA activities but a beginning towards improvement in utilisation and consequently an increase in agriculture production/productivity. The functions for which CADA is directly responsible for their carrying out, are irrigation functions, such as operation and maintenance of irrigation system from headworks to farm gates, OFD works, construction and maintenance of main and link drains, enforcement of Warabandi, conjunctive use, supply of improved seeds, fertilisers, pesticides and irrigation extension, adaptive trials and action research, liasion with agriculture, and R & D institutions/universities; environmental evaluation and monitoring; training of personnel and farmers participation. The functions which CADA should act as a coordinating agency are functions such as supply of inputs and service for agriculture, provision of credit and other functions such as consolidation of holdings and processing, marketing of agricultural produce etc.

The functions assigned to the Command Area Development Authorities (CADA) in order to achieve the stated goals includes modernisation, maintenance and efficient operation of the irrigation system up to the outlet, development and maintenance of the main and intermediate drainage system, carrying out 'on farm development works', consolidation of holdings, enforcement of Warabandi, conjunctive use, selection and introduction of suitable cropping pattern etc. It was against this background that the centrally sponsored Command Area Development Programme was initiated during the Fifth Year Plan. The programme is now almost a decade and half old, which was initially started with 60 major and medium irrigation projects in 16 states (Table 1). At the beginning of the Sixth Five Year Plan the programme was in operation in 76 major/medium irrigation projects. During 1983-84, 29 additional projects were also included but 3 ongoing projects were droped, where on-farm development works were completed. It now includes around 155 irrigation projects covering a culturable command area of about 19 m.ha. in 20 states and 2 Union Territories implemented through 54 CADAs. A massive investment in the Central and State Sectors have been made amounting to around Rs. 2600 crores from inception to the end of Seventh Plan, in which the contribution of Govt. of India alone is around Rs 900 crores. In addition, investments through institutional finance have also contributed significantly towards taking up various activities under this programme. The achievements measured from the point of view of realisation of objectives are, however not highly significant. From a capacity utilisation of around 70% at the end of the Fifth Plan, it has risen to a maximum of around 77% in 1986-87 and came down to 73% in 1987-88 which was, a severe drought year (Table 2). The productivity though has shown considerable improvement in selected projects such as Girna in Maharashtra, Sharda Sahayak in U.P. Lower Bhawani in Tamilnadu, DVC in West Bengal etc. in terms of improvement in annual average growth rate for crops such as paddy, wheat, sugarcane etc. Nevertheless, the increase has been far from satisfactory (Tables 3 & 4).

Achievement

Notwithstanding the functions assigned to the various Command Area Development Authorities at the time of inception of the programme, the present stress on activities has, however, confined itself in most of the states/projects under the programme to mainly construction of field channels and to some extent implementation of Warabandi, land levelling etc. The cumulative achievement from the beginning have been around 11.2 m. ha in case of field channels, 5.2 m. ha. under Warabandi and around 2m. ha. under land levelling and shaping. In spite of coverage under these activities utilisation has not shown commensurate increase (Annexures 1 to 9). This interpretation, however, needs to be made with much ease since utilisation is an aspect which depends on a number of variables such as availability of water in a given year, types of crops that have been grown in the command in that year, the status of the irrigation system delivering water from headworks to farm gates and its management etc. and hence direct linkage of OFD activities on utilisation on year to year basis may not lead to correct conclusions unless other variables are also properly correlated. Even in matters of pace of implementation of these key OFD activities the same have not been satisfactory during the Seventh Plan period.The coverage under these activities were 48% in case of field channels, 54% in respect of Warabandi and 23% in case of land levelling of their planned targets.

As regards the other activities of CADA which have received attention during the Seventh Plan were carrying out adaptive trails, involvement of beneficiary in irrigation water management below minor/outlet, wireless communication system and training of farmers/ field functionaries and officers connected with this programme. But the, majority of the functions such as modernisation, maintenance and efficient operation of irrigation system, the drainage aspect, the consolidation of holdings, conjunctive use etc. have not been followed up with the vigour they deserved.

Constraints

The reasons of such slow progress were many. While the low pace of development of OFD activities may be due to low budget provision, lack of control of CADA's on the departments executing construction of field channels, lack of availability of areas to carry out construction of field channels, problems of consolidation, escalation in cost and flood problem etc. but the main reason appears to be non-development or partial development of the kind of organisation pattern that was expected of CADA to deliver the goods it was supposed to do. The Working Group Report on the Seventh Plan indicated that conceptually while responsibility for increasing agricultural production has been placed under CADA's, functionally they find themselves handicapped as neither the functionaries responsible for water release nor those incharge of extension for agricultural inputs report to them. This is an anomalous situation which was not envisaged when the CAD Programme was launched. As a result, CAD Authorities have confined themselves to the limited task of carrying out 'on-farm development works' and the concept of CAD has deteriorated into being only a field channel construction programme. The backward and the forward linkages for agricultural production and integrated water management, by and large, had not been given the importance they should have been given.

TABLE 1

Irrigation Projects Included under the Centrally Sponsored Command Area Development Programme during Fifth Five Year Plan

Sl. No.	Name of State/Irrigation Projects
	ANDHRA PRADESH
1.	K.C. Canal
2.	Nagarjunasagar
3.	Sreerama Sagar (Pochampad)
4.	Rajoli Bunda Diversion Scheme
5.	Tungabhadra Complex
	ASSAM
6.	Jamuna
	BIHAR
7.	Gandak
8.	Kiul
9.	Badua
10.	Chandan
11.	Kosi
12.	Sone
	GUJARAT
13.	Mahi-Kadana
14.	Shetrunji
15.	Ukai Kakrapar

Sl. No.	Name of State/Irrigation Projects
	HARYANA
16.	Gurgaon Canal
17.	J.L. Nehru L.I. Scheme
18.	Jui L.I. Scheme
19.	Rewari L.I. Scheme
	JAMMU & KASHMIR
20.	Tawi L.I. Scheme
	KARNATAKA
21.	Cauveri Basin Projec
22.	Ghataprabha
23.	Malaprabha
24.	Tungabhadra
25.	Upper Krishna
	KERALA
26.	Chala Kudi
27.	Malam Puzia
28.	Peechi
	MADHYA PRADESH
29.	Barna
30.	Halali
31.	Chambal
32.	Hasdeo
33.	Kharung
34.	Maniyari
35.	Tawa

Sl. No.	Name of State/Irrigation Projects
	MAHARASHTRA
36.	Bagh
37.	Itiadoh
38.	Bhima
39.	Ghod
40.	Purna
41.	Jayakwadi Stg. I
42.	Girna
43.	Upper Tapi
44.	Krishna
	MANIPUR
45.	Loktak L.I. Scheme
	ORISSA
46.	Hirakud
47.	Mahanadi Delta
48.	Solandi
	RAJASTHAN
49.	Bhakra Gang Canal
50.	Chambal
51.	R.C.P. Stage I
	TAMIL NADU
52.	Cauveri System
53.	Lower Bhawani
54.	Periyal

Sl. No.	Name of State/Irrigation Projects
	UTTAR PRADESH
55.	Gandak
56.	Ramganga
57.	Sharda Sahayak
	WEST BENGAL
58.	D.V. System
59.	Kangsbati
60.	Mayurkashi

PROJECTS INCLUDED IN 1979-80

Sl. No.	State	Name of the Project
1.	Goa	Salauli
2.	Jammu & Kashmir	Ravi
3.	Kerala	Neyyar
4.	Kerala	Pothundy
5.	Kerala	Gayathri
6.	Kerala	Walayar
7.	Kerala	Mangalam
8.	Kerala	Cheerakuzhi
9.	Kerala	Vashani
10.	Maharashtra	Mula
11.	Maharashtra	Kukadi
12.	Maharashtra	Pench
13.	Maharashtra	Upper Penganga
14.	Maharashtra	Warna
15.	Maharashtra	Jayakwadi (Stage-II)
16.	Maharashtra	Panzan L.B.C.

TABLE 2

Irrigation Potential Utilisation in the projects under CAD

('000 ha)

	U.I.P.	1973-74			1982-83		
		C	U	% Utilisation	C	U	% Utilisation
1. ANDHRA PRADESH	1676.85	732.21	568.35	78	1125.42	837.98	74
2. ASSAM	65.90	33.00	12.00	36	63.26	46.53	73
3. BIHAR	2295.92	961.12	533.52	55	1880.08	1406.24	75
4. GOA	21.24	-	-	-	-	-	-
5. GUJARAT	954.52	399.73	208.47	52	832.90	342.38	41
6. HARYANA	275.00	74.00	26.00	35	160.00	45.00	28
7. HIMACHAL PRADESH	5.26	-	-	-	4.50	2.40	53
8. J & K	66.78	1.50	0.70	47	26.08	11.80	46
9. KARNATAKA	1740.89	466.09	339.69	73	746.90	615.71	83
10. KERALA	87.73	86.90	65.65	76	87.45	72.55	84
11. MADHYA PRADESH	1257.68	344.23	214.23	62	973.98	585.00	60
12. MAHA-RASHTRA	1494.78	219.70	79.90	35	811.44	295.63	36
13. MANIPUR	48.50	-	-	-	21.00	12.00	57
14. ORISSA	873.83	631.04	624.97	99	873.83	873.83	100
15. RAJAS-THAN	1245.30	1005.52	920.52	91	1139.52	1122.52	98
16. TAMIL NADU	800.35	570.22	570.22	100	664.96	664.96	100
17. UTTAR PRADESH	2489.00	384.48	223.58	58	1851.39	1281.50	69
18. WEST BENGAL	1167.32	774.00	719.00	93	1149.38	787.64	68
TOTAL	16585.85	6683.74	5118.80	76	12433.09	9015.89	72

U.I.P. : Ultimate Irrigation Potential
C : Potential Created
U : Potential Utilised

The above table indicates that in the case of Assam, U.P., Karnataka, Manipur, Rajasthan and U.P., the present utilisation has increased while in all other states, it has decreased. Taking the country as a whole also, while at the beginning of the CAD programme in 1973-74, the utilisation was 76%, but it came down to 72%. In respect of individual projects, Ramanujam (1983) made a study of 27 projects which revealed that only in 12 projects, the percentage of utilisation has been better in 1982-83 than it was in 1973-74. Even among these projects only few have shown noticeable improvement in potential utilisation. The same study indicates that in as many as 14 projects, the area covered by field channels is higher than the utilised potential.

Increase in Productivity

The percentage increase in the yield of various crops obtained in some projects are as follows:

TABLE 3

Yields of Principal Crops in Some Selected Command Areas

(Quintals/hectare)

	State	Crop/Name of the Command	Before O.F.D.	After O.F.D.	Increase	Percentage increase.
		Kharif Paddy				
1.	Andhra Pradesh	Nagarjunasagar Project Left Bank	20.40	45.00(PW)	24.60	120.59
		Nagarjunasagar Project Right Bank	18.85	33.69(79-80)	14.84	78.72
		Sriramsagar	25.82	40.24 (PW)	15.02	59.55
		Tungabhadra	22.81	32.31	10.10	45.47
2.	Bihar	Gandak	30.46	38.34	7.88	25.87
		West Champaran				
		Saran	29.83	34.72	5.39	18.37
		Gopalganj	24.31	29.80	5.49	22.58
3.	Gujarat	Kadana	20.00	22.00	2.00	10.00
		Ukai-Kakrapar	10.00	12.25	2.25	22.25
4.	Maharashtra	Itiadoh	26.00	30.00	4.00	15.38
		Bagh	25.00	30.00	5.00	20.00
5.	Uttar Pradesh	Gandak	10.25	16.90	6.65	64.88
6.	Rajasthan	Chambal	34.93(PW)	39.19(79-80)	4.26	12.19
		Summer Paddy				
1.	Andhra Pradesh	Sriramsagar	29.76	31.57	1.81	6.08
2.	Maharashtra	Itiadoh	40.00	44.00	4.00	10.00
		Bagh	30.00	40.00	10.00	33.33
		Kharif Bajra				
1.	Andhra Pradesh	Tungabhadra	10.47	11.89	1.42	13.56
2.	Gujarat	Kadana	5.16	14.50(PW)	9.34	181.00
3.	Karnataka	Malaprabha	20.00	23.00(79-80)	3.00	15.00
		Ghataprabha	20.00(PW)	23.00(79-80)	3.00	15.00

TABLE 3 — *Contd.*

State	Crop/Name of the Command	Before O.F.D.	After O.F.D.	Increase	Percentage increase
	Wheat				
1. Gujarat	Kadana	25.00	30.00	5.00	20.00
2. Rajasthan	Chambal	12.00	23.06	11.06	92.16
3. Karnataka	Malaprabha	22.50(PW)	35.00(79-80)	12.50	55.55
	Ghataprabha	30.00(PW)	35.00(79-80)	5.00	16.66
4. Rajasthan	Rajasthan Canal Project	20.25	24.26(78-79)	4.01	40.00
5. Uttar Pradesh	Gandak	14.70	19.20	4.50	30.61
6. Madhya Pradesh	Tawa	8.75(d)	12.25(79-80)	3.50	40.00
		15.00	26.52(79-80)	11.52	76.80
	Jowar				
1. Andhra Pradesh	Tungabhadra (kh)	18.01	27.79	9.78	54.30
2. Gujarat	Ukai-kakrapar	6.00	8.07	2.07	34.50
3. Karnataka	Malaprabha(kh)	27.50	35.00(79-80)	7.50	27.27
	Malaprabha(Rabi)	25.00	35.00 -do-	10.00	40.00
	Ghataprabha (kh)	30.00	35.00 -do-	5.00	16.66
	Ghataprabha (Rabi)	30.00	35.00 -do-	5.00	16.66
4. Madhya Pradesh	Tawa	10.00	15.00(78-79)	5.00	50.00
5. Rajasthan	Chambal(kh)	7.58	8.40 -do-	0.82	10.81
	Maize				
1. Andhra Pradesh	Sriramsagar(kh)	17.00	29.17(PW)	12.17	71.59
	Sriramsagar(Rabi)	22.50	37.52(PW)	15.02	66.75
2. Karnataka	Malaprabha(kh)	27.50	35.00(79-80)	7.50	27.27
	Malaprabha(Rabi)	27.50	35.00-do-	7.50	27.27
	Ghataprabha(kh)	30.00	35.00-do-	5.00	16.66
	Ghataprabha(Rabi)	30.00	35.00-do-	5.00	16.66
	Groundnut				
1. Karnataka	Malaprabha(kh)	12.50	18.00-do-	5.50	44.00
	Malaprabha(Summer)	15.00	18.00-do-	3.00	20.00
	Ghataprabha(kh)	15.00	18.00-do-	3.00	20.00
2. Madhya Pradesh	Tawa	7.80	16.88(78-79)	9.08	116.41
	Sunflower				
1. Karnataka	Malaprabha(kh)	5.00	12.00-do-	7.00	140.00
	Ghataprabha (kh & rabi)	10.00	12.00-do-	2.00	20.00

TABLE 3 – *Contd.*

State	Crop/Name of the Command	Before O.F.D.	After O.F.D.	Increase	Percentage increase
2. Rajasthan	Rajasthan Canal Project.	8.60	10.21(77-78)	–	–
	<u>Pulses</u>				
1. Karnataka	Malaprabha(kh & rabi)	3.40	12.00(77-78)	8.60	252.94
	(Summer)	10.00	12.00 -do-	2.00	20.00
	Ghataprabha (kh & rabi)	10.00	12.00 -do-	2.00	20.00
	<u>Gram</u>				
1. Rajasthan	Chambal	6.00	7.15	1.15	19.16
	Rajasthan Canal Project.	10.85	13.26	2.41	22.21
2. Madhya Pradesh	Tawa(Teora)	10.05	17.50	7.45	74.12

d : Desi wheat
pW : Project as a whole
O.F.D : On-farm development

There are no figures available which could indicate the increase in productivity for the command area as a whole before and after introduction of CAD programme in a project. However, some indication can be available from the trend in all India average since the start of CAD programme in 1973-74 for the principal crops.

TABLE 4

Trend in Yield

(kg/ha)

Year	Rice	Wheat	Total food-grains	Sugar-cane (Gur)	Total food-grain production in m. tonnes
1971-72	1141	1380	858	4864	108.4
1972-73	1070	1271	813	5206	105.2
1973-74	1151	1172	827	5244	97.0
1974-75	1061	1338	831	5165	104.7
1975-76	1235	1410	1041	5218	121.0
1976-77	1088	1387	985	5529	111.2
1977-78	1308	1480	1100	5699	120.4
1978-79	1339	1574	1140	5141	131.9
1979-80	N.A.	N.A.	N.A.	N.A.	109.7
1980-81	1336	1630	1023	5784	129.6
1981-82	1308	1691	1032	5840	133.6
1982-83	1230	1836	1041	5621	128.7

The above table indicates that only in case of wheat there is a definite trend in increase of yield. Since major wheat producing states are Punjab, Haryana, and U.P. where irrigation to wheat crops is mostly due to assured water supply from private tubewells, the credit cannot be given to irrigation from canals. Moreover, due to regular increase in actual irrigated area from about 40 m. ha in 1973-74 to 71m. ha in 1990-91, there is bound to be some increase in yield rate. Thus, so far contribution to increase in yield by CAD programme does not appear to be substantial.

Weaknesses

The other issues which are of paramount importance and have been highlighted in the in-depth evaluation study (1987) of the programme carried out by the Indian Institute of Management (IIM), Ahmedabad, at the instance of Union Ministry of Water Resources. The IIM study emphasized on the need to consider removal of uncertainty in the supply of irrigation water as a core function of the programme. In fact, the study considers that the main bottleneck in the CAD programme is the lack of reliability, in the supply of irrigation water to each and every farm holdings. It suggests that there is a need for management approach to make the programme a success in terms of realisation of its basic objectives. Similarly, a number of other evaluation studies carried out by agencies such as WAPCOS, Agriculture Finance Corporation, Institute of Resource Management and Economic Development, Delhi, WALMI, ORG Baroda; Giri Institute of Development Studies, Lucknow etc. have stressed on the lack of reliability of irrigation water supply mainly due to lack of control structures, measuring devices, unauthorised uses, poor maintenance and lack of responsibility centres, lack of equity in water supply due to conflict of interest between head and tail end farmers. The studies also pointed out that the cropping pattern in the command and crop diversification as envisaged in the original project formulation have not materialised in most of the projects. The deviation of cropping pattern is towards less predominance of crop which are efficient from the point of view of the return per unit of water.

FUTURE STRATEGY FOR IMPROVEMENT

The objectives of the programme as envisaged are valid even today. However, there is a need to shift the focus of the programme towards improvement of water use efficiency by resorting to better water management techniques and hence, the following strategies should be adopted for improvement.

1. Control of Irrigation Water

There should be unified control of irrigation water management from head works to farm gates under one single agency to ensure that the agency is responsible for ensuring delivery of water to each and every farm holdings, till such time the farmers organisations are in a position to accept the delivery of water at a point higher in the distribution system such as outlet/minor and distribute among themselves.

2. Software Components

There is also a need to intensify the software components of the programme such as adaptive trials, demonstration, training, wireless communications, Warabandi, farmers participation in irrigation water management and maintenance.

3. Cost Effectiveness

With dwindling financial resources of the states and many competing activities, it has become imperative to seek cost effective solutions to the problem at hand. The estimated cost of potential created at the end of Eighth Five Year Plan is likely to be more than Rs. 30,000 per ha., and hence there is need to concentrate more on higher utilisation of the created potential, which is the main objective of the CAD Programme. Even in the CADP the cost of construction of field channels, the main activity in the CAD Programme varies from Rs. 1000 to Rs. 7000/- per ha depending on the type and extent of lining. It is also felt that construction of field channels *per se* did not mean improvement in utilisation and productivity unless backed up by adequate software components discussed above. These components are cost effective and they are likely to ensure sustenance of gain due to CAD activities. Thus, the future strategy should be towards ensuring reliability of irrigation water supply through unified control, and adoption of management approach.

4. Package of CAD Programme

The package of CAD Programme cannot be designated in isolation but must be related to the construction programme of the irrigation projects. Utilisation of potential cannot be planned unless there is a definite phased programme of creation of potential. Construction and developmental activities must go in tandem which should be properly synchronised and sequenced. Designing of physical programme of CADP should also take into account this aspect keeping in view the availability of financial resources and capability of the organisation to execute the works.

5. Lining of Field Channels

For planning and designing the OFD works below the outlet the entire command of the distributary as a unit should be considered for construction rather than merely the individual field channels. Lining should be in accordance with the needs, and the present Central assistance for selective lining in vulnerable reaches should be permitted upto 50% of the length of field channels because of many constraints *viz.* technical and social. But the states have gone for higher percenatage of lining, in view of the need to ensure that the water courses/field channels carry the designed discharge. Besides specific funds should be earmarked towards renovation/remodelling of field channels which were constructed long back and are in a bad condition due to floods and other reasons.

6. Warabandi

Although considerable area has been brought under Warabandi, yet the actual implementation of field level needs intensification by involvement of beneficiaries *i.e.* farmers in framing the schedule as well as its actual implementation. It is also necessary to encourage for overnight service reservoirs on the field since night irrigation is normally not adopted in most of the CAD Projects and in their absence such reservoirs will do away with the restriction imposed by limiting the running time by individual water course.

7. Land Levelling

The Indian Institute of Management, Ahmedabad study has suggested a low priority to land levelling. However, the important point to keep in mind is that the land levelling itself is a very desirable component in the CADP. But its poor progress is mainly due to small farm sizes, large investments need etc. Therefore, land levelling should be continued in those projects and areas where uneven topography is a serious constraint especially in slope ranging 1-3%.

8. Drainage Network

In view of emerging problem of water logging and salinisation due to rise of ground water table, drainage activities should be taken up on priority basis. Construction of drainage network duly connected upto the main drain in terms of physical and financial commitment must be made implicit to the programme.

9. Adaptive Trials

Adaptive trial is one crucial area where much emphasis in future plan should be given. This would pay rich dividends. Active involvement of Agricultural Universities and Indian Council of Agricultural Research (ICAR) units in adaptive trials and demonstration and generous research grants by CADA on these activities would ensure optimum utilisation/ production per unit of water.

10. Farmer Participation

Farmer participation in irrigation water management continues to be lacking, in spite of the efforts made by the Govt. of India and many state agencies. But there are still cases where farmers organisations have managed water distribution below minor/outlet successfully, improved water use efficiency, paid irrigation charges well in time and even earned profits. However, such cases are very few. In view of these facts the Ministry of Water Resources, Govt. of India, has issued guidelines and State Govts. have been requested to intensify this activity, if necessary through involvement of voluntary agencies. This activity must be intensified and requires a major thrust in the future plans.

11. Agronomical Practices & Crop Cutting Experiments

Greater attention is required for development of agronomical practices which would lead to optimum crop production, preponing of Kharif crop in reservoir backed projects can encourage early maturing variety of paddy so as to leave the field free for being sown with Rabi crops at the appropriate time. Farmers growing paddy should be encouraged to adopt shallow and intermittent submergence as against the traditional practice of continuous and deep submergence. In fact the ICAR, under its coordinated projects on water management has made valuable suggestions to optimise supply of water to crops. This needs to be pursued seriously under lab to land experimentation. In spite of improvement in productivity being one of the objectives of the programme, systematic crop cutting experiments, should be carried out in order to estimate the productivity in the command area. Such crop cutting experiments should be carried out in coordination with Director of Economics and Statistics of the concerned States and should be dovetailed with general crop estimation surveys carried out by such departments.

12. Conjuctive Use

The emerging dichotomy of shortage/non-availability of water over certain areas of the command on one hand and water logging and salinity problem due to excessive water use on the other, necessitates the conjunctive use of water. Ground water should be used not only to supplement the available surface water but also as an effective tool for scientific and efficient management of the water resources in the command to provide reliability of irrigation and remove uncertainty in water supply which would also reduce the water logging and salinity menance.

13. Consolidation of Holdings

It is a work which enables field channels to be constructed and water to be distributed in a more efficient manner. Hence consolidation of holdings should be intensified in order to ensure rectangularisation of field as far as possible.

14. Coordination of Activities

There is a need to ensure multi-disciplinary organisational set up of CADAs in order to achieve the implementation of various activities towards realisation of the objectives of the programme. Functions which should exclusively be carried out by CADA and the ones for which CADA would act as a co-ordinating and monitoring agency need to be clearly spelt out. Based on such functions, we may come out with proper organisational structure of CADA. However, it must be kept in mind that completion of on-farm development (OFD) works is just not the end of CADA activities but a beginning towards improvement in utilisation and consequently an increase in agriculture production/productivity could be possible. The functions for which CADA would be directly responsible for their carrying out, would encompass irrigation functions such as operation and maintenance of irrigation system from headworks to farm gates, OFD works, construction and maintenance of main and link drains, enforcement of Warabandi, conjuctive use; supply of improved seeds, fertilisers, pesticides and irrigation extension, adaptive trials and action research, liaison with agriculture and R&D institutions/universities; environmental evaluation and monitoring functions; training of personnel and farmers participation. The functions which CADA should act as a coordinating agency are such as supply of inputs and service for agriculture, provision of credit and other functions such as consolidation of holdings, processing, marketing of agricultural produce etc.

ORGANISATIONAL SET-UP

The objectives assigned to CAD are to be achieved through establishment of CAD Authority for each command area with a senior officer at its head for effective management through horizontal and vertical coordination of the activities of various developmental departments in the command areas. For this, a three tier organisational set up at state, project and field level would be necessary. At State level there should be a separate CAD Department with full time Secretary assisted by officers of the rank of heads of the departments from Irrigation, Agriculture, Co-operation, Agricultural Engg. etc. The CADA should be a semi-autonomous body with a CADA Board. CAD Commissioner should be the Chairman vested with powers of heads of departments of all relevant departments and CADA should have wings like human resource management, financial management, coordination and agriculture wing which should be headed by experts of the concerned discipline. At field level there should be a construction wing under the Superintending Engineer to carry out OFD works, Warabandi, O&M Wing under Superintending Engineer to maintain the headworks and delivery system of the outlet, agriculture wing under the Joint Director of Agriculture consisting of agronomy and input supply units, and environment wing under an Executive Engineer to study water logging and salinity aspects. CAD authorities should coordinate and strengthen extension activities, enforce suitable cropping pattern, arrange supply of credit and other inputs like improved seeds and fertiliser in time specifically to the weaker group in the command area, link up the activities like construction of link roads, establish market centres, agro-processing and agro-industrial ventures for establishment of effective forward and backward linkage and higher rate of development of the command area.

Monitoring

There is a need to intensify monitoring of various activities of the programme and to evaluate its impact on the overall productivity in the command. Mointoring helps in management which enables timely diagnosis and helps in implementation of on-going projects. The importance of monitoring stems from the fact that through an efficient monitoring mechanism, it is possible to steer the programme in the right direction through mid-course correction. Hence, a monitoring cell at project level should be established which would carry out technical monitoring involving water availability, carrying capacity of the channels, performance of various structures, water distribution, ground water table, salinity and soil status, drainage; financial programme, monitoring on financial allocations and expenditure on various targetted activities and the rates of their execution; physical monitoring of various OFD works and software activities; operational monitoring in terms of potential created and utilisation, area under different crops, water delivery to the cultivators, efficiency, water demand and farm management surveys – to determine area irrigated crop-wise, crops grown in command area, availability and use of inputs, yield of crops, farm income etc.

Evaluation

Periodic evaluation of project at an interval of five years is necessary in order to study the impact of project in terms of achieving of the basic objectives. For such evaluation bench mark data are required to be generated and updated through development of sound and reliable data base. The state should establish a network of centres for collection of scientific data and farmers' response in the command area to provide a feedback mechanism for evaluation and collection of data on planning and management procedure of the irrigation system.

Training of Farmers and Engineers

Training needs of the farmers, field functionaries and officers of the CADA are being presently met through Institutes such as WALMI, Administrative Staff College of India and Organisation such as WAPCOS, WRDTC, University of Roorkee etc. Even then there is need to continue vigorously the training programme in future. There should be 3-4 courses at the State level for the middle officers and an equal number of courses at the National level for senior officers every year. In States where the lower level of hierarchy such as the Canal Inspectors, watermen have not been trained at the recruitment stage and immediately after entering the service, an intensive orientation training should be imparted to them. The CADA should set-up at least one farmers' training centre in each project which should train farmers in storing water on farm, water management, crop water requirement etc.

The suggested organisational set up vested with responsibilities and powers needed at various levels backed up by a physical system capable of delivering the designed discharge through an efficient water management under one agency from headworks to farm gates and active involvement of farmers, the objectives of the programme can prove much effective. The programme objectives formulated at the time of inception are still valid but due to absence of a unified set up to integrate the irrigation and agricultural activities and non-involvement of the farmers have resulted in only marginal achievements by the programme.

Annexure 1

Graph Showing Irrigation Potential Created, Utilised and Field Channel Constructed in Nagarjunasagar, Andhra Pradesh

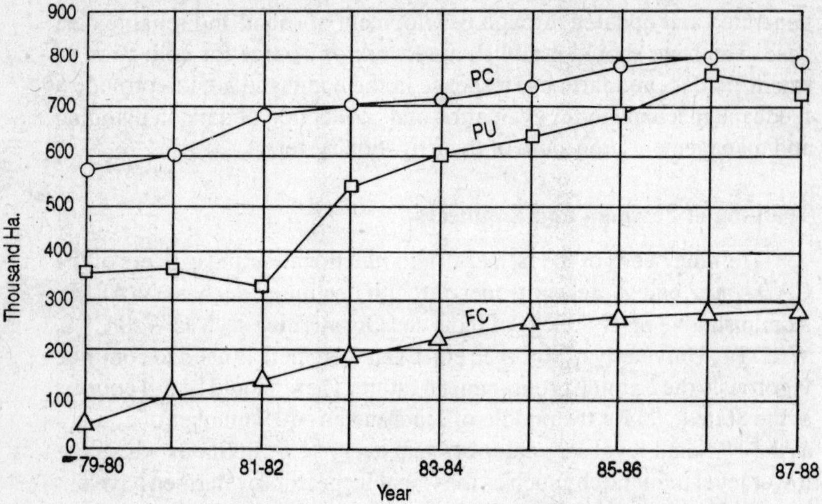

State	Andhra Pradesh
Project	Nagarjunasagar
CCA	895 Th. ha.
Year of inclusion	74-75

Th. ha. (Cumm.)

Year	PC	PU	FC
79-80	572	361	53
80-81	608	369	107
81-82	689	335	138
82-83	711	545	195
83-84	718	611	228
84-85	748	645	261
85-86	788	691	278
86-87	816	770	284
87-88	801	734	287

PC–Irrigation Potential Created
PU–Irrigation Potential Utilised
FC–Field Channel Constructed

Annexure 2

Graph Showing Irrigation Potential Created, Utilised and Field Channel Constructed in Srirama Sagar Project, Andhra Pradesh

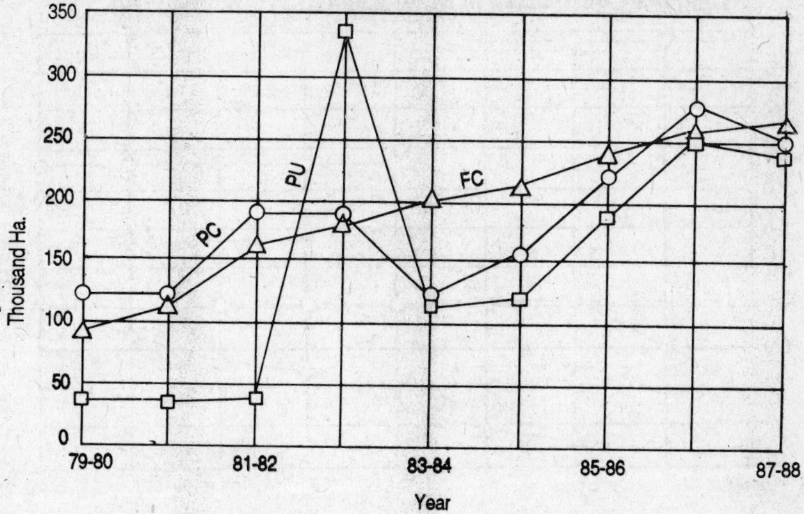

State	Andhra Pradesh
Project	Srirama Sagar
CCA	411 Th. ha.
Year of inclusion	74-75

Th. ha. (Cumm.)

Year	PC	PU	FC
79-80	124	36	94
80-81	124	36	113
81-82	190	39	163
82-83	190	339	181
83-84	123	117	201
84-85	157	121	212
85-86	224	190	239
86-87	280	250	261
87-88	252	240	266

PC–Irrigation Potential Created
PU–Irrigation Potential Utilised
FC–Field Channel Constructed

Annexure 3

Graph Showing Irrigation Potential Created, Utilised and Field Channel Constructed in Mahi Kadana Project, Gujarat

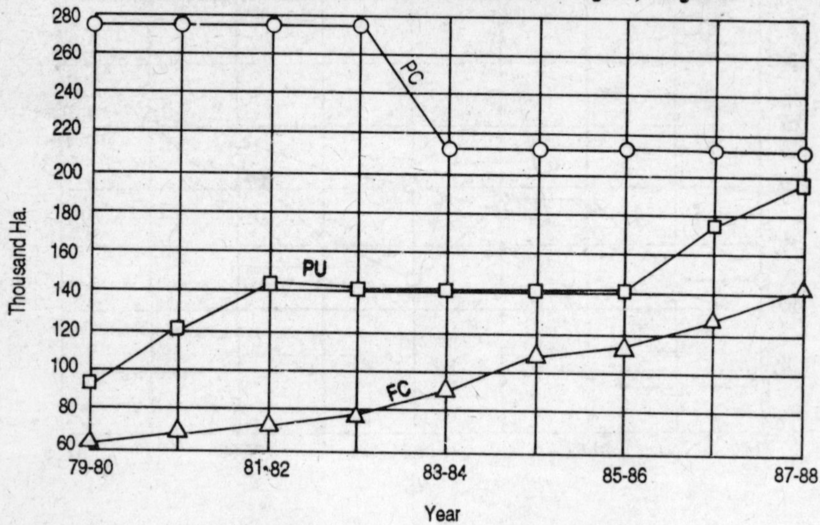

State	Gujarat
Project	Mahi Kadana
CCA	200.4 Th. ha.
Year of inclusion	74-75

Th. ha. (Cumm.)

Year	PC	PU	FC
79-80	275	93	64
80-81	275	122	69
81-82	275	146	73
82-83	275	143	77
83-84	212	143	92
84-85	212	143	110
85-86	212	143	113
86-87	212	176	128
87-88	212	197	146

PC–Irrigation Potential Created

PU–Irrigation Potential Utilised

FC–Field Channel Constructed

Annexure 4

Graph Showing Irrigation Potential Created, Utilised and Field Channel Constructed in Tawa Project, Madhya Pradesh

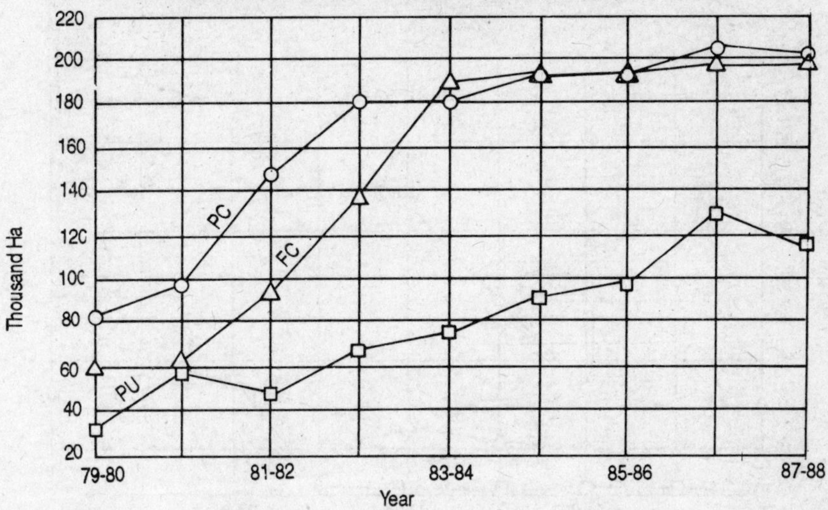

State	Madhya Pradesh
Project	Tawa
CCA	247 Th. ha.
Year of inclusion	74-75

Th. ha. (Cumm.)

Year	PC	PU	FC
79-80	83	31	58
80-81	97	57	62
81-82	147	48	93
82-83	182	66	136
83-84	180	75	190
84-85	192	91	193
85-86	192	98	194
86-87	205	129	196
87-88	202	115	196

PC–Irrigation Potential Created
PU–Irrigation Potential Utilised
FC–Field Channel Constructed

Annexure 5

Graph Showing Irrigation Potential Created, Utilised and Field Channel Constructed in Pench Project, Maharashtra

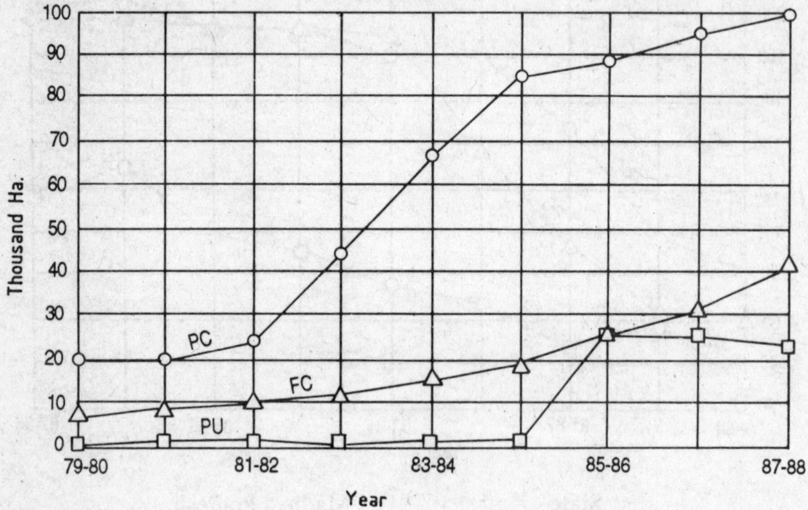

State	Maharashtra
Project	Pench
CCA	62.02 Th. ha.
Year of inclusion	74-75

Th. ha. (Cumm.)

Year	PC	PU	FC
79-80	20	1	7
80-81	20	2	9
81-82	24	2	10
82-83	44	1	12
83-84	67	2	15
84-85	85	2	19
85-86	88	26	26
86-87	95	26	31
87-88	99	23	41

PC–Irrigation Potential Created

PU–Irrigation Potential Utilised

FC–Field Channel Constructed

Annexure 6

Graph Showing Irrigation Potential Created, Utilised and Field Channel Constructed in Sone Project, Bihar

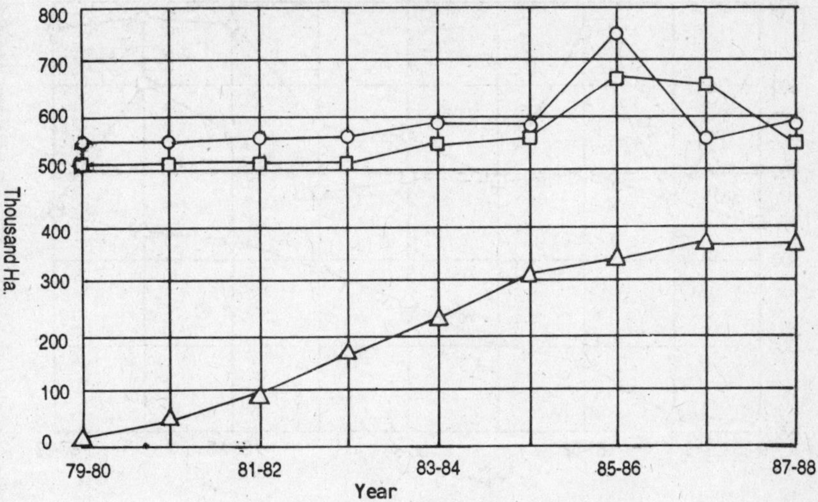

State	Bihar
Project	Sone
CCA	865 Th. ha.
Year of inclusion	74-75

Th. ha. (Cumm.)

Year	PC	PU	FC
79-80	557	514	13
80-81	558	516	46
81-82	559	516	94
82-83	559	516	170
83-84	587	547	230
84-85	587	559	310
85-86	746	671	344
86-87	559	660	365
87-88	584	551	366

PC–Irrigation Potential Created
PU–Irrigation Potential Utilised
FC–Field Channel Constructed

Annexure 7

Graph Showing Irrigation Potential Created, Utilised and Field Channel Constructed in I.G.N.P. Stage I Project, Rajasthan

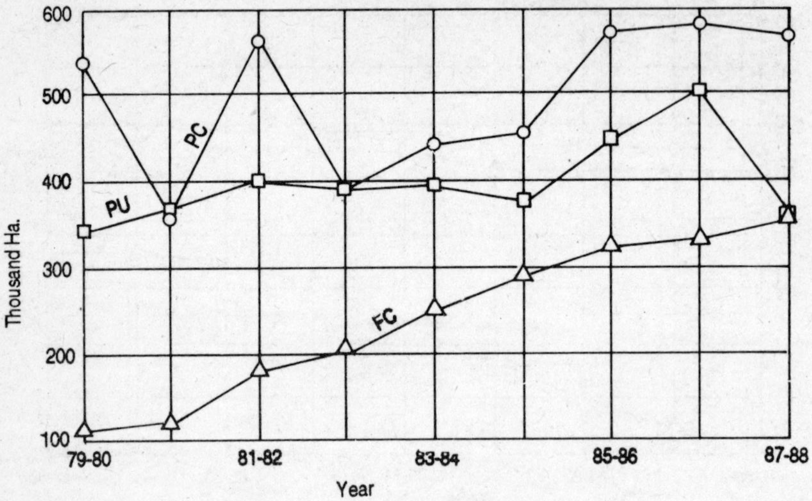

State	Rajasthan
Project	I.G.N.P. Stage I
CCA	540 Th. ha.
Year of inclusion	74-75

Th. ha. (Cumm.)

Year	PC	PU	FC
79-80	539	348	113
80-81	358	361	122
81-82	565	402	182
82-83	396	393	206
83-84	441	398	254
84-85	454	378	294
85-86	573	449	325
86-87	581	506	332
87-88	569	361	357

PC–Irrigation Potential Created
PU–Irrigation Potential Utilised
FC–Field Channel Constructed

Annexure 8

Graph Showing Irrigation Potential Created, Utilised and Field Channel Constructed in Ramganga Project, Uttar Pradesh

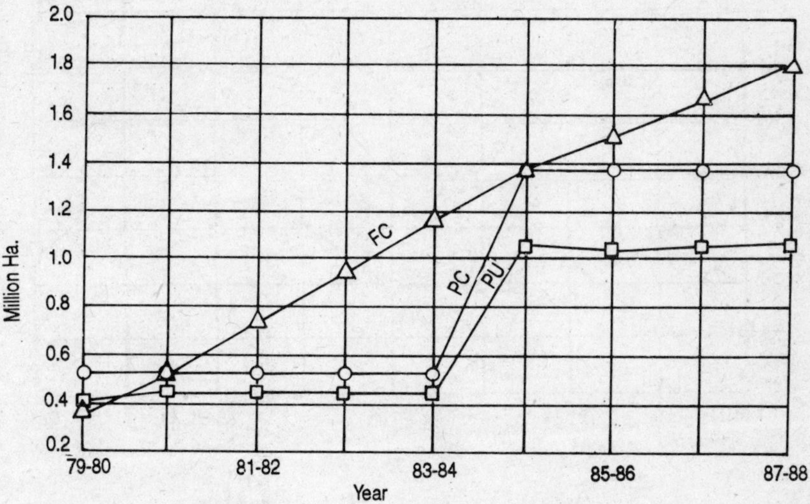

State	Uttar Pradesh
Project	Ramganga
CCA	1897 Th. ha.
Year of inclusion	74-75

Th. ha. (Cumm.)

Year	PC	PU	FC
79-80	540	424	366
80-81	540	441	510
81-82	540	441	739
82-83	540	441	940
83-84	540	441	1162
84-85	1372	1070	1369
85-86	1372	1043	1510
86-87	1372	1060	1664
87-88	1372	1075	1813

PC–Irrigation Potential Created
PU–Irrigation Potential Utilised
FC–Field Channel Constructed

Annexure 9

Graph Showing Irrigation Potential Created, Utilised and Field Channel Constructed in Sarda Sahayak Project, Uttar Pradesh

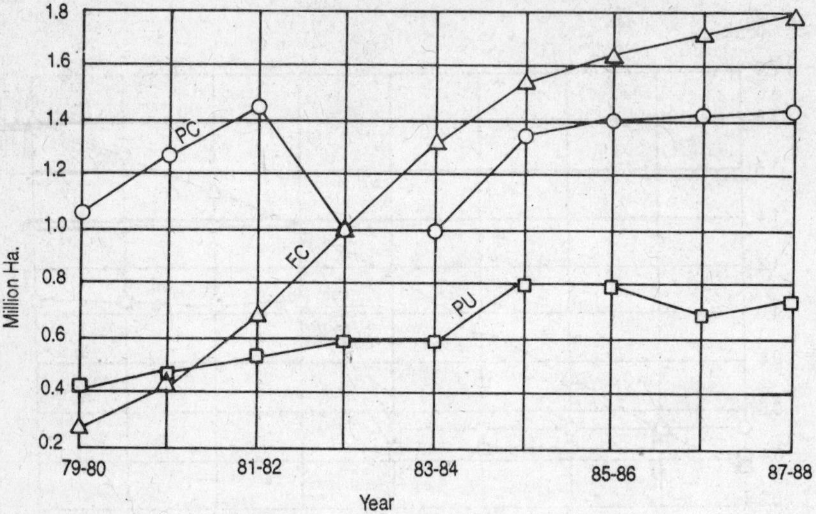

State	Uttar Pradesh
Project	Sarda Sahayak
CCA	2000 Th. ha.
Year of inclusion	74-75

Th. ha. (Cumm.)

Year	PC	PU	FC
79-80	1069	423	279
80-81	1269	468	425
81-82	1456	536	676
82-83	1002	590	1000
83-84	1002	590	1318
84-85	1350	804	1537
85-86	1408	793	1649
86-87	1428	696	1719
87-88	1438	743	1785

PC–Irrigation Potential Created
PU–Irrigation Potential Utilised
FC–Field Channel Constructed

REFERENCES

1. Ramanujam, K. "Nine Years of Command Area Development", Proceedings Vol. I, National Seminar on Impact of CAD Programme on Land and Water Productivity & Economy of Command Area, held at Lucknow, Nov. 1983, pp. 1 to 15.
2. Annual Report 1983-84, Ministry of Agriculture, Govt. of India, New Delhi.
3. Indian Agriculture in Brief, 15th, 17th and 18th editions published by Directorate of Economics & Statistics, Ministry of Agriculture, Govt. of India, New Delhi.
4. Report of the Working Group for VI and VII Plans for CAD, Ministry of Agriculture (1980) and Ministry of Irrigation (1980), New Delhi.
5. Report of the Committee of Ministers on Under-utilisation of Created Irrigation Potential, Govt. of India, Ministry of Irrigation and Power, New Delhi, June 1973.
6. Report of the High Level Committee on the Organisational set up of CAD in States, Ministry of Irrigation, New Delhi, September, 1982.
7. Saksena, R.S., "A Decade of Command Area Development in Major Irrigation Projects", Proceedings, National Seminar on Irrigation Water Management, held at Roorkee, University of Roorkee, Jan. 12-13, 1985, pp. 1-35 to 1-50.
8. Sinha, V.S., "CAD-Infrastructure", Proceedings, National Seminar on Irrigation Water Management, held at Roorkee, University of Roorkee, Jan. 12-13, 1985, pp. II-I to II-II.
9. Singh, Bharat, "Irrigation Management in India", Proceedings, National Seminar on Irrigation Water Management, held at Roorkee, University of Roorkee, Jan. 12-13, pp. I-1 to 1-14
10. Mohan Inder, "Impact of CAD on Utilisation of Created Irrigation Potential – A Study", Government of India, Ministry of Water Resources, CAD Division, New Delhi, May 1990.

CHAPTER 7

DESIGNING WATER USERS ASSOCIATION – STRUCTURE & TRAINING NEEDS; IMPORTANCE OF WATER DISTRIBUTION INSTITUTIONS

"Engineering is not the fundamental problem underlying irrigation development in the LDC's. Engineering principles are known and can be adopted, but the major problem, however, is to discover ways to utilize farmer clients more effectively in operations and maintenance, and development programmes which will create rural transformation. Rural transformation essentially requires changes in farmers' behaviour, motivations and expectations which is hardly possible until institutions exist to provide them with improved production possibilities and incentives...."

Wiener, 1976

Introduction

Irrigation is the basis for a good farm husbandry and better land utilization for a stable and higher crop production. For dependable agriculture, water resources need to be developed and utilized efficiently and judiciously in order to meet the increasing requirements of the food for growing population in India. India is the seventh largest in area and the second most populous country in the world. It has a total area of 329 million hectares of which nearly 145 million hectares constitute the net cropped area–the gross cropped area being 173 million hectares (about 53% of the total). The average size of holding in India is as low as 2.3 hectares. Nearly 67 per cent of its total population is dependent on agriculture which contributes about 42 per cent of the gross national product (GNP) and also contributes directly and indirectly about 60 per cent of the total exports. In the country almost 1/3rd of land area suffers from serious environmental problems and there is a considerable waste land. The extent of waste land is estimated to be more than 100 million hectares which does not include dependent forest areas. Besides, salinity and alkalinity has affected 7.17 million hectares of land. Another 45.5 million hectare is affected by erosion. It is also estimated that the country is losing almost 8000 hectare to ravines every year.

In India, the net irrigated area which was 15.8 per cent of the total cropped area in 1950-51 constitutes about 23 per cent even today. The remaining area is rainfed/dry land farming. The new technology of agricultural production is confined to regions where water resources are good and irrigation is assured. Thus, development of rainfed farming has assumed great importance because rainfed areas are caught in a vicious circle of high risk, low investment, poor technology, and low production. In view of these facts, concerted efforts are needed to focus on rainfed agriculture to achieve a steady rise in the production of coarse cereals, pulses, oilseeds etc. in order to achieve the national objectives of reduction of poverty, unemployment and regional disparities. Hence to sustain dynamism in farming, an optimum use of irrigation water is an imperative necessity. Water is not only a scarce but also costly input, therefore, its wastage means an adverse effect on socio-economic conditions of the farming community and also depriving some other farmers from benefits of irrigation.

Irrigation management[1] is a technological and institutional innovation which is location specific. It is governed by climate, soil, choice of crop-mix, cropping pattern, and social & economic conditions. Water which is a costly input and most important limiting factor in crop production is not considered as important'input' as seeds, fertilizers etc. by majority of farmers particularly by illiterate due to their ignorance. The farmer, by and large is simple, poor and brought up in a very localized environmental conditions, and he is neither an Agronomist, Irrigation Engineer, Sociologist, Soil Scientist, nor an Economist. Moreover, the farmers' cultivation techniques are based for generation on self reliance and for subsistence of his family. However, his sense of responsibility for his family does not allow him to take any risk and therefore, an optimum use of land and water is a pre-requisite. The most important socio-economic factors influencing

1. Irrigation Management is : An Interdisciplinary system process with built-in learning mechanism to improve system performance by adjusting physical, technological and institutional inputs to achieve the desired levels of output (Seckler and Nobe, 1983).

acceptance of irrigation management technology are low levels of income of the farmers, lack of incentives, inadequate knowledge[2] of irrigation management (including proper timings of water application and crop water requirement, critical growth stages etc.), technology, lack of resources, farm credit, equipments and implements, resistance and reluctance to changes, inadequate capacity of the farmers to invest for adoption of new technology, absence of especially structured extension service, small size of scattered and fragmented holdings, illiteracy of the farmers as a constraint in making use of written communication, inadequate infrastructural development, institutional finance etc. Apart from all these factors, non-involvement of the farmers in irrigation development programmes is one of the major limiting factor for optimum use of water.

ORGANISING FARMERS

For improving water courses and achieving control over water quantity and timing at the field outlet farmers need to be organised into effecitve units facilitating their cooperation. The failure of most of the earlier programmes in our country has revealed the inadequacy of any programme which purports to undertake development for farmers without their meaningful programme participation[3]. Without effective farmers' organisations to construct and maintain improved water courses, the benefit of improved seeds, fertilizers, pesticides, improved implements, marketing and agricultural credit is lost. Experience of the developing nations regardless of cultural and social bonds is that irrigation systems[4] have been constructed, maintained and improved only through the building of administrative organisations capable of undertaking activities on

2. Alfred Marshall wrote : Knowledge is the most powerful engine of production; it enables us to subdue nature and satisfy our wants (Shulz, 1981).
3. Farmer involvement/participation means farmer playing an active role in decision-making regarding planning, implementing, operating, maintaining and evaluating projects and programmes designing to improve the productivity, equity and effectiveness of irrigation projects.
4. Huge investments made in the construction of dams and canals have not produced the anticipated economic returns and hence Planning Commission, Govt. of India recommended the establishment of command area development in each State under the Ministry of Agriculture. The basic objectives of establishing these command area development departments and CAD authorities was to see that through proper irrigation management and integrated approach, the investments made in creating the irrigation potential is fully utilized.

behalf of participating farmers. For such organisations, they undertake irrigations system building and improvement. Formation of farmers' organisations could also serve the purpose of mobilisation of rural masses to undertake local developmental work in irrigation management in lieu of already overloaded governmental bureaurcrats attempting to undertake this mammoth effort. For organising the farmers the following principles could be adopted:

(i) Building up from a base of farmer watercourse organisation which are federated into higher units at the level of canal etc. which can serve as linkages to appropriate governmental bureaucracies.

(ii) Formation of organisation must be guided by regulation by the Government.

(iii) Keeping in view the equity of welfare criteria in distribution of water and participation in organisational policy, farmers' organisations could aim to achieve increased agricultural production.

It is in this context of the farmers' non-involvement in irrigation development programmes, particularly in design and operation, that the present Chapter deals with the formation of the voluntary 'Water Users Association' which would ensure active participation of the farmers. This highlights the significances and the necessity for the formation of 'Water Users Association' with a perspective of active involvement of the farmers in irrigation development programme which would help in the optimum use of irrigation water. Briefly, the basic principles for effective irrigation management programme below outlet are:

(i) Organising the farmers;

(ii) Developing an effective linkage between farmers' organisation and development;

(iii) Arranging effective planning and extension work to serve the organisation effectively; and

(iv) Establishing training and evaluation techniques

However, the first principle is covered in this Chapter.

Farmers are generally not prepared to take any kind of risk and therefore, they hesitate to participate actively in the irrigation development programme. However, farmers' active participation can be secured if adequate water supply at the right time and right quantity are assured to them. Unfortunately, in our country, formation of farmers' voluntary organisation does not have any legal support and therefore unless farmers are convinced that their participation in the irrigation development programme will benefit them.

Possibilities of Designing Alternative Organisations

Some of the most important factors responsible for poor management of irrigation systems, under-utilisation of created potential and inefficient irrigation, are the inefficient functioning of farmers' organisations and the non-involvement of the farmers (*i.e.* beneficiaries) in the planning, construction and management of the irrigation systems. However, the success of the farmers' organisations depend on the effective leadership and dedicated efforts of the involved persons.[5]

Keeping in view the given system, values, attitude of the farmers, there appears three possibilities of forming alternative organisations of the farmers which are discussed as under:

> With Independence, several organisational and structural changes have come in, in the urban and rural sectors and the development programmes in the rural sectors are through the Block Development Offices. An unfortunate tendency has been taking root in the minds of the farmers that it is for the Government to look after all the requirements of the people and this has led to apathy, and disinterest among them in continuing to take care of their own distribution systems. People do not cooperate and the traditionally accepted leadership at the village level is no more respected. However, Panchayats have played an important role in rural reconstruction in our country. But the Panchayat System in our country is handicapped due to the bickerings among the elected members of the Panchayat and the Panchayat System has become an arena of conflicts and factionalism.

IRRIGATION PANCHAYATS

According to Irrigation Act of Madhya Pradesh, an Irrigation Panchayat should be established for every village of Chak and at the discretion of

5. Dr. Theodore Shultz States: 'The most important economic resource for India's irrigation development may not be financial capital for new schemes but the acquired abilities of people to do the job .... their knowledge, skills & professional commitment.'

the Collector for a group of villagers in the command area of the canal. The Irrigation Panchyat shall consist of a Sarpanch and two or more members elected by the permanent holders and occupants of the land from among themselves. The functions of the Irrigation Panchayat are:

(i) to assist the officers of the Irrigation Department

-- in detecting and preventing encroachment on canal-lands, prevent damage to irrigation canals,

-- in arranging for the construction of water courses,

-- in recording and checking irrigation,

(ii) to collect Irrigation revenue and remit to the treasur, and

(iii) to arrange for the repair of water courses [Section 61(i) and 62(ii) of Irrigation Act].

Deficiencies of Irrigation Panchayats

The Irrigations Panchayats effectively helped in assessment of irrigation and collection of water revenue. They were also effective in distribution of water where the Irrigation Panchyat was influential to command respect from village farmers and could enforce discimpline. But afterwards the Irrigation Panchyats could not effectively work for want of undisputed leadership and command over local farmers. One of the important reasons is also that there are no financial resources to take up the work of systematic control and distribution of irrigation water from each and every outlet. The Irrigation Panchayats should be allowed a part of collection of water rates for taking up the responsibility of O & M of micro network below 40 ha. outlet. Powers to arrange distribution of water below 40 ha. outlet should be vested with Irrigation Panchayats on R.W.D. System. However, ID & AD officials will help them in preparing R.W.D. schedules for every Kharif/Rabi irrigation season. AD officials will inspect the maintenance work of Irrigation Panchayats before start of Kharif and Rabi Irrigation. Irrigation Panchayats should maintain the accounts of expenditure and progress of works which will be inspected by AD officers who are basically responsible for irrigation water application below 40 ha. outlet.

It is seen that the Irrigation Panchayats are formed after completion of the Project. There is no participation of the farmers groups in the process of planning and execution of the Project. Therefore, sense of personal involvement is absent. Farmers' views were not given importance and weightage it deserved. Similarly, the functions of the Irrigation

Panchayats which is an elected body of permanent holders of the command area are mostly for helping the irrigation department in administration and revenue collections. There is no direct involvement and responsibility of Irrigation Panchayats in operation and maintenance of micro network and drainage systems below 40 ha. outlet and in controlling and regulation of irrigation water on R.W.D. system. The Irrigation Panchayat had no authority and resources to take up the responsibility of O & M of micro network and drainage system below 40 ha. outlet. The permanent holders of the command area are not under desired level of discipline.

Farmers' Involvement in State

Pant & Sharma (1983) have described several cases and small experiments of farmers' involvement in India ranging from 'outlet of pipe committees' in Andhra Pradesh, Water Co-operatives in Gujarat, the Phad System in Maharashtra, the Sttadar System in Bihar. Few of these indigenous systems have been adequately investigated for identifying lessons and principles which might prove useful in India. Detailed study of these systems will be useful in evolving a system for farmers' active participation in Madhya Pradesh.

Cooperative Irrigation Societies

Cooperative is desirable on account of its highly educative influence. On this point, one cannot do better than to quote the Cooperative Planning Committee.

"No influence is so important in the economic education[6] of farmers as their own efforts in Cooperative.... The very attempt on the part of the farmers to solve their problems teaches them basic economic truths.. .. Cooperatives also serve an important function in supplying information on the many factors which affect the economic status of farmers."

Although cooperatives are much desirable on account of their significant educative influence and anticipated improvement in the

6. Association of literacy with technical knowledge scores is more readily understood. A literate farmer with higher education levels has more ready access to knowledge about climate, soil moisture, intake, conveyance, regulation, measurement, and application of right quantity of water at right time etc. through newspapers, posters, extension bulletins and personal contacts with irrigation engineers and other irrigation management experts.

economic status of farmers, yet their performance in the country has been very discouraging. The past experience in the country is that barring a few cases, cooperatives have sown seeds of dissatisfaction. Therefore, on the basis of the performance of the cooperatives together with the growth, we are led to believe that cooperative irrigation societies, if formed, would not be different from other cooperatives in respect of rendering the service to farmers. Hence, we do not favour the formation of 'Co-operative Irrigation Societies'.

WATER USERS' ASSOCIATION[7]

Unfortunately, in our country, more attention has been paid for the development of irrigation resources but the problem of optimum use of water and its scientific management on the farmers field has not received due attention. Much too often the social and economic aspects of water use have been overlooked. Mere creation of the utilization potential and infrastructural facilities is not enough. Farmers' involvement is an adjunct for optimum use of water. To achieve this objective, the farmers need to be educated about the repair and maintenance of the water courses and make their full use for increasing production. But the non-involvement of the farmers, in design and operation of the system causes conflicts and problems. Since the farmers are the actual beneficiaries their participation is essential. Unless they are involved, irrigation offences cannot be checked even with the force of law. The farmers' active involvement in irrigation development programmes can be ensured by a participatory and community-based approach for which an appropriate organisation can be three tier system of an elected 'Water Users' Association'. This pyramid can serve the farmers' community with (i) at the lowest level a 'Chak-Samiti' which can be constituted from the farmers within the chak or the outlet command, and (ii) secondary level can constitute a sub-project committee formed of the representatives of the outlet committees in a distribution system. In this three tier system, on the tertiary level, the farmers' association can represent the farmers at the highest position in the project development. This could be named as 'Project Policy Decision Committee'.

The physical boundaries of the Association could be alongwith the

7. In Indonesia, the purpose of forming the Water Users' Association is to use available water efficiently at tertiary block. The Board of Water Users' Association consists of the following members (i) Chief, (ii) Deputy Chief, (iii) Secretary, (iv) Treasurer, (v) Uluulu (Water Bailiff) and (vi) Chief of the Quarternary block (see Organisational Structure 4 & 5).

hydrologic unit. The forming of water users' association can more appropriately consist of a bottom up approach *i.e.* to organise the farmers alongwith the cultural, physical and social dimensions, which may enable them to participate in irrigation management. It is necessary to provide the water use mechanism by which they can adopt new technologies and programmes. Material support such as equipment, loans, construction materials etc. obviously would benefit to provide incentives. The role of the association would be as follows:

(i) To give legal advise for the water users contracting with the government in order to undertake watercourse and land levelling improvement.

(ii) To provide an assurance that the watercourse would be properly operated, maintained and improved after construction of the physical components.

(iii) To provide a vehicle for the farmers to attain an important identity in the country and give an opportunity for them to develop and assume individual as well as collective[8] responsibilities in the use of scarce natural resource i.e. water. The Association would also provide the water users an opportunity to develop a social consciousness for the use of the resources.

(iv) Water Users' Association would reduce the risk of all users simultaneously sharing the responsibility in a more equitable manner.

(v) To give the water users an opportunity to have an important feedback to the purveyor of water and inform the purveyor of constraints and limitations to which the ultimate users is subjected.

(vi) Associations would provide water users a right of resource directly to the courts where otherwise a conflict of interest may exist.

---

8. Max. K. Lowdermilk, Programme Executive, USAID, New Delhi states: " The most underrated and misunderstood dimension of irrigation development today is that of the individual and collective irrigation behaviour of farmers. Much is known about irrigation technology, the design and construction of dams & canals, crop water requirements and irrigation practices while the social and organisational aspects of irrigation continue to be achilles heel in system development, improvement & operation."

(vii) As a legal entity representing collective goals and duties of farmers within a watercourse.

(viii) Water Users' Association at the chak level in the villages will serve as the first link in the channel of communication between the water users and the governmental agencies with this role, a three tier system could be of the form as:

1. Chak Samiti.
2. Sub-Project Committee.
3. Project Policy Decision Committee.

Level of Formation

The Water Users' Association may be formed at the water course level or at the chak level in the villages. Since all users receiving water from a particular outlet have a common interest in the quantity, quality and distribution of water, this common interest would serve as a link for successful cooperation.

Structure of Association

Water Users' Association could consist of two bodies performing three functions. The first body would be the assembly, consisting of all the water users at the chak level in the Association (Flow Chart 3).

These water users would be shareholders and members of the Association. This assembly would elect office bearers to the second body which would be called the 'Executive of Association', and deciding issues of common interest within the jurisdiction of the Association. However, the executive would have two functions (i) first to manage the Association according to the creating documents and by-laws framed by the Assembly to carry out other decisions by the Assembly and supervise construction and maintenance of the physical structures which would also include hiring the necessary personnel to undertake these works, and (ii) to resolve disputes within the water course among the water users. The executive would manage and operate the Water Users' Association, exercise normal powers to achieve the programme of the Association and have emergency powers for water regulations. It would be responsible for contracting with the Government on the programme, disseminate information on water availabilities and other information pertinent to farmers and carry the issues raised by the farmers back to Government officials. The executive could be organised with the offices of the

Chairman, Secretary and Treasurer. The Chairman may be rotating regardless of the office held by a representative, they would have no additional power of authority by virtue of holding that office over other representatives.

Functions and Powers

The Association could be given the following functions and powers:

(i) Main water course rehabilitation.

(ii) Operation and maintenance of the main wataer course.

(iii) Sanctions for upgrading and maintaining farm's field ditches and outlets.

(iv) Improving 'on-farm management' practices (including land levelling).

(v) Establishing water delivery schedules and supervising water allocation within the water courses.

(vi) Taking decision of tube-well locations in order to optimise the water resources from both surface and ground source.

(vii) Devising assessment methods and then rates and collect assessment.

(viii) The Association could be granted the power to confiscate membership and make assessments in order to undertake emergency repair works.

(ix) In general promote and improve water control and management by water users in an effort to reduce the unnecessary losses and increase agricultural output.

Membership

The formation of the Association could be voluntary, in order to leave the ultimate decision in the hands of the water users and psychologically stimulate their reaction to improving their water use. However, Association once formed, membership should be mandatory for all farmers cultivating lands commanded by the water course.

Voting Rights

Graduated voting system could be adopted. A minimum area of 1 ha. could be fixed to qualify for vote in order to check further fragmentation of land holding. If there are three or four members in a family who hold collectively the minimum amount of land, they would have the right of one vote for the entire family or joint holdings. Graduated voting system is patterned after the practice followed in Mendoza, Argentina and Chille. However, the office bearers of the executive should comprise one from head, two from middle and two from tail end of the water course. But in case of larger water course number would increase in proportion to this scheme.

Assessment

Authority to levy assessment would be granted to the Association. But the assessment could be based on the construction, operation and maintenance costs for improving the systems and allocated among water users either according to the amount of water they used, or the area in hectare under control. The latter would coincide with voting rights of the members.

Registration

All Associations would need be registered. Registration of Association would greatly facilitate communication between Government and the ultimate users *i.e.* farmers.

Federation of Association

Next level of water users association could be federation of associations, which could be formed either at village level or at the minor canal level. The Chairman of the water users associations within the federation area would serve as the member of Federation Executive. Primary purpose of Federation would be to gain greater economies of scale for improvement in the larger area wherever it would be felt necessary. Federation would be in a better position to accumulate the necessary information on water supplies and deliveries and disseminate this information down to the water users association for further dissemination to the irrigators.

Board of Directors

The highest formal level in the hierarchy of water users association would be Board. The Board of Directors would consist of the Chairman of the Federation under a major canal. The Board would deal with the officer incharge of that canal *i.e.* Government side as well as with other officers of various concerned departments.

Executive Council

Executive Council would be on the top of the Pyramid at the provincial level which would be an information body consisting of representative of Boards. The functions of this council would be to coordinate the programmes and activities in improving water use within the major canal's command area. However, it would maintain only *ad hoc* powers granted by the representatives of the Boards.

SPECIAL ORGANISATION FOR SMALL AND MARGINAL FARMERS

About 70% of the land holders in India fall in the category of 'Small' and 'Marginal'. They have engaged the special attention even of the Government of India. For the first time, Government had launched a massive programme involving an outlay of Rs. 2500 million during 1983-84 for assisting this target group of small and marginal farmers to increase their agricultural production. The programme provided subsidies for the development of minor irrigation, land development etc.

The small and marginal farmers, however, have numerous problems and therefore need special organisation for better utilisation of available irrigation water. The present system in most cases does not provide an equal opportunity or assurance of water supply, particularly to marginal and small farmers. Experience gained in Gujarat through various approaches adopted for and focused mainly on the marginal and small farmers, though tried in small areas, indicated encouraging water management practices. The two main approaches have been: (i) formation of water co-operative, and (ii) chak samities. However, of these two approaches, discussed briefly as under formation of chak samities would be a welcome step for mitigating the hardships of the marginal and small farmers.

Water Cooperatives

The Water Cooperative approach has tremendous value in efficient utilisaiton of irrigation water along with beneficiary participation. Efforts need to be made to convince the farmers about benefits of such a society and confidence should be created in their members. Guaranted timely and perdetermined quantity of water supply is basic for this. Suitable financial assistance in the initial period of such a society has to be provided to meet with managerial costs. Most important to a Water Cooperative is the selection of leadership. Mohini water cooperative in

Kakarapar Project, Gujarat started in 1978-79 is a glaring example. The society is given water @25 p/10000 lits. by the Government and the society distributes water among its members on acre basis as per standard rates. The success story of Mohini can be repeated elsewhere also provided the water used by the members is according to advice given by the agronomist. If the proper water management practices are not followed by the members, the society has no advantage. This sort of active participation reduces work of the Government agency to a great extent.

Chak Samities

Formation of chak samities for adequate, equitable and timely distribution of water assumes very great importance in canal irrigation– A group leader at sub-minor level and sub-group leaders at outlet levels to look after rotations, solve problems of maintenance of water courses and ensure correct and equitable distribution to all farmers in the Chak area would be required. Usually such leaders will also act as 'contact farmers' and the messages concerning irrigation use can be conveyed through them more effectively, in T and V system.

In depth study on factors that contribute to the success of farmers organisation in large irrigation projects and conditions which are most congenial for its growth and development are required to have appreciation of problems to be tackled for proper participation of farmers. Pant and Verma (1983) reported five important factors which have great bearing on success of farmers organisation. These are:

1. Right kind of leadership.
2. Availability of adequate and predictable amount of water.
3. Greater interaction and more frequent contact between the officials and farmers and closer involvement and keen interest of the field staff.
4. Easy unanimity among the group members.
5. Incentive in the form of completion of OFD work at the CAD cost.

The OFD works are important but the beneficiary farmers must be vigorously involved in the designing and completion of network to utilise their knowledge and skill and to have them as watching over the quality of construction works (Pant, 1984).

TRAINING AND EXTENSION

General

Utilisation of water for irrigation for maximum production according to the nature of soils and sub-soils, climatic conditions, nature and age of crops, nature of fertilizers and availability of water in the particular period alongwith other necessary supplies and operations is a skilful procedure requiring care and attention.

With the view that this skill should go to each and every individual cultivator doing irrigation and actual production, there must be an ideal, powerful and efficient organisational set up in the field for efficient management of all supplies and operations required right from ploughing of the fields till the harvest and sale of the produce. Any lacuna in any steps will jeopardise the aim of maximum production, however, small and unnoticed the lacuna may be. The percentage of irrigated areas in many states is very small and as such the water, the most valuable asset, must be utilised under a strong and efficient organisational set up only; so that we can reap maximum benefits and food production by its proper and judicious use.

Training of Extension Personnel

Transfer of technical know-how from the research workers to extension personnel is essential for which 2 weeks initial training before each cropping season may be given followed by a day's training in each fortnight. Training should focus on few selected operations covering one or two main crops which need follow up during next two weeks.

Training of In-Service Irrigation Engineers

There is an obvious necessity of putting into practice latest techniques in irrigation methods developed. This task can be better accomplished by the serving engineers, officers in irrigation department by imparting them training in elementary soil science pertaining to crop growth, scientific cropping pattern , economic use of water for various crops, the number and depth of watering as and when required, use of green manures and improved agricultural practices and latest techniques for the reclamation of saline, alkaline and waterlogged lands. Trained irrigation engineer should be able to appreciate the field necessities and work out the distribution of supplies in keeping with the water requirements of crops grown in the command area. Proper emphasis on the agro-irrigational aspects should be given so as to impart the right type of training. Regular in-service training and refresher courses on various subjects concerned with agriculture and irrigation should be arranged to bridge the gap and every practising irrigation engineer should attend these courses once in 5-6 years to refresh his memory and get to know the latest trends in the subject. An intensive in the job type of practical water use training should be given through short term courses of a few weeks duration in each state for each water management practice as is being done in Haryana to create technical confidence.

Farmers' Training

It does little good to irrigate crops when the farmer does not have the adequate know-how to produce a crop. Information on water requirements of crops, cropping patterns, rotational irrigation, time frequency and methods of irrigation are the pre-requisite which need to be made available to farmers. A planned education programme based on field demonstration will go a long way in preparing the farmers for adopting new techniques. However, optimum water use will arise in the minds of the users only when they are alive to the moral responsibility with regards to proper & economical use of water for irrigation. Their moral fibre is to be toned up so as to create in them a sense of cooperative responsibility of enforcing water users etiquette as different from punitive rates which tend to increase corruption.

To organise and train farmers in agricultural skills and improved water management practices, extension service with adequately trained personnel is required on a continuous basis. Experience with irrigation projects shows that where adequate and timely agricultural inputs are not made available, physical improvements often have a short life and intended project benefits are never fully realised.

In brief, the success of any project including irrigation project aimed at increasing agricultural production is highly dependent on effective participation of the real beneficiaries. This is more so where the farm size is small requiring greater manpower and finance to manage water distribution system below pipe outlet. More crucial activities are the maintenance and repair of water courses including field channels and the actual distribution of water among the beneficiaries.

In order to attract the farmers to participate in better water management, they need to be involved in all processes of decision-making so that they are aware of the benefits derived from the activities. The lacuna of educating the farmers in better and economical water use can be overcome by designing Water Users' Association or allowing the water cooperatives or chak samities to hire an agronomist who can constantly guide the farmers in crop planning, crop water requirements, when to irrigate and how to irrigate keeping in view the critical stages of crop growth, etc. In absence of such a help the traditional practices of irrigation are continued by the farmers. The cost of this person can be subsidised by the Government for initial period of 2-3 years.

The Government of Gujarat is envisaging to form a large water cooperative union federating about 200 water cooperative societies in the entire Mahi Command (2 Lakh ha), wherein the above mentioned lacuna will be taken care of.

Keeping in view the given system in our country, it would be desirable to organise the Water Users Association in our country. Though Pt. Jawahar Lal Nehru once said " .. In the Economic Structure of India, cooperation is not even a free choice, it is a necessity", yet it appears that Irrigation Cooperatives may not be successful in India. Therefore, only alternative left is that Water Users' Association would be most appropriate and therefore, for the betterment of small and marginal farmers, Water Users' Association should be formed. Since we began with *Wiener* (1976), we conclude with the statement of Dr. Y.K. Murty (1980) former Chairman of the Central Water Commission and now a consultant for the World Bank. He has summarized the woes of the Indian Irrigaiton in a lecture entitled, "The Irrigation Engineer and the Farmer".

"The farmer who is the king-pin in the process of agricultural development of the country is faced with a number of woes which he is not able to overcome unless there is a revolutionary change in the attitude of the engineers."

IMPORTANCE OF WATER DISTRIBUTION INSTITUTIONS, ORGANISASTION AND TRAINING

Agriculture, by and large predominates our rural as well as the national economy. Increased productivity in agriculture and the means to achieve it are of much significance for our economy. Water is vital for agricuture and agriculture is vital for the livelihood of our mankind. Growth of agriculture assumes critical importance on the fronts of employment, production, income distribution, consumption, adoption of new technology, etc. as the well-being of a majority of population in this developing country depends on a sustained economic development, which is possible if agriculture develops.

Need for Water Distribution Institution

Water is not only scarce but also costly and its wastage means an adverse effect on economic condition of the farmers. Therefore, optimum use of irrigation water is necessary. Water may be surplus in certain parts of the country, but on the whole the utilizable potential of irrigation water from all sources is much less than its requirement. However, the increasinag demand for irrigation water generated by modern agricultural technology obviously suggests the necessity for optimum use of water and scientific management of surface and ground water resources conjunctively. In our country, till now, more attention has been paid towards the development of irrigation resources, but the problem of optimum use of water and its scientific management on the farmers' field has not received due attention. However, with the increase in population to the extent of nearly 85 crores, requirement of foodgrains, fibre, oil seeds etc. has also gone up. The total foodgrains requirement would be nearly 235 million tonnes, by 2000 A.D. in order to feed the growing population, against the present production of nearly 175 million tonnes. To meet this alarming situation caused due to fast increase in population, it warrants a speedy expansion of irrigation resources with improved and scientifc management to exploit ground and surface water resources.

The wastage of water during application is quite considerable which deserves serious attention, and the wastage of water may be minimised which would benefit manifold by:

(i) Additional area may be brought under irrigation,

(ii) Productivity may be increased per unit of water use, and

(iii) Water logging and salinity problems could be averted.

The growing problems in the form of salinity and alkali soils, which have resulted in due to rising water table, are quite alarming. The utilisation of ground water may, however, help in maintaing the groundwater table at lower levels, which could prevent the rise of salts to upper layers of the soil.

In the prevailing institutional set up, water use efficiency in our country ranges from 20 to 40 per cent, which seems to be quite low as compared to other developed countries. Even if we could save losses of water to the extent of 10 per cent by improving the existing operational efficiency, an additional area of 3 million hectares may be irrigated, without creating additional facility. Hence, this is a goal which may be achieved by bringing a shift in emphasis from construction of new projects to rehabilitation of already existing irrigation systems. Moreover, it is more economical to rehabilitate existing irrigation schemes for higher returns than to invest more on new constructions. Apart from this, poor management of water application at the farm level has led to large wastage of irrigation water. Farmers, on the one hand, at the tail reaches do not get their anticipated share of water to increase their farm production, on the other hand, farms in the head reaches are generally found well flooded with water which consequently leads to more wastage of water and creates more environmental hazards.

Keeping in view these facts, extensive efforts are required for equitable water distribution for which an appropriate institutional set-up is needed. The present organisational set-up engaged in water distribution needs to be restructured, which should be re-inforced with the well trained staffs. This seems to be only the way out left for achieving the desired results. The management of re-structured organisational set-up should not only include intake conveyance, timely application of water to crops but it should also include effective drainage systems to drain the excess water from the fields.

The importance and need for the suitable water distribution institution, organisation and training are discussed here and the lines on which the existing institutional arrangements need modernisation in order to improve irrigation efficiency and overall productivity of land. For achieving this, proper maintenance of the conveyance systems is required. Simultaneously, necessary modifications suiting to our land and tradition should be adopted. For example in Taiwan and Japan, every effort has been made to utilise improved seeds, fertilisers, and pesticides with suitable changes on 'On-Farm' development activities.

In our country, the duty of an irrigation engineer ends just after providing water at the outlet only and in fact, irrigation engineer does not bother about the efficient utilisation of the precious input *i.e.* water in the field. The conveyance of water below outlet is left entirely at the discretion of the farmers concerned. Farmers' inadequate knowledge in regard to the modern agronomic and irrigation practices lead to inefficient water use on the farm and due to lack of the coordination and unified approach between the fellow farmers causes retardation in achieving the required benefits. The on-farm developmental activities may be briefly outlined as follows:

(i) Allocation and supply of water to the farmers according to their needs considering its availability at the right time and in their fields.

(ii) Ensuring the supply of allocated water to all farmers more specially to tailenders by improvement of water conveyance and management systems.

(iii) Availability of other infrastructural agencies supporting the agricultural activities.

However, the other institutional and managemental parameters required for the on-farm development activities are:

(i) Land Consolidation.

(ii) Land shaping and levelling.

(iii) Construction of permanent water courses and field channels for reducing cost in opeıation and maintenance.

(iv) Provision of drainage channels and farm roads.

(v) Improvement in cropping pattern and financial assistance to farmers.

(vi) Demonstration on agriculture farms, training and extension facilities.

(vii) Proper distribution of agricultural inputs and diversification of agricultural activities such as animal husbandry, forestry, inland fisheries, marine fisheries, gobar gas and agro-service centres.

(viii) Formation of farmers' association for including cooperative approach among them for consumptive use of irrigation water with proper operation and maintenance of irrigation as well as drainage systems.

(ix) Compulsory levy, so that farmers may use irrigation facilities.

(x) Giving incentives by way of awarding prizes and trophys for all round proficiency.

(xi) Creation of a coordinating body in co-operation of different departments like irrigation, agriculture, revenue and other financial bodies.

(xii) Limiting gestation period of different projects alongwith the on-farm developmental works.

(xiv) Attention on land reclamation and soil conservation works.

(xv) Necessary amendments in the existing laws.

Command Area Development Programmes are in operation in more than 155 irrigation projects covering a culturable command area of about 19 m.ha. in 20 States and 2 Union Territories implemented through 54 CADA's in the country. Of these, three big projects *viz.* Sarda Sahayak (Flow Chart 1). Ramganga and Gandak are in Uttar Pradesh and Bihar and Chambal in Rajasthan. The programme is being undertaken with the object of ensuring a speedy utilization of irrigation potentials, intensive agricultural production and development in the fields of animal husbandry and fisheries including establishment of agro-based industries, growth centres etc. in an integrated and comprehensive manner. This necessitates coordinated action by different development departments functioning in the command area of each irrigation project which are being treated as one unit. In order to ensure effective implementation of programme with command areas in Uttar Pradesh, one statutory authority duly empowered under U.P. Area Development Act 1976 has been created for each project area in U.P. Similar action in other states has either already been taken or is underway. Results from pilot operations in Orissa covering a total of about 5000 ha in various command areas indicate that likely benefits would be 20-30 per cent increase in yield and water savings that would permit 20-30 per cent increase in irrigated areas. The experience on such projects in India suggests that major obstacles to the successful implementation are (i) obtaining rights of way for field channels and drains without compensation and (ii) large number of farmers are ineligible for bank loans due to non-defined land titles.

On-Farm Development

'On-farm' development implies scientific management of soil and water involving such composite efforts as conjunctive water use, suitable land grading and realignment of land holdings for effective water use in order to increase the production potential.

'On-Farm' Development includes:

(i) Execution of field channels, construction of hydraulic structures like culverts, syphons escapes, diversion boxes etc.

(ii) Execution of drainage channels like arterial drains and link drains, remodelling of natural drainages, alongwith link and feeder channels.

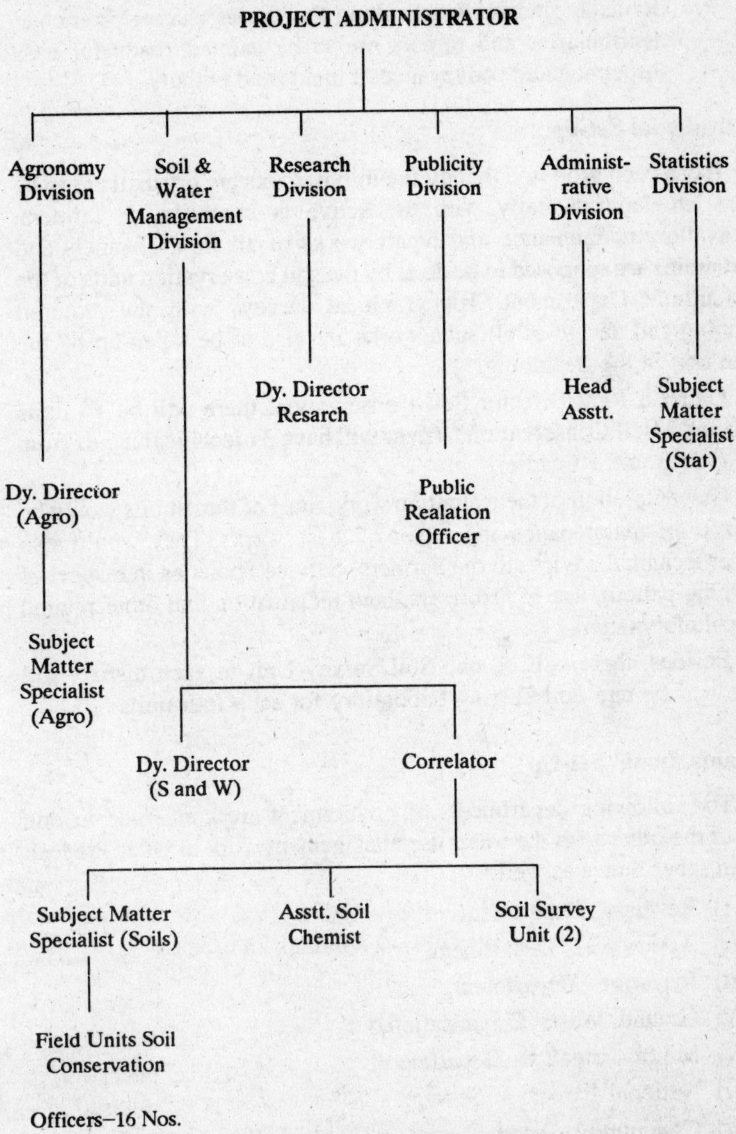

Flow Chart-1: Present Organisational Set-Up of Sharda Sahayak Development Agency.

(iii) Construction of farm roads 3 to 3.5 m width all along the drainage ditches. Roads along the feeder channel branches, distributaries and minors are to be painted roads for easy inspection and conveyance of inputs and outputs.

Institutional Set-up

It has been proposed that all the initial works big or small are to be taken up departmentally with the active co-operation of farmers. Excavation, maintenance and repair works of all field channels and field drains are supposed to be done by the soil conservation units of the Agricultural Department. Topographical surveys with the required planning and design of all such works are also to be taken up by the same unit in the beginning.

Under a Joint Director Soil Conservation, there will be 16 units each and a Soil Conservation Officer will have 31 technical hands from Group I, II and III cadres.

On completion of the execution work, most of these units would be utilized for maintenance and repair of these works. They would also render technical advices to the Farmers' Service Societies in respect of cropping pattern, use of fertilizers, land reclamation and other related agricultural matters.

Besides, there will be one Soil Survey Unit in each district and there will be one Soil Testing Laboratory for each four units.

Organisational Set-Up

The following departments of government are concerned in one way or the other with the water use management work in Uttar Pradesh and in other States as well :

(i) Revenue Department,
(ii) Agriculture Department,
(iii) Irrigation Department,
(iv) Ground Water Organisation,
(v) Minor Irrigation Department,
(vi) National Extension Service,
(vii) Community Development,
(viii) Area Development Authorities, and
(ix) Agricultural Colleges and Universities.

Irrigation Department

A typical set-up of Irrigation Department is shown in the figure below:

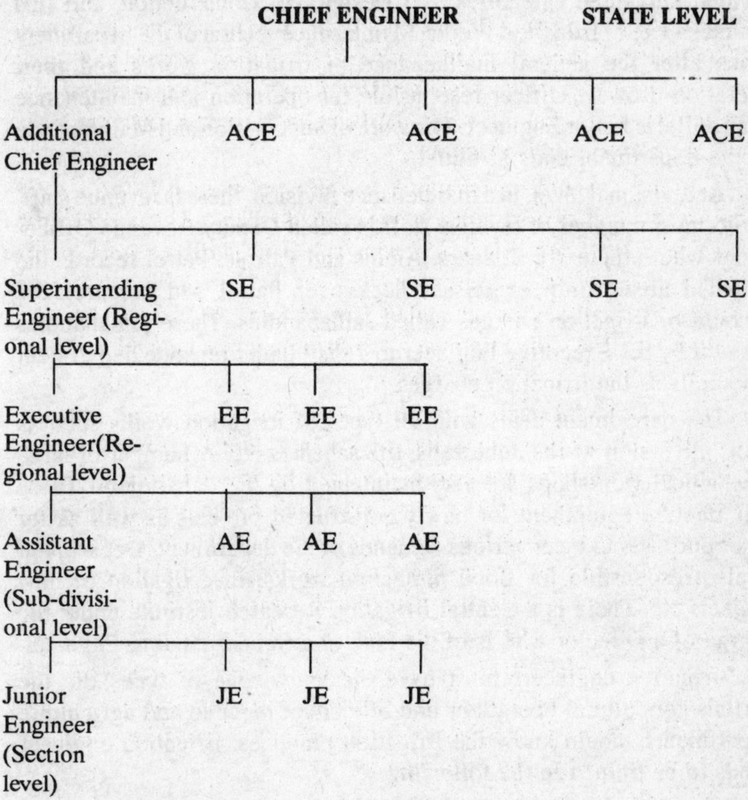

Flow Chart-2 : Organisational Set Up – Irrigation Department

At State level there is Chief Engineer and Additional Chief Engineers. Chief Engineer is the head of department and coordinates the activities of Additional Chief Engineers and deals with government. Every major project is kept under the charge of an Additional Chief Engineer. There are a number of Superintending Engineers under each Additional Chief Engineer who is incharge of a Circle. Circle is divided into Divisions headed by an Executive Engineer. A division is then divided into sub-divisions headed by Assistant Engineers. An

Assistant Engineer has a number of Junior Engineers each incharge of a section (Flow Chart 2).

From functioning point of view, the work of the department is divided into three categories : (i) Design, (ii) Construction, and (iii) Maintenance, of Irrigation Works. Maintenance section of the department looks after the general maintenance of irrigation works and their operation. Lowest Officer responsible for operation and maintenance of an outlet is Junior Engineer. The work of Supervision and Maintenance of the department ends at outlet.

At divisional level, in a maintenance division, there is revenue staff. Seniormost member of revenue staff is called Deputy Revenue Officer under whom there are Ziledars, Amins and Patrols. Patrol records the irrigated area. Amin exercises check over Patrol and prepares the account of irrigation charges called Jamabandies. These jamabandies are sent by the Executive Engineer to Tehsil under revenue department who collects the irrigation charges.

The department deals with all types of irrigation works such as dams, diversion works, tubewells, life schemes etc. A number of large mechanical workshops are also maintained by the department. These manufacture equipment for newly constructed projects as well as for other purposes to meet various demands of the department. Department is also responsible for flood protection works, investigation of new projects etc. There is a Central Irrigation Research Institute under the charge of a Director who is of the rank of a Superintending Engineer.

Irrigation engineers must have the knowledge of types of the various agricultural operations and officers of revenue and agriculture departments should know the irrigation practices. Irrigation engineer needs to be trained in the following:

(i) Period of preparation of land for sowing.

(ii) Periods sowing of crops.

(iii) Periods of each watering.

(iv) Methods of application of irrigation water.

(v) Use of fertilizers.

(vi) Cropping pattern and crop roots.

(vii) Soil and its physical properties.

(viii) Consumptive use.

(ix) Critical periods of crops for irrigation.

(x) Soil-water-plant relationship.

Besides, the training courses should cover the following aspects:

(i) Agriculture, its importance and relationship with other industries.
(ii) Effect of climatic elements on crops.
(iii) Soil, their formation and classification.
(iv) Physical constituent of soil and their properties.
(v) Reclamation of saline, alkaline, waterlogged and sandy soils.
(vi) Soil moisture system.
(vii) Water requirements of common crops.
(viii) Crop rotations, their principles and advantages.
(ix) Surface and sub-surface drainage systems.
(x) Soil and water conservation.
(xi) Mechanical farm equipment including power and machine.

Training programme should also be initiated for administrative personnel in order to develop 'Water Management' awareness among all agencies and personnel having any type of role for increasing food production. The training programme should have a continuing education component.

Assembly

Consisting of all the water users at the chak level (Share -holders and members of the Association)

Assembly would elect office bearers, forming "Executive of the Association."

Executive

Would have two functions:

1. To manage the Association according to by-laws in order to carry out supervision of construction and maintenance of the physical structures (including hiring the necessary personnel to undertake these works).
2. To resolve disputes within the water course among the water users.

And

Would have emergency power for water regulations, and would be responsible for contracting with the Govt. on the programmes, dissemination of information on water availabilities.

Headed by *CHAIRMAN*

Could be rotating regardless of the office held by a representative.

Assisted by Secretary & Treasurer.

Flow Chart 3: Structure of Water Users' Association

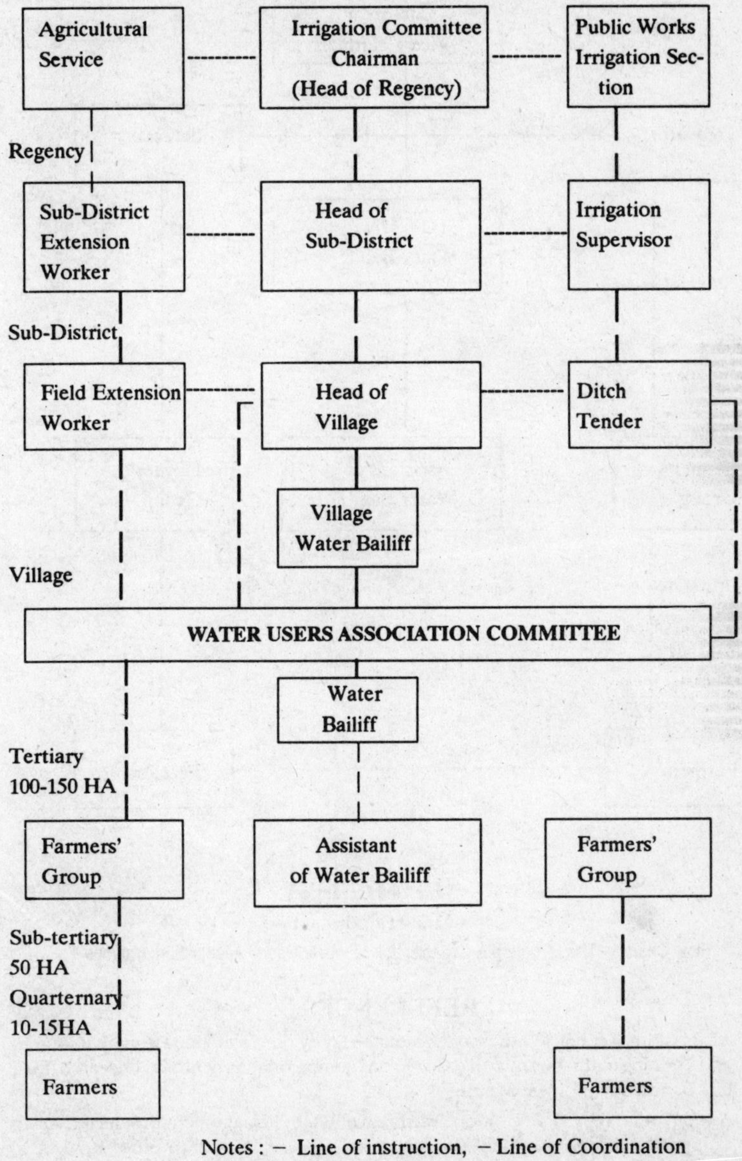

Flow Chart-4: Organisational Structure for Water Users Association (Indonesia)

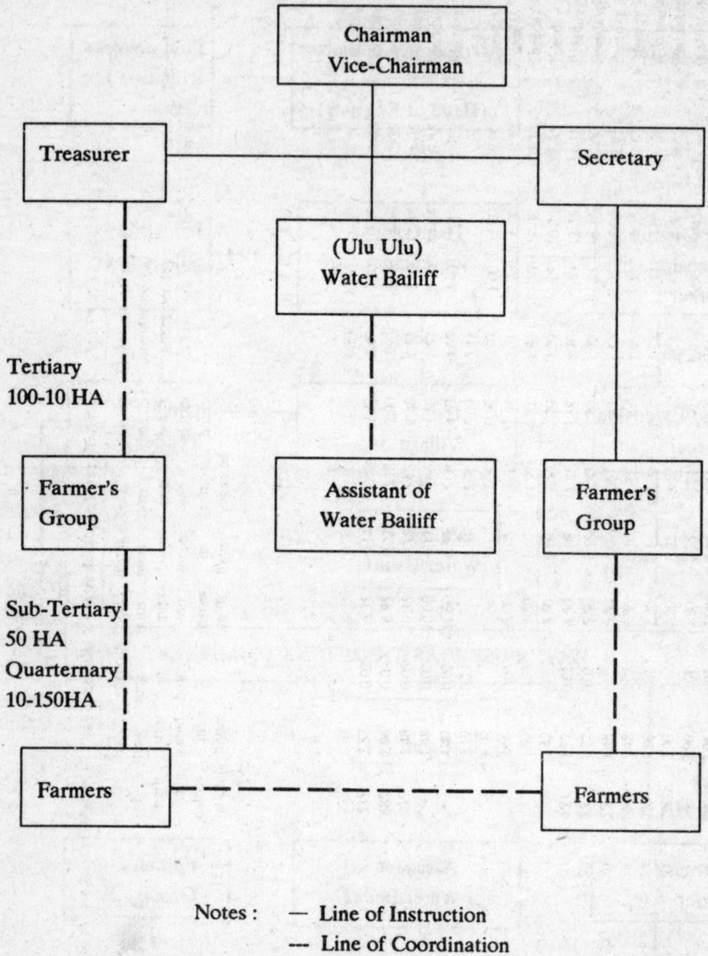

Flow Chart-5: The Structure & Organisation of Water Users' Association, Indonesia

REFERENCES

1. Ali, Hashim, Technical Advisory Committee Study on Water Management Research and Training to the Consultative Group on International Agricultural Research, IAC, Los Banos, Philippines, March 9-17, 1982.
2. Asian Productivity Organization, 'Farm-Level Water Management in Selected Asian Countries', Report of a Multi-Country Study Mission, 12th-28th June, 1979, APC Project Code, OSM/III/79, Tokyo, 1980.

3. Bagadion, Benjamin U., 'Farmers Involvement and Training in Irrigation Water Management and Farm Management', Paper presented at the Workshop on Implementing Public Irrigation Systems, East West Centre, Hawali, August 18-31, 1979.

4. Corey, G.L., 'Irrigation Water Management in India – Farmer Involvement', Unpublished Report, World Bank Mission, New Delhi, India, 1981.

5. Early Alan C., 'Farm Irrigation Constraints and Farmer Responses : Comprehensive Field Survey in Pakistan', Volume - II, Water Management Project, Colorado State University, Fort Collins, Colorado, 1978.

6. Easter, K. William and Welsch, Dalane E., 'Socio-economic Issues in Irrigation Development and Distribution', Economic Report ER 83-5, Department of Agricultural and Applied Economics, University of Minnesota, April, 1983.

7. FAO, 'Farmers' Participation and Organization for Irrigation Water Management', The International Support Programme for Farm Water Management, Land and Water Development Division, Rome, April, 1982.

8. Jayaraman, T.K. 'Farmers' Organizations in Surface Irrigation Projects; Two Empirical Studies from Gujarat', Economic and Political Weekly, Sept., 1981.

9. Johnson, Sam. Jr. Lowdermilk, Max K. Early, Alan, 'Water Problems in the Industrial Food Machines', Water Resources Bulletin 13(6), 1977, pp. 1253-1268.

10. Lowdermilk, Max K. and Lattimore, Dan (ed.), 'Farmer Involvement', Planning Guide No. 2, Water Management Synthesis Project, Agricultural and Irrigation Engineering, Colorado State University, 1982.

11. Murthy, Y.K. 'The Irrigation Engineer and the Farmer', the Fifth Bhaikaka Memorial Lecture, Presented on Feb. 19, 1980.

12. Pant, Niranjan, 'Utilisation of Canal Water Below Outlet in Kosi Irrigation Project: Administrative and Community Level Solutions', Economic and Political Weekly, Review of Agriculture, Vol. XVI, No. 39, Sept. 1981.

13. Pant, N. and Varma R.K. Farmers' Organisation and Irrigation Management, 1983, Ashish Publishing House, New Delhi.

14. Raghuvanshi, C.S. 'Socio-Economic Constratints in Adoption of Water Management Technology – A Case Study of Salawa Command', Proceedings of the Seminar on Water Management Technology Transfer, May 1985, G.B. Pant University of Agriculture and Technology, Pantnagar.

15. Patil, R.G., S.D. Suryavanshi, and P.M. Kapase, An Investigation into the Socio-economic Conditions in Ghod Irrigation Project Area, 1980 Maharashtra.

16. Proceedings of the Seminar on Farmers' Participation in Irrigation Management (A Critical Consideration), Jan. 1986, Jaipur.

CHAPTER 8

INSTITUTIONAL NEEDS FOR WATER CONSERVATION

Water is a scrace national resource which is getting scarcer and yet it is a strategic input in the process of national development. Although we are well gifted with this resource, the national annual precipitation being of the order of 400 M. ham., this amount varies widely in time and space. The result is that while floods occur in some parts of the country, others wither under severe drought. There are situations when the survival of the teeming millions becomes problematic, not to speak of national development. As we approach the 21st century the demand for food, fibre, raw materials, energy and industrial products is bound to increase several fold, also increasing the risks of water shortage. Hence the need for urgency is devising ways and means for conservation of water.

It is of paramount significance that appreciation for conservation of water be developed among the users of water – the farmers, the urban dwellers, the industries and the public at large. A programme of educating the user and the common man about the need to conserve water, in whatever way they make use of it, appears to be an urgent need of the day.

Rain water conservation has received priority in dryland research. Techniques of in-situ moisture conservation and runoff harvesting have been devised. Some of the useful practices for in-situ moisture conservation are : appropriate tillage, mulching, dead furrows, ridging, broad bed and furrows, graded border strips and inter-plot water harvesting. Runoff harvesting and its use on watershed basis has been found to be essential for increasing and stabilising productivity in drylands. However, these practices are difficult to adopt by the dryland farmers due to technical and financial reasons. Consequently a national policy is called for implementation of dryland technology. The strategy and policy matters required in this direction are discussed in this chapter.

General Awareness

Water is an essential constituent of man's life. Man uses water for a multitude of purposes, such as drinking, other domestic uses and sanitation, irrigation, industrial purposes etc. Agricultural use includes irrigation, livestock watering and farm household use. Drinking and other domestic use include supply of water to individual residential complexes. Before use, this water may need to be processed in order to remove all suspended impurities. However, with the advent of modern civilisaiton and technical age, water needs are increasing day by day. Similarly, demand for irrigation water has also increased at a very fast rate mainly due to increasing demand for food-grains, fibre, sugar, vegetables etc. in order to feed growing population. Almost in all industries, there is need for water at some stage of manufacturing process. Just like the water uses for agriculture *i.e.* irrigation and farm household uses, the requirement of water for industrial purposes is also increasing day by day due to phenomenal development of industrialisation and setting up of more and more industries in the country. Thus, all these diverse requirements have to be met from the overall water resources of the country.

Water is also most important single input limiting crop production all over the world. Shortage of water supply for irrigation is increasingly felt, on one hand, because of large scale water demand for growing High Yielding Varieties of crops as well as civic and industrial use and on the other hand, because of difficulty in water resources development[1] as a consequence of high cost and shortage of energy.

The total annual basic water resources of the country are about 140 million hectare meters of surface water resource and 50 million hectare meters of ground water resources. However, on full development of water resources, the total surface water would increase to about 185 million hectare meters and the ground water to about 85 million hectare meters. According to the report of the second Irrigation Commission

1. Water Resources projects include those for irrigation and ground water, land reclamation and drainage, salinity protection and flood control. High priority is attached to the organisation for construction, operation, and maintenance of the projects with emphasis on coordinating use of the physical works with overall agricultural development. It is not alone bringing water to the project area important but also proper drainage should be there so that the excess water is carried away and that soil salinity does not build up. Besides, adequate administrative arangements must be developed. The operating organisation in the project should be able to manage water resources so that water is available at proper times and in adequate amounts.

(1972) utilisable surface and ground water resources of the country are estimated at about 70 million hectare meters and 25 million hectare meters respectively.

PRIORITY CLAIMS FOR DIFFERENT USES

Since quantity of water is limited, problems often arise between conflicting claims. Drinking and other domestic requirements being classified as immediate needs, claims have often been given preference over other water uses. In earlier days, the demand for water was generally smaller in quantity for all these uses, which was met traditionally with wells and handpumps. However, with the population explosion and a mass exodus of people from the countryside to cities, the requirement of water in cities and towns has gone up by leaps and bounds. Water for irrigation being the other traditional use which is estimated to consume nearly 70 per cent available water also claims a preferential treatment over other water use. Since demand for food-grains, sugar, fibres, vegetables, fruits etc. has been increasing and is expected to increase in coming years in order to feed the growing population, which are as much essential as water for survival of the human beings, the importance of irrigation water use cannot be denied. By the turn of century, country's population is likely to reach 98 crores and at the present level of food-grains availability, the food production should be about 235 million tonnes against 176 million tonnes in 1992-93. There are also wide variations in rainfall from one region to another and from year to year in these regions. Hence, there is frequent occurrence of droughts in different parts/regions of the country. This necessitates a widespread use of irrigation and in parts of the drought prone areas, as protective irrigation. Industrial use of water was considered to be relatively of low priority in the past but with the phenomenal growth of industries, the requirement of water has now been increasing but it consumes comparatively a smaller quantity of water.

Despite the fact that the country has irrigation potential of 113 million hectares which may reach 140 million hectares if inter-basin water resource development becomes feasible, crop production in quite a large area would continue to be under limited supply of irrigation water and soil stored rain water. In view of the foregoing facts, we are forced to decide between these conflicting water use, which means to specify very clearly the preference of water use over the others. While it may not be possible to make a general rule in this regard but it can be possible to specify the areas and regions where each kind of water use is to be given importance. It is seen that presently the location of industries are determined by the nearness to the consumers, communication facilities, availability of the raw material, technical knowledge, availability of power and water, other facilities etc. Even then, industries cannot be given priority for use of water in preference to other uses of water. Now-a-days, large areas of fertile agricultural lands are being diverted to industrial complexes either on the basis of regional distribution of industries or on account of the area being very close to large cities/towns. This unplanned growth of industrial complexes vitiate the optimum water use plan. Apart from all these facts, development of industries in fertile agricultural areas and in the vicinity of large cities/towns is certainly going to lead conflicting claims for water use over irrigation water and drinking water requirement of the area, which is bound to result in shortages of water for agriculture, domestic purposes and drinking. This may be faced with acute shortage with the passage of time.

Water Resources Management

For drinking and other domestic purposes, quantity of water use, is comparatively smaller than irrigation water use. Since ground water needs much lesser processing than surface water, therefore ground water should be made available for drinking and domestic purposes. However, in hilly areas, water use needs special consideration. In certain hilly areas surface springs exist and such springs need to be tapped in such areas for drinking water supply in preference to other uses. But in some other hilly areas where no surface springs exist, it may be possible to get ground water from rock joints and fissures. Hence, it would be better to give first priority to drinking for use of such underground water and the second preference should be given to industries. Similarly in sandy soils areas or other scarcity areas, where surface water is not available, ground water may be available in specific areas, *viz.* dry river beds. Drinking should be given first priority for use of such water, even if it needs to be supplied at a longer distance.

However, water use for irrigation should be given first preference in use of surface water in plains fertile areas. There may be some areas which are either waterlogged or there is a tendency of rising of ground water level, in such areas ground water should be used for irrigation purposes and if surface water is available it can be used for meeting the requirement of other purposes. But, in such areas where ground water is low or there is a tendency of further going down of its level, surface water should be used for irrigation even if it has to be conveyed over a long distance for this purpose.

Integrated Water Use Management

Scientific use of surface and ground water, is termed to be integrated and conjunctive water use for deriving maximum benefit from the limited overall quantity of water available. Perhaps, it may require some transfer of water from one area to another, which at times is quite costly but it has to be done in overall interest of economical and best water use. Both surface and ground water may have to be transferred from one area to another. But transfer of surface water is comparatively less costly and easier, whereas transfer of ground water may be uneconomical. However, it is not the apparent cost alone which should be taken into account but due weightage has to be given to the indirect benefits to be derived from this inter-area water transfer. If such transfer of water helps in relieving water-logging condition in an area and replenishes ground water in another area, it makes possible setting up of industries in an otherwise deficient area, then the benefits are much more, than what they would appear to be.

The type and size of industries suitable for an area need a careful consideration. Hence, small scale agro-based industries should be located in a predominently agricultural area, but big industries could be established elsewhere. This practice of establishing/locating industries, apart from creating more and widespread environmental problems, also leads to conflicting claims over water resources and the best use of water is also not possible.

Conservation of Water and Its Reuse

Conservation of water can be possible through minimizing wasteful runoff, minimising losses and recycling.

Minimizing Wasteful Runoff

Huge surface runoffs during rainy season results in several problems like floods, sediment problems, etc. These problems can be tackled by adopting afforestation, soil conservation etc. which help reducing surface water runoff in monsoon season, and increase the absorption of water in the soil. This stored ground water can be available for use during the non-monsoon period. Similarly surplus water, wherever it is possible should be stored for subsequent use by creating storage reservoirs.

Minimising Losses

Measures should be taken for reducing water losses, wherever it can be possible. These measures have to be taken for all types of water use. The losses can be minimised by lining irrigation channels, avoiding wasteful use like over-irrigation and adopting modern improved irrigation practices. Similarly, much water can be saved by educating the consumers, in case of domestic water supply and leakages in water taps/supply need to be avoided. However, in case of industries process which involve economical use of water, need to be adopted.

Recycling and Re-use of Water

Wherever it could be possible, water after being used once, should be reused after reprocessing as may be required. Even if a minor treatment is called for to make it suitable for reuse, it should be done. Thus, all efforts should be to reuse water as much as possible.

WATER CONSERVATION – A NATIONAL NEED

The need for water conservation has been adequately recognised by our planners when they formulated the National Policy (September 1987). This statement states in para 15:

> "The efficiency of utilisation in all the diverse uses of water should be improved and awareness of water as a scarce resource should be fostered. Conservation consciousness should be promoted through education, regulation, incentives and disincentives."

The National Water Poilcy also mentions that water resources available to the country should be brought within the category of utilisable resources to the maximum possible extent. Real conservation lies in the manner of economising use of water and avoiding its wastage. However, this cannot be accomplished unless all persons involved in water utilisation cooperate and have a commitment to the objective of saving water. The first step is to develop awareness among all users about the need for water conservation.

INSTITUTIONAL NEEDS FOR WATER CONSERVATION

Institutional aspects include legal framework to ensure optimal utilisation of water and its minimum wastage; and education to increase awareness for water conservation. In the past, the availability of abundant quality water at reasonable cost has developed tendencies to use more rather than less water. The situation has now changed and it is necessary to restrict free use of water. The constitutional experts and administrators of the country have, therefore, a major responsibility in this regard.

Even though India has sufficiently large water resources but these are not evenly spread in time and space which sometimes causes recurring floods[2] in some areas and droughts in others. But, no efforts have been made for conservation of water, which is highly scarce due to its alternative uses. Although, the principal use of water is for agriculture, yet it is also required for drinking, industrial purposes, navigation, recreation, and energy generation. In view of widely felt shortage of water, there is need for raising water conservation consciousness among the farmers, rural and urban dwellers, industries and public at large. However, administrative measures alone to check the wastage of water in irrigation and water supply cannot be effective without the cooperation of the people.

Rainfall is uncertain which varies from place to place and season to season. Precipitation is confined to only about three or four months in the year and varies from 10 cm. in the western parts of Rajasthan to over 1000 cm at Cheerapunji in Meghalaya. These facts reveal that a large area of the country suffers from water scaracity. Since the principal use of water in our country is for agriculture, therefore, during the last two decades demand for irrigation has increased manifold mainly due to New Technology. Besides, in the recent past, the country has witnessed a phenomenal industrial growth which has also been instrumental for increased demand of water. Also demand for drinking water has rapidly increased due to rapidly increasing population.

Under the prevailing conditions in canal command, water use efficiency in our country varies from 20-40 per cent, which is certainly very low as

---

2. Floods and droughts affect vast areas of the country, transcending state boundaries. A third of the country is drought-prone. Floods affect an average area of around 9 million hectares per year. According to the National Commission on Floods, the area susceptible to floods is around 40 million hectares.

compared to other developed countries. Even 10 percent saving in losses by bringing improvement in the present operational system may provide water to an additional area of 3 million hectares without creating additional irrigation facilities. In this context, there is an urgent need to make concerted efforts for minimizing losses/waste of water[3], and conserve every drop of water and take up measures for water conservation. Also poor management at the farm level has caused a significant wastage of irrigation water. The farmers at the tail reaches of the canal do not get sufficient amount of water for crop production, whereas the fields in the head reach are flooded, consequently leading to wastage which also creates environmental hazards. This requires an effective drainage system to drain the excess water. However, 'on-farm' development requires formation of farmers' association for paving way to the co-operative approach for efficient use of irrigation water with proper operation and maintenance of irrigation as well as drainage system.

An assured and controlled water supply is a basic requirement for steady crop production and water conservation. Also due to uncertainty of water supply, farmers are tempted to store water more than the requirement of the crop as a precautionary measure without realising that too much water can do more harm than good for the growth of plants. In fact, water is wasted due to percolation beyond root zone depth. Hence assured irrigation is one of the important components for economical use of water and thus paving way for water conservation.

WATER SUPPLY SCHEMES AND WASTAGE OF WATER

Broadly, two types of rural water supply schemes are being executed in the country depending upon the nature of sources available and the geography of the area. Potable water may be distributed to the villages either through a piped network or from a single point source with hand-pumps. Piped system works under gravity. Water is also pumped from an underground or surface source. For proper functioning of the water supply system, its efficient and effective management is a pre-requisite, but inefficient control of equipment and supplies have

3. Increasing investments in irrigation will not meet the increasing demand of water, so long farmers allow so much water to be wasted. Irrigation without matching drainage and land consolidation is highly wasteful. Over-irrigation is also increasingly taking lands out of cultivation through salinity, waterlogging etc.

caused maximum wastage of water. Quick restoration of damaged parts is also not possible which results in a considerable wastage of water. Hence, efficient control of equipment and supplies, quick restoration of damaged parts, are necessary for preventing wastage of water.

WATER MANAGEMENT PROBLEMS IN IRRIGATED AREAS

Warabandi system of Irrigation in northern parts of the country does not provide any incentive to the farmers for efficient and economical use of water. They apply more water than the crop requirement, mainly due to the fact that water rates/charges are based on area irrigated. This results in waste of water, which also tends to increase water-logging. A considerable quantity of water is lost due to seepage in the water course. The wastage of water during field application is quite alarming. Therefore, it requires concerted efforts to minimize the wastage. In view of these facts, there is an imperative necessity to minimize water seepage losses by making provisions of concrete lining in field channels which would be helpful in water conservation.

Water management problems are, however, not confined to irrigated lands only. They also exist, though in different forms, in non-irrigated lands. It is worth to note that out of the total area of 170 million hectares under cultivation, nearly 70 million hectares have irrigation facility and thus remaining area of 100 million hectares is rainfed agricultural lands. This needs a great deal of attention, mainly by way of protection against avoidable run-off. It is estimated that the total precipitation is around 400 million hectare meters in the country and out of this about 150 million hectare meters (mhm) enters the soil, which retains around 110 mha.m as soil moisture. It is the remaining 250 mha.m of water which does not find its way into the soil that constitutes the total annual run-off of about 250 mhm in our river systems and around 70 mhm is lost by way of evaporation immediately after precipitation occurs. A pertinent problem which requires an answer is how the excessive run off losses can be reduced? The work involved needs to be treated from Water Conservation angle. A reduction in runoff losses will automatically mean that more water will become availabale for retention within the soil as soil moisture or as ground water. Reduced runoff losses will also save a great deal of top soil from erosion and moderate the incidence as well as the severity of floods.[4] Such a basic administrative reform is needed which will set the pace for similar changes at the State and District levels.

RAINFED FARMING – WATER CONSERVATION PRACTICES

Crops are grown in about 100 m. ha. rainfed area in India. The productivity of these crops depends on the amount and rainfall distribution pattern. The occurrance of drought or flood in one part of the country or other is a regular feature. India receives the largest rainfall per unit area in the world for a country of comparable size. The annual rainfall over India has been computed at 117 cm, 75% of which is received during south-west monsoon season (June to September). Post monsoon season (October to December) accounts for 10-11% of the annual rainfall. The same for winter season (January to February) and pre-monsoon season (March-May) are 3-4% and 10-11% respectively (Sarkar, 1988). The overall water potential of the country, excluding the losses due to evaporation, soil moisture etc. is 178 m. ha. m. from surface water and 42 m. ha. m. from ground water. However, only about 50% of this can be brought to use due to physical and technological limitations (Sachidanandan, 1988). It has been estimated that the maximum amount of exploitable irrigation potential by all types of irrigation is 113 m. ha. m. This would only be sufficient for 50% of the total cultivable area of the country. As such, 50% of the area would be left completely dependent on rainfed farming (India, Planning Commission, 1985 cited by Kanwar, 1988). This preamble is suggestive for efficient rain water management for crops grown under rainfed conditions. Again, the management practices have to be so oriented such that they can serve on a long term basis, as in India we will have to live with rainfed agriculture.

Current Practices

Measuers for soil and water conservation in agricultural lands are synonymous. Any practice which will help in conserving soil will also conserve water. The basic concept of soil and water conservation is to

4. Floods are controlled by effective storage reservoirs, and building flood banks on either side of the river. Reservoirs not only moderate the floods but also serve in power generation, irrigation, drinking water supplies and navigation. Thus, a large number of reservoirs should be built which would help in moderating the floods and conserving water -- a free natural resource.

minimize movement of soil and to have on-farm rain water recharge in the profile. The main programme hitherto followed in India is to construct contour/graded bunding and land shaping in the agricultural lands. Often this will be simple field bunding on ownership basis. It has now been realised that such programme is not yielding desirable results. Another effort is to construct ponds/percolation tanks in the villages, mostly under relief programmes. Of late, development of dry areas on watershed basis is gaining momentum. Government of India has launched a vigorous programme for national dryland agriculture on more than 4000 watersheds in the country. This is based on the experience gained in the earlier programmes.

Water Conservation Practices Developed in Dryland Farming

In dryland research the first priority has been given to absorbing as much water in the soil as it can hold aiming at enhancing productivity of crops per unit of rain water. Thereafter, attempts have been made to supplement the moisture stored in the soil by providing life saving irrigation during dry periods/critical stages of crop growth from the runoff harvested in suitable structures. A brief account of these two aspects is discussed as follows.

In situ moisture conservation

Mechanical structures like contour/graded bunding and bench terracing are the pre-requisites in soil and water conservation in slopy agricultural lands. However, to have uniform and higher recharge of moisture in the profile, inter-terrace land treatments have been found to be effective. Such treatments are:

Tillage : As stated earlier 10-11% of the total rains are received during the pre-monsoon season. Adoption of proper tillage helps the rain water to enter into the soil profile. Besides, this off-season tillage is needed for weed control. Shallow preparatory tillage was found to be beneficial in an Alfisol of Telangana region by increasing the yield of sorghum by 43% over the base yield of 14.3 q ha where direct seeding was resorted to. The effect was, however, more pronounced in sub-normal rainfall years. Excessive tillage could be detrimental to Aridisols due to soil loss in wind erosion. Hard pan below the plough layer and textural profiles having high clay content (due to illuviation) prevent moisture infiltration. Under such situations, deep ploughing (22 cm) helps to increase crop yield, the effect being perceptible during the next two years. Deep tillage is also effective in controlling perennial weeds.

Mulching : Mulching provides physical barrier in movement of moisture from soil into atmosphere. Experiments conducted at several locations have revealed that use of organic mulch in rabi crops increased crop yield to the tune of 30%. Sorghum vertical mulch (placing sorghum stubles in trenches of 40 cm deep, 15 cm wide and protruding 10 cm above the ground level) enhanced available soil moisture by 4-5 cm and increased grain yield of sorghum by 40-50% in Vertisols of Bellary.

Dead furrows : Construction of 'idle furrows', generally called as dead furrows, at 3.6 m interval in groundnut helps in increasing grain yield by about 10% in arid Alfisols at Anantapur.

Flat on grade and ridging : Sorghum and pigeonpea grown on semi-arid Alfisols of Hyderabad gave higher yield by 19 and 24% respectively over control when the crops were sown as intercrops on a grade and ridging was done later.

Broad bed and furrows : Broad bed and furrows with a bed of 100 cm and 50 cm of shallow furrow which has a depth of 15 cm is useful in improving moisture regime and draining the excess water under situations where water stagnation is a problem. This situation arises in high rainfall Vertisol areas. Sorghum yield increased by 26% at Akola under this system over flat sowing.

Graded border strips : Graded border strips of 130 x 11 m with 0.1% grade was found to be effective in deep Alfisols with medium rainfall. Fingermillet yield was increased by 42% due to this treatment at Bangalore.

Inter-plot water harvesting : This practice consists of growing maize and rice in ridge furrow system in Inceptisols of sub-humid areas. Maize is taken on the ridges and water requirement of rice is met by the water harvested in the furrows. Maize and rice yield was increased by 17 and 21% respectively over control.

Inter-row water harvesting : In arid areas having Aridisols, pearl millet yield was increased by 50% by inter-plot water harvesting of 1:1 of cropped to uncropped land (the slope of uncropped land being on both sides), and inter-row water harvesting with a treatment of ridges with runoff inducing substances like tank silt or polyethylene.

Runoff harvesting

In arid and semi-arid tropics runoff is inevitable. Arresting this runoff in suitable water harvesting structures has been the major thrust in stabilising and improving the crop yields from drylands. Water harvesting in large tanks and growing rice under irrigation in the lower reaches is an age old practice prevalent in peninsular India. However, under this system, the donor areas is deprived of the water benefit and an uniform development of agricultural productivity is not possible. To overcome these limitations construction of small storage capacity (about 750 m) farm ponds has been devised with small catchment area of 1-2 ha. Other technique in which water can be directly used for irrigation is the harvesting of runoff in the gullies, in-between the check dams.

Runoff harvesting has also been devised for primary purpose of increasing the ground water recharge. Percolation tanks and submergence bundhies are meant for this. The increased ground water is tapped in dug wells for irrigation. Assured rabi crops are taken in the beds where water is harvested in Kharif season as submergence bundhi.

Strategies

The foregoing discussion is aimed to give a brief overview of the practices developed for increasing moisture regime in dryland soils. Although increase in productivity comes largely from improved agronomic practices, nevertheless *in situ* moisture conservation practices form a better environment for crops to grow. Besides direct beneficial effect of conserved moisture, its interaction with improved practices, particularly judicious fertilizer use, is important.

Moisture conservation strategies should be tailored to rainfall and soil conditions. *In situ* moisture conservation practices deserve serious attention in arid and semi-arid tropics as these practices are primarily meant for increasing carry-over of moisture in short dry spells which is a typical feature of these regions. Runoff management has to be capitalised to mitigate long dry spells and to increase productivity. Fortunately, input responsive cultivars are now available so that water use can be remunerative. In humid and sub-humid areas short dry spell is not uncommon. Therefore, runoff harvesting and management assumes paramount importance for increasing crop productivity and cropping intensity through sequence cropping. In these areas, supplement irrigation for rabi crops would be extremely useful. Runoff is abundant in these areas and it is a matter of technological extension to harvest and use it efficiently.

Planning

While planning for dryland agriculture some facts have to be kept in view. Dryland farmers are poorest of the lot and they have a poor resource base. They have not only small land holdings (about 72% of the dryland farmers have land less than 2 ha), but also it is fragmented. Shortage of fodder in dryland areas has led to shortage of draft power. Country plough and blade harrow are generally used for field preparations.

Under these situations it would be a difficult task for the farmers to go in for deep tillage (once in three years) which can be accomplished by bullock drawn mould board plough or tractor. Availability of implement/ tractor and draft power will be the serious constraints for this important operation in improving crop yield. Similar constraints would be arising in imposing broad bed and furrows and graded border strips. Nevertheless technical guidance in identifying the key lines in the field is also required to be provided.

Experience gained at Chevella (A.P.) and Mittemari (Karnataka) watersheds drive home this point. The Vertisols and the Vertic soils at Chevella were never exposed to land treatments.

INSTITUTIONS FOR WATER CONSERVATION

With the given conditions, high aspirations of the consumers values, attitudes of the farmers and other consumers, possibilities of five alternatives of setting up/forming institutions for water conservation appear to be most convincing. These are :

(i) Department of Water Conservation at National and State level.

(ii) Provincial Water Conservation Bureau.

(iii) Water Users' Association.

(iv) Societies like Indian Water Resources or Simlar Associations.

(v) Consumers Forum.

Different practices can be adopted for conservation of water which are contour trenching, contour pits, deep blasting of hard surface strata, deep holes raising the ground water table and other agronomic practices (like mulching, weeding etc.), re-generation of the vegetation, reduction of the soil salinity etc. However, the practices mentioned above have not been touched, and only possible institutions have been discussed. Organisational structure of these institutions have also been suggested.

1. *A Department of Water Conservation* be set up which will be charged with the responsibility of ensuring that the country's run-off

are reduced to the minimum and that the incidence as well as severity of both droughts and floods is controlled to the maximum possible extent. This department will also pay special attention to the conservation of moisture as well as top soil in rainfed agricultural lands. But it would be a mistake to imagine that the stupendous challenges which we face in the field of water conservation, can be met purely through administrative reforms and government action. While State action is necessary where specialisations and high technologies are involved, in many areas the people can help themselves, provided they are given some basic technical advice and guidance. If the gigantic tasks of water conservation are to be accomplished within the constraints of available resources, and at the speed which the situation demands for, the country must win the race against time to avoid certain disaster – there is no alternative but to mobilise idle man power in the rural sector and convert surplus labour into permanent physical assets like in Mao's China. These physical assets may take the form of proper field levelling, field channels and drains in command areas, contour terraced fields and bunds, millions of small storages – one for every single micro-shed in all rainfed farming areas and denuded non-farm lands. All these are works of a nature that given a technical guidance, can be carried out by the people themselves without bringing in expensive measures and paid labour. Such assets can come into existence only if the people can be motivated[5] to give freely of their surplus time and labour for works which they perceive to be for their common good and the benefit of which they are confident of sharing with other members of the community in a fair and equitable manner. Although our village communities are by and large faction ridden and have no viable institutions. These deadening conditions need to be changed and vibrant self reliant communities brought into existence so that they may tackle them and check the colossal wastage of water, which calls for major political, administrative and social changes in the rural sector. The situation demands that energetic steps are taken for effective water conservation measures village by village, micro-watershed by micro watershed, field by field, which could be possible by enthusing local population to participate in water conservation programmes so that the future of the

5. Increasing agricultural productivity mainly depends on human motivation; human motivation is the vital missing resource. The 80 million owners of land (on 89 million holdings) are the most important national resource. If they can be motivated to invest more into their lands, and use water economically and to work them hard. There would be an immediate and drastic increase in output.

present generation as well as of generations yet unborn, may be secured.

2. *Provincial Water Conservation Bureau*: Water Conservation should be taken up in our country on the pattern of 'TAIWAN' Provincial Water Conservation Bureau (PWCS) which is a Government Organisation. This consists of experts from different departments such as Irrigation, Agriculture, Revenue, Forest and Soil Conservation. PWCS handles the construction of projects whose irrigated area is more than 500 hectares. It is responsible for implementation of flood control works, supervision of Irrigation Associations, Operation and Maintenance Work of Irrigation Systems, Administrative and Financial matters of all Irrigation Associations are also conducted by the P.W.C.S. Similar Institutions/Organisations need to be set up in our country which could take up Water Conservation on war footing.

3. *Water Users and Conservation Association*: Unfortunately, in our country, more attention has been paid for the development of water resources but the optimum use of water and its scientific management on the farmers field has not received due attention. Much too often, the social and economic aspects of water use have been overlooked. Mere creation of irrigation potential and infra-structural facilities are not enough. Farmers' involvement[6] is an adjunct for optimum use of water and water conservation. To achieve this objective, the farmers need to be educated about the repair and maintenance of the water courses and make their full use for increasing production. But the non-involvement of the farmers, in design and operation of the system causes conflicts. Since the farmers are the actual beneficiaries, their participation is essential. Unless they are involved, irrigation offences and wastage of water cannot be checked even with the force of law. The farmers' active involvement in water conservation can be ensured by a participatory community-based approach for which an appropriate organisation can be of three tier system or an elected Water Users and Conservation Association. This pyramid can serve the farmers' community with (i) at the lowest level a 'Chak Samiti' which can be constituted from the farmers within the Chak or the outlet command, and (ii) secondary level can constitute a sub-project committee formed of the representatives

---

6. The farmers' involvement means to take/participate in decisions making for planning, designing, execution, monitoring and evaluation of the programmes in which their experience and knowledge are helpful for the effective improvement of the irrigation systems and water conservation.

of the outlet committees in a distribution system. In this three-tier system, on the tertiary level, the farmers' association can represent the farmers at the highest position in water conservation. This could be named as 'Water Conservation Decision Committee'.

The formation of Water Users' and Conservation Associations can more appropriately consist of a bottom up approach *i.e.* to organise the farmers alongwith the cultural, physical and social dimensions, which may enable them to participate in water conservation. It is necessary to provide the water users with the incentives to improve their water use mechanism by which they can adopt new technologies and programmes. Material support such as loans, construction materials etc. obviously would benefit to provide incentives and these incentives would motivate the farmers for taking up seriously Water Conservation. We suggest the organisational structure, as given in Fig. 1.

A three-tier system can be of the following form :

1. Chak Samiti.
2. Sub-project Committees.
3. Water Conservation Policy Decision Committee.

Level of Formation

The Water Conservation Association may be formed at the water course level or at the chak level in the villages. Since all users receiving water from a particular outlet have a common interest in the quantity, quality and distribution of water, this common interest would serve as a link for successful cooperation.

4. *Indian Water Resources Society* : Evidently, there is a need, for conserving water both in quality and quantity. The dominant sectors of the Society which could potentially contribute towards this urgent need is the utilisation of water by common man. To have him participate in this endeavour, it would be necessary to develop in him a consciousness for conservation of water. The programme directed at the grassroot level is, therefore, needed. A non-governmental, non-profit and voluntary agencies like the Indian Water Resources Society have a role to play in this movement which must ultimately be carried out on the lines of the family welfare campaign.

The objective of the campaign should be to educate people at village level why and how conservation of water and preventing its pollution. It will also help collect field data on the present state of the problem, such as, ways in which water is being wasted, likely amount of wastage, sources of pollution, water needs etc. This will provide the knowledge and experience needed for conducting the water conservation campaign on a larger scale.

The operation may comprise the methods of information, dissemination to develop consciousness among the rural population for water conservation and pollution control. To take up this work a resource preparation team at district headquarters in each State/ Union Territory and field crews at each site would be needed. The resource team will have experts in commercial arts, audio-visual aids and video recording and playing. The crews will comprise demonstrators, skilled help-mates and unskilled helpers which will be headed by experienced persons *i.e.* supervisors at each site. The supervisors will plan operations headed by project coordinator on a whole time basis. The suggested organisational structure is given in Fig. 2.

5. *Consumers Forum* : Consumers forum need to be formed in irrigated area and rainfed agriculture as well, where the farmers are the actual consumers. In canal command (*i.e.* irrigation system), the farmers over-irrigate their crops and thus much water is wasted. Keeping in view the growing demand of water in urban areas and in irrigated areas as well as in unirrigated areas, there is an imperative necessity to motivate the consumers (*i.e.* farmers and urban consumers) to form the consumers forum which should have an 'Advisory Board' assisted by the knowledgeable progressive farmers/consumers drawn from different social and income groups who should educate the rural and urban people to minimise wastage of water. This consumer forum may work on the pattern of 'Consumers Protection Cells' formed recently in big cities' towns under the provision of Essential Commodities Act. The Consumers Protection Cells safeguard the interest of the consumers in the cities and towns. In some areas these are working fairly well and protect the consumers from all fraudulent practices and exploitation. On the same pattern mentioned above the consumers forum for water conservation can be formed in rural and urban areas as well which can take care of minimising the wastage of water. The consumers forum should be authorised to penalise the consumers found wasting water. The suggested organisational structure of the Consumers Forum is given in Fig. 3.

EDUCATION OF FARMERS, CONSUMERS AND ADMINISTRATIVE STAFF

It does little good to irrigate crops when the farmer does not have the know-how to irrigate adequately. He needs information on crop water requirement, rotational irrigation, time, frequency and methods of irrigation so that wastage of water could be minimised. Therefore, a planned education programme regarding water conservation will be much helpful. A sense of water conservation consciousness will arise in the mind of farmers only when they are alive to their moral responsibility as regards to proper economical use of water for irrigation. Their moral fibre needs to be toned up so as to create in them a sense of cooperative responsibility of enforcing water users etiquette as different from punitive rates which tend to increase corruption.

For organising and training the farmers in economical use of water, an extension staff with adequately trained personnel will be required on a continuous basis.

Training of administraive personnel would also be helpful in Water Conservation. This would develop 'Water Management' awareness among all agencies and personnel concerned directly or indirectly with 'Water Resources Management'. Training of the Irrigation Engineers would also help in Water Conservation. However, it would be an immense help in water conservation, if rural and urban population/consumers are educated in economical use of water for minimizing wastage of water.

STRUCTURE OF WATER USERS AND CONSERVATION ASSOCIATION

Assembly

↓

Consisting of all the water users at the chak level (shareholders and members of the Association). Assembly would elect office bearers forming 'Executive of the Association'.

Executive

↓

Would have two functions:

1. To manage the Association according to by-laws in order to carry out supervision of construction and maintenance of the physical structures (including hiring the necessary personnel to undertake these works).
2. To resolve disputes within ithe watercourse among the water users, and would have emergency power for water regulations, and would be responsible for contracting with the Govt. on the programmes, dissemination of information on water availabilities, and ways and means for water- course variation through education, training and incentives.

Headed by

↓

CHAIRMAN

Could be rotating regardless of the office held by a representative.

Assisted by

↓

SECRETARY AND TREASURER

Fig. 8.1

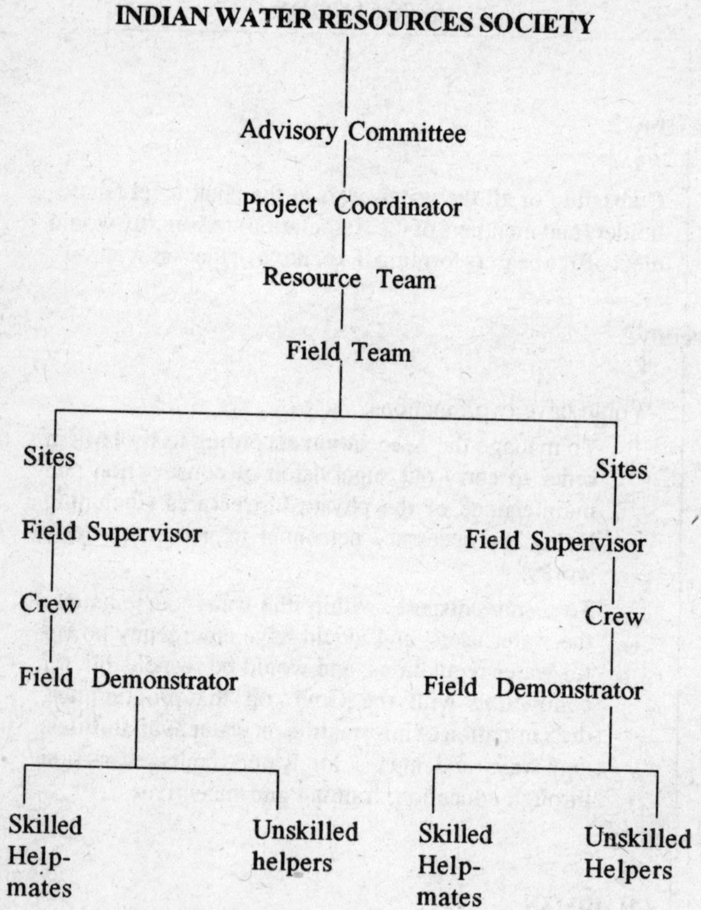
INDIAN WATER RESOURCES SOCIETY
Advisory Committee
Project Coordinator
Resource Team
Field Team
Sites
Field Supervisor
Crew
Field Demonstrator
Skilled Help-mates
Unskilled helpers
Sites
Field Supervisor
Crew
Field Demonstrator
Skilled Help-mates
Unskilled Helpers

Fig. 8.2

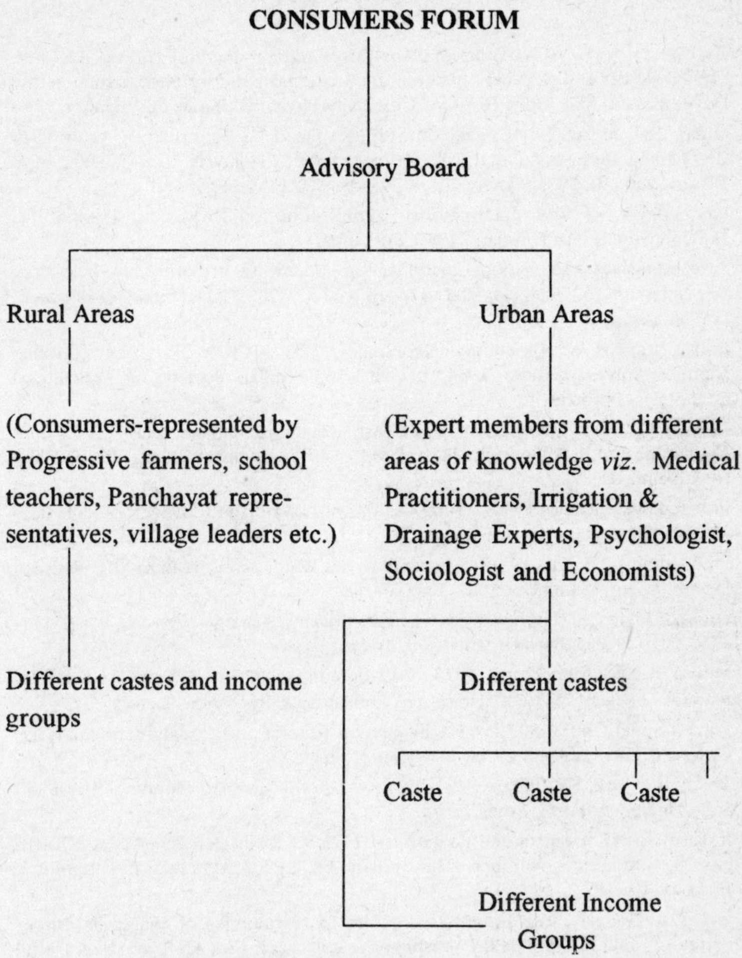
CONSUMERS FORUM
Advisory Board
Rural Areas
Urban Areas
(Consumers-represented by Progressive farmers, school teachers, Panchayat representatives, village leaders etc.)
(Expert members from different areas of knowledge viz. Medical Practitioners, Irrigation & Drainage Experts, Psychologist, Sociologist and Economists)
Different castes and income groups
Different castes
Caste
Caste
Caste
Different Income Groups

Fig. 8.3

REFERENCES

1. Gittinger, J. Price (1974) 'Economic Analysis of Agricultural Projects', pp. 130-147, The Economic Development Institute, International Bank for Reconstruction and Development, The Johns Hopkins University Press, Baltimore and London.
2. Omar, Haji Mohd. Nor Ghazali Bin (1991) 'Financial Performance Analysis of Besut Integrated Agricultural Development Project, Malaysia', Unpublished M.E. Dissertation, WRDTC, University of Roorkee, U.P. (India).
3. Proceedings of the International Symposium on Irrigation Design for Management, 16-18 February, 1987, Sri Lanka.
4. Proceedings of the National Seminar on Modernisation of Canal Irrigation, December 14-15, 1984, pp. VI-1 to VI-13, IWRS, WRDTC, University of Roorkee, U.P. (India).
5. Indian Journal of Agricultural Economics, Vol. XXXIX, No. 3, Conference Number, July-September 1984, pp. 491-553, Indian Society of Agricultural Economics, Bombay.
6. Darra, B.L. & Raghuvanshi C.S. (1990) 'Irrigation Management – A System Approach', Vol. I, Atlantic Publishers and Distributors, Ansari Road, Darya Ganj, New Delhi.
7. Proceedings, Third IWRS Symposium on Watershed Development and Management, Vols. I & II, February, 1990, Kanpur.
8. Proceedings, Second IWRS Symposium on Water Conservation for National Development, December, 1988, Bhopal.
9. Drilon, J.D. Jr. (1971), Introduction to Agri-Business Management, Vol. I, pp. 171-175, Asian Productivity Organisation, Tokyo, Japan.
10. Mishra, S.N. & John Beyer, 1976, 'Cost-Benefit Analysis – A Case Study of the Ratnagiri Fisheries Project', Hindustan Publishing Corporation, Delhi.
11. Puttaswamiah, K., 1980, 'Project Evaluation Criteria and Cost-Benefit Analysis', Oxford & IBH Publishing Co., New Delhi.
12. Tolley, C.S. and F.E. Riggs, 1966, 'Economics of Watershed Planning. The Iowa State University Press, Ames, Iowa.
13. Indian Journal of Agicultural Economics, 1978, October-December, Vol. XXXIII, No. 4, Conference Number, The Indian Society of Agricultural Economics, Bombay-400023.
14. James L. Douglas and Robert R. Lee (1971), 'Economics of Water Resources Planning', Tata McGraw-Hill Publishing Co. Ltd., 12/4, Asaf Ali Road, New Delhi.
15. Proceedings, First IWRS Symposium on Integrated Water Resources Management for Drinking, Agriculture and Industry : Policies and Issues, Jan. 1987, Hyderabad.
16. Proceedings of the Symposium on Waterlogging – Causes and Measures for its Prevention,Volume I & II, Publication No. 118, 45th Annual Board Session, 20-24, Dec., 1972, Central Board of Irrigation and Power, New Delhi.
17. Proceedings of the All India Seminar on Waterlogging and Drainage, Institution of Engineers, Roorkee Local Centre, Dec. 1990.
18. Proceedings of the International Symposium on Water Erosion, Sedimentation and Resource Conservation, Central Soil and Water Conservation R. & T. Institute, Dec. 1990, Dehradun, U.P.

CHAPTER 9

FEASIBILITY STUDY

The preparation of a feasibility study for a dam or small hydro-electric development on canals and irrigation dams outlines the next logical step, after an appraisal study has been approved in a project development study. Many of the same appraisal study's procedural steps occur in a feasibility study. A feasibility study, however, is a higher level study which is based on preliminary plans, better cost and technical data being a few of the upgraded input over the base of the appraisal study.

For cohesiveness in presentation, this chapter is divided into two parts. The first part deals with various feasibility tests and second part is devoted to procedural steps in a feasibility study.

FEASIBILITY TESTS

One must select from several alternatives of proposed projects. Each proposal must pass five feasibility tests. These tests are:

1. Technical or Engineering feasibility,
2. Economic feasibility,
3. Financial feasibility,
4. Political feasibility, and
5. Social feasibility.

The test of technical *i.e.* engineering feasibility is passed if the proposed project is physically capable of performing its intended function. A specific proposal consists of a particular physical system which may not work satisfactorily. Engineering design must be confined to the technologically feasible region (Fig. 9.1)

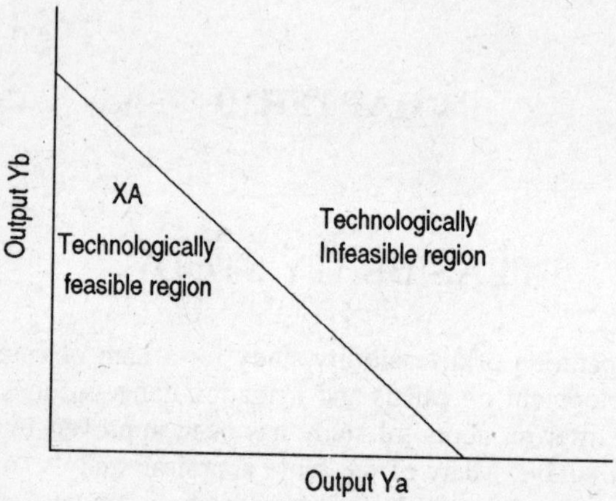

Fig. 9.1: Showing Technologically Feasible Region

The test of economic feasibility (Fig. 9.2) is passed if the total benefits that result from the project exceed those which would accrue without the project by an amount in excess of the project cost. It is important that the comparison should be 'with and without' rather than 'before and after' because many of the after affects may even occur without the project and can thus not properly be used in project justification. However, economic feasibility is contingent on engineering feasibility because a project incapable of producing the desired output is not going to produce the benefits needed for its justification.

The test of financial feasibility is passed if sufficient funds can be raised to pay for project installation and operation. While financial feasibility should always be contingent on engineering feasibility, projects have been constructed in some states/areas which do not work. A project may be economically feasible but financially infeasible because the benefits are insufficiently justified for the beneficiaries to appreciate their true value or are distributed among too many people for payment to be practical. A project may be economically infeasible but financially feasible because someone is willing to pay for the fulfilment of non-economic goals. Financial feasibility also depends on local interests believing estimated economic benefits to the degree that they are willing to raise their portion of the required funds.

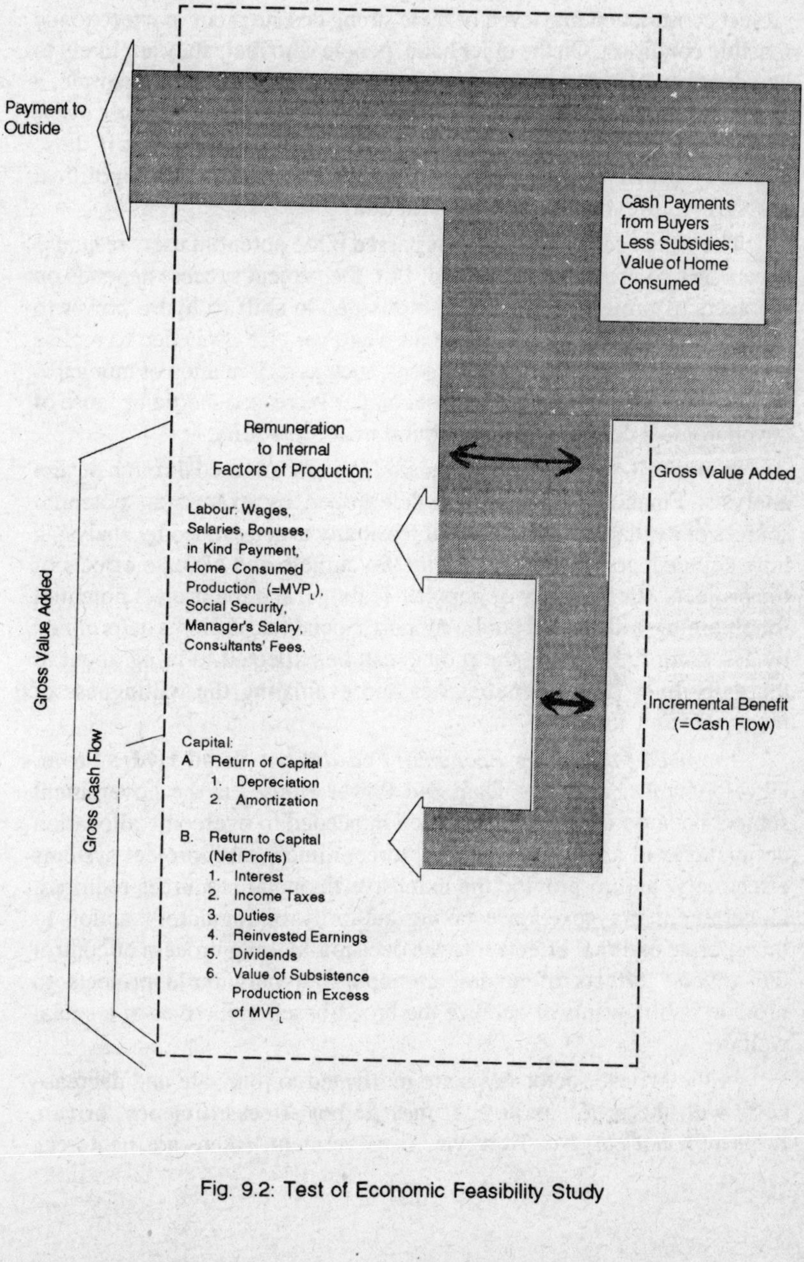

Fig. 9.2: Test of Economic Feasibility Study

The test of political feasibility is passed if the required political approval can be secured. Ordinarily political support follows proof of economic, financial and engineering feasibility. Political pressure for project construction may even be quite strong despite proof of uneconomic feasible condition. On the other hand, people who feel, they are likely to be adversely affected often oppose project installation. For example, a humid region may oppose water export to an arid region. Almost every project harms some one, and if enough people are harmed or if those who are harmed are sufficiently large and vocal, they may use political pressure to prevent project construction.

The test of social feasibility is passed if the potential users response favourably to project construction. But, the project success depends on the users of project output being motivated to shift to hydro power to utilise electrical equipment, or to do whatever else is needed to realise potential project benefits. Some projects, such as recirculation of municipal waste water after treatment, may encounter increased inertia because of psychological connotations or cultural unacceptability.

In nutshell, the engineering feasibility is ascertained through design analysis. Financial feasibility is determined by examining potential sources of available funds. Political feasibility is determined by analysing how key decision-makers assess the favourable and adverse effects of the projects, the intensity of popular feelings, and the project potential for obtaining widespread public support. Social feasibility is determined by assessing the change, the project can be expected to bring about to the daily lives of the beneficiaries and evaluating the willingness of those affected to adapt.

The need for Testing Economic Feasibility: Small Hydro Power Development (Fig. 9.3 – Dam and Power House) is the government subject because of the collective action needed to overcome allocation deficiencies in a market economy, to coordinate multiproject systems effectively, and to provide the extensive financial resources required. Government may excercise taxing authority or regulatory action to incorporate external effects into the decision-making process or control the adverse effects of natural monopoly. It may build projects to provide public wants or achieve the broad-based objectives of a social welfare.

In the private sector firms are motivated to innovate and decrease costs with the profit motive. If they do not effect efficiency, private firms will not survive. However, in goverment, 'there are no forces which operate to reveal the cheapest methods of performing public functions and to induce or compel the government to adopt such methods'. As a result of the lack of market incentives in the public sector, allocations of public funds are often made by the path of momentary least political resistance rather than by objective evaluation. Projects are sometimes taken up which are economically infeasible.

After an appraisal study has identified and selected a potential small hydro-electric project for a feasibility study, several procedures are followed to determine the projects potential feasibility. The steps that must be taken for this analysis are reviewed in the following discussion to provide an overview of the process and indicate the interrelationship of the various steps. Fig. 9.2 reveals to some extent the sequence of steps to be followed in making the feasibility study.

METHOD

The following steps are followed in a feasibility study as shown in Fig. 9.3

1. Project identification.
2. Site identification.
3. Project layout and operational criteria.
4. Environmental factors.
5. Institutional factors.
6. Power and energy generation.
7. Refinement of the preliminary project.
8. Alternate energy source.
9. Major environmental factors.
10. Project financing *vis-a-vis*, Initial power and energy sales.
11. Expected power and energy.
12. Estimated costs of the project.
13. Optimal plant capacity.
14. Final project layout drawings and arrangement.
15. Final environmental requirements.
16. Final institutional requirements.
17. Final project power and energy output.
18. Final project layout and cost estimates.

19. Economic analysis.
20. Financial analysis.
21. Project schedule.
22. Final report and recommendations.

Fig. 9.3: Nagarjunasagar Dam and Power House Distant View

1. Project identification includes knowing the location and source of the project's main features, *i.e.* addition to existing facilities, new dam and reservoir, possible interconnection points to electrical transmission networks and any other feature which might appear to have an impact on the project's cost.

2. After identification of a site (or sites) it is necessary to evaluate the existing site conditions which will include the following :

- Procurement of site plans for any existing development.
- Obtain local topography map.
- Determine the legal access to the site for both project construction and operation.
- Obtain any existing data on site geology and determine the need for additional geologic exploration.
- Review the history of prior developments at or near the site to determine any possible constraints on this or future developments.
- Determine the current status of water rights for hydroelectric development.

3. The preliminary project layout is made after evaluating the site conditions. The preliminary layout should include those evaluations required to determine the expected head on the generating unit. It is also necessary to establish if the water releases from the project are to be dictated by non-hydro-electric requirements. If water users govern the plant operation, the power production can be significantly different if there is operational flexibility permitting optimization of the power output. At this stage of the assessment both the project layout and determination of operation criteria are preliminary and subject to later modification as the study proceeds.

4. Accompanied with the preparation the preliminary layout is the investigation of the major environmental factors which include the following:

- Effects of the project on fish and wildlife resources.
- Changes in the water quality.
- Increase or decrease in recreational benefits.
- Determine if an archaeological investigation is required.
- Impact on visual appearances.

It should be determined which of the above items could be significant in the project development.

5. Also parallel with the preliminary layout preparation is the investigation of the institutional factors which include the following:

- Plan development for accomplishment of the institutional factors.
- Application process for various required Central and State permits and licenses.
- Negotiations with those governmental agencies that may maintain rights at the proposed site.

– Preliminary negotiations for the sale or transmission of the electric energy.

6. A determination is necessary on the potential project's power and energy generation. The hydrologic study is a key element of this part of the study, since it is the basis for determining the project output, benefits and therefore, its economic suitability. The first step is the determination of the average monthly stream flows for a location on the river, near the dam site, and for the longest period possible. Data can be obtained from publications supplemented, when available, by data from State, local agencies or private sources such as utility companies. Where records do not exist or are for short periods, or are inadequate it may be necessary to synthesize records for the site by correlation with nearby stream gaging or precipitation stations. The Crops of Engineers' programme is available to do this by computer. Before using the historic stream flow records, it is necessary to determine if there have been changes in the river system as a result of construction of regulating reservoirs, or of stream depletions for consumptive uses. If so, the historic stream flows should be modified to represent the present development level. Such data are sometimes available as a result of prior work by agencies interested in the watershed. If not, the process can be lengthy and complicated and subject to controversy. A simpler alternative, that may be applicable, is to endeavour and select a recent period of stream flows which will have the same averages as the long term record. This will illustrate the variability of the monthly and yearly data, and will represent the critical dry period. The stream flows adopted can then be used to evaluate the power and energy output of the project, and the size and effectiveness of any reservoir storage which can be provided by a dam. Where a new reservoir and dam are shown to be feasible and effective a cost-benefit analysis will be required to determine the reservoir volume and dam height.

The second aspect of the hydrologic study is the determination of flood volumes, peak discharges, and their frequency of occurrence. From these data are developed the spillway design flood and the lesser floods for planning the construction diversion works. A further requirement is to determine the tailwater curve for the dam or power plant site. This is used generally in its lower range for determining the operating head for the power plant, and in its upper range, which covers flood flows, for the design of the project structures especially the powerhouse and any outlet works.

7. A cursory review is needed in respect of the flow data and power

production based on the given flow. A refinement should be made of the preliminary project layout dimensions or sizes of those project features which affect power generation. This would include:

- Penstock length and diameter.
- Size of tailrace excavation.
- Preliminary estimate of the optimal turbine size and type.
- Head loss through the waterways.
- Tailwater calculated as a function of turbine flow.

8. It is to be identified where the energy is to be used in order to determine the expected cost of power that will be replaced by the proposed project. If the expected user is a non-generating utility (or commercial company) the alternate energy will come from power and energy purchases. If the expected power user is a generating utility, then the alternate energy will likely come from either proposed plant facilities or replacement energy from older less efficient generating facilities. In either case the expected cost of the alternate energy should be evaluated for use in estimating the value of power and energy from the proposed development.

9. On the basis of the refined project layout a review should be made of the environmental factors. An assessment should be made to determine which items could cause significant problems. A plan is developed to resolve these problem areas.

10. After estimation of project capacity, an initial evaluation for the prospects of power and energy sales, and project financing can be started. This will include the following:

- If the project power and energy is to be used by the developer, then the manner in which the power and energy will fit into the developers demand curves is reviewed.
- Identify the various potential power and energy purchases, if any or all of the output is to be sold.
- If feasible make preliminary contacts with potential purchaser to determine the value (order of magnitude) of the energy for use in preparation of an economic assessment.
- Determine if probable project financing will be general obligation or revenue bonds.
- Determine if there are currently any government programmes to assist in project financing, loans or grants for hydro-electric development.

- Determine the suitability for each method of financing and on a preliminary basis the best option to use.

11. Estimates need to be made of the expected project power and energy output for a range of plant capacities in a band around the estimated optimal capacity. A minimum of four or five estimates should be made to establish the relationship between the operation and plant capacity. If it appears suitable to use more than one type of turbine, then power and energy estimates should be made for each type, including multiple turbines. The possibility for developing more power and energy by use of a longer penstock to lower the powerhouse (and afterbay) elevation to obtain a higher operating head should be reviewed.

12. Project costs should be estimated for each plant configuration and total plant capacity. The estimates need only be approximate as it will be the differences between the estimates which will determine the optimal capacity in the economic analysis. The project's estimated costs should include costs for all remedial measures to be taken for environmental effects and any annual operation costs of these items should be included. If detrimental environmental effects occur which cannot be remedied, at all, an annual cost should be assigned to the environmental change and added to the annual operating cost.

For each plant configuration (an unit size) a value of energy can be determined on the basis of the estimated energy output. If there is dependable capacity, this credit should be accounted for with the energy value.

13. Having estimated the total project cost and energy values for each plant configuration, the optimal plant capacity can be determined by adopting the following steps:

- Evaluate the annual costs and benefits over the entire project life.
- Estimate the debt service, on the basis of estimated capital costs and method of financing, for each year for the period 30 to 40 years.
- Estimate annual operation, maintenance and replacement, first year's cost and escalate future years by estimated rate of escalation.
- Power and energy benefits are estimated throughout the analysis in a similar manner.
- Convert the future values of costs to present worth values using

a certain discount rate, cost of money to the developer (the discount rate should be based on opportunity cost).

- For each configuration and capacity determine the ratio of present worth of benefits to present worth of costs, the overall project benefit-cost ratio.

The optimal project is the one having the greatest difference between the total project benefits and the total project costs. If the benefit-cost ratio is less than one for all proposed configurations (and capacities), then the project is not a feasible one.

14. On the basis of the optimal project configuration and capacity, the final project layout drawings are prepared. These drawings will be much less detailed than the final design drawings but should be insufficient detail to allow resolution of all space allocations or construction difficulties. A design specification should be prepared which establishes equipment, building and facility criteria and includes a project design and construction schedule.

15. A final determination should be made of all environmental requirements. All required remedial measures should be identified and associated costs estimated. All expected adverse environmental effects should be specified for later inclusion in the environmental impact statement.

16. A final plan for satisfying the institutional requirements should be prepared. Milestones should be established for all institutional requirements and a schedule established to meet the institutional requirements.

17. A final estimate of the project power and energy output is made. This estimate is prepared in a similar manner as earlier estimates. However, new data on project layout or operating criteria affecting the power output is included in the analysis. This power and energy output estimate should be considered the definite estimate for all further work.

18. A final cost estimate is prepared based on the final project layout. This estimate includes all project costs, construction, development and other indirect costs. The bond issue or loan requirements can be determined from this total project cost estimate. An annual cost of operation is also made.

19. A definitive economic analysis is made based on the final power and energy output estimate and the final cost estimate. This analysis is made in the same manner as the previously described economic

analysis in determination of the optimal plant capacity.

20. A review is made of the project on completion of the final economic analysis. The review includes the following:

- Financing of the project development.
- Costs associated with sale or transmission of the energy.
- Suitability of both the project and the developer for the assumed type of financing.
- Cash flow analysis during both the development period and the initial years of plant operation.

It is not unusual for a project that is economically feasible to have cash flow requirements that preclude project development.

21. A comprehensive project schedule should be prepared. The schedule should include significant milestones for design, purchasing of major equipment items, having a long lead time, construction activities and the process of meeting institutional requirements.

22. To conclude, a final report and recommendations are made on the basis of the foregoing analysis. The recommendations should include any decision to continue the project and further studies which should be performed. Often special studies are required for environmental concern. Thus, benefits and costs can only be estimated with respect to certain goals.

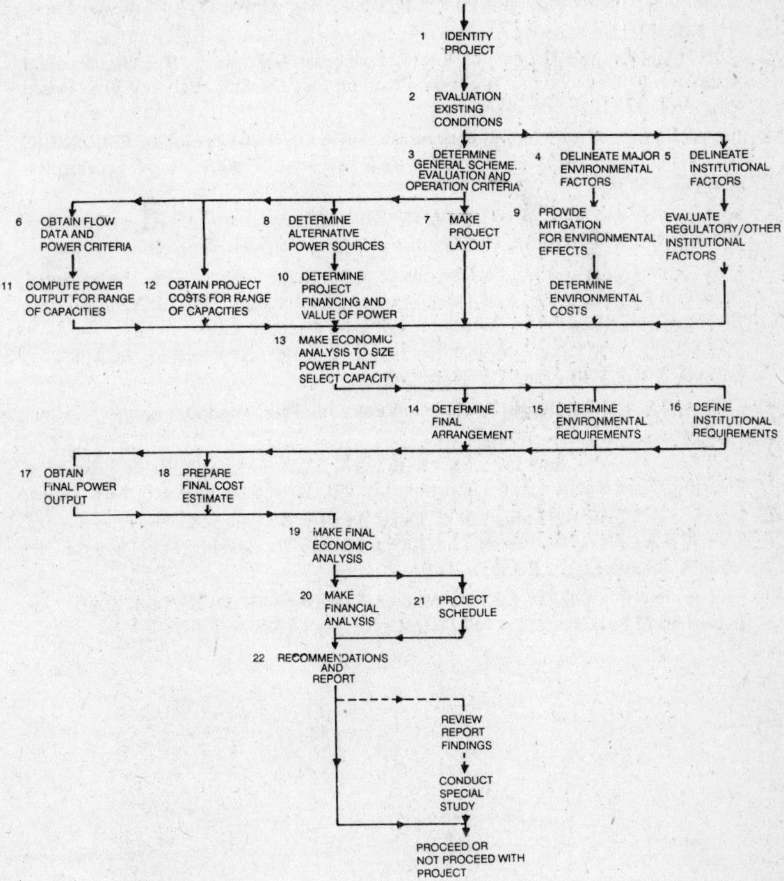

Fig. 9.4 : Generalized Study Flow Chart

REFERENCES

1. H. Bierman and S. Smidt, 'The Capital Budgeting Decision' (New York: The Mac Millan Company, 1960). p. 46.
2. Jack Hirshleifer, Jame C. De Haven, and Jerme W. Milliman, 'Water Supply; Economics, Technology and Policy' (Chicago; The University of Chicago Press; 1960) p. 152.
3. C. H. Oglesby and Eugene L., Grant, Economic Analysis — The Fundamental Approach to Decisions in Highway Planning and Design, Highway Res. Board Proc. Vol. 37 (1958) pp. 48-49.
4. Indian Journal of Agricultural Economics, 1978, October-December, Vol. XXXIII, No. 4, Conference Number, The Indian Society of Agricultural Economics, Bombay-400 023.
5. Mishra, S.N. and John Beyer, 1976, Cost-Benefit Analysis — A case study of the Ratnagiri Fisheries Project, Hindustan Publishing Corporation, Delhi.
6. Price, J. Gittinger, 'Economic Analysis of Agricultural Projects', The International Bank for Reconstruction and Development, Washington, D.C. USA, The Johns Hopkins University Press, Baltimore, 1972, pp. 1-3 and 2-9.
7. Puttaswamiah, K., 1980 'Project Evaluation Criteria and Cost-Benefit Analysis, Oxford, & IBH Publishing Co. New Delhi.
8. Tolley, C.S. and F.E. Riggs, 1966, 'Economics of Water-shed Planning. The Iowa State University Press, Ames, Iowa.
9. James, L. Douglas and Lee, Robert R (1971) Economics of Water Resources Planning, Tata McGraw Hill Publishing Co. Ltd. 12/4, Asaf Ali Road, New Delhi.
10. Mande, O.D. (1980), Evaluation of Social Benefits & Costs of Conjunctive Use of Surface and Ground Waters in Gomti Kalyani Doab, Unpublished M.E. Dissertation, WRDTC, University of Roorkee, U.P.
11. Kumar, Randhir (1979), Socio-Economic Studies of Gomti-Kalyani Doab, Unpublished M.E. Dissertation, WRDTC, University of Roorkee, UP.

CHAPTER 10

MATHEMATICS OF FINANCE

The overall process of national planning is very complex which involves the interaction of many disciplines and many factors to fulfil human needs. Even though in the present context, the main interest is 'Water Resources Development and Management and mathematical aspects of finance'. It must be viewed at this stage that it forms an integral part with the overall planning (Fig. 1) for the well-being of the society.

The well-being of the society even though difficult to define, in short would include the following indicators:

1. Food, clothes, and shelter.
2. Individual and collective security.
3. Luxury and convenience.
4. Good health.
5. Good education.
6. Pleasant working conditions.
7. A clean and unpolluted environment.
8. Cultural and moral standards.

Fig. 1 illustrates the major phases and the cycle of the planning[1] process. The disciplines involved in the process of planning are agriculture, engineering, economics, political science, sociology and management

---

1 Planning is the process by which a manager looks to the future and discovers alternative courses of action open to him. It means the selection from among alternatives of future courses of action for the enterprise as a whole and each department within it. The growing complexity of an enterprise in an increasingly complex environment has made planning, as a management function and thus planning reduces risks.

science. Hence, no one can any longer claim to be an expert in all the disciplines involved. However, there are some very closely linked fields and particularly in a developing country like ours, an inter-disciplinary knowledge is essential.

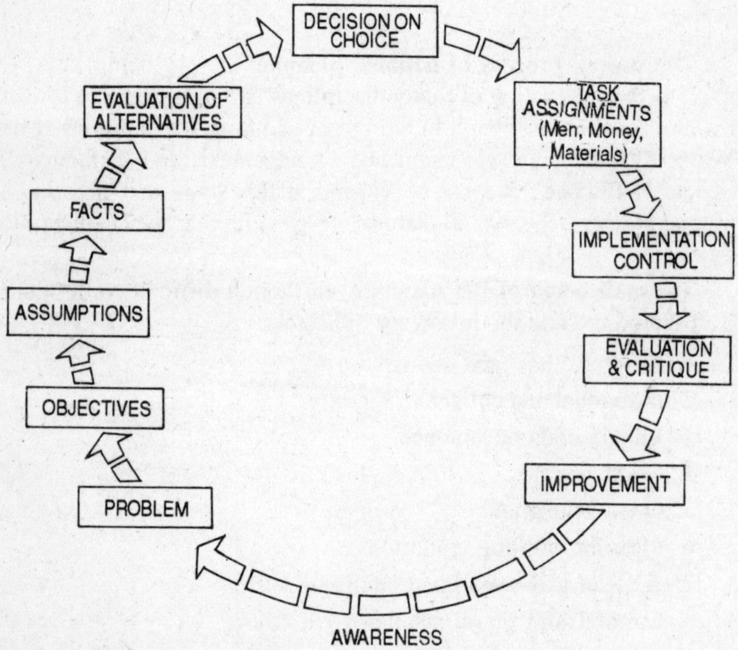

Fig. 10.1: The Planning Cycle

The water resources economics studies at the regional level, in the field of water resources development consist of:

1. The economics of project evaluation, and
2. Supporting micro-economics

The first one deals with benefit-cost analysis and compares alternative projects.

STEPS IN ECONOMIC ANALYSIS

The following steps should be initiated:

1. Explicitly defined alternatives and predictions of resultant physical consequences and their specific monetary value.
2. Choice of a discount rate and its application to convert all predicted time stream of money value into a single equivalent number.
3. Direct comparison of all alternatives.

It is a complex problem to specify an appropriate rate of discounting. However, several assumptions are made in field applications:

1. Only one discount rate should be used in any single economic analysis. The analysis may be repeated several times using different discount rates (sensitivity analysis) but separate discount rates should not be used for the costs and benefits streams in the analysis or for different categories of benefits. In fact, the discount rate is the time rate of decrease in this factor expressed in per cent per time period.
2. The discount rate used does not reflect inflation; all prices used in the analysis are real or constant monetary prices.
3. In theory, the discount rate can be positive, zero or negative, ignoring the concept of discounting (in effect adapting a zero discount rate) does not do away with the problems of trade-offs between present and future consumption (time preference).

A review of literature on discounting reveals at least three distinctive considerations on what sort of views underlie the selection of a single discount rate. In addition, some interesting and persuasive arguments have been developed claiming that, in many cases, discounting should not be applied. The theory to which one subscribes can make a significant difference in the discount rate used – and variation of 2 or 3 per cent points can make the difference between accepting, or rejecting, many large scale projects. The projects whose "bottom lines" are most sensitive to discount rate variations are those for which the benefits and costs coincide least over time. In general, lower rates of discount including a zero rate, will increase the likelihood of approving long-term capital intensive projects, whereas high rates will have the opposite effects.

There seems to be a general agreement that the values of future effects should be discounted to the present value[2] using the same rates. The three principal views of the current basis for the discount rate are summarised as follows:

(i) Opportunity Cost of Capital

This approach is based on the foregone production that results when capital is invested in one project rather than the other, or invested by government in a particular project rather than by the private sector. In this sense, the opportunity cost of capital is directly related to the theory of capital productivity. Invested in plant or equipment, a Rupee's worth of investment should yield net benefits over time. The discount rate is this rate of return.

This approach is also closely related to the financial (or nominal) interest rate, although the latter may include an upward adjustment for inflation. The real (inflation adjusted) opportunity cost rate is affected by changes in real income, the distribution of wealth, taste and technology.

The opportunity cost approach is reported to be used (implicitly) by the World Bank in requiring that to be eligible for loans, proposed projects promise an annual rate of return at least equal to a specified rate which appears to be based on the opportunity cost of capital.

(ii) The Cost of Borrowing Money

Governments frequently have to borrow money, either domestically

---

2. For computation of 'Present Worth', the choice of a discount factor is crucial, which may be determined by the borrowing rate of capital, opportunity cost etc. However, the choice of a social discount factor should be based on 'Social Welfare Criterion'.

or internationally to finance development projects. The financing mechanism used include government debt from borrowing, inflation, or taxation of private consumption. Especially when a country expects to borrow abroad, this approach may be used to set the discount rate.

A risk in this cost of borrowing money criterion is that extremely favourable loans (at very low, subsidized interest rates) will favour projects with long term net benefits and *vice versa*, a high discount rate will favour short-term pay off projects. To the extent that these extremes represent distortions of true scarcity in the economy, they will lead to misallocation of scarce resources.

(iii) The Social Rate of Time Preference

This relies on the ability of society to reflect more accurately than the private market, the present trade offs between present and future consumption. If from Society's view point individuals over-consume in the present rather than save for investment and future production, the social rate of time preference will lead to a lower discount rate than that exhibited by individuals in private markets (the life time of an individual is much shorter than the relevant time horizon of society). Setting this rate actually depends upon the circumstances in the particular country involved (if the soical rate is determined by the political process, this in turn is influenced by elected persons who may have a very short time horizon namely, until next election).

In brief, the actual rate to be used in the economic analysis will be country specific and can probably be established as a matter of government policy. Important factors governing the choice of rate will be the opportunity cost of capital, donor or lending agency requirements, cost of money to the government and governments' current views of the private sector consumption investment mix in relation to its concerns for future generation.

Physical consequences

An irrigation includes the following components of costs:

1. Construction costs,
2. Maintenance costs, and
3. Replacement costs.

Each cost event needs to be predicted by nature and date. The water may be applied to a given cropping pattern and the increase in yield of each type of crop can be predicted year by year. This may increase with the increase in area *i.e.* hectare in first few years and later may be expected to fluctuate with change of weather, and technology and other factors which influence the crop yield. The assignment of a monetary value to all physical consequences is a very complicated process. However, for the time being it is assumed that meaningful monetary values can be assigned. If more consequences fall under intangible class, the economic analysis becomes less reliable.

Cash Flow Diagram

A graphic presentation of each value plotted to time is called Cash Flow Diagram.

For a typical irrigation project

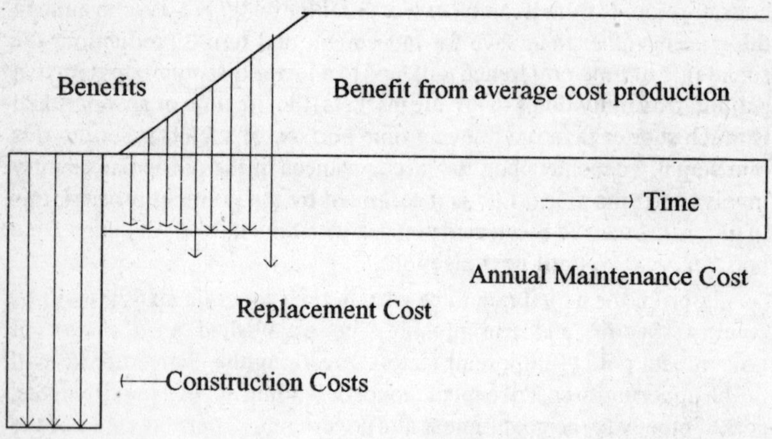

Simplified cash flow diagram

Discounting Factor

Single payment factors: In applying discounting to convert cash flows to a single number suitable for use in comparing alternatives, the basic objective is to convert a value at one date to an equivalent at another date.

Two single payment factors are available for this purpose:

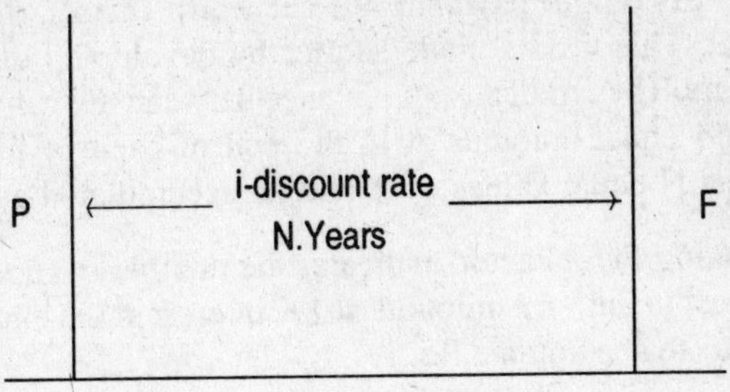

(i) Single payment, compound amount factor:

This indicates the number of rupees which will have to be accumulated of N years for every rupee initially invested at a rate of interest (return) of i per cent.

Let F = future amount

(F/P; i% ; N)

P = present amount

If P rupees were deposited initially after one year:

End of 1 year $F = P(1+i)$

End of 2 years $F = P(1+i)^2$

End of N years $F = P(1+i)^N$

$(F/P, i\%, N) = F/P = (I+i)^N$

(ii) Single payment present worth factors:

Indicates the number of rupees, one must initially invest at i % interest to have Re. 1 after N years.

$$(P/F, i\%, N) = \frac{1}{(1+i)^N} = \frac{P}{F}$$

Uniform annual series factor

All discounting problems can be solved by applying the above two single payment factors. However, additional factors can be developed to greatly reduce the required work. As in the example cited above the irrigation project will produce crops having equal value for each of the 50 years. Fifty single payment present worth factors will have to be worked out. This task is made shorter by developing uniform annual series factors. They indicate equivalence between the value at an earlier date, P, and equal amounts A at the end of each of the N years or between the N equal values of A and an accumulated amount F.

(i) Sinking Fund Factor indicates the number of rupees, one must invest in uniform amounts at 1% interest at the end of each of N years to accumulate Re. 1.

$$F = A\{1 + (1+i) + (1+i)^2 + \dots\dots + (1+i)^N\} \quad \text{Eqn. (I)}$$

Where the last value of A accumulates no interest and the first value of A accumulates interest of N – 1 years.

Multiplying by (1+i) with both the sides of equality:

$$(1+i)F = A\,(1+i) + (1+i)^2 + (1+i)^3 + \dots\dots + (1+i)^N \quad \text{Eqn. (II)}$$

Subtracting I from II, we get

$$iF = A(1+i)^N - A$$

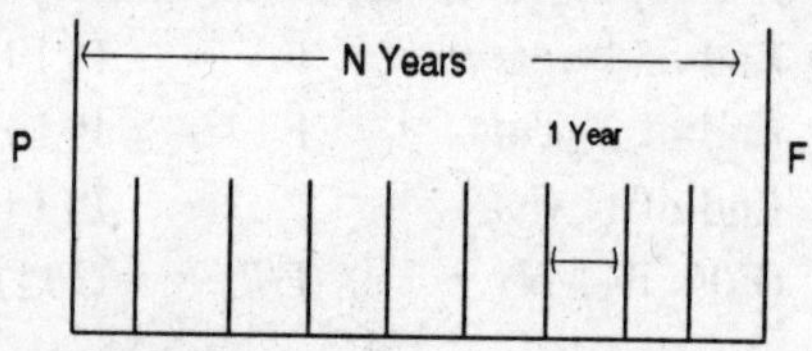

or $F = \dfrac{A\,(1+i)^N - 1}{i}$ A is also called Annuity.

i.e. if we set aside Rs. 1000 every year at 5% interest rate (compound) to provide for some future expenditure, we will have at the end of 20 years:

$$F = \frac{1000\,(1 + 0.05)^{20} - 1}{0.05}$$

$$= \text{Rs. } 33{,}100$$

It is possible that we would be interested in the present value of an annuity running for N years.

We know that

$$F = P(1+i)^N$$

Equating the two and solving for P, we get

$$P = \frac{A(1+i)^N - 1}{i(1+i)}$$

In other words, the present value of Rs. 1000/- per year set aside for 20 years at 5% compound interest will be.

$$P = \frac{1000(21+0.05)^{20}}{0.05(1+0.05)} = \text{Rs. } 12{,}460$$

Therefore, a sum of Rs. 12,460 set aside for 20 years will yield Rs. 33,100 at the compound interest rate of 5%. On engineering problems we often have to provide for a certain fund after a certain period of years.

$$A = \frac{F_i}{(1+i)^N - 1}$$

In order to arrive at the annuity to be provided for the present sum invested for a certain period invested at a certain interest rate:

$$A = \frac{P.i(1+i)^N}{(1+i)^N - 1}$$

This is called the capital recovery factor, e.g. to recover the present capital investment of Rs. 1,00,000/- over 20 years allowing for 7% compound interest, we should recover every year:

$$A = \frac{1{,}00{,}000 \times 0.07(1+0.07)^{20}}{(1+0.07)^{20} - 1} = \text{Rs. } 9{,}440$$

Sources of Funding

The most important funding agencies are:

1. *Institutional Agencies –*

   (a) Cooperatives
   (b) Commercial Banks
   (c) Government Department
   (d) Power Finance Corporation

(e) Industrial Development Bank* of India (IDBI)

(f) NABARD

2. *Non-Institutional and Other Agencies* –

(a) International Development Association (IDA) – a soft lending window of the World Bank,

(b) Asian Development Bank,

(c) Professional, and

(d) Others.

The Commercial Banks and Cooperative Societies also play an important role in lending. However, commercial banks finance projects for not more than 10 years period. Thus, their limit is 7 years to 10 years. Government Departments also finance the medium and long-term projects but their lending contribution is not much. Further, the International Development Association also finances the medium and long term projects and finances the projects of the developing countries which intend to develop their economic base with sustained development either in agriculture or industry. But much preference is given to low developed countries. IDBI is the bank that supports many developments and financial institutions. Also it has continued its thrust in the core sector industries such as fertilisers, petrochemicals, steel, cement and capital goods.

COST-BENEFIT ANALYSIS

This consists essentially of two parts *viz.* (i) calculation of present value of costs and benefits, and (ii) the computation of the indices.

Table 1 provides the formulation of computation of present value of costs and benefits for different patterns of cash flows.

The cost and benefit data from a proposed activity may be summarized by a variety of grand indexes, suitable for use with different decision criteria. They are:

---

*There are almost as many IDBI offices and branches as there are States in India.

(i) Net benefits $= \sum_{t=1}^{n} \frac{B_t}{(1+r)^t} - C_0 + \sum_{t=1}^{n} \frac{C_t}{(1+r)^t}$

where

r = discount rate

n = total number of years activity i.e. action will yield benefits

C_o = initial cost (beginning of first year)

C_t = continuing annual costs

B_t = annual benefits

Table 1 : Formulation of Present Value and Related Computation

Cash flow type 1:

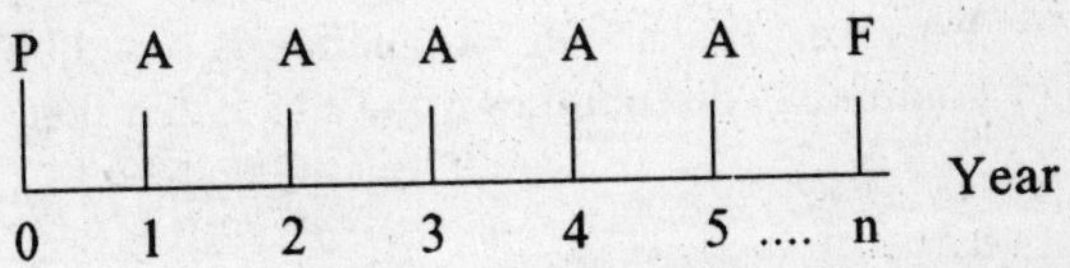

Given	Find	By multiplying	Factor designation
P	F	$(1+r)^n$	
F	P	$(1+r)^{-n}$	present value factor
A	F	$\frac{(1+r)^n - 1}{r}$	
F	A	$\frac{r}{(1+r)^n - 1}$	Sinking fund factor
A	P	$\frac{(1+r)^n - 1}{r(1+r)^{-n}}$	
P	A	$\frac{r(1+r)^n}{(1+r)^n - 1}$	Capital recovery

Cash flow type 2 : Uniform Gradient Series

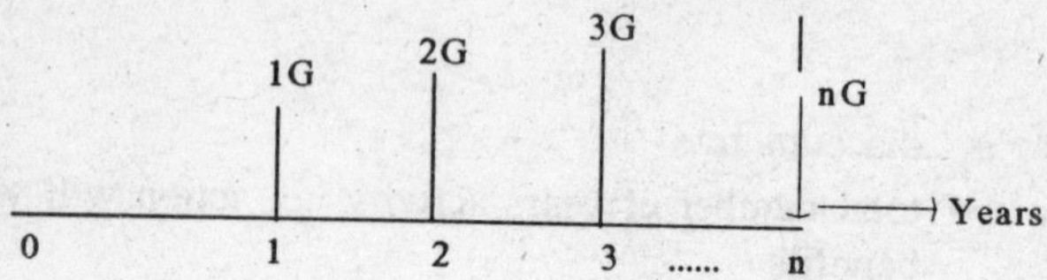

$$P \qquad G \quad \frac{(1+r)^{n+1} - (1+nr+r)}{r^2 (1+r)^n}$$ Gradient series factor

Other uniform Gradient series can be dealt by adopting the uniform Gradient series suitably.

However, the above formulation is based on annual discounting. For continuous discounting it may be noted that

$$\lim_{\substack{n - \alpha \\ t - 0}} (1 + i\,\Delta t)^n \longrightarrow e^{it}$$

Notations:

P = Present value

F = Future value

r = Discount rate

A = Equal annual investment at the end of each year.

The net benefits is a useful decision criterion when the only concern is the absolute amount of benefit. However, in view of opportunity costs (the loss of interest on capital not invested elsewhere), it is more likely that decision-makers will be interested in the benefit per unit of investment (the benefit/cost ratio).

(ii) Benefit- Cost ratio $= \dfrac{\sum_{t=1}^{n} \left(\dfrac{B_t}{(1+r)^t}\right)}{C_o + \sum_{t=1}^{n} \left(\dfrac{C_t}{(1+r)^t}\right)}$

(iii) Net Benefit-Cost ratio = $\dfrac{\sum_{t=1}^{n} (B_t/(1+r)^t) - Co + \sum_{t=1}^{n} \dfrac{C_t}{(1+r)^t}}{C_o + \sum_{t=1}^{n} \dfrac{C_t}{(1+r)^t}}$

(iv) Sometimes the main concern is the amount of initial capital that must be invested relative to net benefits in subsequent years. In this case information may be usefully presented as the capital-output ratio, in which initial costs are divided by discounted benefits minus discounted operating costs :

$$\text{Capital-Output ratio} = \frac{C_o}{\sum_{i=1}^{n} (B_t - C_t)/(1+r)^t}$$

This signifies that we are assuming construction takes one year. If the construction takes several years, the second and subsequent year's construction costs should also be discounted.

(v) Internal rate of return: The internal rate of return is that discount rate at which present value of benefits is equal to the present value of costs

$$\text{i.e.}\ \sum_{t=1}^{n} \frac{B_t}{(1+i)^t} = \sum_{t=0}^{n} \frac{C_t}{(1+i)^t}$$

We can determine i by solving this equation by trial and error. Such a discount rate is called the internal rate of return. The internal rate of return does not separate initial costs from continuing costs i.e. operating costs , as costs are summed starting the first year (t=o). If it is intended to separate initial from continuing costs, then we may calculate the rate of return at which initial costs equal the present value of net benefits during the operation, *i.e.*

$$C_o = \sum_{t=1}^{n} \frac{B_t - C_t}{(1+i)}$$

In this case i is termed the investment rate of return.

There are also parallels between the values for these measures. The following comparison points out these relationships:

TABLE 1

	Project Index			Remarks
	NP_v	B – C ratio	IRR	
if	> O	> 1	and IRR>r	Project acceptable
if	< O	< 1	and IRR<r	Project rejected
if	= O	= 1	and IRR=r	Marginal project

Gittinger (1982) presented a comparative analysis of these three measures. In Table 2 which is an adaptation of Gittinger table, one may distinguish between project selection or ranking under three conditions, independent projects with no constraints on costs, independent projects with an overall constraint on costs, and mutually exclusive projects. For independent projects in the absence of cost constraints, each of the three measures can be used to select or reject projects. However, when there is a constraint on costs for independent projects, such that not all justifiable projects can be selected, only the B–C ratio measure can give correct ranking for project selection. For the B–C ratio ranking to be correct, it must be formulated so that the costs constraint appear in the denominator of the ratio. For mutually exclusive projects (such as two or more projects using the same site) the NPV measure is the only one that will always lead to the correct selection. In all the above cases, 'Correct' selection or ranking is defined as the one that yields the largest present value. More complex rules are required than the above for special situations such as scheduling of projects over time.

TABLE 2

COMPARISON OF THE THREE MEASURES OF PRESENT VALUE

	Net present value	Internal rate of return	Benefit-Cost ratio
Selection or ranking rule for:			
Independent projects:			
No constraint on costs	Select all projects with NPV>O; project ranking not required	Select all projects with IRR greater than cut-off rate of return; project ranking not required	Select all projects B–C 1; project ranking not required
Constraint on costs	Not suitable for ranking projects	Ranking all projects by IRR may give incorrect ranking	Ranking all projects by B–C where C is defined as constrained cost will always give correct ranking
Mutually exclusive projects (no constraint on costs)	Select alternative with largest NPV	Selection of alternative with highest IRR may give incorrect result	Selection of Alternative with highest B-C may give incorrect result
Discount rate	Appropriate discount rate must be adopted	No discount rate required but cut-off rate cf return must be adopted	Appropriate discount rate must be adopted

Source: Adapted from Gittinger (1982)

AMORTIZATION PLAN

Table 3 illustrates how to compute the constant annual amount necessary to repay a loan with interest using the capital recovery factor (also called the partial payment factor or annual payment factor). The amount of each instalment is the same each year, but it consists of varying amounts of interest and principal repayment. There may be two alternatives given as under:

1. Assume the interest during the grace period will be paid when it falls due and assuming the interest due during the grace period will be added to the principal ('Capitalized'). Since the gestation period of the irrigation projects particularly the canal, dam, reservoir etc. is longer as such there is no output of the project in the beginning for several years.
2. Generally, these projects take a longer time for their implementation and much risk and uncertainty are involved. The amortization plan can suitably be formulated by the organisation which intend to receive the loan from the lending institutions. There can be several alternatives for formulating the amortization plan, which should be mutually agreed upon. These amortization plans can be based on:
   - (i) Assuming that no payment of the principal amount will be made during project's life and the entire amount would be paid at the end, if it is agreed upon by the lending institution.
   - (ii) Assuming that interest would be paid every year till the end of project's life and the principal amount would be paid at the end of the project's life.
   - (iii) Assuming that a certain fixed amount for repayment of the principal amount would be paid alongwith the interest on the balance principal amount.

These three alternatives are given in Table 3.

A hypothetical case is presented, with the given alternatives.

Problem 1:

A village water supply scheme is financed by a borrowing of Rs. 30,00,000 at 9% interest for 30 years. The payment conditions are flexible so long as full repayment is made at the end of 30 years. In what form could we repay the loan ? Give an ammortisation plan.

Q. 1. Assuming that no payment will be made during project's life, how much amount should be paid at the end?

Q. 2. Assuming that interest would be paid every year till the end of project's life, how much amount should be paid at the end?

Q. 3. Assuming that a sum of Rs. 1,00,000 or Rs. 1,50,000 or Rs. 2,00,000 or Rs. 2,50,000 + interest every year would be paid, How much should be paid at the end? (Total amount).

Compare all the alternatives and suggest suitable repayment schedule from the point of view of the Financing Agency and receiving organisation as well.

It is required to find out different alternatives for loan repayment.

(1) Future amount $F = P(1 + i)^n$

where i = Rate of interest

n = No. of years

P = Principal amount

F = Rs. $30,00,000\ (1 + 0.09)^{30}$

= Rs. 39803034

(2) Amount of interest per year on Rs. 30 lakhs:

$$\frac{9}{100} \times 30 = 2.70 \text{ lakhs}$$

Total interest for 30 years = 2.70 x 30 = Rs. 81 lakhs

Total amount to be repaid

= Principal + interest

= Rs. 30 + 81 = Rs. 111 lakhs

(3) There are 4 cases. In each case a fixed amount towards principal is paid every year and the interest is paid only at the end *i.e.* after payment of principal amount.

The interest on outstanding balance during loan period is calculated for all the four cases as detailed below:

Qn. 3 Assuming the payment is to be made as follows:

Rs. 1,00,000/- every year

or Rs. 1,50,000/- every year

or Rs. 2,00,000/- every year

or Rs. 2,50,000/- every year

Computation of amount to be paid as per different modes of payment, is presented as under:

TABLE 3

Case I – Payment Made of Rs. 1,00,000 with interest each year

End of yr.	Amount before payment	Principal amount paid	Balance after payment	Interest 9%	Total amount paid at the end (including interest)
1st	30,00,000	1,00,000	29,00,000	2,70,000	3,70,000
2nd	29,00,000	1,00,000	28,00,000	2,61,000	3,61,000
3rd	28,00,000	1,00,000	27,00,000	2,52,000	3,52,000
4th	27,00,000	1,00,000	26,00,000	2,43,000	3,43,000
5th	26,00,000	1,00,000	25,00,000	2,34,000	3,34,000
6th	25,00,000	1,00,000	24,00,000	2,25,000	3,25,000
7th	24,00,000	1,00,000	23,00,000	2,16,000	3,16,000
8th	23,00,000	1,00,000	22,00,000	2,07,000	3,07,000
9th	22,00,000	1,00,000	21,00,000	1,98,000	2,98,000
10th	21,00,000	1,00,000	20,00,000	1,89,000	2,89,000
11th	20,00,000	1,00,000	19,00,000	1,80,000	2,80,000
12th	19,00,000	1,00,000	18,00,000	1,71,000	2,71,000
13th	18,00,000	1,00,000	17,00,000	1,62,000	2,62,000
14th	17,00,000	1,00,000	16,00,000	1,53,000	2,53,000
15th	16,00,000	1,00,000	15,00,000	1,44,000	2,44,000
16th	15,00,000	1,00,000	14,00,000	1,35,000	2,35,000
17th	14,00,000	1,00,000	13,00,000	1,26,000	2,26,000
18th	13,00,000	1,00,000	12,00,000	1,17,000	2,17,000
19th	12,00,000	1,00,000	11,00,000	1,08,000	2,08,000
20th	11,00,000	1,00,000	10,00,000	99,000	1,99,000
21st	10,00,000	1,00,000	9,00,000	90,000	1,90,000
22nd	9,00,000	1,00,000	8,00,000	81,000	1,81,000
23rd	8,00,000	1,00,000	7,00,000	72,000	1,72,000
24th	7,00,000	1,00,000	6,00,000	63,000	1,63,000
25th	6,00,000	1,00,000	5,00,000	54,000	1,54,000
26th	5,00,000	1,00,000	4,00,000	45,000	1,45,000
27th	4,00,000	1,00,000	3,00,000	36,000	1,36,000
28th	3,00,000	1,00,000	2,00,000	27,000	1,27,000
29th	2,00,000	1,00,000	1,00,000	18,000	1,18,000
30th	1,00,000	1,00,000	NIL	9,000	1,09,000

TABLE 3 – *Contd.*

Case II – Payment made of Rs. 1,50,000 with interest each year

End of yr.	Amount before payment	Principal amount paid	Balance after payment	Interest 9%	Total amount paid at the end (including interest)
1st	30,00,000	1,50,000	28,50,000	2,70,000	4,20,000
2nd	28,50,000	1,50,000	27,00,000	2,56,500	4,06,500
3rd	27,00,000	1,50,000	25,50,000	2,43,000	3,93,000
4th	25,50,000	1,50,000	24,00,000	2,29,500	3,79,500
5th	24,00,000	1,50,000	22,50,000	2,16,000	3,66,000
6th	22,50,000	1,50,000	21,00,000	2,02,500	3,52,500
7th	21,00,000	1,50,000	19,50,000	1,89,000	3,39,000
8th	19,50,000	1,50,000	18,00,000	1,75,500	3,25,500
9th	18,00,000	1,50,000	16,50,000	1,62,000	3,12,000
10th	16,50,000	1,50,000	15,00,000	1,48,500	2,98,500
11th	15,00,000	1,50,000	13,50,000	1,35,000	2,85,000
12th	13,50,000	1,50,000	12,00,000	1,21,500	2,71,500
13th	12,00,000	1,50,000	10,50,000	1,08,000	2,58,000
14th	10,50,000	1,50,000	9,00,000	94,500	2,44,500
15th	9,00,000	1,50,000	7,50,000	81,000	2,31,000
16th	7,50,000	1,50,000	6,00,000	67,500	2,17,500
17th	6,00,000	1,50,000	4,50,000	54,000	2,04,000
18th	4,50,000	1,50,000	3,00,000	40,500	1,90,500
19th	3,00,000	1,50,000	1,50,000	27,000	1,77,000
20th	1,50,000	1,50,000	NIL	13,500	1,63,500

TABLE 3 – *Contd.*

Case II – Payment made of Rs. 2,00,000 with interest each year

End of yr.	Amount before payment	Principal amount paid	Balance after payment	Interest 9%	Total amount paid at the end (including interest)
1st	30,00,000	2,00,000	28,00,000	2,70,000	4,70,000
2nd	28,00,000	2,00,000	26,00,000	2,52,000	4,52,000
3rd	26,00,000	2,00,000	24,00,000	2,34,000	4,34,000
4th	24,00,000	2,00,000	22,00,000	2,16,000	4,16,000
5th	22,00,000	2,00,000	20,00,000	1,98,000	3,98,00(
6th	20,00,000	2,00,000	18,00,000	1,80,000	3,80,000
7th	18,00,000	2,00,000	16,00,000	1,62,000	3,62,000
8th	16,00,000	2,00,000	14,00,000	1,44,000	3,44,000
9th	14,00,000	2,00,000	12,00,000	1,26,000	3,26,000
10th	12,00,000	2,00,000	10,00,000	1,08,000	3,08,000
11th	10,00,000	2,00,000	8,00,000	90,000	2,90,000
12th	8,00,000	2,00,000	6,00,000	72,000	2,72,000
13th	6,00,000	2,00,000	4,00,000	54,000	2,54,000
14th	4,00,000	2,00,000	2,00,000	36,000	2,36,000
15th	2,00,000	2,00,000	NIL	18,000	2,18,000

Case IV – Payment made of Rs. 2,50,000 with interest each year

End of yr.	Amount before payment	Principal Amount paid	Balance after payment	Interest 9%	Total amount paid at the end (including interest)
1st	30,00,000	2,50,000	27,50,000	2,70,000	5,20,000
2nd	27,50,000	2,50,000	25,00,000	2,47,500	4,97,500
3rd	25,00,000	2,50,000	22,50,000	2,25,000	4,75,000
4th	22,50,000	2,50,000	20,00,000	2,02,500	4,52,500
5th	20,00,000	2,50,000	17,50,000	1,80,000	4,30,000
6th	17,50,000	2,50,000	15,00,000	1,57,500	4,07,500
7th	15,00,000	2,50,000	12,50,000	1,35,000	3,85,000
8th	12,50,000	2,50,000	10,00,000	1,12,500	3,62,500
9th	10,00,000	2,50,000	7,50,000	90,000	3,40,000
10th	7,50,000	2,50,000	5,00,000	67,500	3,17,500
11th	5,00,000	2,50,000	2,50,000	45,000	2,95,000
12th	2,50,000	2,50,000	NIL	22,500	2,72,500

COMPARISION OF DIFFERENT MODES OF PAYMENT

When both principal and interest are paid after 30 years................................ Rs. 3,98,03,034

When only interest is paid every year and principal amount paid at the end of life *i.e.* 30 years.............. Rs. 111,00,000

Amount borrowed (Rs.)	Mode of Payment (in Rs.)	Last payment at the end of Year	Total amount paid at the end (in Rs.)	Remarks
30,00,000/-	1,00,000 + Interest every year	30th Year	71,85,000	Long term Repayment suits to borrowing organisation
30,00,000/-	1,50,000 + Interest every year	20th Year	58,35,000	Moderate term Repayment suits to both borrowing agency & lending agency
30,00,000/-	2,00,000 + Interest every year	15th Year	51,60,000	Short term repayment suits to Lending Agency
30,00,000/-	2,50,000 + Interest every year	12th Year	47,55,000	Short term repayment most suitable to Lending Agency

Conclusion:

1. It is seen from the abstract that if the lending agency is a Public Sector Organisation, then borrowing agency can conveniently settle the repayment of the borrowed amount.
2. If the lending agency is a private organisation, then the efforts would be made to recover the borrowed amount from the borrower at an earliest possible time.
3. A mutual repayment finally agreed upon between the lending agency and the borrower would suit the most.

From the point of view of the borrower the alternative with the capital & interest repayment after the end of 30 years is suitable due to the current trend of inflation and escalation of prices. It is worthwhile to keep the loan pending for as long a period as possible as for any sum at a future date is much less than its value compared to present.

The plan which suits our financial need is the most attractive.

Problem 2:

A water supply project is completed on Ist January 1981 at a capital cost of Rs. 1,00,000/-, the useful life of the project is assumed to be 20 years. The value of the project investment at the end of period is nil. Rate of interest is 7%. The annual cost of maintenance is Rs. 5,000/- for first five years, Rs. 10,000 for the next five years and Rs. 15,000/- for next 10 years. The water sold during the first 10 years is 1,00,000 lit/year and 20,00,000 lit per year for the last 10 years.

At what constant rate the water should be sold to liquidate the project within 20 years without loss or profit ?

Solution:

The cash flow is in both directions. The only unknown factors is x, *i.e.* the price of water.

First calculate the present worth of cash outflow, all reduced to present worth at 7% interest. The outflows are taken in slabs of expenditure, i.e. 5 years, 5 years and 10 years.

Present value of Annuity of Re. 1/- per year at 7% during 5 years :

$$P = \frac{1(1+0.07)^5 - 1}{0.07(1+0.07)^5} = 4.1 \quad \text{for 5 years} \quad 7.02 \text{ for 10 years}$$

Also present value of Re. 1 at 7% paid at the end of 5 years:

$$P = \frac{F}{(1+i)^N} = \frac{1}{(1+0.07)^5} = 0.713 \text{ or say } 0.71$$

At the end of 10 years

$$P = \frac{1}{(1+0.07)^{10}} = 0.5083 \text{ or Say } 0.51$$

Cash Flow Pattern for the Scheme

Year	End of year payment	Outflow 1981 value	Inflow for 1981 value End of year receipt	
1980	1,00,000	1,00,000	–	–
1981	5,000		10,00,000 x	x 7.02
1982	5,000			
1983	5,000 (x 4.1)	= 20,500		= Rs 70,20,000 x
1984	5,000		–	
1985	5,000		–	
1986	10,000		–	
1987	10,000		–	
1988	10,000 x 4.1 x 0.71	= 29,200	–	
1989	10,000		–	
1990	10,000		–	
1991	15,000		20,00,000 x	
1992	15,000		–	
1993	15,000		–	
1994	15,000		–	
1995	15,000 x 7.02 x 0.51	= 53,500		x 7.02 x 0.51 = Rs. 71,50,000 x
1996	15,000		–	
1997	15,000		–	
1998	15,000		–	
1999	15,000		–	
2000	15,000		20,00,000 x	
		2,03,200		1,41,70,000 x

∴ 1,41,70,000x = 2,03,200 Hence x = 0.014 Paise per litre

Problem 3:

A piece of construction equipment costs Rs. 30,000. It has an expected life of 10 years and no salvage value. Cost of maintenance, fuels and lubricants, taxes, insurance etc. are estimated as Rs. 8000.00 for the first year and to increase by Rs. 500.00 each year. Find the uniform annual cost of owning and maintaining the equipment if the interest rate is 12%.

Problem 4:

As a Water Resources Project Manager, one is charged with the responsibility of purchasing a machine for the project. The related data about the alternative machines are as follows:

	Machine A	Machine B	Machine C
Present investment (Rs.)	10,00,000	12,00,000	15,00,000
Total annual cost (Rs.)	2,00,000	1,50,000	1,20,000
Life (years)	10	10	10
Salvage value (Rs.)	50,000	1,00,000	1,20,000

Select the best machine assuming 12% normal rate of return per year.

1. Given data

Solution:

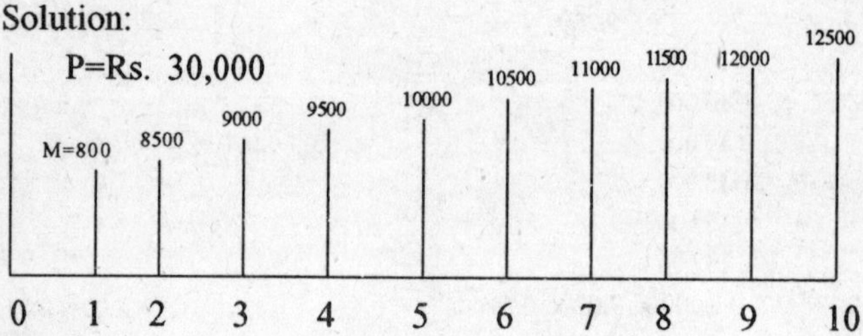

P	=	Rs. 30,000
M	=	Rs. 8,000
N	=	10 years
G	=	Rs. 500
i	=	12% or 0.12

(a) Uniform annual cost of owning the equipment

$$P\,(1+i)^n = \frac{A[(1+i)^n - 1]}{i} \quad \text{qr} \quad A = \frac{Pi\,(1+i)^n}{[(1+i)^n - 1]}$$

$$A = \frac{30000 \times 0.12 \times (1+0.12)^{10}}{[(1+0.12)^{10} - 1]} = \text{Rs. } 5309.52$$

Uniform annual cost of owing the equipment = Rs. 5309.52

(b) Uniform annual cost of maintaining the equipment

where, M = cost of maintenance, fuels etc.

G = growth or increase in cost.

$$= M + G\left[\frac{I}{i}\ \frac{n}{i}\ \left\{\frac{i}{(1+i)^{n}--1}\right\}\right]$$

$$= 8000 + 500\left[\left\{\frac{1}{0.12} - \frac{10}{0.12}\right\}\frac{0.12}{(1+0.12)^{10} - 1}\right]$$

= Rs 9792.36

2. **Given data**

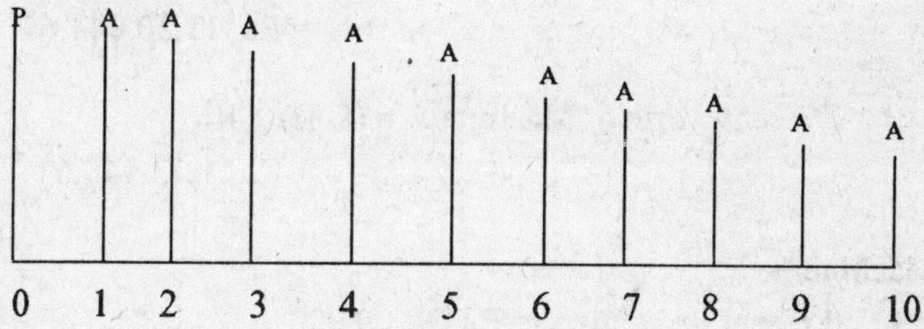

P	=	Present investment (Rs.)
A	=	Total annual cost (Rs.)
S	=	Salvage value (Rs.)
n	=	life (years)

	Machine A	Machine B	Machine C
P	Rs. 10,00,000	Rs. 12,00,000	Rs. 15,00,000
A	Rs. 2,00,000	Rs. 1,50,000	Rs. 1,20,000
S	Rs. 50,000	Rs. 1,00,000	Rs 1,20,000
n	10 years	10 years	10 years

(a) Machine A:

I. Present investment = Rs. 10,00,000

II. Salvage value (S) = Rs. 50,000

Present worth of salvage value $= \frac{S}{(1+i)^4} = \frac{50000}{(1+0.12)^{10}}$

= Rs. 16,058

III. Annual cost:

Future value of annual cost $= F_n = \frac{A[(1+i)^n - 1]}{i}$

$$F^{10} = \frac{2,00,000\ [(1+0.12)^{10} - \ ]}{0.12} = \text{Rs. } 35,09,747.014$$

Present worth of $F_{10} = \frac{F_{10}}{(1+i)^n} = \frac{3,509,747.014}{(1+0.12)^{10}}$

= Rs. 11,30,044.61

Present worth of Machine A = (I–II) + III

= Rs 21,13,946.61

(b) Machine B:

I. Present investment = Rs. 12,00,000

II. Salvage value = Rs. 1,00,000

Present worth of salvage value $= \frac{S}{(1+i)^n}$

$$= \frac{1,00,000}{(1+0.12)^{10}} = \text{Rs. } 32,197.32$$

Present worth of salvage value =

III. Annual cost:

Future value of annual cost

$$F_n = \frac{A[(1+i)^n - 1]}{i} = \frac{1,50,000\ [(1+0.12)^{10} - 1]}{0.12}$$

= Rs. 26,32,310.26

Present worth of $F_{10} = \frac{F_{10}}{(1+i)^n} = \frac{26,32,310.26}{(1+0.12)^{10}}$

= Rs. 8,47,533.45

Present worth of machine B = (I-II) + III = Rs. 20,15,336.13

(c) Machine C:

I. Present investment = Rs 15,00,000

II. Salvage value = Rs. 1,20,000

$$\text{Present worth of salvage value} = \frac{S}{(1+i)^n}$$

$$= \frac{1,20,000}{(1+0.12)^{10}} = \text{Rs. } 38,636.79$$

III. Annual cost:

$$\text{Future value of annual cost } F_n = \frac{A\,[\,(1+i)^n - 1\,]}{i}$$

$$F_{10} = \frac{1,20,000\,\{(1+0.12)^{10} - 1\}}{0.12} = \text{Rs. } 21,05,848.208$$

$$\text{Present worth of } F_{10} = \frac{F_{10}}{(1+i)^n} = \frac{21,05,848.208}{(1+0.12)^{10}}$$

$$= \text{Rs. } 6,78,026.76$$

Present worth of Machine C = (I–II)+III = Rs. 21,39,389.97

Summary:

Machine	Present Worth Value (Rs.)	Rank
A	21,13,946.61	II
B	20,15,336.13	I
C	21,39,389.97	III

The minimum Present Worth Value of the machine will be considered which indicates the best machine.

Hence, the best machine is machine B with the Present Worth Value of Rs. 20,15,336.13.

Problem 5:

A field study data of 150 farmers (by adopting an *Intensive Survey Method*), were used to prepare the financial crop budgets for a Dam's financing, which included inputs use, output expected, gross and net returns per hectare data. While preparing the financial crop budgets, present conditions and future possible outcomes in the light of improved technology taken into account.

The field data revealed the following facts:

Investment cost....	Rs. 2965.65 lakhs...	Ist Year
	Rs. 9885.50 lakhs...	2nd Year
	Rs. 6919.85 lakhs...	3rd Year

O&M from 4th year onward @ 2% of the investment cost.
Production cost : Rs. 7759.06 lakhs per year from 4th year onward
(including management cost)
Life of the Project: 50 Years

Q. 1. Compute Net Present Worth and B – C ratio of the project.
2. Compute Internal Economic Rate of Return (Use Interpolation Method)
3. Project be tested sensitivity to determine the effect of changes in the levels of the most critical 3 sets of variables:

(i) Cost of construction up by 10 per cent
(ii) benefits down by 10 per cent, and
(iii) combined impact of both costs and benefits *i.e.* costs up by 10% and benefits down by 10%.

Compare results before and after senstivity analysis.

Life of the project	Investment cost (10^5 Rs.)	O & M (10^5 Rs.)	Production cost (10^5 Rs.)	Total cost (10^5 Rs.)	Gross benefit (10^5 Rs.)	Incremental benefits (10^5 Rs.)	Present Worth of Incremental Benefits 35% DF	Present Worth of Incremental Benefits 30% DF
1	2	3	4	5 = (2+3+4)	6	7	8	9
1	2965.65	–	–	2965.65	–	–2965.65	–2196.778	–2281.270
2	9885.50	–	–	9885.50	–	–9885.50	–5424.143	–5849.408
3	6919.85	–	–	6919.85	–	–6919.85	–2812.518	–3149.681
4	–	395.42	4655.436	5050.856	10360.386	5309.53	1598.531	1859.014
5	–	395.42	5819.295	6214.215	12950.4825	6735.7675	1502.167	1814.138
6	–	395.42	6595.201	6990.621	14677.2135	7686.5925	1269.788	1592.479
7	–	395.42	7371.107	7766.527	16403.9445	8637.4175	1056.933	1376.513
8	–	395.42	7759.06	8154.48	17267.31	9112.83	826.066	1117.137
9	–	395.42	7759.06	8154.48	17267.31	9112.83	611.856	859.336
10	–	395.42	7759.06	8154.48	17267.31	9112.83	453.227	661.028
11	–	395.42	7759.06	8154.48	17267.31	9112.83	335.724	508.483
12	–	395.42	7759.06	8154.48	17267.31	9112.83	248.684	391.141

Contd.

Life of the project	Investment cost (10^5 Rs.)	O & M cost (10^5 Rs.)	Production cost (10^5 Rs.)	Total cost (10^5 Rs.)	Gross benefit (10^5 Rs.)	Incremental benefits (10^5 Rs.)	Present Worth of Incremental Benefits 35% DF	Present Worth of Incremental Benefits 30% DF
1	2	3	4	5 = (2+3+4)	6	7	8	9
13	–	395.42	7759.06	8154.48	17267.31	9112.83	184.210	300.871
14	–	395.42	7759.06	8154.48	17267.31	9112.83	136.452	231.444
15	–	395.42	7759.06	8154.48	17267.31	9112.83	101.076	178.034
16	–	395.42	7759.06	8154.48	17267.31	9112.83	74.871	136.949
17	–	395.42	7759.06	8154.48	17267.31	9112.83	55.460	105.346
18	–	395.42	7759.06	8154.48	17267.31	9112.83	41.081	81.835
19	–	395.42	7759.06	8154.48	17267.31	9112.83	30.431	62.335
20	–	395.42	7759.06	8154.48	17267.31	9112.83	22.541	47.950
21	–	395.42	7759.06	8154.48	17267.31	9112.83	16.697	36.887
22	–	395.42	7759.06	8154.48	17267.31	9112.83	12.368	28.373
23	–	395.42	7759.06	8154.48	17267.31	9112.83	9.162	21.825
24	–	395.42	7759.06	8154.48	17267.31	9112.83	6.786	16.789
25	–	395.42	7759.06	8154.48	17267.31	9112.83	5.027	12.914
26	–	395.42	7759.06	8154.48	17267.31	9112.83	3.724	9.934

27	–	395.42	7759.06	8154.48	17267.31	9112.83	2.758	7.642
28	–	395.42	7759.06	8154.48	17267.31	9112.83	2.043	5.878
29	–	395.42	7759.06	8154.48	17267.31	9112.83	1.513	4.522
30	–	395.42	7759.06	8154.48	17267.31	9112.83	1.121	3.478
31	–	395.42	7759.06	8154.48	17267.31	9112.83	0.830	2.676
32	–	395.42	7759.06	8154.48	17267.31	9112.83	0.615	2.058
33	–	395.42	7759.06	8154.48	17267.31	9112.83	0.456	1.583
34	–	395.42	7759.06	8154.48	17267.31	9112.83	0.338	1.218
35	–	395.42	7759.06	8154.48	17267.31	9112.83	0.250	0.937
36	–	395.42	7759.06	8154.48	17267.31	9112.83	0.185	0.721
37	–	395.42	7759.06	8154.48	17267.31	9112.83	0.137	0.554
38	–	395.42	7759.06	8154.48	17267.31	9112.83	0.102	0.426
39	–	395.42	7759.06	8154.48	17267.31	9112.83	0.075	0.328
40	-	395.42	7759.06	8154.48	17267.31	9112.83	0.058	0.252
41	-	395.42	7759.06	8154.48	17267.31	9112.83	0.041	0.194
42	-	395.42	7759.06	8154.48	17267.31	9112.83	0.031	0.149
43	-	395.42	7759.06	8154.48	17267.31	9112.83	0.023	0.115

Contd.

1	2	3	4	5 = (2+3+4)	6	7	8	9
44	-	395.42	7759.06	8154.48	17267.31	9112.83	0.017	0.088
45	-	395.42	7759.06	8154.48	17267.31	9112.83	0.012	0.068
46	-	395.42	7759.06	8154.48	17267.31	9112.83	0.009	0.052
47	-	395.42	7759.06	8154.48	17267.31	9112.83	0.007	0.040
48	-	395.42	7759.06	8154.48	17267.31	9112.83	0.005	0.031
49	-	395.42	7759.06	8154.48	17267.31	9112.83	0.004	0.024
50	-	395.42	7759.06	8154.48	17267.31	9112.83	0.003	0.018
						Σ 400450.4975		
							−1820.006	−202.651

Total Σ Inv. cost = Rs 19771

Note : DF means discount factor.

$$\text{Average Incremental benefit} = \frac{\Sigma \text{ Incremental benefits}}{50}$$

$$= \frac{400450.4975}{50}$$

$$= \text{Rs. } 8009.0095 \text{ lakhs}$$

$$\text{Total Investment Cost} = \text{Rs. } 19771 \text{ lakh}$$

$$\text{DF (i) for starting} = \frac{\text{Average incremental benefit}}{\text{Total Investment Cost}}$$

$$= \frac{8009.0095}{19771}$$

$$= 0.405089$$

$$= 40.5089\%$$

IERR = lower discount factor + difference between higher DF and lower DF

$$\times \frac{\text{(PW of total incremental benefit at lower DF)}}{\text{Sum of the Present Worth i.e. at higher and lower D.F.}}$$

$$= 30 + (35-30) \times \frac{-202.651}{(-1820.006 - 202.651)}$$

$$= 30.50092$$

$$= 30.50\%$$

Note: Minus signs are ignored.

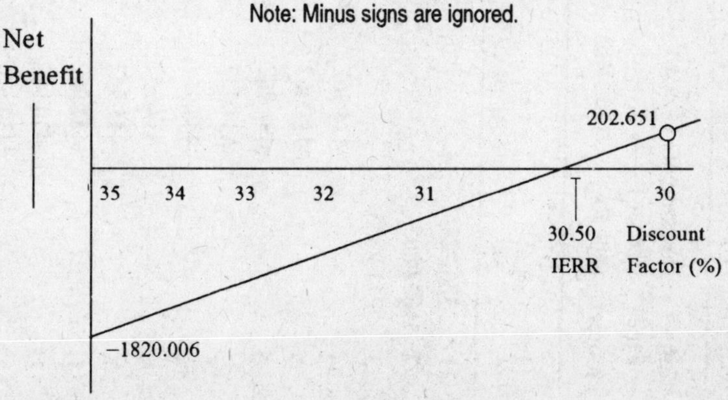

(2) Cost of construction up by 10%

Life of the project	Investment cost (10^5 Rs.)	O & M (10^5 Rs.)	Production cost (10^5 Rs.)	Total cost (10^5 Rs.)	Gross benefits (10^5 Rs.)	Incremental benefits (10^5 Rs.)	PW of incremental benefits	
							30% DF	25% DF
1	2	3	4	5 = (2+3+4)	6	7	8	9
1	3262.215	-	-	3262.215	-	–3262.215	–2509.3962	2609.772
2	10874.05	-	-	10874.05	-	–10874.05	–6434.3491	–6959.392
3	7611.835	-	-	7611.835	-	–7611.835	–3464.6495	–3897.2595
4	-	434.962	4655.436	5090.398	10360.386	5269.988	1845.1693	2158.5871
5	-	434.962	5819.295	6254.257	12950.4825	6696.226	1803.4884	2194.2193
6	-	434.962	6595.201	7030.163	14677.2135	7647.051	1584.2871	2004.6285
7	-	434.962	7371.107	7806.069	16403.9445	8597.876	1370.2188	1803.1053
8	-	434.962	7759.06	8194.022	17267.31	9073.288	1117.2896	1522.2451
9	-	434.962	7759.06	8194.022	17267.31	9073.288	855.6074	1217.7961
10	-	434.962	7759.06	8194.022	17267.31	9073.288	658.1595	974.2369
11	-	434.962	7759.06	8194.022	17267.31	9073.288	506.2766	779.3895
12	-	434.962	7759.06	8194.022	17267.31	9073.288	389.4435	623.5116
13	-	434.962	7759.06	8194.022	17267.31	9073.288	299.5719	498.8093

14	-	434.962	7759.06	8194.022	17267.31	9073.288	230.4399	399.0474
15	-	434.962	7759.06	8194.022	17267.31	9073.288	177.2615	319.2379
16	-	434.962	7759.06	8194.022	17267.31	9073.288	136.3550	204.3123
17	-	434.962	7759.06	8194.022	17267.31	9073.288	104.8885	204.3123
18	-	434.962	7759.06	8194.022	17267.31	9073.288	80.6834	163.4498
19	-	434.962	7759.06	8194.022	17267.31	9073.288	62.0642	130.7599
20	-	434.962	7759.06	8194.022	17267.31	9073.288	47.7417	104.6079
21	-	434.962	7759.06	8194.022	17267.31	9073.288	36.7244	83.6863
22	-	434.962	7759.06	8194.022	17267.31	9073.288	28.2495	66.9490
23	-	434.962	7759.06	8194.022	17267.31	9073.288	21.7304	53.5592
24	-	434.962	7759.06	8194.022	17267.31	9073.288	16.7157	47.8474
25	-	434.962	7759.06	8194.022	17267.31	9073.288	12.8582	34.2779
26	-	434.962	7759.06	8194.022	17267.31	9073.288	9.8909	27.4223
27	-	434.962	7759.06	8194.022	17267.31	9073.288	7.6084	21.9379
28	-	434.962	7759.06	8194.022	17267.31	9073.288	5.8526	17.5503
29	-	434.962	7759.06	8194.022	17267.31	9073.288	4.5020	14.0402
30	-	434.962	7759.06	8194.022	17267.31	9073.288	3.4631	11.2322
31	-	434.962	7759.06	8194.022	17267.31	9073.288	2.6639	8.9857
32	—	434.962	7759.06	8194.022	17267.31	9073.288	2.0492	7.1886

Contd.

Life of the project	Investment cost (10^5 Rs.)	O & M (10^5 Rs.)	Production cost (10^5 Rs.)	Total cost (10^5 Rs.)	Gross benefits (10^5 Rs.)	Incremental benefits (10^5 Rs.)	PW of incremental benefits 30% DF	PW of incremental benefits 25% DF
1	2	3	4	5 = (2+3+4)	6	7	8	9
33	–	434.962	7759.06	8194.022	17267.31	9073.288	1.5763	5.7509
34	–	434.962	7759.06	8194.022	17267.31	9073.288	1.2125	4.6007
35	–	434.962	7759.06	8194.022	17267.31	9073.288	0.9327	3.6806
36	–	434.962	7759.06	8194.022	17267.31	9073.288	0.7175	2.5445
37	–	434.962	7759.06	8194.022	17267.31	9073.288	0.5519	2.3556
38	–	434.962	7759.06	8194.022	17267.31	9073.288	0.4245	1.8844
39	–	434.962	7759.06	8194.022	17267.31	9073.288	0.3266	1.5076
40	–	434.962	7759.06	8194.022	17267.31	9073.288	0.2512	1.2060
41	–	434.962	7759.06	8194.022	17267.31	9073.288	0.1932	0.9648
42	–	434.962	7759.06	8194.022	17267.31	9073.288	0.1486	0.7719
43	–	434.962	7759.06	8194.022	17267.31	9073.288	0.1143	0.6175
44	–	434.962	7759.06	8194.022	17267.31	9073.288	0.0880	0.4940
45	–	434.962	7759.06	8194.022	17267.31	9073.288	0.0677	0.3952

46	–	434.962	7759.06	8194.022	17267.31	9073.288	0.0520	0.3162
47	–	434.962	7759.06	8194.022	17267.31	9073.288	0.0400	0.2529
48	–	434.962	7759.06	8194.022	17267.31	9073.288	0.0308	0.2023
49	--	434.962	7759.06	8194.022	17267.31	9073.288	0.0237	0.1619
50	–	434.962	7759.06	8194.022	17267.31	9073.288	0.0182	0.1295
		Σ=21748.1				Σ=396564.425	Σ=98.3775	Σ=2304.8242

$$\text{Average incremental Benefit} = \frac{\Sigma \text{ incremental benefits}}{50}$$

$$= \frac{396564.425}{50M}$$

$$= \text{Rs. } 7931.2885 \text{ lakhs}$$

$$\text{Total investment cost} = \text{Rs. } 21748.1 \text{ lakhs}$$

$$\text{DF =i for starting} = \frac{7931.2885}{21748.10} = 0.3646$$

$$= 35\%$$

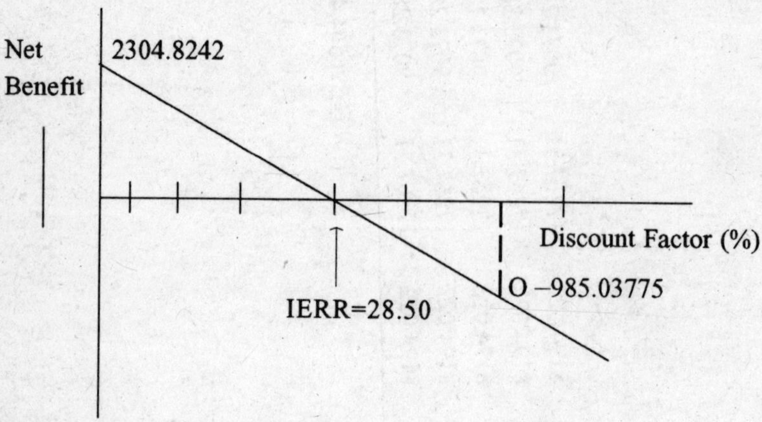

$$\text{IERR} = 25 + (30-25) \times \frac{(2304.8242)}{(-985.3775 - 2304.8242)}$$

$$= 28.50\%$$

Calculation of BC Ratio & Net Present Worth

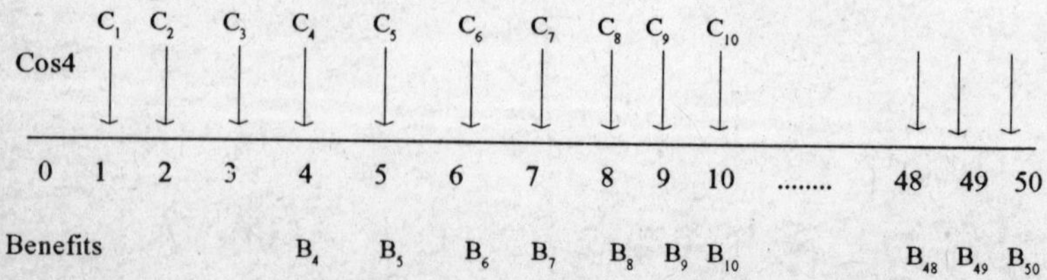

C_1 = Rs. 3262.215 lakhs B_4 = Rs. 10360.386 lakhs per year
C_2 = Rs. 10874.05 ” B_5 = Rs. 12950.4825 ”
C_3 = Rs. 7611.835 ” B_6 = Rs. 14677.2135 ”
C_4 = Rs. 5090.398 ” B_7 = Rs. 16403.9445 ”
C_5 = Rs. 6254.257 ” B_8 = Rs. 17267.31 ”
C_6 = Rs. 7830.163 ”
C_7 = Rs. 7806.069 ”
C_8 = Rs. 8194.022 ”

Present worth of cost = $PC_1 + PC_2 + PC_3 + PC_4 + PC_5 + PC_6 + PC_7 + PC_8$

$$= \frac{3262.215}{(1.12)^1} + \frac{10874.05}{(1.12)^2} + \frac{7611.835}{(1.12)^3} + \frac{5090.398}{(1.12)^4} + \frac{6254.257}{(1.12)^5} +$$

$$\frac{7830.163}{(1.12)^6} + \frac{7806.069}{(1.12)^7} + \frac{\dfrac{8194.022\,(1.12^{47}-1)}{0.12\,(1.12)^{47}}}{(1+0.12)^7}$$

= Rs. 61527.736 lakhs

Present worth of benefits = $PB_4 + PB_5 + PB_6 + PB_7 + PB_8$

$$= \frac{10360.386}{(1.12)^4} + \frac{12950.4825}{(1.12)^5} + \frac{14677.2135}{(1.12)^6} + \frac{16403.9445}{(1.12)^7} +$$

$$\left[\frac{\dfrac{17267.31\,(1.12^{43}-1)}{0.12\,(1.12)^{43}}}{(1+0.12)^7}\right]$$

B-C = Rs. 93381.4596 lakhs

$$\text{Ratio} = \frac{93381.4596}{61527.736}$$

= 1.518

Net Present worth = 93381.4596 – 61527.736
= Rs. 31853.7236 lakhs

(3) Benefits down by 10%

Life of the project	Investment cost (10^5 Rs.)	O & M (10^5 Rs.)	Production cost (10^5 Rs.)	Total cost (10^5 Rs.)	Gross benefits (10^5 Rs.)	Incremental benefits (10^5 Rs.)	PW of incremental benefits 25% DF	PW of incremental benefits 30% DF
1	2	3	4	5 = (2+3+4)	6	7	8	9
1	2965.65	-	-	2965.65	-	–2965.65	–2372.52	–2281.2692
2	9885.50	-	-	9885.50	-	–9885.50	–6326.72	–5849.4083
3	6919.85	-	-	6919.85	-	–6919.85	–3542.9632	–3149.6814
4	-	395.42	4655.436	5050.856	9324.3474	4273.4914	1750.4221	1496.2681
5	-	395.42	5819.295	6214.715	11655.4342	5440.7193	1782.8149	1465.3439
6	-	395.42	6595.201	6990.621	13209.49215	6218.8712	1630.2340	1288.3692
7	-	395.42	7371.102	7766.527	14763.55005	6997.0231	1467.3821	1115.0898
8	-	395.42	7759.06	8154.48	15540.579	7386.099	1239.1818	905.4580
9	-	395.42	7759.06	8154.48	15540.579	7386.099	991.3454	696.5061
10	-	395.42	7759.06	8154.48	15540.579	7386.099	793.0763	535.7741
11	-	395.42	7759.06	8154.48	15540.579	7386.099	634.4611	412.1338
12	-	395.42	7759.06	8154.48	15540.579	7386.099	507.5689	317.0260

13	—	395.42	7759.06	8154.48	15540.579	7386.099	406.0551	243.8662
14	—	395.42	7759.06	8154.48	15540.579	7386.099	324.8441	187.5894
15	—	395.42	7759.06	8154.48	15540.579	7386.099	259.8753	144.2995
16	—	395.42	7759.06	8154.48	15540.579	7386.099	207.9002	110.9996
17	—	395.42	7759.06	8154.48	15540.579	7386.099	166.5202	85.3843
18	—	395.42	7759.06	8154.48	15540.579	7386.099	133.0561	65.6802
19	—	395.42	7759.06	8154.48	15540.579	7386.099	106.4499	50.5233
20	—	395.42	7759.06	8154.48	15540.579	7386.099	85.1559	38.8641
21	—	395.42	7759.06	8154.48	15540.579	7386.099	68.1247	29.8954
22	—	395.42	7759.06	8154.48	15540.579	7386.099	54.4998	22.9965
23	—	395.42	7759.06	8154.48	15540.579	7386.099	43.5998	17.6896
24	—	395.42	7759.06	8154.48	15540.579	7386.099	34.8799	13.6074
25	—	395.42	7759.06	8154.48	15540.579	7386.099	27.9039	10.4672
26	—	395.42	7759.06	8154.48	15540.579	7386.099	22.3231	8.0517
27	—	395.42	7759.06	8154.48	15540.579	7386.099	17.8585	6.1936
28	—	395.42	7759.06	8154.48	15540.579	7386.099	14.2868	4.7643
29	—	395.42	7759.06	8154.48	15540.579	7386.099	11.4294	3.6649

Contd.

Life of the project	Investment cost (10^5 Rs.)	O & M (10^5 Rs.)	Production cost (10^5 Rs.)	Total cost (10^5 Rs.)	Gross benefits (10^5 Rs.)	Incremental benefits (10^5 Rs.)	PW of incremental benefits 25% DF	PW of incremental benefits 30% DF
1	2	3	4	5 = (2+3+4)	6	7	8	9
30	–	395.42	7759.06	8154.48	15540.579	7386.099	9.1435	2.8191
31	–	395.42	7759.06	8154.48	15540.579	7386.099	7.3148	2.1686
32	–	395.42	7759.06	8154.48	15540.579	7386.099	5.8519	1.6681
33	–	395.42	7759.06	8154.48	15540.579	7386.099	4.6815	1.2832
34	–	395.42	7759.06	8154.48	15540.579	7386.099	3.7452	0.9871
35	–	395.42	7759.06	8154.48	15540.579	7386.099	2.9962	0.7593
36	–	395.42	7759.06	8154.48	15540.579	7386.099	2.3969	0.5841
37	–	395.42	7759.06	8154.48	15540.579	7386.099	1.9175	0.4493
38	–	395.42	7759.06	8154.48	15540.579	7386.099	1.5340	0.3456
39	–	395.42	7759.06	8154.48	15540.579	7386.099	1.2272	0.2658
40	–	395.42	7759.06	8154.48	15540.579	7386.099	0.9818	0.2045
41	–	395.42	7759.06	8154.48	15540.579	7386.099	0.7854	0.1573
42	–	395.42	7759.06	8154.48	15540.579	7386.099	0.6283	0.1210
43	–	395.42	7759.06	8154.48	15540.579	7386.099	0.5027	0.0931

44	–	395.42	7759.06	8154.48	15540.579	7386.099	0.4021	0.0216
45	–	395.42	7759.06	8154.48	15540.579	7386.099	0.3217	0.0508
46	–	395.42	7759.06	8154.48	15540.579	7386.099	0.2574	0.0424
47	–	395.42	7759.06	8154.48	15540.579	7386.099	0.2059	0.0326
48	–	395.42	7759.06	8154.48	15540.579	7386.099	0.1644	0.0251
49	–	395.42	7759.06	8154.48	15540.579	7386.099	0.1318	0.0193
50	–	395.42	7759.06	8154.48	15540.579	7386.099	0.1054	0.0148
Σ=19771.00						Σ=320761.362	Σ=584.137	Σ=1591.6901

$$\text{Average incremental benefit} = \frac{320761.362}{50}$$

$$= \text{Rs. } 6415.22724 \text{ lakhs}$$

$$\text{Total investment cost} = \text{Rs. } 19771 \text{ lakhs}$$

$$\text{DF (for starting)} = \frac{6415.22724}{19771}$$

$$= 0.32447 \text{ or say } 32\%$$

$$\text{IERR} = 25 + (30 - 25) \times \frac{(584.1370)}{(-1991.6901 - 584.1370)}$$

$$= 26.13\%$$

Calculation of B–C Ratio & Net Present Worth

assume i=12%

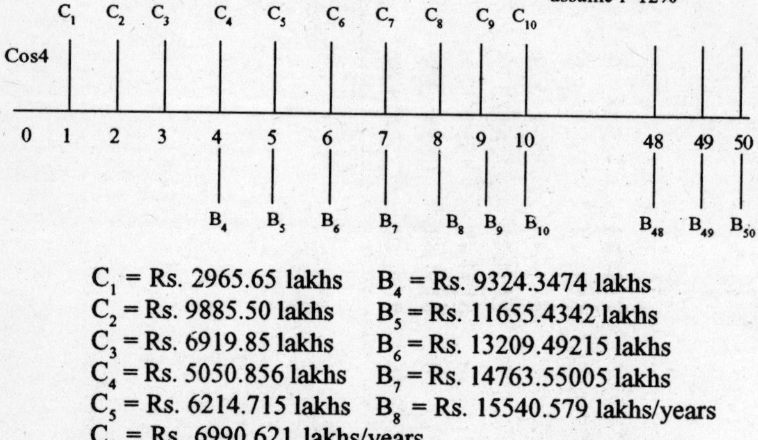

C_1 = Rs. 2965.65 lakhs B_4 = Rs. 9324.3474 lakhs
C_2 = Rs. 9885.50 lakhs B_5 = Rs. 11655.4342 lakhs
C_3 = Rs. 6919.85 lakhs B_6 = Rs. 13209.49215 lakhs
C_4 = Rs. 5050.856 lakhs B_7 = Rs. 14763.55005 lakhs
C_5 = Rs. 6214.715 lakhs B_8 = Rs. 15540.579 lakhs/years
C_6 = Rs. 6990.621 lakhs/years
C_7 = Rs. 7766.527 lakhs
C_8 = Rs. 8154.48 lakhs

Present worth of Cost = $Pc_1 + Pc_2 + Pc_3 + Pc_4 + Pc_5 + Pc_6 + Pc_7 + Pc_8$

$$= \frac{2965.65}{(1+0.12)^1} + \frac{9885.50}{(1+0.12)^2} + \frac{6919.85}{(1+0.12)^3} + \frac{5050.856}{(1+0.12)^4} + \frac{6214.715}{(1+0.12)^5} +$$

$$\frac{6990.621}{(1+0.12)^6} + \frac{7766.527}{(1+0.12)^7} + \left[\frac{\dfrac{8154.48\,(1.12^{43} - 1)}{0.12\,(1.12)^{43}}}{(1+\ 0.12)^2}\right]$$

= Rs. 59748.937 lakhs

Present worth of benefits = $PB_4 + PB_5 + PB_6 + PB_7 + PB_8$

$$= \frac{9324.3474}{(1+0.12)^4} + \frac{11655.4342}{(1+0.12)^5} + \frac{13209.49215}{(1+0.12)^6} + \frac{14763.55005}{(1+0.12)^7} +$$

$$\left[\frac{\dfrac{15540.579\,(1.12^{43}-1)}{0.12(1.12)^{43}}}{(1.12)^7}\right]$$

= Rs. 86,442.832 lakhs

$$\text{B-C Ratio} = \frac{66442.832}{59748.937} = 1.447$$

Net Present Worth = 66442.832 – 59748.937

= Rs. 6,693.895 lakhs

(4) Costs up by 10% and benefits down by 10%

Life of the project	Investment cost (10^5 Rs.)	O & M (10^5 Rs.)	Production cost (10^5 Rs.)	Total cost (10^5 Rs.)	Gross benefits (10^5 Rs.)	Incremental benefits (10^5 Rs.)	PW of incremental benefits	
							25% DF	20% DF
1	2	3	4	5 =(2+3+4)	6	7	8	9
1	3262.215	-	-	3262.215	-	–3262.215	–2609.772	–2718.513
2	10874.05	-	-	10874.05	-	10874.05	–6959.392	–7551.424
3	7611.835	-	-	7611.835	-	7611.835	–3897.260	–4404.997
4	-	434.962	4655.436	5090.398	9324.3474	4233.949	1734.226	2041.835
5	-	434.962	5819.295	6254.257	11655.4343	5401.177	1769.858	2170.612
6	-	434.962	6595.201	7030.163	13209.4922	6179.329	1619.874	2069.445
7	-	434.962	7371.107	7806.069	14763.5501	6957.481	1459.090	1941.705
8	-	434.962	7759.06	8194.022	15540.5790	7346.557	1232.548	1708.574
9	-	434.962	7759.06	8194.022	15540.5790	7346.557	986.838	1423.812
10	-	434.962	7759.06	8194.022	15540.5790	7346.557	788.831	1186.510
11	-	434.962	7759.06	8194.022	15540.5790	7346.557	631.064	988.758
12	-	434.962	7759.06	8194.022	15540.5790	7346.557	504.852	823.965
13	-	434.962	7759.06	8194.022	15540.5790	7346.557	403.881	686.636

Contd.

14	-	434.962	7759.06	8194.022	15540.5790	7346.557	323.185	572.198
15.	-	434.962	7759.06	8194.022	15540.5790	7346.557	258.484	476.832
16.	-	434.962	7759.06	8194.022	15540.5790	7346.557	206.787	397.360
17.	-	434.962	7759.06	8194.022	15540.5790	7346.557	165.430	331.133
18.	-	434.962	7759.06	8194.022	15540.5790	7346.557	132.344	275.944
19.	-	434.962	7759.06	8194.022	15540.5790	7346.557	105.875	229.954
20.	-	434.962	7759.06	8194.022	15540.5790	7346.557	84.700	191.628
21.	-	434.962	7759.06	8194.022	15540.5790	7346.557	67.760	159.690
22.	-	434.962	7759.06	8194.022	15540.5790	7346.557	54.208	133.075
23.	-	434.962	7759.06	8194.022	15540.5790	7346.557	43.368	110.896
24.	-	434.962	7759.06	8194.022	15540.5790	7346.557	34.693	92.413
25.	-	434.962	7759.06	8194.022	15540.5790	7346.557	27.755	77.011
26.	-	434.962	7759.06	8194.022	15540.5790	7346.557	22.204	64.176
27.	-	434.962	7759.06	8194.022	15540.5790	7346.557	17.763	53.480
28.	-	434.962	7759.06	8194.022	15540.5790	7346.557	14.210	44.567
29.	-	434.962	7759.06	8194.022	15540.5790	7346.557	11.368	37.139
30.	-	434.962	7759.06	8194.022	15540.5790	7346.557	9.095	30.949
31.	-	434.962	7759.06	8194.022	15540.5790	7346.557	7.276	25.791

Contd.

Life of the project	Investment cost (10[5] Rs.)	O & M (10[5] Rs.)	Production cost (10[5] Rs.)	Total cost (10[5] Rs.)	Gross benefits (10[5] Rs.)	Incremental benefits (10[5] Rs.)	PW of incremental benefits	
							25% DF	20% DF
1	2	3	4	5 =(2+3+4)	6	7	8	9
32.	-	434.962	7759.06	8194.022	15540.5790	7346.557	5.821	21.492
33.	-	434.962	7759.06	8194.022	15540.5790	7346.557	4.656	17.910
34.	-	434.962	7759.06	8194.022	15540.5790	7346.557	3.725	14.925
35.	-	434.962	7759.06	8194.022	15540.5790	7346.557	2.988	12.438
36.	-	434.962	7759.06	8194.022	15540.5790	7346.557	2.384	10.365
37.	-	434.962	7759.06	8194.022	15540.5790	7346.557	1.907	8.637
38.	-	434.962	7759.06	8194.022	15540.5790	7346.557	1.526	7.198
39.	-	434.962	7759.06	8194.022	15540.5790	7346.557	1.221	5.998
40.	-	434.962	7759.06	8194.022	15540.5790	7346.557	0.977	4.998
41.	-	434.962	7759.06	8194.022	15540.5790	7346.557	0.781	4.165
42.	-	434.962	7759.06	8194.022	15540.5790	7346.557	0.625	3.471
43.	-	434.962	7759.06	8194.022	15540.5790	7346.557	0.500	3.893

44.	-	434.962	7759.06	8194.022	15540.5790	7346.557	0.400	2.411
45.	-	434.962	7759.06	8194.022	15540.5790	7346.557	0.320	2.009
46.	-	434.962	7759.06	8194.022	15540.5790	7346.557	0.256	1.674
47.	-	434.962	7759.06	8194.022	15540.5790	7346.557	0.205	1.395
48.	-	434.962	7759.06	8194.022	15540.5790	7346.557	0.164	1.162
49.	-	434.962	7759.06	8194.022	15540.5790	7346.557	0.131	0.969
50.	-	434.962	7759.06	8194.022	15540.5790	7346.557	0.105	0.807
$\Sigma = 21748.1$						$\Sigma = 316925.787$	$\Sigma = 721.055$	$\Sigma = 3796.073$

Average incremental benefits $= \dfrac{316925.787}{50}$

$=$ Rs. 6338.51574 lakhs

Total investment cost $=$ Rs. 21748.1 lakhs

DF (for starting) $= \dfrac{6338.51574}{21748.1}$

$=$ 30%

IERR $= \dfrac{20 + (25 - 20) \times 3796.073}{(-721.055 - 3796.073)}$

$=$ 24.20%

Calculations of B-C Ratio and Net Present Worth:

PW of cost $=$ Rs. 61527.736 lakhs

PW of benefits. $=$ Rs. 66442.832 lakhs

B-C Ratio $= \dfrac{66442.832}{61527.736} = 1.405$

Net present worth $=$ 66442.832 - 61527.736

$=$ Rs. 4915.096 lakhs

Summary

Comparison of net present worth (NPW), B – Cratio and internal economic rate of return of the project before and after sensitivity analysis:

Conditions		B – C Ratio	NPW (lakhs Rs.)	IERR
Before Sensitivity Analysis		1.563	33632.523	30.50
After Sensitivity Analysis	Cost of construction up by 10%	1.518	31853.724	28.50
	Benefits down by 10%	1.447	6693.895	26.13
	Costs up by 10% and Benefits down by 10%	1.405	4915.096	24.20

The present worth technique is described to be easier and more direct. But it cannot be used to rank projects in order of economic desirability unless all require equal investment.

The rate of return technique has the advantage that it does not require a pre-determined discount factor but the complexity of trial and error solutions, many time misleads. However, interpolation method can easily be used for computing the internal rate of return.

The B – C ratio method is universally accepted. However, if incremental benefit and cost analysis is not adopted it gives misleading results.

The annual cost method has the same advantages and disadvantages, when benefits cannot be evaluated, the method cannot be used.

For details regarding NPW, B – C ratio and IRR, see Chapter 11 ''Economic Evaluation of Water Resources Projects''.

REFERENCES

1. James, L.D. and Lee, R.R. (1971), 'Economics of Water Resources Planning', Tata Mc-Graw Hill Publishing Company Ltd., New Delhi.
2. Irrigation Commission (1972), Report of the Irrigation Commission, Govt. of India.
3. Mande, O.D. (1980), Evaluation of Social Benefits and Costs of Conjunctive Use of Surface and Ground Waters in Gomti Kalyani Doab, unpublished M.E. Dissertation, WRDTC, University of Roorkee.
4. Mishra, S.N. and Bayer John (1976), 'Cost-Benefit Analysis – A Case Study of the Ratnagiri Fisheries Project', Hindustan Publishing Corporation (India), New Delhi.

CHAPTER 11

ECONOMIC EVALUATION OF WATER RESOURCES PROJECTS

Policy makers are much concerned about the best use of scarce capital and to maximise the economic returns or profitability of the capital investment to the whole society or economy, regardless who in the society contributes the resources and who receives the benefits. Since capital investment in the developing countries is intended to accomplish a specific objective, therefore, a well defined time sequence of investment should be made. For effective marshalling the necessary technical services, facilities, and resources for economic development, a coordinated approach at all possible levels, both in the process of planning and execution of projects/plans are required. This requires a systematic evaluation of programmes/projects which becomes a normal administrative practice in all branches of public activity. In view of the scarcity of capital, investment is subjected to careful appraisal before decisions on investment allocation are made. Evaluation[1] of development programmes/projects implies the application of the fact-finding process to the problems and methods connected with the implementation of these programmes. By evaluating the progress of a programme/project, it becomes easier to locate needs, identify some of the barriers to its success and thus, suggest ways and means to overcome these obstacles. Thus monitoring[2] and evaluation of

1. Evaluation assesses overall project effects, both intentional & unintentional and their impact. It involves comparisons requiring information from outside the project either in time, area, or population (Casley & Lury, 1982).
2. Monitoring is the provision of information and the use of that information, to enable management to assess progress of implementation and take timely decisions to ensure that progress is maintained according to schedule .... Monitoring is an internal project activity, an essential part of good management practice and therefore an integral part of day-to-day management.

the plans/projects are important aspects on which the success of a plan/ project depends.

Irrigation projects have many special characteristics, which make the task of economic analysis more difficult. In fact, technical analysis is not done in isolation. The technical aspects begin with engineering and technical specifications and covers the requirements of the projects as to quality and specifications of each type of components of machinery/ design, accessories, construction materials, labour, power, fuel, transport etc. However, an economic study assigns a value to each physical consequences and proceeds through a series of mathematical operations to condense these values into aggregate worth. Thus, assigning the value is the first step in the economic analysis and find a common value unit and to assess profitability of a project. Each monetary value must be identified by both amount and time. Hence, amounts in different time periods are made equivalent by multiplying future amounts by a factor[3] becoming progressively smaller into the more distant future.

The investment is, therefore, subjected to an analysis of economic justification. Though the analytical methods are of great help in identifying which project will improve the quality of life of the people for whom the projects are to be constructed. But, it is not intended that the economic analysis[4] will replace other judgements but rather it is to reinforce and provide one more tool by which judgement can be sharpened. The economic analysis thus provides a framework within which all aspects of the economic considerations of the projects are applied in a coordinated and systematic manner.

---

3. The discount rate is the time rate of decrease in this factor expressed in per cent per time period.
4. The economic analysis should be based on benefits and costs calculated at efficiency prices.
Efficiency prices can be estimated as per the following relationship:

$$EP = MP \times CF$$

where, EP = Efficiency price
MP = Market price
CF = Conversion factor

Conversion factors have been computed by the World Bank separately for traded and non-traded goods in some of its recent publications, *e.g.* Colin Bruce; Social Cost-Benefit Analysis: A Guide to Country and Project Economists to the Derivation and Application of Economic & Social Accounting Prices, World Bank Staff Working Paper No. 239. The International Bank for Reconstruction and Development, August, 76.

In brief, there are three stages in evaluation:

1. The first stage is one which covers evaluation before any change is brought out or any further change occurs in the existing situation, *i.e.* before the programme is implemented, which is in fact to establish a 'bench mark'. Evaluation at this stage is called 'pre-project' or 'ex-ante' evaluation, which assesses the technical, economic, financial and social feasibility of the project.
2. The second stage evaluation is conducted when the project/programme is in operation. This evaluation is called 'concurrent', which is very useful because it identifies loop-holes, or pitfalls and reasons of slow progress. This also suggests remedial measures for accelerating the progress of the project during the remaining period of its operation.

   In line with normal evaluation practice, a mid-term review/evaluation should be undertaken in order to assess the performance[5] of the project.
3. Finally, the third stage evaluation is conducted at the end, *i.e.* after the programme/project has run its full course, in order to assess the achievements. This evaluation is called 'ex-post'. Such an evaluation at the end determines the usefulness of the project/programme in its totality.

The time element in evaluation is also an important factor on which the utility of evaluation studies depends. Nevertheless, the 'pre-project' (or 'ex-ante') appraisal helps to ascertain the feasibility of the projects by means of discounting techniques *viz.* benefit-cost ratio, internal economic rate of return, internal financial rate of return, capital recovery etc. The concurrent evaluation which is done simultaneously, when the project is in operation, helps to identify flaws or pitfalls.

DISCOUNTING TECHNIQUES

The procedure of systematic use of discovering[6] factors to compare

5. Too many projects have floundered, at considerable loss to the investors, and indeed to the National Economy through waste of scarce resources, because the investment decisions were taken without clearly defined objectives and in-depth techno-economic feasibility studies.

alternatives (either different sizes of the same project or different projects) is called a discounting technique.

Four conceptually correct discounting techniques are:

1. Net Present Worth (NPW)
2. Benefit-Cost Ratio (B – C ratio)
3. Internal Rate of return (IRR)
4. Annual Cost Method.

Net Present Worth

The most simple discounted cash flow measure of project worth is net present worth (often abbreviated as NPW). This is simply the present worth of the incremental net benefit or incremental cash flow stream. The net present worth may also be computed by finding the difference between the present worth of the benefit stream less the present worth of the cost stream.

In other words, net present worth can be computed by subtracting the total discounted present worth of the cost stream from that of the present worth of the benefit stream. Thus, to work out the incremental net benefits, gross costs are deducted from gross benefits. In short, it is the discounted algebraic sum of benefits minus costs over projects' life.

$$PW = \sum_{t=1}^{n} \left[\frac{P}{F}, i\,\%\,t\right] \left[B_t - C_t\right]$$

The formal selection criterion for the net present worth measure of project worth is to accept all independent projects with a zero or greater net present worth when discounted at the opportunity cost of capital.

Benefit-Cost Ratio

A second discounted measure of project worth is the benefit-cost

6. The process of finding the present worth of a future income is called "discounting".

ratio. This is the ratio obtained when the present worth of the benefit stream PW_b is divided by the present worth of the cost stream PW_c.

The benefit-cost ratio[7] is not commonly used in developing countries. This is because the value of the ratio changes depending on where the netting out in the cost and benefit streams occurs. The cost and benefit streams should be discounted at the opportunity cost of capital, which may range from 12 to 15 per cent.

To compute the benefit-cost ratio, the present worth of the benefits is divided by the present worth of the total costs (*i.e.* investment cost plus the operation and maintenance, replacement etc.). The present worth PW_b of annual benefits B_t is:

$$PW_b = \sum_{t=1}^{n} \left[\frac{P}{F} \; i\,\%, t \right] B_t$$

The present worth PW_c of the costs C_t is:

$$PW_c = \sum_{t=1}^{n} \left[\frac{P}{F} \; i\,\%, t \; C_t \right]$$

Internal Rate of Return

Another way of using the incremental net benefit stream or incremental cash flow for measuring the worth of a project is to find a discount rate that makes the net present worth of the incremental net benefit stream or incremental cash flow equal to zero. This discount rate is called the 'Internal Rate of Return', which is the maximum interest that a project could pay for the resources used if the project is to recover its investment and operating costs, and still break even. It is the 'rate of return on capital outstanding per period while it is invested in the project'.

7. The absolute value of the benefit-cost ratio will vary depending on the discount rate chosen. The higher the discount rate, the smaller the resultant benefit-cost ratio and if a high enough rate is chosen, the benefit-cost ratio will be driven down to less than 1. It is important to note that the best project has the largest net benefits and not the largest benefit-cost ratio.

The internal rate of return is that rate of discount at which the net present value of benefits of a project becomes equal to zero.

More explicitly, the formula for the internal rate of return can be written as follows:

$$NPW(B) = \sum_{t=0}^{T} \frac{B_t - C_t}{(1 + r)^t} = 0$$

where,

B_t = benefits in each year
C_t = costs in each year
r = discount rate or internal rate of return.

The internal rate of return is stated to be determined through a trial and error procedure. Given the time stream of benefits and costs, one may arbitrarily choose a value x for r, discount the benefits and costs streams, sum up them up respectively and may find the difference between the two sums. If the difference is positive *i.e.* the net present worth of benefits is positive, the value of r is raised and the procedure is repeated until the net present worth becomes equal to zero. The internal rate of return, thus, calculated does not on its own provide a decision rule for choosing a project. However, its cumbersome computation can be made easier and shortened to some extent by adopting the following procedure:

Calculate the average benefits of the project *i.e.* gross benefits divided by the project's life. Then the average benefit is divided by the investment cost of the project which is generally much larger than the average benefits. This value may be choosen to begin with and discount the benefits and costs stream. This procedure reduces the computation to some extent.

The Internal Rate of Return is a very useful measure of project worth of return. If this is limited only to the economic analysis, then it results the "Economic Rate of Return."[8]

For computing the Internal Rate of Return, interpolation method can also be adopted, which can be applied through a trial and error in order to find that discount rate which will make the net present worth of the incremental net benefit stream equal to zero. The accurate

8. The Economic or Financial rates of return should always be rounded to the nearest whole percentage point, since the underlying projections never can justify the implication of greater precision.

Interpolation[9] is the method of finding a desired value between two values.

Thus, to begin with a certain discount factor can be used to estimate the internal rate of return. This discount factor is used to determine the present worth of the incremental net benefit stream. On getting the discounted present worth of the incremental net benefit stream as positive, at a certain discount rate, it signifies that the present worth of the project benefit is greater than the present worth of the cost. Hence, it is considered that the project pays a higher rate of interest and still recovers the resources invested. When the present worth of the incremental net benefit stream is negative, it signifies that at this discount rate the present worth of the cost stream is greater than the present worth of the benefit stream. The project does not pay such a high rate of interest and we need another estimate of the internal rate of return that is on the lower side.

The following formula can be adopted for interpolating[10] the value of the internal rate of return lying between discount rates too high on the one side and too low on the other.

$$\text{Internal rate of return} = \text{Lower discount rate} + \text{Difference between the discount rates (i.e. higher and lower discount factors)} \times \left[\frac{\text{Present worth of incremental net benefits stream at the lower discount rate}}{\text{Sum of the present worths of the incremental net benefits stream at the two discount rates, signs ignored}}\right]$$

The error introduced by interpolation is usually slight and it disappears when the result is rounded to the nearest whole percentage point.

---

9. In practice, it is better never to interpolate between intervals greater than five percentage points because wider intervals can easily introduce an interpolation error.

10. Adapted from J.P. Gittinger "Economic Analysis of Agricultural Projects."

Annual Cost Method

The annual cost method converts all benefits and costs into equivalent uniform annual figures. Decision rules resemble with those for the present worth method because each annual cost is a present worth times a constant capital-recovery factor.

EVALUATION OF DISCOUNTING TECHNIQUES

Each of the four discounting methods if used correctly select the same project, given the same data. However, each technique has its own advantages and disadvantages associated with it which should be kept in mind while selecting a particular method to apply in a given analysis.

The present worth method does not require an additional set of computations to apply the incremental cost principle. Therefore, this technique is described to be 'simpler, safer, easier and more direct'. Some experts are of the view that this method is 'logically prior to others, therefore its use' is recommended. The simple, direct expression of net present worth is conceptually straightforward and easily understood. But if one is dealing with a large numbers resulting it to be harder to visualize, it may lead to more frequently to numerical errors. Furthermore, the present worth method cannot be used to rank projects in order to economic desirability unless all projects under examination require equal investments.

The internal rate-of-return technique is a very useful measure because it does not require a pre-selected discount rate. Thus, internal rates of return are intuitively meaningful to many investors, as the resulting rates can be compared with those of many other types of investment. On the other hand, this technique cannot escape criticism mainly because of: (1) it gives ambiguous results due to dual solutions, (2) necessity of calculating incremental rate of return for inter-dependent projects, (3) the danger of people's accepting overall as contrasted with incremental rates of return as indicators of rank, and (4) the complexity of the required trial-and-error solutions. However, the advantages discussed above are important enough to make the internal rate-of-return method a valuable analytical tool.

The benefit-cost ratio method is almost universally used by Central and State water resources agencies and are expected to be used frequently. Krutilla and Eckstein based their analysis on benefit-cost mehtods, and Marglin's work shows it to be consistent with economic theory. On the other hand, the use of the benefit-cost ratio without applying the required incremental benefit-cost analysis can lead to serious errors. Interdependent projects should, therefore, not be ranked according to their benefit-cost ratio because each enlargement must pass the incremental benefit-cost ratio test. Nevertheless, the fact remains that the benefit-cost ratio method can lead to the same results as other correct discounting techniques.

One shortcoming of the Net Present Worth and the Benefit-Cost Ratio is that they depend upon an externally given social rate of discount. However, the Internal Rate of Return has an advantage in that it does not depend upon an externally given social rate of discount. It is difficult to find an appropriate social rate of discount.

The annual-cost method makes use of the constant multiples of the present-worth method and has the same advantages and disadvantages (except for the use of smaller numbers). But, the annual cost is sometimes preferred because more people are accustomed to thinking in terms of annual costs than the present worths.

Generally, one is faced with a question, which method should be used? The answer depends primarily on the purpose of the analysis. When one is working in a situation of a larger proportion of unquantifiable benefits, it becomes impracticable to use benefit-cost or internal rate of return techniques. Costs alone must be compared by using the present worth or annual cost method. There are complex problems which one has to face in calculating the internal rate of return or benefit-cost ratio and there is every possibility of more errors of interpretation, but computational work is a smaller segment of the total analysis.

Evaluation Under Uncertainty

The irrigation projects like most other projects are subjected to uncertainty in more than one way.

1. There may be uncertainty with respect to the data used in the analysis, which may be under-estimated, over-estimated or only a rough approximation. A part of the data may have been obtained through improper sampling and still other data collected with much care and by a good estimation procedure is subjected to uncertainty due to its estimated value. Thus, the uncertainty of the basic data used into the projections of projects benefits and costs reflects to uncertainty of the profitability computations of the NPW, B – C ratio and the IRR.

2. The project lies in future and the future is always uncertain by virtue of its nature. For example, unexpected events in future may adversely affect the projects' profitability. The unexpected events like natural calamity, technological innovation and so on, may reduce the project life. Thus, uncertainty due to unexpected future events cannot be incorporated in the analysis, whereas uncertainty related to project data can be incorporated.

The first type of uncertainty due to the expected variations of the project data around estimated values can be measured, but the second type of uncertainty caused due to unexpected events cannot be measured. Therefore, sometimes the first type of uncertainty is referred to 'risk' in order to distinguish it from uncertainty of an unexpected event.

The expected variations in the values of the project variables estimated from the basic data leads to variation in the project's profitability and hence the extent of variation in the NPW, B – C ratio and the IRR should be determined in order to test whether or not these values *i.e.* NPW, B – C ratio and the IRR are within the acceptable range for selecting the project. It is also likely that the project's profitability may vary more with respect to some variables than others.

Although there is no completely satisfactory method of handling project uncertainty, yet it can be done at various levels of analytical analysis. Nevertheless, there are three approaches for handling the project uncertainties. These are:

1. Traditional approach
2. Probability analysis
3. Sensitivity analysis

Traditional Approach

In the traditional approach, project uncertainty is handled by computing a 'minimum' value of NPW and IRR of a given project through over-estimating costs and under-estimating the benefits of the project. Generally a higher social rate of discount is adopted which takes care of risk and uncertainty. Still another approach is to consider a shorter life of the project. However, the shortcoming of this approach is that it may turn out to be 'over-conservative', which may even eliminate potentially profitable projects.

Probability Analysis

Probability analysis approach is the most advanced in dealing with project uncertainties which rejects the utility of a single value estimate of NPW and IRR, but it attempts to prepare a probability distribution of the values of the NPW and the IRR of a project. The probability of a given value of the NPW and the IRR indicates the likelihood of its being achieved. Based on the probability distribution of the NPW and the IRR, the decision maker considers the most probable value of the NPW or the IRR which the project can achieve. The decision maker selects the project if this value satisfies his choice criteria. The approach of the probability distributions of the values of the project variables, on which the probability distribution of the NPW and the IRR is dependent, requires that the probability distribution of the values of the project variables should be first prepared. This can be done either for all the variables or for those which, based on the sensitivity analysis, are found to be most sensitive. After doing all this, the NPW or the IRR are calculated for different probabilities which are simultaneously summed up to give probabilities of the respective NPW or the IRR.

Sensitivity Analysis

The third approach for the handling of project uncertainties is by employing the sensitivity analysis.

One of the advantages of the economic analysis of a project is that it may be used to test what happens to earning capacity of the project if something goes wrong. Since project estimates can be subjected to a considerable degree of variation and fluctuation and that the projections of costs and benefits can possibly be put to a high degree of uncertainty, therefore, projects/dam sites should be tested for sensitivity to determine the effect of changes in the levels of the most critical variables. The re-examination of results to see what happens under the changed variables of costs and benefits should be done in order to assess 'how sensitive is a project's/dam's internal economic return to an increase in construction cost or decreased benefits, or combined impact of costs up and benefits down by certain percentages.

Sensitivity analysis may involve three sets of variables:

(i) Cost of construction of project/dam up by 10 per cent or more.

(ii) Benefits down by 10 per cent or more.

(iii) Combined impact of both costs and benefits, *i.e.* if costs are up by 10 per cent and benefits are down by 10 per cent or more.

(iv) Costs of construction up by 20 per cent.

(v) Benefits down by 20 per cent.

(vi) Combined impact of project costs up by 20 per cent and benefits down by 20 per cent.

To illustrate the sensitivity analysis based on farmgate prices and international prices is also presented (hypothetical case Table 1, 2 & 3) in order to highlight their impact on the overall feasibility of the projects/dams.

Sensitivity analysis reveals that 10 per cent increase of construction costs of dams brings down the internal economic rate of return and similarly 10 per cent down in benefits influences internal economic return of dams site. However, the combined impact of these two critical variables further brings down the internal economic.

Sensitivity analysis may also be attempted with 20 per cent costs or benefit–one each at a time (costs up by 20 per cent ; benefits down by 20 per cent), and combined impact of project costs up by 20 per cent and benefits down by 20 per cent can also be attempted to show how far the project is sensitive to these parameters.

TABLE 1

Sensitivity Analysis of Proposed Dams with 10% (Farmgate Prices)

Dams Code No.	Internal Rate of Return (IRR) before sensitivity analysis, %	Intenal Rate of Return (IRR) with costs up by 10%	Per cent fall of IRR	Internal Rate of Return (IRR) with bene-fits down by 10%	Per cent fall of IRR	Internal Rate of Return if costs up by 10% & bene-fits down by 10%	Per cent fall of (IRR)
A	27	24	11	24	11	22	19
B	24	21	13	21	13	18	25
C	34	31	9	31	9	28	28
D	7	6	14	6	14	4	43
E	17	14	17	14	18	12	29
F	13	12	8	12	8	10	23
G	31	28	10	28	10	25	19
H	28	26	7	25	11	23	18
I	18	16	11	16	11	14	22
J	23	20	13	20	13	17	16

TABLE 2

Internal Economic Return of Proposed Dam-I Initial Costs and Benefits
(With International Price)

Year	Investment	O&M	Production Cost	Total	Gross Benefits	Incremental Benefits	DF12%	Present worth at 12%	DF11%	Present Worth at 11%
1	7453925	.00	.00	7439.25	.00	— 7439.25	.893	— 6642.19	.901	— 6701.96
2	24797.50	.00	.00	24797.50	.00	—24797.50	.797	— 19768.42	.812	— 20125.81
3	17358.25	.00	.00	17358.25	.00	—17358.25	.712	— 12355.26	.731	— 12691.83
4	.00	991.90	2540.00	3531.90	7898.00	3566.10	.636	2266.32	.659	2349.01
5	.00	991.90	2740.00	3731.90	8190.00	4458.10	.567	2529.65	.593	2763.98
6	.00	991.90	3120.00	4111.90	9282.00	5170.10	.507	2619.33	.535	2763.98
7	.00	991.90	3120.00	4111.90	10374.00	6262.10	.452	2832.66	.482	3015.98
8	.00	991.90	3120.00	4111.90	10920.00	6808.10	.404	2749.68	.434	2953.98
9-50	.00	991.90	3120.00	4111.90	10920.00	285940.10	3.337	22717.67	3.895	26516.55
	49595.00	46619.29	145680.00	241894.40	504504.00	262609.60	—	— 3050.56	—	725.45

Benefit-cost ratio at 12% DF = .951
Net present worth at 12% DF = -3050.56
Net present worth at 11% DF = 725.45
Internal rate of return = .112% or say 11.0%

TABLE 3

Internal Economic Return of Proposed Dam-I-Initial Costs and Benefits

(With International Price)

Year	Investment	O&M	Production Cost	Total Cost	Gross Benefits	Incremental Benefits	DLF 12%	Present Worth at 12%	DF13%	Present Worth at 13%	DF14%	Present Worth at 14%
1	2200.95	.00	.00	2200.95	.00	−2200.95	.893	−1965.13	.885	−1947.72	.877	−1930.63
2	7336.50	.00	.00	7336.50	.00	−7336.50	.797	−5848.61	.783	−5745.42	.769	−5645.06
3	5135.55	.00	.00	5135.55	.00	−5135.55	.712	−3655.38	.693	−3559.07	.675	−3466.22
4	.00	293.46	2100.00	2393.46	3512.60	1119.14	.636	711.23	.613	686.36	.592	662.59
5	.00	293.46	2440.00	2733.46	4053.00	1319.54	.567	748.74	.543	716.15	.519	685.29
6	.00	293.46	2540.00	2833.46	4593.40	1759.94	.507	891.64	.480	845.27	.456	801.75
7	.00	293.46	2540.00	2833.46	5133.80	2300.34	.452	1040.56	.425	977.71	.400	919.22
8	.00	293.46	2540.00	2833.46	5404.00	2570.54	.404	1038.20	.376	966.85	.351	901.04
9-50	.00	293.46	2540.00	2833.46	5404.00	107962.60	3.337	8577.53	2.876	7392.69	2.493	6409.13
	14673.00	13792.62	118840.00	147305.60	249664.80	102359.10		1538.77		332.81		-662.90

Benefit-cost ratio at 12%	=	1.055
Net present worth at 12%	=	1538.770
Benefit-cost ratio at 14%	=	.973
Net present worth at 14%	=	-662.90
Net present worth at 13%	=	332.806
Internal rate of return		= .133% or say = 13.0%

The wider repercussions of the Irrigation Projects may be examined through the project impact surveys which may cover the following aspects:

- Farm income (farm budgets),
- Income distribution,
- Employment,
- Returns to labour,
- Migration, and
- Regional impact.

SOCIAL BENEFIT-COST ANALYSIS

"The method of project-appraisal which attempts to account for all the direct/indirect impacts of a project is appropriately termed 'Social Benefit-Cost Analysis'

Genesis

The criterion which was initially adopted for project[11] appraisal was to examine whether or not a project was productive. The productivity was considered in terms of Govt. receipts from sale of water. But, it was soon realised that this criterion was too harsh for irrigation projects as very few projects could satisfy it. Therefore, with a view to assessing the benefits of irrigation projects (to follow Central Water and Power Commission's benefit-cost study of Hirakund Dam Project) and to evolve a more comprehensive criteria than the direct financial returns accruing to Government being the investing authority, the Planning Commission initiated studies of 5 major irrigation projects in 1958. These projects were:

1. Sarda canal in Punjab and U.P. region.
2. Gang canal in Rajasthan and Madhya Pradesh region.
3. Tribeni canal.
4. Damodar canal in West Bengal, Bihar and Orissa region, and
5. Cauvery-Mettur Project in the Southern coastal region.

These studies were carried out under a 'Committee of Direction' which was headed by Prof. D.R. Gadgil. These were completed by the

---

11. The whole complex of activities involved in using resources to gain benefits constitute the 'PROJECT'.

middle of 1961. The Report of the Committee highlighted the benefits accruing from irrigation in terms of double/multiple cropping, better quality crops, higher yields, increased income and employment. Indirect benefits also accrued from irrigation in the establishment of processing industires, expansion of consumer industries and trading in them. The Committee, therefore, recommended that benefit-cost ratio should be used for assessing the feasibility of new irrigation projects instead of traditional criterion of 'productivity' *i.e.* direct financial return to Government. The Planning Commission, Govt. of India, considered the report in Oct. 1964 and accorded their acceptance of the suggested change in criteria for assessing the feasibility of major and medium irrigation works. In accordance with another suggestion made by the committee, the Planning Commission also constituted a "Working Group" consisting of irrigation experts, economists, and planners for preparing a Manual of standard procedures and methods for working out the benefit-cost ratio.

The Irrigation Commission (1972) appointed by the Govt. of India also examined, interalia, the aspects of benefit-cost analysis and recommended for calculating the B-C ratio, the criterion 'Before Introduction of Irrigation' and 'After Irrigation'. This method has been followed for appraising irrigation projects in Planning Commission and Central Water Commission. Only such irrigation projects which have a B-C ratio of 1.5 or more are approved. This criterion of a minimum ratio of 1.5 was suggested in 1964 by a Committee set up by the (then) Ministry of Irrigation and Power, Govt. of India, for suggesting ways and means of improving financial returns from irrigation projects. However, the Committee did not specify any reasons for this recommendation. The Irrigation Commission also upheld this decision of a minimum B-C ratio of 1.5. The Commission also recommended the lower limit of B-C ratio of 1 to cover such projects which are intended to provide protective irrigation in drought prone or backward/tribal areas and also schemes for modernisation of existing works for improving their efficiencies, or to provide carry over storages over the years to improve dependability of water.

Limitations of the Current Method

Current method is based on 'before and after' concept, which is not a correct approach because even without a project some changes in agricultural production are likely to occur with the passage of time. Hence, in view of this fact, in terms of 'before and after' even such changes wrongly get attributed to the project which are even are not actually caused by it. Therefore, the proper way is to analyse the situation based 'on with & without project'.

There are three major limitations of the current method:

1. The annual cost – a component of total cost is composed of interest on capital, depreciation, operation and maintenance and replacement (OMR) costs. Interest is worked out on the total investment and not on decreasing investment (*i.e.* diminishing balance) due to depreciation. In other words, it amounts to recovery of cost more than actually invested, which is not justified. The correct method to account for is to calculate interest on the balance cost at any point of time, then the present value of all recovered costs[12] plus interest is equal to the initial investment.
2. According to current method of benefit-cost analysis, project selection is based on benefit-cost ratio. A smaller project costing, say Rs. 50 crores with a benefit-cost ratio of 3.0 is obviously preferred compared to another big project costing Rs. 80.0 crores, which may have a lower benefit-cost ratio 2.0. This is quite misleading. Although the bigger project would be much larger than that of the smaller project. Hence, the maximisation of benefit-cost ratio is not the correct approach for project selection. In fact, the correct underlying objective is maximisation of the present value of all net benefits over the life of the project, by adopting a reasonable and appropriate discount factor. This approach would also reflect society's preference for present consumption over future consumption.
3. Finally, the current method of benefit-cost analysis does not reflect the true socio-economic impact of a project. For example, cement, steel, foreign exchange etc. are scarce, therefore, the real worth of these is much greater than that of their market prices. Further, to illustrate, every project yields some 'social' benefits (in addition to economic goods/services) like:

12. This is nothing but the capital recovery factor because the component of capital and interest (which constitute the annual cost) can be easily obtained by multiplying the initial investment with the capital recovery factor:

$$crf = \frac{I(1 + i)^n}{(1 + i)^n - 1}$$

(i) Increased employment
(ii) Redistribution of income
(iii) National self sufficiency
(iv) Conservation of foreign exchange.

However, these cannot be accounted for in the current method of benefit-cost analysis. Presently, the only 'social' provision is to sanction a project with a lower benefit-cost ratio of unity, if it is to benefit drought prone, backward/tribal area. But this provision is rather qualitative which is hardly sufficient for project planning in a developing country striving for overall social welfare and progress. Hence the existing method of project appraisal has many shortcomings.

The profitability of any project is highly sensitive to the rate of discount. For example, a project which may appear quite profitable and attractive with a discount rate of 10%, may be reduced to unprofitable with a discount rate of 20%, and may be rejected. Therefore, a proper choice of discount rate is most crucial for project-appraisal.

Social Rate of Discount defined

The social rate of discount[13] is the rate at which the weight or importance attached to a unit of project benefit declines over time.

For the sake of convenience, the social rate of discount is assumed to remain constant during the life of a project. But, for benefit-cost ratio or net present worth calculations, the most appropriate rate is the opportunity cost of capital – that rate which will just result in all the capital in the economy being invested if all possible projects were undertaken which yield that much or more return. Normally, it is felt that the society has a longer time horizon, therefore its discount rate would be lower. Thus, a lower discount rate should be used for public projects than for private projects.

The present value of a project's benefits and costs will depend very much on the magnitude of the social rate of discount. A higher social rate of discount will reduce the net present value of a project and a lower rate will increase it.

---

13. The dependence of the social rate of discount (SRD) rests with the facotrs in the following form:

$$SRD = [(1+g)^{-e} - 1] + PTP$$

where, g is the growth rate of per capita consumption, 'e' is the elasticity of diminishing marginal utility of consumption and 'PTP' is the pure time preference rate.

The Social Rate of Discount

The project life lies in the future and the costs are incurred and benefits earned at different points in time, which raises the problem of reducing future costs and benefits to the present in order to make them comparable with each other. This problem can be handled by employing a *social rate of discount.*[14]

It may be questioned why should a tonne of wheat produced in 1985 be attached a higher weight than a tonne of wheat produced in 1993. It is logical, because (i) individuals as well as social groups attach a time preference which favours the present more than the future. Given every thing else, a tonne of wheat to-day is considered to be more valuable than a tonne of wheat to-morrow, and (ii) with the increase of income of an individual and society, the marginal utility of an additional tonne of wheat declines. At the income level of 1993, the utility of an additional tonne of wheat would be lower than its utility at the income level of 1985, provided the income level is rising over time.

Benefit-Cost Ratio

The benefit-cost ratio is used almost exclusively as a measure of social benefit *i.e.* for economic analysis and most commonly for water resources projects. It is never used for private investment analysis.

Benefit-cost ratio is computed, that is to say:

$$\text{B-C} = \frac{\text{Present worth of benefits}}{\text{Present worth of costs}}$$

The formal mathematical statement of the B-C ratio is as follows:

---

14. There are several factors commonly accepted for determining the social rate of discount. Some of these are:

    1. Present level of consumption of the society
    2. Expected growth of population
    3. Expected growth of consumption
    4. Diminishing rate of marginal utility of consumption
    5. Society's time preference *i.e.* society's preference for current consumption.

$$\text{B-C ratio} = \frac{\sum_{t=1}^{n} \frac{B_n}{(1+i)^n}}{\sum_{t=1}^{n} \frac{C_n}{(1+i)^n}}$$

where,

B_n = benefits in each year

C_n = costs in each year

n = number of years (or economic useful life of the project)

i = interest (discount) rate.

The computation of the benefit-cost ratio with a simple irrigation example is illustrated in Table 4. It is assumed that a small earth fill dam is to be built over the period of two years with a total cost of Rs. 13,500,000. After implementation, there is an annual operation and maintenance cost of Rs. 6,00,000 per year. The analysis is carried for seven years in order to minimize cumbersome calculations. At the end of seven years, it is assumed that the dam at that point has a 'salvage value' of Rs. 3,31,000. The salvage value is treated as a 'benefit' in the last year of the project.

Choice of a Discount Rate

To compute the B-C ratio, one has to choose a discount rate. Hence, there are three alternatives. Probably the best discount rate to use is the 'opportunity cost of capital'. Although, theoretically it appears to be good, yet it is difficult to apply as a practical working tool. Since nobody knows what the opportunity cost of capital really is? In most developing countries (including India) it is assumed, to be somewhere between 12 and 15 per cent. For illustration the opportunity cost of capital is assumed to be 12 per cent.

Another discount rate which sometimes is chosen for the computation of B-C ratio is the borrowing rate for the project to be financed. A third rate often suggested is the social rate of return – a rate which more adequately reflects the time preference of the society as a whole than does the opportunity cost of capital.

Another accounting convention can be introduced in order to

avoid any confusion. The accounting convention is that all costs and benefits are discounted for the first year and for each year thereafter. Even the World Bank usage is to discount both costs and benefits beginning with the first year, which has been adopted in computing B-C ratio in this illustrative example. Thus, by dividing the present worth of the gross benefits by the present worth of the gross costs, the B-C ratio is:

$$\frac{\text{Present worth of gross benefits}}{\text{Present worth of gross costs}} = \frac{\text{Rs. 17,394,00}}{\text{Rs. 15,217,00}} = 1.1$$

It is worth to point out that the total of the discount factors cannot be taken and multiply it by the total of the cost or benefit stream to come out with the present worth. Suppose the benefit-cost ratio worked out is less than one, then the present worth of the benefits at the assumed discount rate is less than the present worth of the costs and one is not recovering his investment. Hence, it is better to put the money in a bank at the assumed interest rate than to invest it in the project. Further, it must be noted that the absolute value of the benefit-cost ratio will vary depending on the discount rate chosen (Table 6). The higher the discount factor, the smaller the resulting benefit-cost ratio, and if a high rate is chosen the benefit-cost ratio will be driven down to less than one. In practice, it should never be done to compute the benefit-cost ratio using gross costs and gross benefits, but rather to compare the present worth of the net benefits with the present worth of the investment cost plus operation and maintenance costs,[15] (Table 5). This is adopted in

15. In United States of America it is a common practice to evaluate a project on the basis of its 'average annual net benefit'. Both the present worth of the benefits and the present worth of the costs are multiplied by the capital recovery factor to find their average annual equivalents.

$$\text{Average annual net benefit} = \left[\text{Present worth of benefits at 12\%} \times \text{Capital recovery factor at 12\% for 7 years}\right] - \left[\text{Present worth of costs at 12\%} \times \text{Capital recovery factor at 12\% for 7 years}\right]$$

Rs. 4,77,000 = (Rs. 15,382,000 x 0.219) − (Rs. 13,204,000 x 0.219)

United States of America where the benefit-cost ratio has been a common measure applied to assess the 'national economic development' effect[16] of water resources projects. If the beneficial effects, both quantifiable and non-quantifiable are judged to exceed the adverse effects, considering both quantifiable and non-quantifiable, the project/programme is considered to be justified.

Which Price to Use?

While making an appraisal of a project, the evaluation of 'costs' and 'benefits' is done using market/controlled prices of various inputs and outputs. This does not seem to be appropriate because resources like cement, steel and foreign exchange are very scarce and hence their real worth is much greater than that indicated by their market/controlled prices. Therefore, for proper project appraisal, it is necessary to adopt social benefit-cost analysis. This is all the more important for irrigation projects as they make tremendous socio-economic impacts.

Social benefit-cost analysis requires the use of 'shadow prices and their accurate determination is not an easy task. Nevertheless, despite of all its imperfections, inaccuracies and scope for controversy, social benefit-cost analysis is a better method of project appraisal.

It is worth to note that the whole question of shadow prices refers only to economic analysis. In financial analysis, actually the market prices are used. For various reasons, markets are imperfect, because there may be price controls, institutional rigidities, imperfect information about prices offered by competing sellers or buyers and so forth. Therefore, the use of market prices may introduce a significant error into the economic analysis of a project. The price of foreign exchange may be too low, which may favour projects, with a high import, or the wages paid to labour may be too high, tending to favour capital intensive projects over labour intensive projects. To avoid these biases in the economic analysis of projects, the shadow prices should be used instead of the market price. *For purposes of operational project analysis, a shadow price may be defined as that price which would prevail in the economy if it were in perfect equilibrium under conditions of perfect*

16. Each water resources project has three distinct impact:
    1. Effects on national economic development.
    2. Effects on environmental quality.
    3. Effects on regional development.

competition. Generally, there are three areas where shadow prices should be used. These are:

1. Foreign exchange-rate of exchange should be used
2. Commodities, which are important in world markets – World or International price must be used
3. Unskilled agricultural labour-marginal value product should be computed.

World market prices of wheat is more nearly a true measure of the 'value' of wheat than a domestic price. Rather, shadow prices should be used for all agricultural products irrespective of the consideration whether the product is intended for exports or domestic consumption. However, vegetables, cassava, meat and the like should be priced at the domestic price level. Agricultural unskilled labour's wages should be determined by the marginal value product of the labour.

Social effects of the Projects/Dams

If the principal aim of a project is to develop a more equitable distribution of income in the target population, emphasis should be placed on the extent to which it meets this goal. Similarly, if the objective is to generate employment, a thorough assessment of the job-creating impact of the project is required. Some of the following aspects/indicators should be incorporated in the assessment of social benefits.

(i) *Income distribution:* The extent to which, as a result of the project, the income of the poorest section of the population is expected to improve relative to that of the other section, should be recorded.

(ii) *Employment* : The extent to which the project can reduce under-employment and unemployment is required to be assessed. This can be quantified in terms of the number of man-years of work created by the project, with a distinction being made between permanent employment and employment during the construction phase. When a deliberate attempt is made to substitute machinery by labour, the cost (in financial terms) should be shown.

(iii) *Access to land:* If the project includes the land reform element, the distribution of land, and utilisation rights by type of tenure, 'without' and 'with' the project, should be covered.

TABLE 4

Benefit-Cost Ratio of Earth Fill Dam Small Scale Irrigation Project

(Thousand Rs.)

Year	Project costs: Capital costs	O&M costs	Production costs	Gross costs	D.F. 12%	Present worth at 12% DF	Total value of production (=Gross benefits	D.F. 12%	Present worth at 12% DF
1.	7500	-	-	7500	0.893	6698	-	0.893	0
2.	6000	-	-	6000	0.797	4782	-	0.797	0
3.	-	600	700	1300	0.712	926	6000	0.712	4272
4.	-	600	700	1300	0.636	827	6000	0.636	3816
5.	-	600	700	1300	0.567	737	6000	0.567	3402
6.	-	600	700	1300	0.507	659	6000	0.507	3042
7.	-	600	700	1300	0.452	588	6000	0.452	2712
						331*	(0.452)	150.000	
Total	13500	3000	3500	20000	4.564	15217	3[illegible]331		17394

$$\text{Benefit-cost ratio at 12\%} = \frac{17{,}394{,}000}{5{,}217{,}000} = 1.1$$

$$\text{Net present worth at 12\%} = \text{Rs. } 17{,}394{,}000 - \text{Rs. } 15{,}217{,}000 = \text{Rs. } 2{,}177{,}000$$

*Salvage value.

TABLE 5

Comparison Between Net Benefits and Investment (Including Operation and Maintenance Cests)

(Thousand Rs.)

Year	Project costs			D.F. 12%	Present worth at 12%	Total value of Production (gross benefits)	Production Costs	Net Benefits	D.F. 12%	Present worth at 12%
	Capital costs	O&M costs	Total costs							
1.	7500	-	7500	0.893	6698	-	-	-	0.893	-
2.	6000	-	6000	0.797	4782	-	-	-	0.797	-
3-7.	-	600	600	2.874	1724	6000	700	5300	2.874	15232
						331*		331*	(0.452)	150
	13500	3000	16500	4.664	13204	30331	3500	26831	4.564	15382

$$\text{Benefit-Cost Ratio} = \frac{\text{Rs. }15382000}{\text{Rs. }13204000} = 1.2$$

Net Present Worth at 12% = Rs. 15,382.00 – Rs. 13,204,000
= Rs. 2,178,000

* Salvage Value

TABLE 6

Benefit-Cost Ratio of Earth Fill Dam Small-Scale Irrigation Project — A Comparative Analysis

(Thousand Rs.)

Year	Projects' gross costs	D.F. 6%	Present worth at 6% D.F.	D.F. 12%	Present worth at 12% D.F.	D.F. 18%	Present worth at 18% D.F.	Total value of production (Gross benefits)	Present worth at 6% DF	Present worth at 12%DF	Present worth at 18%DF
1.	7500	0.943	7072.5	0.893	6698	0.847	6352.5	-	-	-	-
2.	6000	0.890	5340.0	0.797	4782	0.718	4308.0	-	-	-	-
3.	1300	0.840	1092.00	0.712	926	0.609	791.7	6000	5040	4272	3654.0
4.	1300	0.792	1029.60	0.636	827	0.516	670.8	6000	4752	3816	3096.0
5.	1300	0.747	971.10	0.567	737	0.437	568.1	6000	4482	3402	2622.0
6.	1300	0.705	916.50	0.507	659	0.370	481.0	6000	4230	3042	2220.0
7.	1300	0.665	864.50	0.452	588	0.314	408.2	6000	3990	2712	1884.0
								331*	220.12	150	103.9
	20000		17286.2		15217		13580.3	30331	22714.12	17394	13579.93

Benefit-cost ratio at 6% D.F. = 22714.12 ÷ 17286.20 = 1.31

Benefit-cost ratio at 12% D.F. = 17394000 ÷ 15,217.00 = 1.10

Benefit-cost ratio at 18% D.F. = 13579.93 ÷ 13580.30 = 0.99

*Salvage value

(iv) *Internal migration:* In countries with serious metropolitan growth problems, it is much useful to attempt evaluation of the probable impact of the project on rural-urban migration.

(v) *Nutrition and health :* If the proposed project is likely to be located in an area with recognized nutritional or health problems, its expected impact on these problems should be assessed. If a quantitative assessment is possible, the nutritional effects may be best described in relation to expected levels of daily protein and calories intake relative to present levels. In evaluating the health impact of irrigation and drainage projects, any potential adverse effects, for instance from malaria or schistomiasis, should be studied.

COSTS AND BENEFITS OF THE PROJECT

Economic analysis of projects is undertaken to compare costs with benefits and determine which among various alternative projects have an acceptable return. The costs and benefits of a proposed project, therefore, should be identified. Furthermore, once costs and benefits are known, they must be priced and their economic values determined. In project analysis, the objectives of the analysis provide the standards against which costs and benefits are defined. Quantifiable benefits and costs can be computed from the incremental production of crops' produce and costs to incur on production.

To compute the costs of crops production the inputs used for 'Without Dams' and 'With Dams' or 'Without Project' and 'With Project' condition should be considered for crop production. Similarly benefits for 'Without Project' and 'With Project' for crop production should be considered.

Components of Costs

While working out the costs of inputs, wages of human labour, cost of bullock labour/use of machinery, seeds, manure, fertilisers, pesticides, if any, irrigation, cost on account of transportation of inputs, interest on capital etc. for both conditions, *i.e.* 'Without Project/Dams' and 'With Project/Dams' are taken into account.

Benefits

For working out the benefits from crop production, farm gate prices or economic efficiency prices (*i.e.* shadow prices) should be adopted to arrive at the total benefits.

Quantifiable benefits to be used in the economic analysis can be computed from the incremental production of cereals, wheat, maize, barley and other crops, like sesames, alfalfa, fruits and vegetables, coffee, etc.

Further, the cost of production of crops should be based on the field data collected from the farmers interviewed which need to be adopted for estimating the production cost of crops in a situation of the created facility *i.e.* 'With the Project'. All benefits and costs are, however, calculated based on certain base year prices, but with suitable changes/adjustments for calculating the farm gate prices or economic efficiency prices. These prices should be used to calculate the gross benefits from crop production and new plantations. For example, a project life of dams of 50 years may be assumed. Since some technological improvements will occur even in the absence of the dams/projects, the 'Without project', situation reflects correspondingly increased production *i.e.* incremental benefits. On the basis of the costs and benefits stream, the internal economic return can be worked out and Net-Present Worth, Benefit-Cost Ratio of each Project/Dam may be determined.

The build-up costs (production) and benefits may be adopted from the financial crop budgets. The costs and benefits flow smoothly from crop budgets for computation of Net Present Worth, Benefit-Cost Ratio and the internal economic return.

Derivation of the Cash Flow

It can safely be assumed that the proposed projects when implemented would earn a stream of gross benefits through increased crop production. The investment cost, operation and maintenance, and production cost, when subtracted from the gross benefits, yield the net benefits.[17] This left over *i.e.* balance is a residual, which may be negative during first few years after implementation of the project. The residual is available (i) to recover the investment made in the project–the return of the capital, and (ii) to compensate for the use of the money involved in the project – the return to capital. This residual is the 'Cash Flow'.

17. After deducting the capital investment, and payment of operation and maintenance cost from gross returns the balance is residual return which is termed as 'Cash Flow'.

The total cost is composed of:

(i) Investment cost of dams/irrigation (*i.e.* canal) projects.

(ii) Operation and maintenance cost.

(iii) Production cost (including interest on capital/management charges)

The investment cost can be worked out from the available information and the production cost from the financial crop budgets. The gross benefits can be adopted from the crop budgets. For the computation of the internal economic return, it may be assumed that construction of projects/dams, is likely to take five to seven years and therefore investment cost may be assumed with a phasing of (say for five years):

– 10% in the first year of the total investment cost
– 25% in the second year
– 35% in the third year
– 20% in the 4th year
– 10% in the 5th year.

Keeping in view of the present situation, there is every likelyhood that 10% physical and price contingencies provided in the cost[18] estimates of project/dams may fall short. Also, the assumption is that the entire amount of investment in a particular year will not be at a point of time but in some instalments and therefore, in each year interest may be charged for six months only. However, operation and maintenance cost should be charged @2% of the investment from sixth year onward for the project/dam life.

The cost of production/cultivation per hectare includes cost of seeds, manure, fertilisers, pesticides, inter-culture, labour and machinery use, water charges, harvesting, transportation and interest on the working capital for six months in case of each cereal and vegetable crop except the plantation crops *viz.* citrus, coffee and tea (for these interest is charged for one year *i.e.* till their economic life). Besides, the management charges should also be accounted for, as the farmer is the Supervisor and Manager of his farm and also provides all the required labour except on some peak operational occasions when he hires labour. For

18. Gittinger suggests 'Since future price increases can affect costs only until work is completed, the overall inflation contingency allowance is built-up by applying the appropriate year and price increase factors to the unexpected costs at each year end (Gittinger, J. Price, Economic Analysis of Agricultural Projects, p 103).

estimating the total production cost, the cost per hectare, should be multiplied with the total cropped area in each project/dam's command.

The financial crop budgets prepared for each crop also give the gross benefits which can be estimated by multiplying the cropped area with the gross benefits of each crop. It can safely be assumed that at the full development about 60% of the total benefits would be achieved in the sixth year, 75% in the seventh, 85% in the eighth, 95% in the ninth and 100% in the tenth year only. Since, coffee, tea and citrus would yield benefits in the fourth year only after plantation, these have been considered in the fourth year and onward. However, intercropping between rows of plantations may yield benefits.

PROJECT CONSTRUCTION PERIOD AND OTHER PARAMETERS

(a) Project Construction Period

It can be assumed that the construction of projects/dams may take five to seven years to complete. The investment can be considered as discussed earlier, which should be determined as per time schedule expected for construction and its completion.

(b) Project Development Period

After completion of the construction of the project and commissioning thereof, it can be safely assumed that a period of five years or so would be needed for full development and realisaiton of 60%, 75%, 85%, 95% and 100% of the total benefits may be possible in the sixth, seventh, eighth, ninth and tenth year respectively of the project. This assumed rate of growth cf development appears to be slow, but may be adopted on the safer side.

(c) Net Annual Incremental Benefits

The cash flow *i.e.* annual incremental benefits should be computed by subtracting the total costs (investment cost, operation and maintenance cost, and cost of crop production) from the benefits. The present worth of these incremental benefits should be worked out in order to calculate the internal economic return/internal financial return.

(d) Annual Costs

Different components to be adopted for working out annual costs and computing net benefits stream are:

(i) For estimating annual costs, investment cost of construction of projects/dams should be taken into account.

(ii) Operation and maintenance cost @2% may be assumed.

(iii) Production cost of crops based on the future development potential should be included in the annual cost as a component of the total annual cost. However, annual cost of crop production should be based on the Farm Crop Budgets.

(e) Interest Rate

Interest rate[19] @12% (or the prevailing rate of interest in the project area) may be considered as a component of production cost of crops for the period of 6 months in case of annual/short duration crops other than plantation crops. But in case of plantation crops interest for one year should be charged.

(f) Discount Rate

For calculating the net present worth and benefit-cost ratio, 12 to 15% discount factor may be adopted which should be determined by the 'opportunity cost' of the capital.

(g) Life of the Project

The life of the proposed dams of 50 years and 100 years of canals may be considered for the economic analysis. This is the period for which provision for the capacity of the canals/dams may be made.

FARMGATE PRICES

Farmgate prices in a competitive situation should, in the long-run, equal the cost of production plus a reasonable return to all factors of production (land, labour, capital and management). For example, the government's decision not to allow wheat or rice or maize imports may

19. The only difference between the interest rate and discount rate is that the interest rate assumes looking from the present to the future, whereas discounting looks backward i.e. from the future to the present.

reduce total wheat, or rice or maize supply to that produced locally while total demand may remain fairly constant. The supply shortage which may follow could cause prices to rise. But, as local wheat/rice/maize production increases over time to satisfy demand, prices should adjust to the competitive level and returns to wheat/maize/rice producers will normalize.

Retail price information is equally important to the public. Properly collected retail prices could form the basis for calculating the marketing margins. Market price information in conjunction with farm management and farm cost data can provide farmers and businessmen with improved bases for making investment and resource allocation decisions.

Justification for Use of Farmgate Prices

Farmgate prices may be used in the economic analysis which may appear to be the best to value the output *i.e.* crop produce because it is at the point of first sale. Farmgate price is the price, the farmer receives when he sells his product at the boundary of his farm. Since agriculture in our country is the most important sector in the economy and will most likely continue to hold that role in the coming years, the value of its output will significantly effect the National economy and gross domestic product (GDP) of the economy. Although, Agricultural Production Statistics of area and production are useful to determine output charges, production variations and productivity over time, yet the measurement of agricultural sectors' economic growth cannot be determined by the changes in physical quantities alone. Hence, the prices of physical outputs, provides the basis for determining the value of production. The aggregate monetary value of production increases as the proportion of high value crops rises.

Farmgate prices in a competitive market equal the cost of production plus a reasonable return to factors of production in the long run. But, it would be presumptuous to assume that the farmgate prices of any particular product is at that level at any specific time. Therefore, a good beginning point is the farmgate harvest price at the peak of the harvest season, which may perhaps be very close to the lowest price during the seasonal fluctuation cycle. Hence, farmgate prices can be adopted/used due to the following reasons:

For various reasons, markets in our country are imperfect, therefore, imperfect information about prices offered by competing sellers, do exist. Since these imperfections exist, therefore, the use of market prices may introduce an error into the economic analysis of the projects/dams. Hence, to avoid these biases in the economic analysis of the proposed projects/dam, the farmgate prices can reasonably be used instead of the market and world market prices *i.e.* international market prices. Apart from this, the Govt. programmes of agricultural development are also focused on reducing continued dependence on imports, therefore, use of farmgate prices may avoid biases in the analysis. Apart from this, the consumers of the country may have preference for local/home produce for consumption. It is also much important to note that the imperfections have been introduced into the world market by the existence of commodity agreements, which sometimes may pose a problem to decide which price to choose *i.e.* which world market price to use for economic analysis. Also, some kind of considerations like the appropriate grades, the allowance for costs of marketing from the farmgate to the point applied where the world market is offered, for example, at the port. In view of these complexities, farmgate prices may be used.

Calculations to Determine Farmgate Prices: The calculation of farmgate prices should be made by working backward of the farmers' market prices collected by the Government Department/non-Government organisation. The margins or price differentials are affected primarily by product perishability, cost of transportation, time spent in marketing, and the number of intermediary in the marketing chain. The farmgate prices can be computed by estimating the effect of these factors which are the best estimate of true farmgate prices. These calculations may give the following results:

(i) Farmers' market prices for non-perishable products such as grains, may be reduced by 10 per cent to account for transportation, bagging and imputed labour cost.

(ii) Perishable products mainly vegetables, may have an additional 10% reduction to account for extra losses resulting from in transit damage and spoilage caused by holding and storage.

(iii) Perishables mainly fruits which are normally transported long distances and are generally sold through a broker or commission agent, may have an additional margin of 10-15%. Based on these costs, the margin between the farmgate and farmers' market price is estimated to average 30 per cent. To illustrate, farmgate prices for agricultural products (Yemen Arab Republic) are given in the following Table:

TABLE 7

Estimated Farmgate Prices for Major Agricultural Products, Using 1985 Average Prices Collected by the Agricultural Statistics Department, MAF*

Yemen Arab Republic

Product	Average market price	Marketing costs	Farmgate price
		YR per kilogram	
Cereals (10% margin)			
Sorghum	5.91	0.59	5.32
Millet	7.07	0.71	6.36
Maize	5.40	0.54	4.86
Wheat	6.42	0.64	5.78
Barley	4.76	0.48	4.28
Vegetables (20% margin)			
Potatoes	8.80	1.76	7.04
Tomatoes	9.24	1.85	7.39
Onions	5.98	1.20	4.78
Okra	12.24	2.44	9.77
Cucumber	7.73	1.55	6.18
Radish	5.84	1.17	4.67
Dry legumes	11.77	2.35	9.42
Other vegetables	10.56	2.11	8.45
Fruits (30% margin)			
Grapes	20.13	6.00	14.13
Bananas	17.31	5.19	12.12
Citrus	23.88	7.16	16.72
Dates	9.74	2.92	6.82
Papaya	8.21	2.46	5.75
Mango	23.62	7.09	16.53
Apricot	24.19	7.25	16.94
Watermelon	4.17	0.83	3.34
Muskmelon	6.27	1.25	5.02
Other fruits	23.12	6.94	16.18

Contd..

* MAF indicates Ministry of Agriculture and Fishery.

YR = Yemen Rials.

Product	Average market price	Marketing costs	Farmgate price
		YR per kilogram	
Meat (10% margin)			
Sheep - Kg.	72.05	7.21	64.84
Calf - Kg.	65.02	6.50	58.52
Goat - Kg.	58.38	5.84	52.54
Kid - Kg.	62.30	6.23	56.07
Beef - Kg.	49.94	4.99	44.92
Camel - Kg.	29.42	2.94	26.48
Chicken (balladi) each	44.80	4.48	40.32
Chicken (commercial)	19.86	1.99	17.87
Eggs (balladi)	-	-	-
Eggs (commercial)	0.84	0.084	0.76
Industrial Crops (10% margin)			
Coffee	48.74	4.87	43.87
Tobacco	17.30	1.78	16.02
Sesame	17.44	1.74	15.70

INTERNATIONAL PRICE

India is basically an agricultural oriented economy. The population of the country may touch a high at 980 millions by 2000 A.D. The country has imported food grains in the past and may continue to import some products in coming years. Therefore, it would be better if the international prices of agricultural commodities are considered/ adopted to work out the feasibility of the projects. In case of Internationally traded commodities, it is more likely to project a real situation of the economy. Country which depends to a greater extent upon a major component of import commodities, probably it has a more complicated economy. Therefore, it is the responsibility of the Government to keep on top the production of commodities and price trends under control. The World Bank has also a commodity group which studies likely future trends in production and prices. The results of these researches are available to Member Government for project analysis whether or not the fundings would be available for the project from the World Bank alone. The Major International Commodity Association also maintains groups which study products and price trends. Finally, some agencies in some of the developed countries make available studies of production and price trends of commodity's interest to them. These are usually available without imposing restrictions on Government of developing countries. The Marketing and Inspection Directorate of Ministry of Agriculture, Govt. of India also publishes elaborate and detailed commodity's studies for most of major crops traded in International markets.

The countries which import the major proportion of food products to feed their population, should adopt the cheapest prices for all the imported commodities all over the world. The country may import the agricultural commodities to feed the growing population of the country, from those countries which can supply the products comparatively at lower prices. Hence, in view of these facts, for computing the Net Present worth, Benefit-Cost Ratio and Internal Rate of Return for different projects should be based on the International prices to quantify the output. The returns from the emerging cropping pattern, on the implementation of the projects based on the International prices should be worked out. The International prices can be considered keeping in view the reports and data available from different sources which may range generally from 70-75% of the farmgate prices. However, for the vegetables and fruits which are not traded and imported from other countries, the farmgate prices can be adopted because the International prices have no relevance in case of the fruits and vegetables. Besides, the home production of fruits and vegetables may be sufficient to feed the country's population.

FINANCIAL CROP BUDGETS

The field data collected from farmers by adopting an "Intensive Survey Method" or "Cost Accounting Method" should be used to prepare the financial crop budgets which may include inputs use, output expected, gross and net returns per hectare. While preparing the financial crop budgets, present conditions and future possible outcomes in view of improved technology should be taken into account. The financial crop budgets should be prepared for all cereal crops, fruits and vegetables, cotton, coffee, etc. assuming that farmers will adopt new methods of cultivation, provided extension workers disseminate the new technology among the farmers. The crop budgets, which also include the cost of production/cultivation per hectare, may indicate that net returns per hectare are highest for fruits and vegetables, garlic, and cotton, but cereals *viz.* wheat, maize, barley, sorghum etc. comparatively earn low returns per hectare. Besides these facts, the cost of cultivation per hectare for vegetables and fruits, cotton, garlic etc., may also be quite high which may show that higher doses of critical inputs like fertilisers, pesticides, and water are required for cultivation of these crops and these crops are labour intensive.

The average farmgate prices for a particular base year may be used for input and output in the preparation of financial crop budgets and it may be assumed that the impact of inflation both on inputs and output would be equal. Since improved technology of seeds-water-fertiliser, which is generally considered a risk by the farmers at the introduction stage, the possible outcomes of this may be kept in view in the preparation of financial crop budgets. Also intensive use of labour per hectare is expected which would increase the demand of labour for crop production. This may also push up the demand for hired labour.

While preparing the financial crop budgets for future situation, the size of holdings, farmers belief and perception alongwith their financial condition should be kept in view. Inter-cropping may be suggested/ proposed in case of plantation crops which start bearing fruits in third year or after third year.

The financial crop budgets prepared for each crop should also give the gross returns (*i.e.* benefits) per hectare. The gross benefits may be assumed to be at the full development,

- 60% benefits of the total would be achieved in the sixth year if construction of the project takes 5 years
- 75% in the seventh year
- 85% in the eighth year
- 95% in the ninth year
- 100% in the tenth year.

REFERENCES

1. H. Bierman and S. Smidt, 'The Capital Budgeting Decision', New York: The MacMillan Company, 1960, p. 46.
2. Jack Hirshleifer, James C.De Haven, and Jerome W. Milliman, 'Water Supply Economics, Technology and Policy', Chicago; The University of Chicago Press; 1960, p. 152.
3. C.H. Oglesby and Eugene L., Grant, 'Economic Analysis — The Fundamental Approach to Decisions in Highway Planning and Design', Highway Res. Board Proc. Vol. 37 (1958), pp. 48-49.

4. Indian Journal of Agricultural Economics, 1978, October-December, Vol. XXXIII, No. 4, Conference Number, The Indian Society of Agricultural Economics, Bombay-400023.
5. Mishra, S.N. and John Beyer, 1976, 'Cost-Benefit Analysis – A case study of the Ratnagiri Fisheries Project', Hindustan Publishing Corporation, Delhi.
6. Price, J. Gittinger, 'Economic Analysis of Agricultural Projects', The International Bank for Reconstruction and Development, Washington, D.C. USA, The Johns Hopkins University Press, Baltimore, 1972, pp. 1-3 and 29.
7. Puttaswamiah, K., 1980, 'Project Evaluation Criteria and Cost-Benefit Analysis', Oxford & IBH Publishing Co., New Delhi.
8. Tolley, C.S. and F.E. Riggs, 1966, 'Economics of Water-shed Planning', The Iowa State University Press, Ames, Iowa.
9. James, L. Douglas and Lee, Robert R (1971), 'Economics of Water Resources Planning', Tata McGraw Hill Publishing Co. Ltd., 12/4, Asaf Ali Road, New Delhi.
10. Mande, O.D. (1980) 'Evaluation of Social Benefits & Costs of Conjunctive Use of Surface and Ground Waters in Gomti Kalyani Doab', Unpublished M.E. Dissertation, WRDTC, Uni. of Roorkee, U.P.
11. Kumar, Randhir (1979), 'Socio-Economic Studies of Gomti-Kalyani Doab', Unpublished M.E. Dissertation, WRDTC, University of Roorkee, U.P.

CHAPTER 12

FINANCIAL ANALYSIS

Analysis of financing alternatives need to distinguish between financing initial construction and repayment by the beneficiaries. A large project typically utilizes many sources of funds and repayment procedures are agreed upon both by lending institution and the loan borrowing agency. Thus, the overall financial structure requires to be formulated in financial analysis.

Financial feasibility quantifies a project's ability to obtain funds for implementation and repay these funds on a self-liquidating basis. For a project to be feasible, the anticipated project receipts must exceed the project disbursements, funds must be available, and the project must be able to service the debt. These items depend on the project's characteristics, the sponsor and purchaser, the requirements of those providing funds, and the overall credit market as it affects the cost of borrowing.

An important part of establishing financial feasibility is the anticipated borrowing cost. The cost of capital is the return expected by potential investors and other market, and economic costs. The costs are the sum of the real interest rate that compensates the lender for surrendering the use of funds, the purchasing power, risk premium that compensates for expected inflation, the business and financial risk, and the marketability risk associated with low-liquidity of long-term debt.

The purpose of the financial analysis is to concentrate on the sources of funding.

Distinction Between Financial & Economic Analysis : A water supply project may be financially feasible which implies that necessary funds can be generated to pay for it. This can be through water charges and taxes. But, it does not mean that the project is best of all the available alternatives or that the proposed construction is appropriate. Besides, a project may be economically feasible (Table1) even though it cannot be financed. Also, the debt limit of an agency or organisation's jurisdiction may prohibit borrowing of additional funds to finance a project. There may be several instances to quote where the beneficiaries of the project may be so widespread that no institutional framework exists to set charges and collect funds for repayment. Apart from this, only differential inflation should be included in an economic analysis, whereas general price inflation should be covered in the financial analysis since a bond issue or appropriation based on current prices may not be adequate at the time funds are expended.

ANNUALIZED COST

To compare costs which occur over a period of time and in varying amounts of expenditure it is necessary to have a common time basis. This is obtained by reducing each expenditure to an equivalent uniform annual series of payments (debt service). The largest item of the annual cost for the new project is a function of the initial capital cost. The magnitude of this cost is related to the life of the project, type of financing, and the interest rate of the money used for the project construction. The annual cost for repayment of the construction cost *i.e.* a capital recovery factor is:

$$crf = \frac{i\,(1+i)^n}{(1+i)^n - 1}$$

where,

i is the annual interest rate (per cent)

n is the payment life (years).

It is not necessary to compute the crf given by equation above as financial tables are available which include all normal interest rates and for time periods extending over a 100 years.

The annual cost for financing the construction cost then becomes:

Annual financial cost = Total construction cost x crf

For example, if the original cost was ten lakh Rupees and the loan or bond repayment period was assumed to be 40 years with financing to be

TABLE 1

A Comparison of Financial and Economic Efficiency Analysis

	Financial	Economic
Focus	Net returns to equity capital or to private group or individual.	Net returns to Society.
Purpose	Indication of incentive to adopt or implement.	Determine if government investment is justified on economic efficiency basis.
Prices	Market or administered (may assume that markets are perfect or that administered prices have compensated for imperfections).	May require 'shadow prices' (*e.g.*, monopoly in markets, external effects, unemployed or underemployed factors, overvalued currency).
Taxes	Cost of production.	Part of total societal benefits.
Subsidies	Source of revenue.	Part of total societal cost.
Loans	Increase capital resources available.	A transfer payment; transfers a claim to resource flow.
Interest or loan repayment	A financial cost; decreases capital resources available.	A transfer payment.
Discount rate	Marginal cost of money; market borrowing rate.	Opportunity cost of capital; social time preference rate.
Income distribution	Can be measured net returns to individual factors of production such as land, labour, and capital.	Not considered in economic efficiency analysis. Can be done as separate analysis or as weighted efficiency analysis.

made with money at 6 per cent, the annualized cost for this would become:

The crf for 6 per cent for 40 years is = 0.06646

Annual financial cost = 10,00,000 x 0.06646

= Rs. 66,460

Other items included in the financial cost analysis are operation and maintenance, administration and replacement. The amount of these are generally estimated at the time of making an economic assessment of the project. Dependent upon the owner's practices, other items included, such as insurance, taxes, etc. Any of the foregoing cost may be assumed in the analysis to be constant or escalated to include effects of inflation dependent upon the owner's practices.

Each cost included in the annual cost analysis is regarded to be either a constant value for the life of the project or treated as an equivalent uniform annual cost by using a unifom series of annual payments reflecting the life of the project and the cost of money. If the owner finances the project from internal funds, then the annual cost is based on a required rate of return rather than the interest rate of borrowed money.

Lastly, the extent to which they must bear the burden of project repayment affects the beneficiaries benefits and costs. If the beneficiaries are required to repay a very little of the project costs, they have an incentive and may like the project, even if the project may not pass the test of economic feasibility. Thus, financial incentives put hindrance in planning from the overall viewpoint when those benefitting are required to pay so little of the costs.

Government Financing

Funds for financing the initial construction of public sector (government) projects are appropriated from the general budget which ultimately come from tax revenues or borrowing. This ends up with the increase in the national debt. Government cost sharing practice divides the burden of this cost between the beneficiaries. However, the part of the funds required to be repayed by the beneficiaries depends on the agency constructing the project and the type of the benefits received. But the repayment needs allocation of the total project cost among different project purposes and setting specific charges from allocated costs.

State and Local Financing

Funding Options: If a water resources development project is likely to be taken up, the authorities may apply for Central grants or loans, seek aid through state appropriated funds for small project development programmes. A local government seeking financial support for a small water resources project raises the first cost by a combination of loans and grants from the central or sometimes the state government. Sometimes the funds are raised from the sale of bonds. Even the Power Finance Corporation raised Rs. 620 crores by issue of bonds within the country in 1990-91. However, after completion of the project, it will gradually pay off the loans over the years of project life and incurred bonded indebtedness. State governments in tribal and backward areas desirous to take up development projects particularly water resources development projects may obtain funds through the respective Ministries of the Central Government or may mobilise funds at State level.

GENERAL FINANCING METHODS

An investor-owned project may be financed, but not limited to, bonds preferred stock or common stock. There are many types of bonds which specify the callability and refunding of the bonds. The bond holder does have the first priority on the assets of the firm in any liquidation action but does not have a voting power on the firm's operation. The cost of the borrowed money *i.e.* interest on the bond, is related to the financial strength of the firm and the relative amount of prior bond issues.

Preferred stock that may be issued by an investor-owned utility is lower in priority to corporate assets than bonds in a liquidation proceeding. The interest paid may be more or less than the bond interest dependent upon the strength of the corporation, the corporation's financial structure and the financial market. Some preferred stock issued have voting power and some don't. Common stock issued by the investor utility has a variable rate of interest and a voting power in the company operation.

An investor-owned utility would not issue bonds, preferred stock or common stock for starting construction of any small low-head hydroelectric project. Their request to the money market is made at intervals that the corporate finance managers believe is prudent to augment their cash flow for all current construction and operational needs. The types of funding requested, bonds, stock or short term loan, is based on the corporate financial structure, debt ratio and financial market conditions. Accordingly, the interest rate used in determining the annual cost of the construction cost is a variable which is a composite of the financial costs of outstanding bonds, stocks and any other financial burden which may be in effect during the construction period.

General Obligation Bonds

These bonds are secured by the issuer's pledge of its full faith, credit and taxing power. The issuer of the bonds will raise taxes, if necessary to cover bond service (payment of interest and principal amount). However, the bond holders can go to court and force the payment, if the issuer is not willing to do so.

General obligation bonds offer the buyer the greatest security and thus, sell the bonds at lowest interest rates. Despite this financial advantage for the seller, sometimes it is advantageous to use another type of bonds. State general obligation bonds are backed up by taxes from sources other than real estate.

The two most common methods of borrowing by a public entity is by use of either general obligation bonds or revenue bonds. The general obligation bond is secured by the taxing power of the entity issuing the bonds. If at any time the revenue from the project is inadequate to cover the bond repayment and all other annual costs, then the entity may take steps by imposing a tax or increasing the taxes to make up the deficiency. As the general obligation bond is a legal obligation on all property owners within the entity, approval of the voters must be obtained for issuance of this type of bond.

Revenue Bonds

Revenue Bonds are payable from revenues collected from project beneficiaries, which are used in case when it is inadvisable or impossible to sell general obligation bonds. However, the revenue bonds are outside the statutory debt limit placed on state and most local governments. These bonds can be used by agencies which have no power of taxation or when there are prohibitions against the extension of state credit facilities. These have rather a distinctive characteristic in view of the fact that instead of being secured by the full faith and credit of the issuer, these are supported only by a pledge of gross or net revenues from a specific enterprise such as a *hydropower facility* or *municipal water supply*, which limits the use of revenue bonds to revenue-producing projects. However, revenue bonds cannot be used in case benefits are widespread like from flood or water quality control. Since revenue bond security is less than that of general obligation bonds for a comparable project, the interest rate paid on revenue bonds is higher.

Thus, a bond reserve fund is usually created in connection with the sale of revenue bonds. Excess revenues are accumulated to provide for payment of interest and principal amount when due in the event that pledged revenues are temporarily insufficient. But the common practice is that the reserve fund should be equal to at least one year's total requirements of interest and principal amount.

Revenue bonds may be restrictive in that their security for bond repayment is dependent upon the revenue of a single project. If the revenue bond is of the general type then the repayment is obtained by marketing revenue of the entity. Revenue bonds must also be approved by the voters in the entity but approval is at a lower rate than obligatory bonds, generally only a simple majority. There are instances whereby revenue bonds may be issued solely on the authority of a governing body, such as a Board of Directors, and property owners' approval is not required. As prepayment of the revenue bonds is not secured by the entities' taxing power, but only by the revenue from the budget, then the margin of safety required for bond repayment is high to insure against unforeseen adverse conditions.

Assessment Bonds

Assessment bonds are backed by liens against specific real property. The total cost of the project (after completion of its construction) is apportioned among benefiting property owners based on proportional to benefits received in terms of area, assessed value etc. On receiving his bill the individual property owner may either pay immediately or agree to an assessment bond's being sold which he will pay off over the next 10 to 20 years. However, if refused to pay on scheduled time gives right to the bond's owner for compensation through sale of the property. These bonds are best for small drainage, water supply or waste-water treatment projects serving limited areas.

It is usual that all public entity bonds are tax free, that is the interest received by the bond holders is exempt from central income taxes and state income taxes in the state of issuance. There are occasions when the type of public entity is a private or investor-owned utility. These financing methods include the following:

1. Taxable Revenue Bonds.
2. Tax-exempt Revenue Bonds.
3. Internal Cash Flow.

With the central government funding a loan, the money is granted in the early stage of development and prior to start of construction. This money is available as required throughout the construction period. When bonds are issued for the development these are issued prior to start of construction for the total construction costs. The proceeds from the bond issue are then invested on short term basis until required by the construction progress for payments.

Debt Service Interest Rate

The debt service is the annual cost for repayment of the financial obligation assumed by the owner for the project construction costs. The interest rate on the borrowed money is a function of whether the project owner is a public entity or it is an investor-owned project. Financing by a public entity is usually at a lower interest rate than for an investor-owned project.

Debt Service Repayment Period

The life of a small hydroelectric project may be determined by either the length of time before expiry of the project license or equipment life, whichever is the shortest time. Equipment's life may be taken as 50 years unless the owner's experience indicates another value. There may be conditions for the sale of bonds of a public entity which dictate a shorter repayment period. Normally the bond repayment period will vary from 25 to 40 years. The time value used by an investor-utility will generally be either the expiry of the operating license or equipment life.

FINANCIAL ALTERNATIVES

There are possibly six methods of financing a small hydroelectric development. The developer may have more than one of these methods available for financing dependent upon the status of the developer, that would have an interest rate of approximately nine per cent or more. Normally the repayment period for a bond issue of this type is upto 40 years.

Internal Cash Flow

A private utility would fund the construction costs of a small hydroelectric development by internal cash either available or made available by short term loans or sale of securities in the money market.

Financial Annualized Cost

Each of the previously discussed financial alternatives will result in a different annualized cost which is chargeable to financing the hydroelectric development. For simplification an assumption is made for the following examples. This assumption is that the loan amount is identical for all cases. The total construction cost which must be funded always includes the interest during construction. In the several financial alternatives discussed the interest during construction may not necessarily be the same for all alternatives. The loan amount is assumed to be Rs. 43,88,000. If bonds were used as a method of financing, the bond issue would be for this amount. A private utility would consider this amount as required from its cash flow.

In this section the term 'annual cost' includes only the financial charges. When an economic assessment is made for the project, the project annual cost includes additional indirect and direct costs.

Taxable Revenue Bonds

The use of taxable revenue bonds is a conventional source of funding by many public entities. Central tax laws currently provide that if the power from the project is purchased by an investor-owned utility, upto Rs. 10,00,000 of bonds can be sold that are exempt from central income tax. Under this condition it is currently estimated that such bonds could be sold at an interest rate of seven per cent. Bonds for the amount in excess of Rs. 10,00,000 are subject to central income tax and would carry an interest rate of about ten per cent. The term of both the tax-exempt and the taxable bonds may be upto 40 years. To sell revenue bonds the power purchaser must pledge to retire the bonds. This pledge could be provided for in the purchase agreement which is negotiated with a power purchaser prior to the bond sale.

Tax-Exempt Revenue Bonds

The use of tax-exempt revenue bonds for funding may be used if the power purchaser is a public utility district.

Revenue bonds, 40 years,
10 per cent, crf = 0.1023
Annual Debt Service = Rs. 43,88,000 x 0.1023
= Rs. 4,48,900
Total annual cost of financing = Rs. 5,23,900

For a 6 per cent discount rate the present worth of this alternative is Rs. 78,82,800.

Entire funding may be accomplished by issuance of tax-exempt bonds for a 40 year repayment period.

Tax-exempt bonds, 40 year,
7 per cent, crf = 0.07501
Annual Debt Service = Rs. 53,88,000 x 0.7501
= Rs. 4,04,200
Total cost of financing = Rs. 4,04,200

For a 6 per cent discount rate the present worth of this alternative is Rs. 60,81,700.

Taxable Revenue Bonds

Tax-exempt revenue bonds in the amount of Rupees 10 lakh may be issued and the balance of the funding by taxable revenue bonds.

Tax-exempt revenue bonds,40 years,
7 percent, crf = 0.07501
Annual Debt Service = 10,00,000 x 0.07501
= Rs. 75,010

For a 6 per cent discount rate the present worth of this alternative is Rs. 54,72,300.

Internal Cash Flow

Assume a private developer has a remaining time of 45 years before the project license expires. The developer elects to have the construction costs funded prior to elapse of license and also requires 8 per cent return on the investment.

A 45 year funding period, 8 per cent
return *i.e.* crf = 0.08259
Annual Debt Service = Rs. 53,88,000 x 0.08259

= Rs. 4,45,000

Total annual cost of financing = Rs. 4,45,000

For a 6 per cent discount rate the present worth of this alternative is Rs. 68,77,800.

Annual Debt Servie as Related to Financial Feasibility

The debt sevice payments plus other escalating and constant annual costs are then summed to estimate total annual cost through the project financing period. Total annual cost divided by average energy production yields the expected cost of power generation.

A brief example of a municipal utility project is presented to illustrate the method, assume:

- Completed cost equals Rs. 60,00,000
- Annual O&M in the first year of operation equals Rs. 1,35,000
- Cost of financing is approximately 6 per cent
- 30-year financing period

Then, the capital recovery factor is crf = .07265 and annual debt service is approximately Rs. 4,35,900.

Table 2 shows the results of the cost-of-service calculations.

Over the 30-year financing period used in this example, the cost of service approximately doubles. Over this same period, the value of energy which was close to the original cost of services and escalated at the same rate as O&M increased by a factor of about five per cent. This example illustrates how inflation will generally enhance the project's long-run annual value.

Planning the Debt Structure

Borrowing to finance the small hydro power projects or water resources development requires coordination with the overall financial capabilities of the supporting agencies. In this context, each agency must schedule its debt service obligation to provide coverage from expected income sources. Several agencies/organisaitons can join for sharing the financial burden of the projects, where it is not possible for any one to support and afford alone.

Debt Service and its Coordination: The debt service for each new bond issue requires to be coordinated with previous debt service commitments in order to have the maturity schedule coincide as closely as possible with expected revenues or tax receipts. This flexibility is gained through choices among serials and sinking fund bonds, different types of serials, callable and noncallable bonds and different maturity lengths.

However, serial bonds and sinking fund differ by method of redemption. Sinking-fund bonds are sometimes called term bonds, which is mainly due to the reasons that all principal becomes due in a lump-sum at maturity. Annual payments must be made to a sinking fund in order to accumulate sufficient funds to redeem sinking fund bonds. This, when invested at compound interest, will produce the required amount of principal when it becomes due. But individual bonds within an issue of serial bonds have different maturity dates so that the bonds may be retired in more uniform annual instalments.

Joint-Venture Financing

There has been growing demand for central funds and therefore, a fierce competition has caused states to seek new approaches for financing small, medium and large hydro-electric projects and water resources development. For example, Tehri Project and Narmada are joint ventures which are in collaboration of Russian and World Bank respectively. The Rs. 3000 crore Soviet-aided Tehri Dam across Bhagirathi river in Uttar Pradesh is reported to be located in the seismical active zone. Sometimes, it may be desirable to convert the escalating cost of service into a levelized cost. This can be accomplished by discounting and summing the cost of service stream to the first year of operation and then calculating the constant annual cost, which is equivalent to the summed costs. Since the procedure would only be used to compare the cost of the hydro project to an alternative available to the power purchaser, the appropriate interest rate to use in these calculations is the weighted average cost of capital to the power purchaser. IF the levelized cost of the hydro plant is less than the cost of the power purchaser's alternatives, it should be possible to negotiate a marketing agreement that allows project implementation.

TABLE 2

— Cost of Service Calculation
— Construction Cost, Rs. 60,00,000
— Financing, 30 years, 6 Per cent
— First year O&M Cost, Rs. 1,35,000
— Annual Escalation of 6 Per cent

Year of Operation	Bond Amortization	Operation & maintenance	Total annual cost	Average annual energy production (Millions of (KWH)	Cost of service (KWH)	Value of energy (KWH)
	Rs.	Rs.	Rs.			
1	435,900	135,000	570,900	22.500	2.537	2.500
2	435,900	143,100	570,900	22.500	2.573	2.650
3	435,900	151,686	587,586	22.500	2.611	2.809
4	435,900	180,787	596,687	22.500	2.651	2.977
5	435,900	170,434	606,334	22.500	2.694	3.156
6	435,900	180,606	616,560	22.500	2.740	3.345
7	435,900	191,900	627,400	22.500	2.788	3.546
8	435,900	202,990	638,890	22.500	2.833	3.753
9	435,900	215,169	651,069	22.500	2.893	3.984
10	435,900	228,079	663,979	22.500	2.951	4.223
11	435,900	241,764	677,664	22.500	3.011	4.477
12	435,900	256,270	692,170	22.500	3.076	4.745
13	435,900	271,646	707,545	22.500	3.144	5.030
14	435,900	287,945	723,845	22.500	3.217	5.030
15	435,900	305,222	741,122	22.500	3.233	5.652
16	435,900	323,535	750,435	22.500	3.375	5.991
17	435,900	342,947	778,847	22.500	3.461	6.350
18	435,900	363,524	799,424	22.500	3.552	6.731
19	435,900	385,335	821,235	22.500	3.649	7.135
20	435,900	408,455	844,355	22.500	3.752	7.563
21	435,900	432,963	898,863	22.500	3.861	8.017
22	435,900	458,941	894,841	22.500	3.977	8.498
23	435,900	486,477	922,977	22.500	4.099	9.008
24	435,900	515,666	951,566	22.500	4.229	9.543
25	435,900	546,606	982,506	22.500	4.366	10.122
26	435,900	579,402	1,015,902	22.500	4.512	10.723
27	435,900	614,166	1,050,066	22.500	4.666	11.373
28	435,900	631,016	1,080,916	22.500	4.830	12.055
29	435,900	690,077	1,125,977	22.500	5.004	12.779
30.	435,900	731,482	1,167,382	22.500	5.188	13.545

REFERENCES

1. Gittinger, J. Price (1974) 'Economic Analysis of Agricultural Projects', pp. 130-147, The Economic Development Institute, International Bank for Reconstruction and Development, The Johns Hopkins University Press, Baltimore and London.
2. Omar, Haji Mohd. Nor Ghazali Bin (1991) 'Financial Performance Analysis of Besut Integrated Agricultural Development Project, Malaysia', Unpublished M.E. Dissertation, WRDTC, University of Roorkee, U.P. (India).
3. Proceedings of the International Symposium on Irrigation Design for Management, 16-18 February, 1987, Sri Lanka.
4. Proceedings of the National Seminar on Modernisation of Canal Irrigation, December 14-15, 1984, pp. VI-1 to VI-13, IWRS, WRDTC, University of Roorkee, U.P.
5. 'Indian Journal of Agricultural Economics', Vol. XXXIX, No. 3, Conference Number, July-September 1984, pp. 491-553, Indian Society of Agricultural Economics, Bombay.
6. Darra, B.L. & Raghuvanshi C.S. (1990), 'Irrigation Management' – A System Approach', Vol. I, Atlantic Publishers and Distributors, Ansari Road, Darya Ganj, New Delhi.
7. Proceedings, Third IWRS Symposium on Watershed Development and Management, Vol. I & II, February, 1990, Kanpur.
8. Proceedings, Second IWRS Symposium on Water Conservation for National Development, December, 1988, Bhopal.
9. Drilon, J.D. Jr. (1971), 'Introduction to Agri-Business Management', Vol. I, pp. 171-175, Asian Productivity Organisation, Tokyo, Japan.
10. Mishra, S.N. & John Beyer, 1976, 'Cost-Benefit Analysis – A Case Study of the Ratnagiri Fisheries Project', Hindustan Publishing Corporation, Delhi.
11. Puttaswamiah, K., 1980, 'Project Evaluation Criteria and Cost-Benefit Analysis,' Oxford & IBH Publishing Co., New Delhi.
12. Tolley, C.S. and F.E. Riggs, 1966, 'Economics of Watershed Planning', The Iowa State University Press, Ames Iowa.

CHAPTER 13

COMPLEMENTARY INPUTS – PROJECTED FERTILISER CONSUMPTION, ORGANISATIONAL SET UP AND DISTRIBUTION OF FERTILISER AND IRRIGATION WATER

"Nutrient removal by crops is on the increase with increasing crop production and prodcutivity. Although fertiliser consumption has also increased considerably, an annual gap of about 10 m.t. (55 kg/ha) of nutrients (NPK) still exists between nutrient removal and supply through fertilisers. The gap which varies widely (21-88 kg/ha) among different agro-climatic regions of the country, if not bridged timely will pose major threat to sustainable agriculture. To highlight the extent of problem, this chapter gives an overview of estimated nutrients removal, fertiliser consumption and gap to be bridged in different regions. Projections by 2000 A.D. have also been given."

INTRODUCTION

In an agrarian country like India, fertiliser has long been recognised as one of the critical inputs for increasing production. With the advent of planned development in the country, strenuous efforts have been made to increase agricultural production by improving availability of the critical inputs alongwith an efficient distribution system. However, extension and promotion have helped in dissemination and creating awareness among farmers of increasing role of critical inputs like fertilisers, pesticides and improved seeds.

India is the seventh largest country in area and the second most populous in the world. Of the total area (329 million hectares), nearly 145 million hectares constitute the net cropped area – the gross cropped area being 173 million hectares. Nearly 67 per cent of our population is dependent on agriculture. Agriculture contributes about 42 per cent of the gross national product (GNP). Agriculture also contributes about 60 per cent of the total exports, and earns foreign exchange from agricultural exports which facilitates imports of capital goods, machinery and spare parts for expanding industrial base. Many traditional export items are dependent on the performance of agriculture. Thus, the performance of agriculture greatly determines the level of economic activities in other sectors of the economy.

Besides food, agriculture also supplies important raw material to several processing and manufacturing industries. Hence, continuous growth in agriculture production in a country like India with limited scope for bringing additional land under cultivation is an imperative necessity which is possible only if there is a continuous growth in productivity. However, continuous increase in use of improved certified seeds in the country has increased by 23 times over the last three decades. Similarly consumption of fertilisers has maintained a steady upward trend over the past years. From a mere 66 thousand tonnes (in terms of NPK nutrients) in 1950-51, the fertiliser consumption reached a level of nearly 11.57 million tonnes in 1988-89. There is still vast scope for increasing fertilizer consumption.

The need to raise productivity for growth in agriculture was recognized in our country since long. Till mid-sixties, however, efforts to raise productivity through increased use of various inputs had only limited success due to certain reasons. Break-through in agricultural research beginning with the evolution of High Yielding Varieties (HYV) and improvement in wheat, rice and maize production dramatically altered production conditions for cultivators in the second half of the sixties. Since most of arable land in the country is already under cultivation, more intensive cultivation is the crux for the required growth in agricultural production which is increasingly dependent on greater use of the chemical fertilizers and irrigation.

The gains of the 'Green Revolution' in agriculture are attributable mainly to the availability of three primary inputs–irrigation, high yielding varieties, and fertilizers. The spectacular gains have consequently been confined, in particular to areas where surface and ground water could be tapped, and land-holdings are economically viable. These areas, amounting to less than 21 per cent of the cultivated area, account for over 60 per cent of the country's total fertilizer consumption. However, fertilizer consumption in the remaining 79% of the cultivated area being rain-fed lands, is on an average a fraction *i.e.* about one-sixth of the rate of fertiliser consumption in the irrigated areas. Countries whose fertiliser consumption rates are many times higher than ours, use fertilisers mainly on one crop per year and that one crop is rainfed. For example, the United States of America, with 8 per cent more arable land under permament crops than India, has half as much irrigated arable land, yet fertilizer consumption per hectare in the USA is about seven times higher than in India.

The state with the highest fertilizer consumption rate is Punjab. In 1983-84, the average consumption of fertilizers in Punjab was about 149.3 kg. per hectare, against the national average of 44.9 kg. per hectare. However, this rate seems insignificant in comparison with 255 kg. per hectare of the U.K. and 626 kg. per hectare of the Netherlands, both countires with one cultivation season in the year. If comparison with developed countries seems inappropriate, Punjab's fertilizer consumption rate may be compared with that of UAR – a country that is similar, in that it is a developing nation whose arable lands are all irrigated. With an average of nearly 160 kg. per hectare, UAR's consumption is still higher by about 53 kg. per hectare than that of the Punjab. During 1989-90, Maharashtra occupied the third rank in fertiliser consumption in the country, next to Uttar Pradesh and Andhra Pradesh. According to the review made by the Fertiliser Association of India, the share of Maharashtra state in total fertiliser consumption in the country turned out to be 10 per cent, thus recording the highest quantum increase of 0.291 million tonnes among all the states. The review, however, indicates that Punjab topped per hectare consumption of gross cropped area with 159 kg. followed by Andhra Pradesh 131 kg., Uttar Pradesh 83 and Maharashtra 60 Kg. per hectare. These four states accounted for 51 per cent of all-India consumption.

The year 1989-90 witnessed an increase in the consumption of fertilisers from 11.036 million tonnes in 1988-89 to 11.571 million tonnes. But the consumption per hectare of gross cropped area rose to 65.4 kg as against 62.4 kg. in 1988-89. The Fertiliser Association of India (FAI) review revealed that phosphatic fertilisers consumption came down from 2.25 million tonnes in 1988-89 to 1.80 million tonnes in 1989-90.

Despite the fertiliser consumption growing by 5 per cent during 1989-90, the FAI review says, six states – Uttar Pradesh, Bihar, Karnataka, Madhya Pradesh, Assam and Kerala showed a negative growth rate of 1.23 lakh tonnes. The major shortfall was in Uttar

Pradesh and Bihar (44,000 tonnes each), Karnataka (21,000 tonnes) and Madhya Pradesh (11,000 tonnes). The drop in consumption in Assam and Kerala was a negligible 3,000 tonnes.

The importance of the fertilizer sector in the national economy cannot be overemphasised. It continues to be the most important input, next only to water, in agriculture production. The new technology has created an enormous demand for purchased inputs such as fertilizers and pesticides for which a new marketing structure is required, with a view to make available these inputs to farmers in right quantity, at right place, time and at a reasonable price. This input is required in increasing quantities to enable to feed the teaming millions in this country. With this view the Government has been planning and approving huge investments in the fertilizer sector. The present installed capacity of nitrogenous fertilizers manufacturing is around 5.2 million tonnes. With the completion of the projects in hand, this capacity will go upto nearly 9.25 million tonnes. Creation of additional capacity of nearly 2.2 million tonnes of nitrogen has been contemplated to cater to the growing demand for fertilisers in the Eighth Plan Period.

Purpose

Fertilizers and manures are used to supplement the nutrients required to increase the crop production. These are also needed to restore and maintain the soil fertility. However, more than one fertilizer is needed in order to supplement more than one nutrient for which a mixture of fertilizers is used. Not all the fertilizers are compatible, therefore this nature needs to be identified.

In fact fertilizer has dual purpose of 'feeding the soil' and 'feeding the crop'. The idea underlying 'feeding the soil' is to improve the fertility of the soil by adding efficient nutrients. In feeding the crop, the amounts of nutrients needed during crop growth is added to the rooting medium of the crop. But there are also some losses which are made up by further increase in the fertilizer rate.

The use of fertilizers in production is required because of (a) low levels of soil fertility, (b) low level of plant nutrient use, (c) alternative use of major organic manurial resources, (d) possibility of quick production response, (e) dependence of many technological changes in agriculture and increased use of plant nutrients, and (f) the possibilities of enlarging the supplies of fertilizers by increasing domestic production by inputs. Thus, the increased production of fertilizer is as important as producing it efficiently and lowering the unit cost to the extent possible. This is especially necessary in the context of increasing plant and input cost, and the necessity to keep down the consumer price *i.e.* the price to be paid by the farmer.

Fertiliser is a complementary input, thus its use along with irrigation[1] promotes intensive use of inputs, particularly use of high yielding varieties seeds and fertilizers.

COMPLEMENTARY INPUTS

Complementary inputs complement each other in that one adds/ helps to the contribution of other when the resources (*i.e.* fertilizer and irrigation in this case) are limited in amount.

Consumption of fertilisers in the country has been increasing steadily. Now there is better availability through increasead domestic production and streamlined distribution coupled with measures taken by Government for increasing its demand. At the beginning of the First Plan, fertilizer consumption was only about 66,000 tonnes of nutrients and in 1979-80, it was nearly 53.0 lakh tonnes. In 1974-75, there was a decrease in fertilisers consumption due to hike in prices. After recovering from this set-back, the fertilisers consumption has continued to rise which increased to 11.6 metric tones (65.4 kg/ha) in 1989-90. The average annual increase during the three years ending 1978-79 was 20 per cent, which was mainly due to reduction in their prices. Now, a dual pricing policy of fertilisers has been announced for the benefit of marginal and small farmers. There are, however, wide differences in per hectare consumption of fertilizers in different states ranging from 2.04 kg. in Assam to 149.3 kg. in Punjab with the average for the country being about 44.9 kg. per hectare (nutrient) in 1983-84. Further, fertiliszer consumption continues to be concentrated in about 60 districts (out of a total of 405), which account for about 50 per cent of the overall fertilizer consumption.

FERTILISER USE

Fertiliser (NPK) consumption has increased from 66 thousand tonnes (0.55 kg/ha) in 1951-52 to 11.6 m.t. (65.4 kg/ha) in 1989-90. It is, however, much below than that of many developed and developing

1. Irrigated areas are potential places for increasing fertiliser application because of fertilisers' complementary character.

countries. Moreover, there is also a wide variation (6 to 120 kg/ha) in fertiliser consumption in different agro-climatic regions (Table 1). Fertiliser use (kg/ha) is maximum in Zone 6. The Gangetic Plain Regions (3,4,5 & 6) having less than 30% gross cropped area, consume the lion's share (45%) of fertiliser. Average fertiliser consumption of the zones is about 96 kg/ha which was over 50% more than the country's average consumption of 62.3 kg/ha during 1988-89.

The fertiliser use in Plains and Hill Regions, particularly in Regions 11 and 12, is also high. The Plateau and Hill Regions (7, 8, 9 & 10) occupying more than 45% of gross cropped areas have relatively low fertiliser consumption (42 kg/ha) which is 2/3 of national average.

The fertiliser consumption in the remaining zones is much below than the national average. Thus, more than half of area comprising Hill Regions of Himalayas, Plateau and Hill Regions, Western Dry Region and Islands Region have relatively low fertiliser consumption.

TABLE 1

Region-wise Fertiliser (NPK) Consumption (1988-89)

Region No.	Gross cropped area	Fertiliser consumption	
	(m/ha)	m.t.	Kg/ha
1	3.17	0.16	51
2	6.18	0.11	18
3	7.03	0.57	81
4	15.58	1.30	83
5	14.99	1.40	93
6	13.87	1.67	120
7	15.94	0.36	23
8	20.77	0.62	30
9	22.84	0.86	38
10	21.49	1.57	73
11	11.89	1.31	110
12	5.23	0.40	76
13	9.86	0.65	66
14	8.16	0.05	6
15	-	-	-
All India	177.0	11.03	62

FERTILISER IMPORTS

Imported fertilisers are no longer as cheap as they used to be. The international market for fertilizers is extremely sensitive to an increase in demand from countries like India and China.

Import of fertilisers during 1984-85 touched all time high of 6.9 million tonnes of material consisting of about 1.99 million tonnes of N, 0.75 million tonnes of P_2O_5 and 0.86 million tonnes of K_2O. As a result, the import bill for fertilisers increased from Rs. 365 crores in 1983-84 to approximately Rs. 1,435 crores in 1984-85. Besides, the increase in the quantity imported, this sharp increase in the import bill was also caused by consequent increased f.o.b. prices as also the increase in the value of dollar. It is expected that there will be likely more and more imports in the coming years.

NUTRIENT BALANCE IN AGRO-CLIMATIC REGIONS

Nutrient removal by crops has increased by over four times during the last four decades putting four-fold pressure on soil. Although supply of nutrients through fertilisers also increased by over 11 m.t. since 1950-51 but it is still much lower in comparison to nutrient (NPK) removal (22 m.t.) resulting in a yearly negative balance of about 10 m.t. Considering projected removal of about 28 m.t. by 2000 AD, this gap is unlikely to be narrowed down much with estimated nutrient (NPK) supply of about 18 m.t. through fertilisers.

The gap is being partially bridged by using other sources like organic manure, bio-fertilsers and green manuring. However, due to increasing demands for food, fodder, fuel and fibre (Table 2), use of these sources is becoming limited.

TABLE 2
Important projections by 2000 A.D.

Particulars	Projections
Human population (millions)	1000
Livestock population (millions)	700
Foodgrain requirement (million tonnes)	240
Fuelwood requirement (million tonnes)	200
Livestock fodder requirement (million tonnes)	700
Fertiliser requirement (million tonnes)	20

A wide variation in fertiliser use, nutrient removal and availability of other sources of nutrients exits in different agro-climatic regions. As a result, nutrient gap also varies widely among different regions. Prior to making location specific measures to bridge the gap in each region, information on extent of nutrient removal, fertiliser consumption and nutrient gap in each region, is urgently required.

Removal

There are 13 essential plant nutrients which are taken from the soil. Depending upon the plant requirements, these nutrients have been grouped into primary, secondary and micro-nutrients. Keeping in view the widespread deficiencies, 5 nutrients (N, P, K, S & Zn) are of great importance and discussion is therefore confined to these nutrients only.

Nutrient concentration in plant is influenced by soil, climate, crop, variety and management factors which ultimately affect the nutrient removal by crop. Crop removal of nutrients is directly related with the yield. Cereals though have relatively low nutrient concentration, remove more nutrients from soil due to higher yields.

As the nutrient content in plants is affected by a number of factors, variation in calculations of nutrient removal in individual case is obvious. Nutrient removal has been calculated by taking average values for each crop as wide variation exists in reported nutrient concentrations of different crops determined by different workers.

Primary Nutrients

Nitrogen, phosphorus and potassium are called primary nutrients as they are primarily supplied in bulk through fertilisers because soil cannot provide them in required quantities. These are also termed as fertiliser elements as they are generally supplied through fertilisers.

Annual NPK removal at the present production level is around 21 m.t., out of which over 13 m.t. is by foodgrains only (Table 3). Removal of nutrient (NPK) per ha of gross cropped area is relatively more in cereals (110 kg) in comparison to pulses (70 kg). It indicates that cereal-cereal cropping systems are more exhaustive. A wide variation in crops grown, cropping intensity and crop productivity have a great influence on NPK removal in different agro-climatic regions. Per ha NPK removal ranged between 33 to 183 kg/ha in different regions with an average of 117 kg/ha (Table 4). There are five regions (5, 6, 8, 9 & 10) where annual NPK removal exceed 2 m.t. which account for nearly 60% of the total removal.

TABLE 3

NPK removal by important group of crops (1988-89)

Crop group	Removal (m.t.)
Cereals	11.61
Pulses	1.60
Oilseeds	2.73
Fruit & vegetables	0.95
Fodder crops	2.10
Cash and plantation crops	1.80
Total	20.79

TABLE 4

Region-wise Nutrient (NPK) removal by crops (1988-89) *

Region No.	Name of region	Nutrient removal (000 tonnes) Cereals	Pulses	Oilseeds	Others	Total removal 000	tonnes/kg/ha
1.	Western Himalayan Region	211	7	26	65	309	97
2.	Eastern Himalayan Region	283	3	29	130	445	71
3.	Lower Gangetic Plains Region	612	20	76	203	911	129
4.	Middle Gangetic Plains Region	1299	56	85	375	1815	116
5.	Upper Gangetic Plains Region	1648	108	167	540	2553	170
6.	Trans-Gangetic Plains Region	1746	101	175	518	2540	183
7.	Eastern Plateau & Hills Region	776	81	165	304	1326	83
8.	Central Plateau & Hills Region	1128	541	424	356	2449	118
9.	Western Plateau & Hills Region	912	269	312	656	2149	94
10.	Southern Plateau & Hills Region	1346	91	614	585	2636	123
11.	East Coast Plains & Hills Region	975	54	356	476	1861	156
12.	West Coast Plains & Ghat Region	306	21	69	268	664	127
13.	Gujarat Plains & Hills Region	243	83	186	348	860	87
14.	Western Dry Region	124	78	48	15	265	33
15.	The Islands Region	-	-	-	-	-	-
Total		11609	1603	2732	4839	20783	117

*Nutrient removal/consumption in the region very low.

Source: Adopted from Fertilizer News, 36(2): 27-30 1991, Research Paper titled "Fertilizer use in Different Agro-Climatic Regions of India," by Biswas, B.C. and Tewatia, R.K.

These regions cover the main foodgrains and oilseeds producing areas and account for 55% of the total production. Nutrient removal ranged between 116 to 183 kg/ha in Indo-Gangetic Plain regions (Zones 3 to 6) which account for over 40% of Country's foodgrain production. Likewise NPK removal ranges between 83 to 123 kg/ha in. Plateau and Hills Regions (Zones 7 to 10) which are responsible for over 45% of total oilseeds production in the country. Nearly 40% of the cotton and sugarcane production also comes from these regions. There are 5 regions (3, 5, 6, 11 & 12) in which nutrient removal is relatively higher (>125 kg/ha) due to relatively higher crop productivity.

However, present annual NPK removal is likely to increase by over 5 m.t. in next 10 years. By 2000 AD, per hectare nutrient removal would increase by 23 kg reaching to the level of 140 kg. Increase is likely to vary widely (6 to 50 kg/ha) among different regions. But NPK removal is likely to exceed 3 m.t. in at least 4 regions (Zones 5, 6, 8 & 10) which will account for nearly one half of the total removal by 2000 AD. In 6 regions (3, 5, 6, 10, 11 & 12) per ha NPK removal is likely to exceed 150 kg per annum. Besides, wide variation (39 to 211 kg/ha) in nutrient removal is likely to continue among different regions.

TABLE 5

S Removal by Important Group of Crops (1988-89)

Crop group	S Removal (m.t.)
Cereals	0.57
Pulses	0.10
Oilseeds	0.21
Others	0.22
Total	1.10

Mg deficiency has also been reported from some areas but it is unlikely to be of major concern in near future. At present, removal of S by crop production is a little above 1 m.t. (Table 5). In spite of the fact that the removal of S by oilseeds is 3-4 times more than cereals, more than half of total removal is by cereals only because of their higher production. Annual removal of S by oilseeds is around 0.2 m.t. against 0.57 m.t. by cereals.

Removal of S in different regions varies widely (2 to 11 kg/ha) due to variation in crops and their yield levels. Per hectare removal is considerably more in Indo-Gangetic Plains Regions then other regions.

Secondary Nutrients

Among secondary nutrients (Ca, Mg, S), importance of S in Indian agriculture is being increasingly realised due to increasing reports of S deficiency from different areas of the country. It is now recognised as the 4th major plant nutrient.

Although the S removal per unit of gross cropped area in different regions seems to be moderate, its total removal per ha per annum in intensively cultivated area is quite high which ranges from 30 to 72 kg. This is why S deficiency is generally being observed in areas of intensive cropping and higher productivity. Annual crop removal of sulphur is likely to be around 1.33 m.t. by 2000 AD. Loss of S through leaching and erosion is additional (Table 6).

Micro-nutrients

Among micro-nutrients (Zn, Fe, Cu, Mn, B, Co, Mo) deficiency of Zn particularly in intensively cultivable areas is increasingly being reported followed by Fe. Although micro-nutrients are required by plants in smaller quantity, annual removal of about 11 thousand tonnes of Zn and 1.1 lakhs tonnes of Fe is found to be by foodgrains and oilseeds (Table 7). This removal is likely to increase by 20-25% by 2000 AD.

TABLE 6

Region-wise S Removal by Crops (1988-89)

Region No.	S removal	
	(000 tonnes)	Kg/ha
1	16	5.0
2	21	3.4
3	44	6.3
4	87	5.6
5	125	8.3
6	148	10.7
7	69	4.3
8	151	7.3
9	122	5.3
10	137	6.4
11	88	7.4
12	33	6.3
13	44	4.5
14	17	2.1
15	-	-
All India	1102	6.2

TABLE 7

Zn and Fo Removal by important Group of Crops (1988-89)

S. No.	Group of crops	Removal (00 tonnes)	
		Zn	Fe
1.	Cereals	8.86	72.1
2.	Pulses	0.45	12.1
3.	Foodgrains (1+2)	9.31	84.2
4.	Oilseeds	1.78	28.8
	Total (3+4)	11.09	113.0

During 1988-89 about 0.65 m.t. of S was added through S containing fertilisers and materials indicating an addition of 3.7 kg S per ha of gross cropped area. As the production of Zn is not in organised sector, its production cannot be estimated. It is, however, reported that approximately 40,000 tonnes of zinc sulphate is produced annually against the demand of 60,000 tonnes.

TABLE 8

Projected regionwise NPK removal by 2000 AD

Region No.	Nutrient removal (2000 AD)		Increase over (1988-89)		
	m.t.	kg/ha	m.t.	kg/ha	% increase
1	0.42	126	0.11	29	35
2	0.59	86	0.14	13	31
3	1.18	163	0.27	34	30
4	2.38	149	0.56	32	31
5	3.14	204	0.58	33	23
6	3.15	211	0.61	15	24
7	1.65	99	0.32	16	24
8	3.11	140	0.66	22	27
9	2.64	102	0.49	8	23
10	3.34	154	0.71	31	27
11	2.29	176	0.43	20	23
12	0.93	177	0.27	50	41
13	1.29	126	0.43	39	50
14	0.33	39	0.07	6	27
15	-	-	-	-	-
All India	26.44	140	5.65	23	27

KRIBHCO'S fertilizer plant at Hazira in Gujarat: The worlds largest in the cooperative sector.

A view of the Nampur-III plant of the Hindustan Fertilizer Corporation in Assam.

NEW PROJECTS IN SEVENTH PLAN

The Seventh Five Year Plan also envisaged commissioning of seven more new projects or expansion of existing projects. With the completion of these new nitrogenous and phosphatic fertiliser projects during the Seventh Plan, the fertiliser industry registered a spectacular growth with the capacity reaching a level of 95 lakh tonnes of nitrogen and 29 lakh tonnes of phosphate by the end of the plan. (Fig. Kribhco's Fertilizer Plant at Hazira and Nampur Plants).

Apart from timely completion of new projects, the emphasis during the Seventh Plan was on optimising production from the existing fertiliser plants. The two important steps initiated to improve performance of existing plants were the identification of equipment problems and implementation of remedial measures by way of debottlenecking, rehabilitation and modernisation of ailing units.

Provisions of captive power facilities at the units facing recurring shortage or instability of power supply were another important measures to improve performance. Captive power plants were installed at Durgapur, Barauni, Bhatinda, Panipat and Talchar. Captive power facilities were also being provided as an integral part of the new nitrogenous plants to insulate them completely from the vagaries of grid supply.

Percentage of fertilisers production of north zone alone is given in the Table 9 (Page 357).

TABLE 9

Proportion of Production in North Zone with Break-up in Constituent States (Production in thousand tonnes)

	Zone/State	No. of Plant	Nitrogenous % of production		No. of plants	Phosphate % of production	
			1983-84	1984-85		1983-84	1984-85
	North Zone	7	28.7	30.4	9	5.4	6.9
(i)	Haryana	1	15.6	15.6	1	18.3	22.6
(ii)	Punjab	2	33.4	33.4	2	22.1	31.2
(iii)	U.P.	4	50.8	56.5	5	27.2	42.8
(iv)	Delhi	-	-	-	1	32.2	30.0

An enhanced consumption of fertilizer nevertheless has to be achieved if India is to attain a goal of producing 235 to 240 million tonnes of foodgrains by the end of the century, which is estimated to be the requirement of population of about 980 million *i.e.* 98 crores by 2000 A.D.

To produce 240 million tonnes of foodgrains in order to feed our burgeoning population estimated at 98 crores by 2000 AD, the country will require nutrients of around 20 million tonnes. Consequently, the current domestic production of 8.5 million tonnes of fertiliser nutrients (NPK) will have to be more than doubled by the end of this decade.

FUTURE STRATEGIES – ROLE OF EXTENSION AND PROMOTION SERVICES

From the initial stage of transforming subsistence agriculture to the present phase of technologically developed agriculture, extension and promotion services can be broadly grouped into three distinct phases:

1. Initial Phase
2. Phase II – Horizontal integration of critical inputs services alongwith application of fertilisers.

To increase the country's fertiliser production capacity in the most cost effective way, strategy must centre around:

(1) Modernisation and expansion of existing facilities to optimum levels by revamping and retrofitting.

(2) Building new units at existing production centres to take advantage of existing costly infrastructure.

(3) New grassroot facilities near areas where fertiliser consumption has impressive growth.

(4) Increased and effective use of indigenous resources with the help of emerging technologies.

A vigorous implementation of the above strategies will help to optimise domestic fertiliser production with the least possible strain on foreign exchange. The alternative of not being able to produce enough food for our population, would mean having to import foodgrains.

3. Phase III – Vertical integration of farm output resulting into more use of fertilisers.

During the first phase *i.e.* upto early 60's serious efforts were made to convince the farmer, who is the focal point of all development, that application of fertiliser in adequate quantity for any crop in any type of soil would result in better yields. To demonstrate various methods and mass media were extensively used. This resulted in the acceptance and increased adoption of critical inputs like fertiliser. However, with the experience gained in early 60's and from the feedback, it was increasingly realised that High Yielding Varieties (HYV), plant protection measures and water management practices are all important inputs, which are required alongwith fertilisers to increase the productivity. In brief, a complete package of agricultural inputs and services contributed significantly, which resulted in the 'green revolution'. This second phase can be traced from the second part of 60's to the beginning of 80's. In the third phase, our farming has progressed well with the integrated use of critical farm inputs, particularly with the consumption of higher levels of fertilisers, and more and more facility of irrigation. Consumption of fertilisers and other inputs is significantly higher in Punjab, Haryana, Western Uttar Pradesh, coastal districts of Andhra Pradesh, Sugarcane belts in South Gujrat and Maharashtra, and the irrigated green belt in Tamil Nadu. Intensive farming is being practised in these areas which has resulted in high crop productivity, almost matching the laboratory yields.

Between 1980-81 and 1988-89 the installed capacity of nitrogen almost doubled from 4.6 million tonnes to 8.147 million tonnes. The P_2O_5 capacity increased from 1.33 million tonnes to 2.7 million tonnes during the period.

TABLE 10

Consumption and Production of Fertiliser During the Period 1971-72 to 1983-84

Year	Nutrient	Consumption (Feb-Jan.)	Production (Apr-March)	Gap *i. e.* short-fall	Total gap of all nutrients
1971-72	N	1998	949	849	1418
(Apr-March)	P_2O_5	558	290	268	
	K_2O_5	301	-	301	
1976-77	N	2457	1862	595	1071
	P_2O_5	635	478	157	
	K_2O_5	319	-	319	
1977-78	N	2913	2000	913	1616
	P_2O_5	867	670	197	
	K_2O_5	506	-	506	
1978-79	N	3420	2173	1247	2167
	P_2O_5	1106	778	328	
	K_2O_5	592	-	592	
1979-80	N	3498	2224	1274	2268
	P_2O_5	1151	763	388	
	K_2O_5	606	-	606	
1980-81	N	3678	2164	1514	2510
	P_2O_5	1214	842	372	
	K_2O_5	624	-	624	
1981-82	N	4069	3143	926	1974
	P_2O_5	1322	950	372	
	K_2O_5	676	-	676	
1982-83	N	4224	3430	794	1973
	P_2O_5	1436	984	452	
	K_2O_5	727	-	727	
1983-84	N	5236(a)	3485	1751	3252
	P_2O_5	1757(a)	1055	702	
	K_2O_5	799(a)	-	799	

(a) Provisional.

Projected Fertiliser (NPK) consumption 2000 A.D

Projections regarding fertiliser (NPK) use by 2000 A.D. have been made by various workers which ranges between 18 to 22 m.t.. But it is unlikely that fertiliser consumption will exceed 17.6 m.t. (Table 11). It will require over 50% increase (11.6 m.t. to 17.6 m.t.) in next 10 years.

TABLE 11

Projected region-wise Fertiliser (NPK) Consumption (2000 A.D.)

Region No.	Fertiliser Consumption (2000 A.D)		Increase over (1988-89)	
	m.t.	kg/ha	m.t.	kg/ha
1	0.30	90	0.14	39
2	0.28	41	0.17	23
3	0.81	112	0.24	31
4	2.05	129	0.75	46
5	2.07	134	0.67	41
6	2.28	143	0.61	23
7	0.68	41	0.32	18
8	1.24	56	0.62	26
9	1.59	61	0.73	23
10	2.30	106	0.73	33
11	1.85	142	0.54	32
12	0.68	129	0.28	52
13	1.19	116	0.54	50
14	0.28	33	0.23	27
15	-	-	-	-
All India	17.60	93	6.57	31

By 2000 A.D. an average increase of 31 kg/ha in fertiliser consumption has been estimated over 1988-89. The extent of increase will be different in the different regions. The projections in Table 11 indicate that the maximum increase in fertiliser consumption (kg/ha) is likely to come from the Plains and Hill Regions (Zones 11, 12 & 13), followed by Gangetic Plains Regions (3, 4, 5 & 6)

Gap

Present nutrient gap (NPK removal by crops – NPK supply through fertilisers) and likely gap by 2000 A.D. have been shown as follows (Table 12).

TABLE 12

Region-wise Nutrient (NPK) Gap (Crop Removal – Supply through Fertilisers)

Region. No.	Present gap (1988-89) m.t.	Present gap (1988-89) kg/ha	Projected gap (2000 A.D.) m.t.	Projected gap (2000 A.D.) kg/ha
1	0.15	46	0.12	36
2	0.34	55	0.31	45
3	0.34	48	0.37	51
4	0.52	33	0.33	20
5	1.16	77	1.07	70
6	1.18	63	0.87	55
7	0.97	60	0.97	58
8	1.83	88	1.87	84
9	1.39	57	1.05	61
10	1.06	50	1.04	48
11	0.51	46	0.44	34
12	0.26	51	0.25	48
13	0.21	21	0.10	10
14	0.21	27	0.05	6
15	-	-	-	-
All India	9.79	55	8.84	47

Annual negative balance (gap) of about 9.8 m.t. of NPK exists at the present production level. A wide variation (0.15 to 1.83 m.t.) in nutrient gap exists among the regions. There are 5 regions (5, 6, 8, 9 & 10) where nutrient gap is considerably high (> 1 m.t.). The regions account for two-third (6.6 m.t.) of total NPK gap in spite of the fact that these regions consume the lion's share of fertiliser (55%) in the country. NPK gap varies considerably (21 to 88 kg) among different regions with average value of 55 kg. The data in Table 12 reveals that annual negative balance of over 50 kg/ha exists in nearly 70% of total gross cropped area in the country. If the gap is not bridged timely it will result in continuous depletion of nutrients over the years and thus making the soil less productive.

Projections (Table 12) reveal that annual NPK gap will be reduced by 1 m.t. in the country provided estimated fertiliser consumption of about 17.6 m.t. is achieved by 2000 A.D. Per ha NPK gap is also likely to come down to 47 from 55 kg. But wide variation in nutrient gap (6 to 84 kg/ha) among different regions is likely to continue.

Besides, NPK, a net negative balance of 0.5 m.t. of S per annum has been estimated. This is likely to increase in future due to shift from use of S containing fertilisers like Ammonium Sulphate and SSP towards the use of 'S free' fertilisers like urea and DAP. Likewise micro-nutrient deficiencies particularly that of Zn and Fe are also likely to engulf more areas in coming years, present use of organic manure and other sources so far is unlikely to check the micro-nutrient deficiency in intensively cultivated areas.

Bridging the Gap

It is difficult to estimate exact zonewise nutrient gap (negative balance) when the information on nutrient additions through other sources like organic manure, crop residues, irrigation water, rainfall etc. and nutrients losses through leachig and erosion are not available. Organic manures which were the primary source of nutrients in traditional agriculture still supplies some amount of nutrients and nutrient gap of 50 to 80 kg/ha which exists in most of the intensively cultivated regions is unlikely to be bridged by these sources.

Increasing demand of cow dung as the source of fuel due to increasing population is a major constraint in availability of organic manure. Installation of biogas plants which supply both organic manure and fuel, need to be encouraged. Large scale plantation of quick growing plants should be taken up. Growing of green manures like pigeon pea and dhaincha which supply firewood should also be encouraged. Unless the alternate source of energy is made available, availability of organic manure is unlikely to improve.

Due to livestock malnutrition in almost all parts of the country, the quality of organic manure produced is also degrading. India is painfully proud of sustaining 16% of the world's livestock on 2.4% of geographical area. However, the malnutrition in livestock is much severe than human beings. Inadequate fodder fed to livestock is also of poor quality, thus it reflects in organic manure produced.

Biological nitrogen fixation of about 50 to 60 kg N/ha by most leguminous and pulses crops has also been estimated. But how much is really available to the next crop cannot be estimated. Moreover, due to increasing pressure on land, it is unlikely that farmers will grow more pulses by replacing main crop. Therefore, short duration pulses should be popularised *viz.*, summer moong *i.e.* mixed cropping which besides increasing pulses production will help in improving soil fertility.

The use of organic manure may partially maintain soil fertility by growing green manures. But a large increase in food production would be needed to feed the ever-growing population which is likely to double in next 30 years. To remain self-sufficient, foodgrains production should also double during the same period. Since there is no scope of future increase in area, only alternative left, is to increase the productivity. Thus, sustaining foodgrains production in coming years will be much more challenging. Hence concreted efforts need to be made to make certain that poor soil fertility does not limit the crop production. This will require increased efficient and integrated use of all sources of the plant nutrients.

FERTILIZER DISTRIBUTION AND ORGANISATIONAL SET UP

The organization and management for fertilizer distribution is different from distributional system of other consumer goods, initially fertilizers were channelled to the farmers through Government Depots. This function, however, increasingly went to the cooperative institutions as a result of the recommendations made by the Famine Enquiry Commission (1945), the Second Foodgrains Policy Committee (1947), the Planning Commission (1952), the National Development Council (1958), the National Committee on Agricultural Administration (1958), and the working group on cooperative policy (1957). By mid 1960's cooperatives had not only predominated but a substantial monopolitic role in the distribution system of nitrogenous fertilizers in many states. In 1965 out of about 61,000 retail outlets of fertilizers, 78% were in the cooperative sector, 18% in the hands of private agencies and 4% Government system.

In general, distribution of fertilisers in the country is dominated by the private trade (see Flow Chart 1).

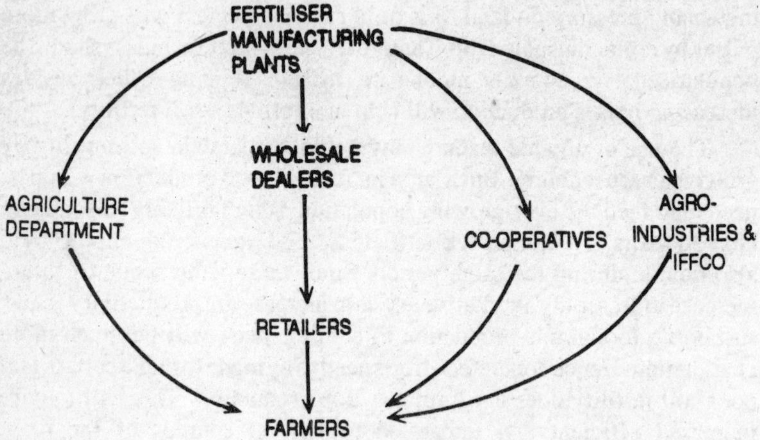

Flow Chart 1: of Distribution of Fertilisers

Patterns of Fertilisers Distribution

Physical-distribution policies are a potent instrument in the demand-stimulation process.[2] The narrow view of physical distribution starts with the fact that going concerns have much less freedom in choosing the components of their physical distribution system. However, the broad perspective would make channels of distribution just one aspect of the larger problem of physical distribution. In fact, the physical distribution objective is getting the right goods at the right places at the right time for the least cost. In brief a basic output of a physical distribution system is the level of customer service. Viewed in this context, following is a brief review of the existing physical distribution of fertilisers in the country and Uttar Pradesh.

Fertiliser distribution/consumption in physical terms is based on

2. Kotler, Philip (1972) "Marketing Management : Analysis, Planning and Control", Second Edition, Prentice Hall of India, Pvt. Ltd., New Delhi.

infra-structural facilities under normal conditions. For example, of the total fertiliser distribution/consumption, U.P. consumed 20.86% in 1980-81 and thus U.P. ranked third in respect of fertilisers consumption (Table 13), whereas it topped in consumption of fertilisers in physical terms. However, fertiliser consumption per hectare was highest in Punjab, followed by Tamil Nadu. Uttar Pradesh consumed the largest quantity of fertilisers (in physical terms) but per hectare consumption was only 48 kg. in 1980-81. Western Uttar Pradesh which also covers the Meerut area, consumed as much as 60 kg. per hectare which is just nearly half of Punjab's average.

Fertilisers are distributed by the private dealers, IFFCO, Department of Agriculture, Co-operative Societies, Agro-Industries, etc. in the country. It was observed that out of 1,93,211 metric tonnes fertilisers distributed in 1979-80 in Meerut Division, Meerut District alone consumed 24.55 per cent followed by Bulandshahar District, being 21.63 per cent of the total fertilisers distributed. Saharanpur District assumed the third place wherein about 21 per cent of fertiliser was distributed. It was lowest in Ghaziabad District *i.e.* 12.7 per cent of the total fertilisers distributed. However, in Muzaffarnagar District, it was 19.84 per cent of the total distribution of fertilisers. In 1980-81, the fertilisers distributed in Bulandshahar District was as much as 25.08 per cent of the total fertilisers (*i.e.* 222538 metric tonnes) distributed in the Meerut Division. Meerut District assumed the second position accounting for 24.27 per cent of the total distribution followed by Saharanpur District which shared 20.13 per cent of the total fertilisers distributed in Meerut Division. In Muzaffarnagar District, it was only 18.55 per cent of the total distribution. Again, it was lowest in Ghaziabad District which accounted for 11.97 per cent of the total distribution. Further, in 1981-82 Meerut District assumed the first place in fertiliser distribution which accounted for 24.21 per cent of the total distribution. However, the distribution in Bulandshahar District slumped down to second position in respect of total fertilisers distributed in Meerut Division. It was only 22.22 per cent of the total fertilisers distributed. Saharanpur District assumed the third place which accounted for 21.75 per cent of total fertilisers distributed. But, there was no change in respect of Ghaziabad District which consumed the lowest fertilisers *i.e.* 12.49 per cent of the total distribution. Keeping in view the use of fertilisers, it is seen that there was an increasing trend in fertilisers distribution. It increased from 1,93,238 metric tonnes in 1979-80 to 2,31,509 metric tonnes in 1981-82 which is about 1.2 times more than the distribution of fertilisers in 1979-80. In 1982-83, there was highest consumption of fertilisers in Bulandshahar District of 59237 metric tonnes *i.e.* 22.97 per cent followed by Meerut accounting for 21.59 per cent (*i.e.* 55,666 metric tonnes) of the total fertiliser distributed in Meerut Division.

TABLE 13

Consumption of Fertilisers in Different States (1980-81)

Sl. No.	State	Consumption ('OOO M tonnes)				Percentage of total consumption
		N	P	K	Total	
1.	Andhra Pradesh	399.4	130.9	45.3	575.6	10.44
2.	Assam	7.0	1.0	1.3	9.3	0.17
3.	Bihar	160.4	29.6	14.6	204.5	3.71
4.	Gujarat	204.1	117.2	35.5	356.9	6.47
5.	Haryana	187.4	31.3	12.1	230.3	4.17
6.	Karnataka	193.1	80.9	69.8	343.9	6.24
7.	Madhya Pradesh	121.7	59.2	15.9	196.8	3.57
8.	Maharashtra	264.6	91.3	65.1	421.0	7.63
9	Rajasthan	106.6	23.0	5.5	135.1	2.45
10.	Tamil Nadu	292.4	84.4	114.5	491.3	8.91
11.	Uttar Pradesh	860.6	209.3	80.6	1150.5	20.86
12.	Kerala	41.7	23.4	32.4	97.5	1.77
13.	Orissa	51.7	15.9	8.8	76.4	1.38
14.	West Bengal	167.3	70.8	44.7	282.8	5.13
15.	Himachal Pradesh	12.3	2.3	1.6	16.2	0.29
16.	Punjab	518.3	206.7	28.6	753.6	13.66
17.	Jammu & Kashmir	15.7	4.0	1.0	20.7	0.37
18.	Others	73.8	32.3	46.7	153.1	2.78
	Total	3678.1	1213.5	624.0	5515.5	100.00

Source: Fertilisers Statistics 1981-82, Fertiliser Association of India, New Delhi.

A typical example of 'Fertiliser Distribution' by different institutions and organisations is presented below pertaining to Saharanpur District, Uttar Pradesh, and in almost all other states, the same pattern of fertilizer distribution is followed with some minor variation/change.

1. Agriculture Department,
2. Co-operative Societies,
3. State Agro-Industries,
4. Private dealers, and
5. Sugarcane Co-operative Societies.

A study conducted[3] by the author jointly with Shri Tauseef Ahmed, a Research Scholar, in Roorkee Block, Distt. Saharanpur (now Hardwar) revealed that the private trade handled as much as 63.46% of the total distribution of fertilisers, whereas cooperative societies handled only 18% followed by State Agro-Industries (9%). However, the Agriculture Deptt., distributed only 3.32% of the total fertilizer distributed to the farmers.

In foreign countries, 20% to 25% of the retail selling price is the marketing cost[4] (comprising costs of transport, storage, distribution margin, and sales promotion). Of this 10% to 15% is cost of sales promotion. In India, only a fraction, of 1% to 2% out of the marketing cost of 17% to 20% is spent on sales promotion, including technical services to the customer. The bulk of marketing cost goes on transport, storage and distribution margins.

IRRIGATION WATER

Irrigation contributes substantially to the agricultural price stability, by removing to a large extent the elements of uncertainty in the agricultural production. The development of irrigation, however, involves heavy investments, but its purpose is to suitably change the availability of water in a stream both in space and time so that the available water is put to its most beneficial use.

---

3. Ahmed, Tauseef and C.S. Raghuvanshi (1981), 'Distribution of Fertilizers', Indian Journal of Marketing, Dec. 1981, Vol. XII, No. 4, pp. 28 to 32.
4. F.J. Heredia, 'Expanding the Market for Fertilizers: New Opportunities in Changing Agriculture', pp. 65, Proceeding to the 7th Alumni Conference, 1972, I.I.M., Ahmedabad.

Organisational Set Up

The following departments of government are concerned in one way or the other with the water distribution and management in Uttar Pradesh and other states as well:

1. Revenue Department,
2. Agriculture Department,
3. Irrigation Department,
4. Ground Water Organisation,
5. Minor Irrigation Department,
6. Block Development Agency,
7. Area Development Authorities, and
8. Agricultural Colleges and Universities.

However, organisational set up of Irrigation Department in U.P., which is charged with the function of the distribution of irrigation water is that the Chief Engineer is responsible for direction and controlling at the State level, assisted by Additional Chief Engineers. Chief Engineer coordinates the activities of Additional Chief Engineers, and deals with the Goverment. Every major project is kept under the charge of an Additional Chief Engineer. Further, the Superintending Engineers in the capacity of incharge of a certain circle work under the control of Additional Chief Engineers. Circle is divided into Divisions headed by an Executive Engineer. A division is then divided into sub-divisions headed by Assistant Engineer, who is further assisted by Junior Engineers – incharge of a section.

From functioning point of view, the work of the department is divided into three categories (i) Design, (ii) Construction, and (iii) Maintenance of Irrigation Works. Maintenance section of the departments look after the general maintenance of irrigation works and their operation. Junior Engineer is responsible for operation and maintenance of an outlet, at the lowest level. The work of supervision and maintenance of the department ends at the outlet (See Flow Chart, on the next page).

But the water distribution segment of a tubewell comprises a delivery tank, water distribution channels & field channels. Water distribution channels tend to become an important cost of tubewell irrigation as the capacity of a tubewell increases. Thus, in the case of a public tubewell the capital cost of the water distribution system (excluding the cost of field channels that are constructed and maintained by the

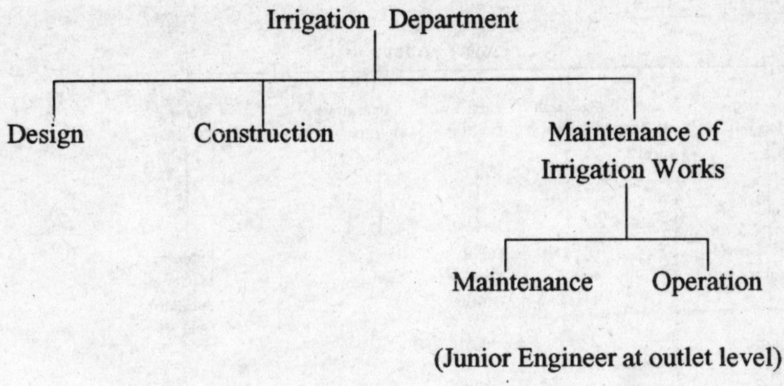

farmers themselves) becomes a substantial cost, especially if the command area of a tubewell is unduly extended either because of a desire to diffuse the benefits of public investment over a larger number of beneficiaries or because of low intensity of demand for tubewell water. Evidently, the distribution system is *cateris-paribus* much smaller for a tubewell providing productive irrigation for supporting intensive cultivation in the command area, and it still becomes smaller if the tubewell is deployed in an augmentation role so as to augment water supply in a surface water canal.

The present organisational set up of Sarda Sahayak Development Agency, U.P. is presented on the following page.

The organisational set-up for distribution of irrigation water and its management, is almost the same in all states except with a minor change. However, the role of each government department in distribution of water is discussed as under:

Revenue Department

Under the provision of U.P. Land Revenue Act (1901) controlling of all non-judicial matters connected with the land revenue in Uttar Pradesh other than matters connected with settlement is vested in the State Government and the control of all judicial matters and of all matters connected with settlement is rested in the Board of Revenue.

State has been divided into divisions, divisions into districts and districts into Tehsils which are also called sub-divisions of the districts.

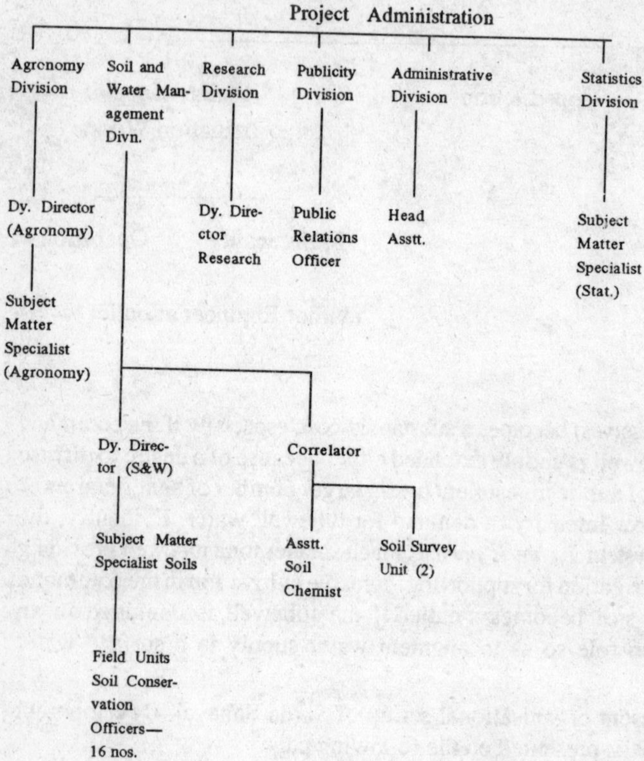

Head of Division is Commissioner who exercises authority over all the revenue offices in his division. Head of the district is Collector who exercises power and discharges his duties throughout his district. He maintains a map and a field book of each village in his district and records changes in the boundaries of each village or field and corrects needed errors annually. Assistant Collector of first class is incharge of sub-division. Head of Tehsil is called Tehsildar. In tehsil, Kanungo is responsible for supervision, maintenance and correction of annual revenue registers. Lekhpals are kept in each Taluka for preparation of revenue records.

Records of rights of each village is maintained in annual register. It shows all persons cultivating or otherwise occupying any land. Any change in possession of land either by succession or by transfer is intimated by the person getting possession to Tehsildar for making necessary changes in records. All disputes regarding boundary of fields, possession of the field and rent are decided by revenue courts. All agrarian reforms are carried out by revenue department. It collects rent *i.e.* revenue of fields and irrigation charges from farmers.

Agriculture Department

Agriculture department is headed by Director who is responsible for overall administration. There are Joint Directors and Deputy Directors working under him to control over different branches of agriculture. For example, there are Deputy Directors for agriculture implements, fertilizers, seeds, composts and aforestations etc. At district level, there is District Agriculture Officer under whom there are Agriculture Inspectors /Supervisors who come in direct contact with the Cultivators.

This department arranges seeds, fertilizers and pesticides etc. and supplies to cultivators through Block Development Officer but does not supervise its utilisation in the field. Utilisation part is left entirely on the farmers. It advises the farmers on request. One Agriculture Inspector/ Supervisor called Agriculture Development Officer from Agriculture Department is posted at block in the district. He renders advise at block level. In case of some insect pests or agricultural disease he is supposed to inspect the crop on information and suggests measures. He also arranges insecticides and pest control chemicals etc. needed for control. The department maintains field soil testing laboratories at regional level which carry out testing of soils to assess its fertility level, pH value etc. and advises application of fertilizer doses.

There are Soil Survey Divisions who carry out soil survey in the State for soil classification from the point of view of their irrigability and productivity. So far a small area of the State has been mapped. There are some Soil Conservation Divisions which take measures for conservation of soil. They also undertake field levelling at the cost of farmers.

Irrigation Department

For details, See Chapter Water Distribution Policies and Warabandi.

Agricultural Colleges and Universities

Agricultural Colleges and Universities in the country also impart knowledge on water use and management at Graduate and Masters level. They further educate the farmers and give them latest knowledge of water use *i.e.* particularly method of irrigation and timings of irrigation, which are not only helpful in boosting up production but also help in efficient use of water resources. Research work to evolve new seed varieties and agricultural technology is also done by Agricultural Universities, like Pantnagar University in U.P. and P.A.U. Ludhiana in Punjab. Refresher Courses for serving personnel are also run by some institutions like Water Resources Development Training Centre, University of Roorkee, and WALMIS in different States, with a view to apprise field personnel with the latest development and knowledge in water use and management.

Contorl on Cropping Pattern

In the present water distribution system in Uttar Pradesh there is no control over the cropping pattern that may be adopted by the cultivators in any particular command area with the result that extreme shortage of water is frequently felt in areas having excessive sugarcane cultivation. In some states like Maharashtra where block system is prevalent, the irrigation is allowed on a certain pre-determined cropping pattern and the maximum area for heavy water using crops allowed to be irrigated in any particular command is decided beforehand according to the availability of supplies. This sanction is given on long term basis *i.e.* six years or sometimes even longer and this system incorporates various policies pertaining to crop pattern, safeguarding land from water logging, maximising utilisation of the run off of the river during monsoon etc. Water supply is assured for these sanctioned blocks and rates are charged on the basis of area of the blocks. When additional supplies are available, the area outside the blocks can also be irrigated but they do not have any rights for getting supplies.

Pesticides

Although, the pesticides are not the complementary inputs, yet briefly their role in increasing production is discussed. The High Yielding Varieties are highly susceptible to insects and pests. The pesticides are yield saving inputs and with the expansion of area under high yielding varieties, the use of pesticides has also increased. With the process of adoption of New Technology more and more pesticides use by farmers is likely to increase in coming years. It is , therefore, an imperative necessity to provide these facilities to the farmers. Alone provision of fertilizers to increase agricultural production would not be sufficient, unless pesticides

are also provided to the farmers on cheaper rates at the time when these are required by the farmers at the right time and place, and at reasonable prices.

REFERENCES

1. Ahmad, Tauseef and C.S. Raghuvanshi (1981), 'Distribution of Fertilisers – A Study of Institutional Role', Indian Journal of Marketing, Vol. XII, No. 4.
2. Griliches, Z. (1959), 'Distribution Lags, Disaggregation and Regional Demand Function for Fertiliser', Journal of Farm Economics, Vol. 41, No. 1, pp. 90-102.
3. Hiranath, C.R. (1963), 'Marketing and Distribution of Fertiliser through Cooperative', Fertiliser Marketing News, Vol. 14, No. 1, pp. 10-11.
4. Parthasarathy, N.S. (1980), 'Fertiliser Marketing Infrastructure to Meet the Challenges of the Eighties', Fertiliser News, Vol. 25, No. 12, pp. 46-61.
5. Percy, P.F. (1981), 'Fertiliser Distribution and Marketing in Seria Leon in the Decade to 1990 and 2000 A.D. Some Aspects', FAO/FIAC, Rome.
6. Sikder, B.P. (1980), 'Handling and Distribution of Fertiliser in Bulk – Indian Experience', Proceedings of F.A.O. Seminar 1980 on Fertilisers in India in the Eighties, Part-II, MKTG II-3(11)/1-11.
7. Venkatappiah, B. (1968), 'Fertiliser Credit and Distribution: New Perspective and Old Problems', Proceeding of Seminar on Fertiliser Credit and Distribution, Fertiliser Association of India, New Delhi.
8. Jain, B.K. & Dr. (Miss) B. Swaminathan, 'Handbook on Fertiliser Technology', The Fertilizer Association of India, New Delhi.
9. Jain, B.K. & Satya Nand (1980), 'Productivity in the Indian Fertilizer Industry', Fertilizer News, the Fertilizer Association of India, New Delhi, p. 67.
10. Fertilizer News, The Fertilizer Association of India, Special Number on Fertilizer Marketing in Rainfed Agriculture together with Annual Review, 1984-85.
11. 'New Opportunities in Changing Agriculture', Proceedings of the 7th Alumni Conference, March 17th & 18th, 1972, Delhi, Indian Institute of Management, Ahmedabad.
12. Garg, S.P., Technical Memorandum, 39, U.P. Irrigation Research Institute, Lucknow, Uttar Pradesh.
13. Dhawan, B.D. (1979), 'Development of Tubewell Irrigation in India', Institute of Economic Growth, University Enclave, Delhi - 110007.
14. Indian Journal of Agricultural Economics, July-September, 1984, Vol. XXXIX, No. 3, Indian Society of Agricultural Economics, Mahatma Gandhi Road, Fort, Bombay.
15. Indian Journal of Agricultural Economics, October-December, 1985, Vol. XL, No. 4, Indian Society of Agricultural Economics, Mahatma Gandhi Road, Fort, Bombay.
16. 'Institutional Framework on Improved On-Farm Water Management in Pakistan', Special Report prepared by Water Management Research Project Staff, Colorado State University, U.S.A.

17. Proceedings of the Symposium on Social and Non-Economic Factors in Water Resources Development, Water Resources Series No. 47, United Nations.
18. Biswas, B.C. and Tewatia R.K., 'Micro-nutrient Status in Indian Agriculture', Fertiliser News 33 (11), 29-35 (1988).
19. Biswas, B.C. and Tewatia, R.K., 'Fertiliser Use in Different Agro-climatic Regions of India', *Fert. News*, 36 (2): 27-30 (1991).
20. Biswas, B.C. and Tewatia, R.K., 'Role of Sulphur in Balanced Plant Nutrition — Indian Experience', Paper presented in the International Symposium on the "Role of Sulphur, Magnesium and Micro-nutrients in Balanced Plant Nutrition", April 3-10, 1991, Chengdu, PRC (1991).
21. *Fertiliser Statistics* 1989-90, FAI, New Delhi (1990).
22. *Regional Statistics* (1988-89), FAI, New Delhi.
23. Swaminathan, M.S., 'Agriculture for 21 Century', *Kisan World*, January 11-12, 1991.
24. Tandon, H.L.S., 'Sulphur Research and Agricultural Production in India', FDCO, New Delhi (1986).

CHAPTER 14

LAND REFORMS AND THEIR SIGNIFICANCE IN EQUITABLE DISTRIBUTION OF WATER

INTRODUCTION

The very meaning of the term 'Land Reforms' varies from time to time. To some, for example, it means taking away land from the big land holders including government's vacant lands and distributing the same to the landless while to others it means land to the tiller. In the traditional and generally accepted sense land reform means the redistribution of property or rights in land for the benefit of landless agricultural labourers. However, in broadest sense land reform means 'any improvement in the institutions of land tenure and ownership'. On the whole land reforms consist of an integrated programme of measures meant to eliminate obstacles in socio-economic development that arise out of the defects in the agrarian structure.

The imbalance between the distribution of control over land, and the number dependent on it breeds social and economic inequalities. It also leads to unequal access to developmental activities, institutional facilities, decision-making process etc. Furthermore, the existing imbalance offers great social injustice in respect of land tenure system including the share-cropping between tenants and owners. These situations call for an appropriate land reform measures. A more radical the land reform the greater will be the equity of effect. Several studies made by FAO and other agencies for Asian countries showed the effects of differences between distribution of land holding size and yields (16, p. 215). The effects revealed that reduction in either holding size or inequity in land holding distribution is an important factor for increasing productivity and employment. Land reform measures should, therefore, be focused on three basic objectives, *viz.* (i) higher productivity, (ii) higher employment opportunities, and (iii) equity justice. Thus, an appropriate Agrarian Reform Policy is an important strategy for rural development as well as a move for promoting egaliterian goals for peasants. For balanced and sustained development of agricultural and rural economy, phasewise transition towards redistribution of land including other complementary programmes in terms of credit, extension services, High Yielding Varieties and overall improvements in technology, are imperative. Also it is evident that without effective measures to implement land reform measures and policy for equitable land distribution, it will be extremely difficult to improve the socio-economic conditions of the poor.

Land reform is not only a political slogan but an activator of technological diffusion and growth in the agrarian sector, obviously, an inquisitive mind is apt to ask why emphazise land reforms? Japanese had it but what is the necessity of this type of institutional reform? Before deliberating on the reforms made in India, it is better to discuss the necessity of land reforms in the country.

Compulsion for land reform, which has happened in countries with widely different historical and cultural background such as Japan/Iraq/ Cuba/Bolivia etc. basically emanates from two sources. Firstly, serious supply-demand imbalance in land. Secondly, from the fact that in the initial stage of growth land represent, by and large, the sole source of production in the economy. Ownership and terms governing tenancy vitally affects the life of millions, hence any government gets concerned about the subject.

However, the professional economists neglected the subject of land reforms because it concerns with the institutional framework of the society which they usually perceived as given. Now in the recent past attempts were made to examine the economic base of land reforms. In this attempt the work of N. Georgesca Roger entitled, 'Economic Theory and Agrarian Economics' (Oxford Economic Paper XII, 1960, pp. 1-40) which has been examined and extended by Dandekar is quoted:

> ".... defines over-population to be the situation in which, under conditions of full employment, the marginal productivity of labour falls short of minimum subsistence of the worker. In the more extreme situation, the marginal productivity of labour may even reach zero before the conditions of full employment are realised.... Most underdeveloped countries do show such signs

> of over-population in a more or less extreme form. The process of economic growth consists in accumulating more and more land capital resources so that marginal productivity may progressively rise – first above the zero and then above the minimum subsistence. It is then that the condition of over-population ceases to exist."

From the point of view of land reforms, Dandekar continues to elaborate Roger's approach (quote):

> "It should be recognized further that in the countries concerned, the agricultural sector is usually much more acutely over-populated than is the economy as a whole. This is because the non-agricultural sector in these economies is usually organised on the capitalist principles and hence does not permit workers in, unless they can contribute to the production more than the wages, they received in return. Consequently, the entire residual population is thrown on the agriculture which by its nature and tradition employs or accommodates whatever population is thrown on it without reference to the marginal productivity of labour conceived as a part of the problem of economic growth, the agrarian problem consists in holding on this population until an increasing part of its is withdrawn to the non-agricultural sector and in the meanwhile in employing it usefully so as to maximise the total output of the agricultural sector ... That capitalism cannot offer solution to this problem is easily demonstrated. Because capitalism, understood as an economic system regulated by profit maximisation, cannot offer employment to labour beyond the point where its marginal production is equal to marginal cost, therefore labour remains unemployed. Apart from its social consequences, this is obviously not even an economic solution for, though it maximises the profit-rent of the capitalist entrepreneur, it fails to maximise the total output of the agricultural sector."

Viewed from this angle a non-capitalist type farming, or conversly speaking individual peasant holding, offers opportunities though at a wage rate, less than the marginal productivity to a very large number of farmers – family workers etc. Thus, land reforms promote maximisation of total output that has an economic rational in a typical economy that LDC's represent.

SIGNIFICANCE OF LAND REFORMS IN INDIA

1. Promotion of incentives to invest, earn more by which process capital formation can be accelerated.
2. Social Justice: Tiller of the soil be given an economic status. Concentration of economic power that a large ownership of this productive resource represents is not conducive for the growth of democracy. Therefore, land to the tiller is a motto to obtain social justice.

Viewed from this point of view, the concept represents two institutional reforms: One is related to agrarian relations and the other to the size of the unit of cultivation. The latter component has quite often been objected upon the arguments, will not this redistribution of ownership reduce productivity by dividing up large estates? This is really very important and hence it is proposed to discuss it later in the context of land ceilings as a measure in land reforms in India.

In different countries land reform measures have been introduced to meet different requirements of individual countries. According to U.N. Survey, the programme of utilisation of land incorporates several reformative policies. In Canada and Australia, it has been done with the basic objectives of conferring ownership rights on tenants. In Spain, it has embraced a much wider field with a view to improve both the economic conditions of farmers and output of the farm. On the other hand in Italy land reforms include measures for the improvement of the social condition both for moral and civic reasons as also for economic considerations. The objective set forth in the Agricultural Land Law of Japan reads out, 'In recognition of the fact that agricultural land shall be most appropriately owned by none other than the cultivators thereof.'

If all these land reforms discussed above are to be catalogued into suitable categories, it is interpreted that either one or more of the following aims are intended to be achieved.

(i) To provide an opportunity for the development of farmer's personality. In agrarian economies land has economic and prestige value. Without possessing land of their own, even a small piece of land, people have no status and suffer from a sense of injury.

(ii) To provide an opportunity for the development.

(iii) To eliminate the exploitation of one class with another.

(iv) To remove the inhibitions at institutional level towards augmenting agricultural output, both total and per unit of land.

(v) To increase and stabilise the volume of farms employment through a wiser distribution of the ownership of land.

(vi) To bring about a fair and equitable distribution of agricultural income.

In our country where land and labour productivity is very low, a change in ownership of land can substantially result in capital accumulation but not on a scale sufficient to meet the requirements of successful agriculture. However, redistribution of land can help to free the landless from the bondage and to create in him the 'pride of possession'. After living without incentive and for generations oriented mainly towards sheer survival ownership of a few plots of land gives them a measure of self-respect, incentive and above all, a sense of equality-pre-conditions for higher productivity.

Land reform in India represents a grand design to revolutionize the relations between the government, the owner, and the cultivator of the land, change the size of farms in an economically meaningful way and thereby revolutionize investment technology and productivity in conjunction, of course, with other major policies. However, one would be benefitted by a reference to the then Prime Minister's Inaugural Address to the Chief Ministers' Conference on Land Reforms on 26th-27th Sept. 1970 (quote).

> "....During this period, we have had unmistakable evidence, and clear warning of the awakening and impatience in the country size....The people in this country have entrusted their destiny in our hands. We owe it to them to think deeply and honestly over recent developments. Why is social discontent in the country-side on the increase? Why is it erupting into violence with greater frequency? The answer to these questions is obvious, but it bears repetition. The land reform measures implemented have failed to match the legitimate expectations which were first fostered on millions of cultivators during the national movement. We have yet to create an equitable tenurial system for the village poor... in short, we have yet to create institutional conditions which would enable small farmers, tenants and landless labourers to share in the agricultural New Deal."

This paragraph has been quoted in order to highlight the reasons, of course, as visualised by the party in power *i.e.* the government, why land reform has become a problem of national importance and national urgency. Concurrently, it admits failures in a very striking manner. As a student of economics, however, these reform measures have to be understood with academic coolness and political overtures.

Land reforms have succeeded when they were initiated by authoritarian rulers, while in Japan, Taiwan and partially in Korea, land reforms were more or less imposed, efforts even through partial democratic methods ended in a stalemate in Mexico. This is because, under a dictatorship or an authoritarian rule, there are hardly any interference of politicians or the village elites and also no legal limitations. On the contrary, in democratic countries like India, implementation of land reforms presents many serious problems from vested interests *viz.* rich land owners, established commercial and political interests. In some cases, even, there are interference from foreign forces (as in Philippines). In India, it is a pity that even though land reforms form an important and integral part of the policy matter of the Central Government aimed at rural poverty alleviation, neither the Centre nor the States appeared to be serious to their implementation.

The First Five Year Plan set out a broad outline of the policy to be followed by the State governments; the policy was elaborated in the Second Plan:

(i) To remove such impediments in the way of agricultural production as came from the character of the agrarian structure and to create conditions for evolving as speedily as possible an agrarian economy with high levels of efficiency and productivity.

(ii) To establish an egalitarian social order and eliminate social inequalities.

The Third Plan envisaged the implementation of the Policy evolved during the earlier plans. This period is characterized by Legislative measures on the various aspects. At the time of the Fourth Plan it was realised that the entire policy needs to be oriented having regard to the technological developments in agriculture and the social requirements of the time, is a reflection of the pressing need to be effective and realistic. To review the progress of land reform measures, to identify weakness and gaps in the land laws and their implementation and to review the land policy in the context of technological developments in agriculture -- a Central Land Reform Committee was set up in 1970 with Union Minister of Agriculture as its Chairman. As a result of this reoriented policy and directives from the Committee, land ceiling and redistribution was accelerated.

The Draft Fifth Plan observed: 'The objectives of land policy have been to remove such non-motivational and other impediments to increase agricultural production as arise from the agrarian structure inherited from the past and also to eliminate all elements of exploitation and social injustice within agrarian system so as to, ensure equality of tenurial status and opportunity to all sections of the rural population' (Draft Fifth Plan, Vol. II, p. 42).

The various reformative measures when placed together reveal that reforms of the following type were introduced:

(i) *Abolition of Intermediaries*: This topped the list in priority. The system of Zamindari/Jagirdari/Talukdaries in all covering 40% of the area of the country had to be done away forthwith. Owners of large holdings resorted to delatory tactics through courts. However, this could be through. Legislative provisions, had yet to be enacted (1970) for abolition of some of the remnants of intermediary tenures in some states as temporarily settled estates in Assam, intermediary interests in Tata Nagar, Zamindari in Bihar, Sripandar Vogai lands in Kerala etc. The main problem faced by the government is to bring about uniformity in the rights of tenants and rationalisation of assessment payable by them, and the build-up of effective land revenue and land reform agencies in the former zamindari areas. Meanwhile, with the abolition of intermediary tenures like Zamindaris, Jagris, Inams, etc. more than 20 tenants have been brought in direct contact with the State.

(ii) *Tenancy Reforms*: Three types of cultivating tenants existed. These were occupancy tenants; non-occupancy tenants *i.e.* tenants at will, and sub-tenants. These continued even after the abolition of intermediary tenures. Various measures have been taken to give security to the tenant; fixation of fair rent and eventually to bring them in direct contact with the State. Further, the right of resumption by the land-owner from his tenants has been further curtailed.

(a) In all tenancy laws, 'personal cultivation' includes cultivation through servants or labourers provided they are paid in cash or kind but not in crop share. Personal supervision is not made essential; supervision by any member of the family is allowed. Residence in the locality concerned is also not required. Thus, owing to several reasons, tenancy reforms have not been able to eliminate absentee-landlordism.

(b) One major obstacle in tenancy reforms had been the so-called 'voluntary surrender' of tenancy rights by the tenants. A large number of landowners have been able to engineer such surrenders and regain tenanted land. Obviously, it could become difficult for the tenants to resist pressures put on them due to their social status and financial position. Besides, all states have enacted laws on fair rent. The conferment of ownership on the tenants had been implemented in Andhra Pradesh (Telangana region), Gujarat, Haryana, Himachal Pradesh, Karnataka, Kerala, Maharashtra, Madhya Pradesh, Orissa, Rajasthan, Tripura and Uttar Pradesh. But, where ownership was conferred on tenants, future leasing of land was prohibited and all leases in contravention of this prohibition were declared invalid. However, there is no reason to believe that the demand for land has declined or will decline in future and therefore, there would be little demand for land on lease from the landless. Also, no measures have been taken where the pressure on land can be reduced through improved opportunities in sectors other than agriculture. Secondly, population growth continues unabated and shows no signs to slow down.

(iii) *Ceiling on Land Holdings*: The entire range of porblem relating to ceiling has been covered at the later stage, in a way continuation of this.

(iv) *Consolidation of Holdings*: Indian farming was known for its absentee landlordism and for smallness and fragmentation all over the world and evidence of this is available in the Report of the Royal Commission on Agriculture in India. Consolidation, unlike other land reform measures does not relate to tiller-owner dimension of the problem. However, it proposes to do away with the scatteredness of the operational holdings. With varying degrees of success each State in India has gone ahead with this programme.

Consolidation of land holdings stands for amalgamation and redistribution of fragmented land so as to reduce the number of plots and make them more compact. It provides for giving every title holder a compact area equivalent in value to what he held before in scattered plots. Thus, consolidation of land holdings has a seven-fold objective; restore economic viability of holdings, increase potential for more efficient use of water, evolve better cropping pattern, improve resource use efficiency, reduce wastage of land area used for embankments and boundaries etc. cut down litigation over boundaries, and increase potential for comprehensive village planning. Consolidation of land holding laws were enacted in all states other than Kerala and Tamil Nadu. But consolidation has been linked to village planning in Andhra

Pradesh, Himachal Pradesh and Rajasthan. In Uttar Pradesh and Punjab, consolidation is considered as an integrated programme of village reconstruction including laying inter-village roads, and building schools and hospitals.

Impediments in Implementation

Implementation of land reforms is beset with numerous difficulties. These are political, social, economic and legal. Here only the more significant ones have been listed:

(i) *Defective Laws*: Legislative measures adopted from time to time contained many exemptions and allowed flexibility to states and thus the entire aim of putting the agricultural land within the orbit of land reforms has been defeated. Some argue that this element was an off-shoot of the lack of political will radically alter the tiller-ownership relationship.

(ii) *Inadequate Application*: Time lag between the intention to alter the existing land-owner-tiller relationship, enactment into laws and its application has often helped the owner to make fake transfers taking out the land from the legal ambit. This trend got further incentive from the inadequate administrative support. Regarding implementation and the required coordination, it may be quoted extensively with advantage, from the 5th Report on the Progress in Land Reforms of the United Nations.

The basic record being the village record of titles, is defective which have led to evasion of the ceiling laws. Implementation of tenancy reforms has also been hampered due to inadequate land records. Further, the right of resumption continued in Assam, Bihar, Haryana, Punjab and Tamil Nadu. In some states like Bihar, Haryana, Orissa, Punjab and Rajasthan, landlords could resume land upto the ceiling limit. In other states, the resumable area was fixed below the ceiling limit. In many states, the law also required a minimum area to be left with the tenant. But the right of resumption often led to insecurity of tenancy and the harassment of tenants:

> "... While on the one hand the nature of the land reform programme would indicate the nature of the administrative organization required for its implementation, on the other hand administrative factors such as the nature of the existing administrative structure, the availability of personnel, the existence

or otherwise of land records would dictate the scope, timing and phasing the programme. For instance, an integrated programme would require large number of trained personnel in a number of different fields. In the absence of such personnel, it would be useless (and even harmful) to introduce, with a programme, since it would be deemed to failure. Similarly, the granting of individual ownership would require an adequate and accurate system of land records ... the production of which through cadastral survey and land registration would take a long time."

After Independence the rural sector remained under a bureaucracy meant originally to rule and not serve; land records were anything but adequate.

These two deficiencies in conjunction with class-caste ridden social structure aggravated the situation of non-implementation. Under the Constitution, the main responsibility for enactment of land legislation and its implementation is that of the state governments wherein local pressures are bound to cause difficulties. Uniformity received strength after the meeting of the Central Land Reforms Committee (CLRC) held on 3rd August, 1971, under the chairmanship of the then Minister of Agriculture.... Hence, it is better to give their main recommendations later.

Thimmaiah and Aziz[1] outlined the causes of failure in implementation of Land Reforms in Karnataka which are: (i) Caste System and its interaction with State power and bureaucracy. Caste System contributes to the failure of Land Reforms in two ways: it weakens class consciousness among the potential beneficiaries and inhibits growth of a supporting peasant movement, and (ii) Caste alliances of the rich land-owners with bureaurcracy, and those in State power work against the effective implementation. Further, the role of Caste System in contribution to the failure of Land Reforms has been highlighted. The Inam Abolition is explained in Caste Terms. The owners of Inam lands were mainly Brahmins, absentee owners, and the tenants of these lands belonged to the dominant majority castes who constituted the vote banks after Independence. It suited the political interests of those in power *i.e.* the non-Brahmins landed interest *viz.* Vokkaligas and Lingayats, to bring in legislation for abolition of Inams. But the bureaucracy was controlled by Brahmins, and this contributed to the delay in implementation.

1. Thimmaiah, G. and Abdul Aziz, 1984, "Political Economy of Land Reforms", Ashish Publishing House, New Delhi-26.

Though, legislation for abolition of Inam lands was passed in 1947, it was made into an Act only in 1954.

If the delays in the implementation of Inam legislation are attributed to Brahmins bureaucracy, which had a vested interest in Inams. The delays in initiating a radical Ceiling Legislation upto the early 1970's are attributed to the dominance of the land owning Lingayat group in State power. The growing power of the dominant non-Brahmin caste groups is illustrated by the facts on the changing composition of the Karnataka Legislation Assembly by caste. While the share of Brahmins in the Legislative Assembly declined since 1952, the Lingayats and Vokkaligas held dominant position in the Assembly with more than 60% of the Legislature. There was also a shift from non-Agricultural to Agricultural groups. Thus, the dominance of non-Brahmins land-owners in State power contributed to delays in radical ceiling legislation while resulting in a stiff tenancy legislation. The contrast is traced to the interplay of Caste politics. While ceiling legislation affects the land owning Vokkaligas and Lingayats, the tenancy legislation affects the Brahmin absentee landlord's and the Vokkaligas-Lingayat coalition in State power had less to lose by a stiff tenancy legislation. The more radical ceiling legislation of the early 1970's is attributed to the installation of non-dominant minority backward group in power, reduced the strength of dominant landlord caste groups in legislature and the support of a Brahmin bureaucracy which by this time lost its landed interests.

As regards the implementation of the 1974 Act, the post-1977 period implementation suffered a set back as compared to the pre-1977 period. This is explained mainly in terms of a number of factors; the renewed power of the dominant majority caste group, the growing share of the dominant majority caste groups in bureaucracy, and the conversion of land Tribunals into an institution for distribution of spoils among politicians.

CEILINGS ON LAND HOLDING: THE CONTROVERSY

Emphasis on ceiling on land ownership underwent metamorphic change between the 1950's and the 1970's. Some lessons appear to have been learnt from the past. The policy of ceiling would be able to make contributions of the following types:

1. Meeting the widespread desire to possess a land.
2. Reducing glaring inequalities in ownership and use of land.[2]

---

2. After nearly 35 years since Acharya Vinoba Bhave launched the 'Bhoodan' and later the 'Gramdan' movement, only about half the total land donated to the Sarvodaya leader has been distributed so far.

3. Reducing inequalities in agricultural incomes.
4. Enlarging the sphere of self-employment.

While obtaining the above mentioned results, it has to be ensured that the ceiling does not lead to the establishment of uneconomic holding; in other words the size must be efficient to adopt and work under the given technology (in the foreseable future) with a degree of efficiency should not suffer with size disabilities.

In this context, the yardsticks for determining the minimum farm size, three norms are available, a bullock unit, a labour unit and an income unit; ceiling may be a multiple of such holdings. Usually three types of the family holdings (determined by any one of the three norms listed above) were recommended. These three norms are discussed as follows:

(a) *Bullock Unit*: The family farm should be of a size as to employ fully the indivisible inputs especially a pair of bullock.

(b) *Labour Unit*: The family farms should be of a size that it would employ fully the labour of the farm family (manpower of an average sized family) without the need to work outside the farm.

(c) *Income Unit*: It should provide a minimum income for a civilized life, for example Rs. 3500 per annum per family.

On a deeper probe, it can be established that farm size should be determined by any of the above noted yardsticks which will vary from region to region and in the same region according to the level of technological development.

Whatever may be the yardstick, a nation characterised with deficits in most of the products, the ceiling on land holdings has to be such as not to introduce size disabilities. Thus, the issue of maximum permissible ownership is linked with the determination of the minimum size since ceiling is viewed as an aid to production. The Congress Agrarian Reforms Committee defined an economic holding as one, under the given agro-economic conditions, that would provide a reasonable standard of living in addition to full employment for a family of normal size and at least a pair of bullocks (that it should need all the three norms listed above). The Planning Commission replaced the norm of economic holding with that of a family holding equivalent to a plough unit/or to a labour unit working with such assistance as is customary in agricultural operations. The exact area of a family holding was to be fixed in each region separately according to various factors such as type of soil, nature of crop etc. In May, 1955 the Planning Commission set up a Panel on Land Reforms which recommended: "The limit should be three family holdings for an average family in which the number of members does not exceed five. Due additional family holding should be allowed for each additional member subject to a maximum of six family holdings."

Since no central direction was given 'prior to Central Land Reforms Committee', each State was free to adopt its norms fully utilising the defining factor of the local condition with the result that:

(a) In some States family was taken as the unit and in some other individual.

(b) Relative valuation of different types of land (irrigated and unirrigated land) was tackled differently.

(c) Various kinds of exemptions were provided in the name of efficiently managed farms/plantations etc.

(d) Under different laws transfers were disregarded differently *i.e.* in Andhra Pradesh, Uttar Pradesh, Himachal Pradesh and West Bengal, all transfers after the prescribed date, were null and void or disregarded, but in Bihar, Delhi, Manipur and Tripura transfers were made through registered documents for valuable considerations.

As a consequence the levels of ceilings fixed in different States varied, a glimpse of which can be had from the following tables:

TABLE 1

State	Level of ceilings (Acres)
1. Andhra Pradesh	10.93 to 131.17
2. Gujarat	7.69 to 53.44
3. Karnataka	10.93 to 87.45
4. Rajasthan	8.91 to 136.00

Source: Note on ceiling on Agricultural Holdings considered by the Central Land Reforms Committee held on April 16, 1971. In fact, a perusal of the said document makes an interesting reading as how sincerely the land ceilings were drawn-up.

No doubt that effective action under land ceilings could not make much headway which can be ascertained from the following details :

TABLE 2

State-wise Details (June 30, 1992)

(In Lakh Acres)

States/UTs	Area declared surplus	Area taken poss-ession	Area distri-buted	Beneficiaries (in Lakhs)
Andhra Pradesh	7.29	5.49	5.04	4.19
Assam	6.10	5.49	4.62	4.03
Bihar	4.75	3.96	2.77	3.27
Gujarat	2.52	1.55	1.32	0.29
Haryana	1.21	1.15	1.13	0.38
Himachal Pradesh	2.84	2.82	0.03	0.04
J & K	4.56	4.50	4.50	4.50
Karnataka	2.71	1.56	1.15	0.30
Kerala	1.35	0.93	0.64	1.40
Madhya Pradesh	3.21	2.75	1.83	0.70
Maharashtra	7.04	6.24	5.26	1.33
Manipur	0.02	0.02	0.02	0.01
Orissa	1.73	1.62	1.49	1.27
Punjab	1.38	1.05	1.02	0.27
Rajasthan	6.07	5.50	4.38	0.76
Tamil Nadu	1.82	1.71	1.46	1.21
Tripura	0.02	0.02	0.02	0.02
Uttar Pradesh	5.38	5.06	3.64	3.14
West Bengal	12.69	12.01	9.36	20.44
D&N Havell	0.09	0.09	0.06	0.03
Delhi	0.01	Neg.	Neg.	Neg.
Pondicherry	0.02	0.01	0.01	0.01
Total	72.81	63.53	49.75	47.59

Since the inception of Land Ceiling Programme in the country, a total of 72.81 lakh acres of land have been declared surplus under the various ceiling laws. Of this 49.75 lakh acres have been distributed.

RECOMMENDATIONS OF THE CENTRAL LAND REFORMS COMMITTEE

The Central Land Reforms Committee gave a new dimensions to the programme of land reforms by recommending certain uniformity in ceiling laws plugging many of the known loopholes; it recommeded a lower ceiling unit. For fixing the norms were clearly laid down, exemptions were taken-out. More significant is their recommendations to fix ceiling in various States within certain limits. In the following paragraphs, their recommendations regarding the ceiling on land holdings as finalised in their meeting held on 3rd August, 1971 are given as under.

(i) Ceiling should be applicable for the family, as a whole, the term 'family' being defined so as to include husband, wife and minor children.

(ii) Where the number of members in the family exceeds five, additional land may be allowed for each member in access of five in such a manner that the 'total area to the family does not exceed twice the ceiling limit for a family'.

(iii) The ceiling for a family of five members may be fixed within the range of 4.05 to 7.29 hectare of perennially irrigated land or irrigated land capable of growing two crops. Since agro-climatic conditions vary from area to area the committee only laid down the range within which states were free to fix the ceiling.

(iv) For various categories of land, conversion ratios should be fixed taking into account availability of water, productivity, soil classification, crops grown etc. However, an absolute ceiling for a family even in the case of dry lands was put at 21.86 hectare thereby limiting sizeable variations.

(v) Exemptions in the existing laws in favour of mechanised farms, well managed farms, etc. were to be withdrawn.

(vi) Exemptions in favour of plantations of tea, coffee, cardamom, rubber etc. should be carefully examined in consultation with the Ministers concerned and State Governments. Thereafter, this and other types of exemption should be discussed with the Chief Ministers in order to formulate the national policy.

Since then, *i.e.* after the Central Land Reforms Committee's recommendations and consequent changes in the socio-political atmosphere, ceiling laws of most States have been amended and the present position with regard to the ceiling is indicated (as illustrated only a few States have been listed) in the following Table 3:

TABLE 3

Sl. No.	State	Level of ceilings (hectares)
1.	Andhra Pradesh	4.05 to 21.85
2.	Bihar	6.07 to 18.21
3.	Haryana	7.25 to 21.85
4.	Himachal Pradesh	4.05 to 21.14 (in certain specified areas upto 28.33 hectares)
5.	Punjab	7.00 to 21.80
6.	Uttar Pradesh	7.25 to 18.21

Bhoodan Yagna

The total land donated to the Sarvodaya leader, who had launched the 'Bhoodan' and later the 'Gramdan', still remains undistributed and thus, 988237.65 acres of land awaits distribution.

According to latest estimates, 909888.26 hectare of land has been distributed till now, out of the 1898125.90 hectare received in 'Bhoodan'.

Bihar, which had led in the land donation movement with a tally of 858165.99 hectare is the major defaulter with 604211.74 hectare still to be distributed. However, out of more than 8.50 lakh hectare donated during the mid-fifties, only about 343832.79 hectare were found to be fit for cultivation. Of this, only 253954.25 hectare have been distributed and about 89878.54 hectare of culturable and 514333.20 hectare of unculturable land is still to be distributed.

The next major defaulter is Rajasthan. In this State, out of the 243408.50 hectare received in Bhoodan, only 56880.97 hectare have been distributed among the landless. According to the report furnished by the State Government, distribution work was in progress in the Chhattergarh area in Bikaner District. This area, it may be mentioned, has recently come under the command area of the Indra Gandhi Nahar Pariyojna. Earlier, it was all more or less desert. The State Government has also reported that records of 20242.92 hectare out of the donated land were being verified from the Revenue record.

Although the donation in Gujarat was modest *i.e.* only 54436.03 hectare, the distribution too has been very poor – only 10984.21 hectare.

Out of the 166088.66 hectare received in Madhya Pradesh, 67906.48 hectare are still to be distributed out of which about 23076.92 hectare are said to be unfit for cultivation.

Orissa appears to have registered the best achievement with 231566.80 hectare out of the 256625.10 hectare received in bhoodan. The reconstituted State Bhoodan Yagna Committee has decided to distribute the remaining land within three years and to plant trees etc. on land found unsuitable for cultivation.

In Maharashtra, a total of 44534.0 hectare has been donated, out of which 33757.09 hectare have been distributed.

Uttar Pradesh has achieved the best results, better than that of Orissa even of the176688.66 hectare donated, as much as 170365.18 hectare have been distributed.

Small areas were donated in some other States too, like Assam, Haryana, Karnataka, Punjab and Tamil Nadu.

Size and Productivity: But for the recent years, a great debate followed, during the Second Five Year Plan and immediately following years, concerning the size desirability that would be introduced due to lowering of the ceilings. At the back of the argument was the commonly accepted notion that size and productivity are highly correlated dimensions and any reduction in size would, if so affected mean lowering the productivity of farm efficiency. The Farm Management Survey, initiated in India on a national scale in 1954, revealed that this politically sensitive issue could be examined scientifically. However, it is not feasible to attempt a detailed review of each one of the argument for and against size and productivity relationship.

Without going into the methodological series, of some important studies conducted by Internationally known Economists *viz.* Dantwala, Raj Krishna, Hanumantha Rao, A.K. Sen and Khusro, revealed by and large an agreement in academics on certain issues:

(i) Farm size can be defined either in terms of a single input, say hectare (*i.e.* acreage) or in terms of output, farm efficiency either in terms of output per unit of a single input acreage or as output per unit of cost of all inputs. Both these sets suffer with limitations and a policy maker has to make a decision in the light of yardsticks that are intended to be used.

(ii) As farm size (acreage or hectare) expands, gross output per acre declines. There are certain studies contributing to the idea of constant return to scale. In any case not many have disputed this contention.

To quote from the 'Studies in Farm Management in West Bengal Report for 1954-55 to 1956-57' (Economic Weekly, Annual Number, February, 1961, p. 326):

'Farms of moderately large size rather than the biggest ones are observed to have earned the maximum profit. The clue to the successful performance of these farms lies in the adoption of multiple and diverse cropping pattern which combines in a satisfactory manner growing of different crops. The farms that have earned the maximum profit out of all the farms in the three years have farms size 9 and 12 acres .... usually the farms of moderate size are observed to earn maximum profit per acre while it is mostly the small farms[3] that have incurred very high loss per acre' (Explanation : This loss has been ascribed to total or partial crop damage due to drought and flood).

(iii) As farm size expands (acreage), net profit per acre increases which stands in sharp contrast to that of decline productivity with increase in size. This is so because small farms have a surplus in overheads/home labour and when a share price is placed such home produced inputs per acre cost goes up and their profitability (not the yield per acre) goes down.

Taking a broader view of the situation the impression of constant returns to scale is quite strong. If such is the case, then it dispels the fear that land ceiling can adversely affect agricultural productivity efficiency. Of course, below a minimum the ceiling may adversely affect the 'Cut-Off' point which has to be kept in view.

With the introduction of seed-fertiliser-irrigation break-through, usually captioned as the "Green Revolution" the High Yielding Varieties Programme (HYVP), the possibility to further lower down the ceiling has gained impetus. For, some time, it was feared that the adoption of `New

3. If small holdings have proved productive in countries like Japan and Taiwan, it does not necessarily mean that they would be successful in India too. There are many other factors in Japan and Taiwan which contributed to the success of small farms: climate, timely rain, adequate irrigation facilities, labour use, supply of improved seeds, fertilisers, insecticides, efficient organisational set-up and technical guidance.

Technology' may get a setback due to the recommended lowering of ceiling by the Central Land Reform Committee. The All India Survey was launched to adversely affect the productivity efficiency of farms consequent to the lowering of ceiling on farm holdings. On the contrary, indications are that the "New Technology" carries potents of radical lowering of ceilings in regions endowed with better infra-structure *i.e.*, endowed with an assured irrigation/financing facilities.

Thus, the present day controversy on land ceiling is more on the inter-sectoral income parity *i.e.*, the level of income that an agriculturist has the moral right to claim to earn from his land keeping in view the level permissible to his urban counterpart (entrepreneur).

Before concluding this, let it be clear that importance of ceilings on farm holdings without care to intersectoral balance issue, and to place it below a critical minimum may create serious economic and social problems. But, to keep the ceiling too high, will forfeit the main objectives of the land reforms. Effective carriage of the philosophy of 'land to the tiller' plus adequate infrastructure facilities specially suited to small farmers like adequate provision of irrigation[4], fertilizers, seed and cash finance and linked with the facility of efficient marketing institution are the most urgent needs of the nation. Thus, the programme of land reform has to be an integrated business and should not be viewed in isolation.

ROLE OF LAND REFORMS IN EQUITABLE DISTRIBUTION OF WATERS

The average size of holding in India is as low as 2.1 hectare and that too is handicapped with scattered plots/fields of the farmers. Besides, the condition is further aggravated on account of defective laws of inheritance which accelerates the fragmentation of holdings of the farmers. Further, the imbalance between the distribution of control over land and the number dependent on it breeds social and economic inequalities. It also leads to unequal access to irrigation water more particularly to surface water *i.e.* canal, and also to developmental activities, institutional facilities, decision-making process. Moreover, caste system also contributed to the failure of equitable distribution of water.

4. Dantwala, M.L. and C.H. Shah (1971), 'Evaluation of Land Reforms (with special reference to the Western Region of India), published by the Indian Society of Agricultural Economics, Bombay-400 001.

The failure in the redistribution of land to the poor through land reform is well documented in several early studies by the erstwhile Research Programmes Committee of the Planning Commission, Government of India. Subsequent studies have also revealed the failure in the redistribution of land to the marginal and small farmers through land reforms.

Implementation of land reforms could not successfully be affected with the seriousness it was expected because of loopholes and deficiencies in laws, insufficient administrative machinery, prolonged litigation, lack of awareness among them about their rights and lack of regular monitoring of land reforms programmes at the State level. Therefore, land reforms could not contribute much in equitable distribution of water, which mainly happened due to:

(i) Defective land laws.
(ii) Inadequate application.
(iii) Smallness and fragmented holdings.
(iv) Improper land levelling and shaping.
(v) On-farm development.

Consolidation of Holdings

Legislative measures adopted from time to time allowed flexibility to States and thus, entire efforts of consolidation of holdings have been defeated. The purpose to do away with the scatteredness of the operational holdings and put it in one or two compact blocks is also lost due to defective laws of inheritance. Since after every 10 to 15 years again the problem of scatteredness and fragmented holdings would arise. Such a situation does not contribute much in equitable distribution of water. A farmer with 3 or 4 chaks of his holdings can neither have his own tube-wells nor boring in each chak nor he (farmer) can afford to have expensive irrigation by adopting small scale lift technology. In fact, consolidation of holdings is a work which enables field channels to be constructed and water to be distributed in a more efficient manner. Therefore, a very effective consolidation of holdings can be much helpful in equitable distribution of water. The fragmented holdings further aggravate the situation and become a stumbling block in unequal distribution of water due to lack of reliability in the supply of canal water to each and every farm holding as these farms cannot have their own irrigation.

Land Levelling for Uniform Distribution of Water

Land levelling is a very crucial component in the water distribution. But its poor progress is mainly due to small farm sizes, large investment needs etc. Therefore, land levelling needs to be done in those areas and projects where uneven topography is a serious constraint especially in slopes ranging from 1 to 3 per cent.

Land reforms could hardly help in land levelling and therefore, irrigation water is not being uniformly and efficiently used by the farmers. Irrigation water is most efficiently utilised by crops, if it is distributed evenly on surface of the soil. Low lying or high lying patches of the plots are the obstacles in uniform distribution of water because in our country gravitational irrigation is adopted which does not help in equal distribution of water. The farmers because of their illiteracy and ignorance do not have the adequate knowledge of the land levelling and shaping, and also do not have the knowledge of the benefits of land levelling and shaping. Thus, improper land levelling and shaping adversely affects the equal distribution of water.

Fragmented and Small Holdings

Land reforms' application has often helped the owner to make fake transfers taking out the land from the legal ambit. This trend further got incentives from the inadequate administrative support which has come in the way in an equal distribution of irrigation water. Similarly, the smallness and fragmented holdings are a stumbling blocks in the way of equal distribution of irrigation water because a small and marginal farmer cannot afford to have his own irrigation systems each block or field of fragmented holdings. In some cases, the size of holding is so small that the marginal and small farmers cannot afford even to have the small scale lift technology because it is not economical. Unfortunately, in our country, the irrigation cooperatives have neither been adopted by the farmers nor could either be taken up by the farmers with the legal support of Government support.

Factionalism

In several parts of the country, the consolidation of holding has either been not favoured or seriously implemented. It has often resulted in the factionalism or groupism in the rural areas and thus the consolidation of holding rather being a boon to the farmers has adversely affected the equal distribution of irrigation water.

The 'Bhoodan' launched by Late Acharya Vinoba Bhave could also not contribute much because of the fact that a large amount of land still awaits redistribution of the land received as donations from the big landlords or the big farmers. It has also been found that after redistribution of the donated land was either waste land or not suitable at all for cultivation purposes. The landless labours who have received the donated lands in 'Bhoodan' for cultivation purposes could not take up the cultivation because the size of the holding is very uneconomical. Such a situation is rather unsuitable for equal distribution of water.

To conclude the statement of Sri B. Venkatappiah, Ex-Member Planning Commission, Government of India, (while addressing the Indian Society of Agril. Eco. 29th Annual Conference, Dec. 30, 1969, Waltair.) is quoted:

"The individual studies on small farmers show that, while their handicaps differ from area to area, the major disadvantages are: fragmentation of holdings, insecutiy of tenure, inadequate and untimely supply of inputs including water, lack of credit facilities and unsatisfactory arrangement for marketing and storage. The studies also show that with support from irrigation, the new technological development makes it perfectly possible for even a small farm of say 1.21 to 2.02 hectares to be converted into a viable unit."

REFERENCES

1. Dantwala, M.L. & C.H. Shah (1971), 'Evaluation of Land Reforms (with special reference to the Western Region of India)', Indian Society of Agricutural Economics, Mahatama Gandhi Road, Fort, Bombay.
2. Comparative Experience of Agricultural Development in Developing Countries of Asia and the South-East since World War-II and Proceedings of International Seminar held at New Delhi October 25-28, 1971, Indian Society of Agricultural Economics, Bombay.
3. Indian Journal of Agricultural Economics, Conference Number, Oct.-Dec., 1984 Indian Society of Agricultural Economics, Mahatma Gandhi Road, Fort, Bombay.
4. Indian Journal of Agricultural Economics, Conference Number, July-Sept., 1976, Indian Society of Agricultural Economics, Mahatma Gandhi Road, Fort, Bombay.
5. Asian Productivity Organization, 'Farm-level Water Management in Selected Asian Countries', Report of a Multi-Country Study Mission, 12th-28th June, 1979, APO Project Code OSM/III/79, Tokyo, 1980.
6. Corey, G.L., 'Irrigation Water Management in India — Farmer Involvement', Unpublished Report, World Bank Mission, New Delhi, India, 1981.
7. Easter, K., William and Welsch, Dalane E., 'Socio-Economic Issues in Irrigation Development and Distribution', Economic Report BR 83-5, Department of Agricultural and Applied Economics, University of Minnesota, April, 1983.

8. Jayaraman, T.K., 'Farmers' Organizations in Surface Irrigation Projects: Two Empirical Studies from Gujarat', Economic and Political Weekly, Sept., 1981.
9. Lowdermilk, Max K. & Lattimore, Dan (ed.), 'Farmer Involvement', Planning Guide No. 2, Water Management Synthesis Project, Agricultural and Irrigation Engineering, Colorado State University, 1982.
10. Pant, Niranjan, 'Utilisation of Canal Water Below Outlet in Kosi Irrigation Project, Administrative and Community Level Solutions' Economic and Political Weekly, Review of Agriculture, Vol. XXI, No. 39, Sept., 1981.
11. Raghuvanshi, C.S., 'Socio-Economic Constraints in Adoption of Water Management Technology — A Case Study of Salawa Command', Proceedings of the Seminar on Water Management Technology Transfer, May, 1985, G.B. Pant University of Agriculture and Technology, Pantnagar.
12. Proceedings of the Seminar on Farmers' Participation in Irrigation Management (A Critical Consideration), Jan., 1986, Jaipur.

CHAPTER 15

ECONOMIC PRICING OF WATER: ECONOMIC AND FINANCIAL CRITERIA FOR FIXATION OF IRRIGATION CHARGES

WATER PRODUCTION FUNCTION FOR PRICING OF IRRIGATION WATER

Introduction

Agriculture's role in economic development requires that it expands production greatly through various increasing processes. Such a role requires development of new technology suited to the highly varied and specific conditions of developing countries. For this purpose, a widespread system of adaptive research is required. Once 'New Technology' is developed, it creates an enormous new demand for purchased inputs such as fertilisers and pesticides. In the process of development, the structure of demand for farm products changes which requires a vast new marketing structure. Failure of this structure to develop stifles an important aspect of agricultural development. Marketing and distribution firms have an important and expanding role to play in fostering technological change through risk reduction and education as well as through traditional task of distribution services.

Apart from material inputs *viz.* fertilisers, pesticides, improved implements and machineries, improved seeds supported by other services like credit, insurance, storage, marketing and processing are also required. In addition to this, an appropriate price policy is a crucial factor in the strategy of agricultural development which is manifested on account of firstly, modern agriculture increasingly involves the use of costly inputs as part of improved technology and hence an assured minimum price becomes a necessary condition for sustained agricultural production.

Secondly, price policy is also an important tool for facilitating crop planning. Finally, price policy can be geared towards ensuring that the relevant income levels of the farming community are not eroded by continuing unfavourable terms of trade between agricultural and non-agricultural sector. In the context, of development of agriculture, the major targets of scientific price policy are increased production and productivity, for which technology still remains the prime mover.

The fixing of price of principal farm products is becoming more of a charade than a rational exercise. The Agricultural Prices Commission[1] makes its recommendations before the start of each season after taking an objective assessment of relevant factors. The Union Agriculture Minister then convenes a Conference of Chief Ministers who overwhelm him with the pitched demand, for price well above the Agricultural Prices Commission's recommendations.

PRICE POLICY

Agricultural price policy is being used as an effective instrument for promoting agricultural development. This is done by announcing support prices for a number of crops, fully backed by institutional arrangements for government intervention in case the market prices tend to fall below this level. In respect of the two important cereals *viz.* rice and wheat, this policy has yielded rich dividends. Buffer stocks are built up through procurement at support prices which sustain the public distribution system. Enforcement of this policy over the years has demonstrated that agricultural development is directly related to the price policy through which the farmers are assured of a minimum support price.

Agricultural Inputs and Output Commission gives considerable emphasis to such policy measure which can induce increases in productivity, and to bring about such improvements in market structure which makes price policy much more effective. In making such recommendations on the non-price recommendations, receive very little attention from the public or policy makers. As a result, discussions which hinge around the level of price support in isolation, lose to overall perspective of price policy within the broad framework of agricultural policy. This Chapter covers that in the dynamic context of the developmental needs of the economy, the non-price recommendations of the Agricultural Inputs & Output Commission become an integral part of positive price policy. As the key to higher agricultural production lies in improving the efficiency of irrigation water and good water management at the field level, this aspect of agricultural technology is discussed in relation to Price Policy. The objective of agricultural price policy as enunciated by the terms of reference of the Agricultural Inputs and Output Commission also emphasises the developmental aspect of the price policy in as much as it states (i) the need to provide incentives to the producer for adopting improved technology for development of production pattern broadly in the light of national requirements, (ii) the need to ensure rational utilisation of land, water and other production resources, and (iii) likely effect of the price policy in the rest of the economy, particularly on the cost of living, level of wages, industrial cost structure etc. It is a known fact that one of the main planks of the agricultural price policy is to stimulate the production process through the adoption of technology and the rational use of such production resources as land, water etc.

POLICY FOR WATER CHARGES

Part of the responsibility of the managers engaged in water resources projects is to determine charges for project output *i.e.* irrigation water. The project manager needs guidelines to select a fair price and persuasive reasons to justify his decision to those required to pay. Prices are charged for two reasons:

(i) *Financial*: Enough money must be raised to recover the cost incurred in providing a good or service, *i.e.* water.

(ii) *Economic*: The quantity of goods the people buy depends on the price. If the price exceeds the marginal cost, full economic utilisation will be prevented. If the price is less than the marginal cost, an apparent demand will suggest an expansion which cannot be justified on economic grounds, only if price equals marginal cost, then market forces encourage the economic level of production.

Pricing also has a social function related to multi-dimensional nature of 'Social Welfare'. In addition to affecting economic efficiency, price levels influence income distribution, economic stability, the foreign trade balance and other social goals. Prices can be reduced to effect income redistribution, encourage more rapid utilization of project output during the building period, encourage substitution of project output for imports to improve the trade balance and encourage reinvestment by project beneficiaries.

A brief review is presented below regarding the pricing of water in developed countries and developing countries (like India) which highlight the various issues involved in pricing of water. Such a review will help in delineating the important aspects of pricing.

The United States of America seems to have done the pioneering work in the field of irrigation pricing. The Reclamation Act of 1902 required the users to pay the construction cost in a period of 10 years. No interest was to be charged. However, in due course of time when costlier projects were to be taken up, the forms of repayment had to be made liberal. In 1914, this period was lengthened to 20 years. In 1926 this was again extended to 40 years.

The Reclamation Project Act of 1939 drastically revised the policy itself from repayment of cost to charge based on the concept of 'ability to pay'. The Act authorised allocated-costs to be repaid from power revenues. This had brought in the possibilities to undertake more irrigation projects. Repayments were then based on the irrigators' 'ability to pay' over a period of 40 years. The said Act also modified the criteria for feasibility. The laying down of benefit-cost criteria, with the underlying principles of 'benefits and costs' to whomsoever they may accrue was a bold step in the said Act and revolutionalised the project economics. The flood control and navigaiton costs were non-reimbursable, and twenty-three years later, the Act of 1962 provided for a development period upto 10 years, during which payments were deferred.

Howe, C.W. (1971) in his Benefit-Cost Analysis for water system planning, pointed out that as a matter of social equity, it is considered necessary that the persons, who benefit from public investments should pay for these services. Of course, this obligation may not apply when the beneficiaries or the users cannot be easily identified or segregated, and also when objectives other than economic development are included.

Young and Bredehoeft (1972) in their economic model to simulate the response of irrigation water users to variations in water supply and costs, used the concept that in benefit based pricing it is necessary to determine the value of water in the production process. According to them, 'the response of the water using firm to alternative supply and cost conditions depends on its production possibilities and on the revenues and costs associated with these conditions. The concept of 'willingness to pay' is the most rational of imputing value of intermediate goods.

Davis, R.K. and S.H. Kanke (1972) studied pricing and efficiency in water resources management, and indicated that pricing of irrigation water should be done on the basis of normative economic theory of marginal cost pricing.

In 1973, Water Resources Council, U.S.A. published 'Principles and Standards of Water and Related Land Resources' wherein it is laid down: 'Reimbursement and cost sharing policies shall be directed generally to the end that identifiable beneficiaries bear an equitable share of cost commensurate with beneficial effects received in full cognizance of the planning objectives. Since existing cost sharing policies are not entirely consistent with this approach to planning water and land resources, these policies are being thoroughly reviewed, after which changes will be recommended. 'The Council also recommended the residual imputation method for imputing the value of agricultural water supply.'

Birgmann and Boussard (1976) summarised the various principles of irrigation water pricing as follows, on the basis of specific objectives:

(a) to cover only the working costs of the system,

(b) to provide total or partial reimbursement of public investment and to cover the working expenses,

(c) to charge marginal cost, and

(d) to allocate the benefits of irrigation between farmers and the community at large.

Major, D.C. (1977) in his "Multi-Objective Water Resources Planning" noted that long-term marginal cost pricing represents a more realistic situation. From the national point of view the construction of a new project provides a small increment to the total irrigation potential.

Young, R.A. (1979) conducted an economic analysis of Federal Irrigation Policy and suggested that while using the procedure of residual imputation, some of the assumptions and pitfalls should be borne in mind, which are:

(a) If any of the variable resource is inadvertantly omitted, or not adequately accounted for, its contribution gets assigned to water with consequent increase in the value of water.

(b) If any of the inputs are subsidized, or there is price support to commodities, the value of water gets inflated.

(c) Euler's postulate holds good under ideal conditions at a particular level of resource use and for a particular mix of inputs.

(d) The assumption that the marginal productivity of other inputs equal their marginal productivity is seldom achieved for want of proper information as well as other uncertainties inherent in agriculture.

PRICING IN INDIA

As far back as 1959, National Council of Applied Ecnomics Research in their report summarised that the only sound basis for fixing irrigation rates is the net additional benefit after irrigation over net benefit before irrigation. The condition of majority of cultivators who own small holdings is to be kept in mind by the State while fixing water rates.

The Irrigation Commission of India (1972) reviewed the irrigation rates and the considerations on which these are fixed. The Commission noted the fact that irrigation is included in the State list of the Constitution and the primary responsibility to look after the said subject is that of the States. There is considerable diversity in the system for levying irrigation charges in different States. The rates charged are generally based on crop area basis. In some States the charges are levied on year to year basis. In eastern part of the country, long term agreements upto ten years are made. There is no uniform basis for having irrigation charges. The Planning Commission and other Central authorities have been impressing upon the State Governments for a rational pricing system. However, social and political forces have been active against increase in the water rates. Though, there have been some revision, these are minor compared to the problem size. The water charge varies not only from State to State, but from one part to another and from one project to another.

The Commission, therefore, recommended benefit or income based pricing, rather than cost based price. 'The irrigator is primarily interested in the net gain from irrigation, and to him, the cost incurred in making water available is of little consequence. His willingness to pay for water varies in proportion to the gain that he expects from its use. From the irrigator's point of view, therefore, water rates should be related to the benefit, which irrigation confers, rather than to the cost of irrigation projects'.

Seckler, D. (1981) in his 'The Era of Irrigation Management in India' advocated the principle of equal rights for the use of water by all the inhabitants of the village. Water rights in the form of coupons are given to each family. The farmer then has the right to use the water, or trade off with other users for consideration of money through the water users association. This system has been tried in a small project, 'Sukhomajri' in a village of Haryana of same name and the system is named after the village.

Padhi, G.N. (1983) studied in detail the 'Pricing Policy of Irrigation Water' and arrived at the following conclusions:

(i) Pricing on the value or productivity of water in crop production is preferred to a cost-based pricing.

(ii) The benefit from use of water in crop production is equitably shared by the users and investors. The user is allowed full share for his contribution to national objectives.

(iii) Social equity demands discriminatory pricing to account for risk and income distribution effects. National/regional párameters should be prescribed.

(iv) Recovery of cost need not be an objective. The impact of pricing on cost recovery should be exhibited in the feasibility studies. A lower discount rate than that used for economic evaluation need be prescribed for project feasibility.

(v) Pricing policy guidelines should be prescribed for rationality and uniformity in pricing. The present water charges (Table 5) are much on the lower side and there is need for upward revision. (The price suggested by Padhi are given in Table 3).

(vi) Crop area based pricing would not be an effective way for eliminating over irrigation. Demand based allocation and distribution should be enforced.

The Managers engaged in Water Resources Projects output are particularly responsible to determine the charges of irrigation water and hence the Project Managers are responsible to decide a fair price with a persuasive reason to justify their decision to those required to pay the irrigation charges. Pricing also has a social function related to multi-dimensional nature of 'social welfare'. In addition to effecting economic efficiency, price levels influence income distribution, economic stability, the foreign trade balance and other social goals.

FINANCIAL REQUIREMENT

In perfect competition, the financial and economic functions of irrigation charges are satisfied. For fixation of price P and the output O, marginal cost equals the average cost at the point of intersection and the product of P and O equals the total cost. Thus the financial requirement is satisfied. Since the marginal cost equals the price, the economic requirement is also satisfied.

However, if the economies of large-scale production are large or say total demand is small, the optium scale may be almost as large as total market demand. The optimum O is still determined by the point where marginal costs equal marginal benefits. The price satisfying the economic requirement is P_1. But, only the average cost resulting P_2 for producing O need be charged to satisfy the financial requirement. Marginal cost pricing will produce a profit equal to $(P_1 – P_2)Q$, which if large enough, may justify an additional production unit. If demand is smaller than the optimum production-unit size, the marginal-cost curve intersects the demand curve at an output level where average cost exceeds marginal cost (Fig. 1). The price P_1 will satisfy the *economic requirement*. But the price would have to be P_2 or the average cost, in order to satisfy financial requirement.

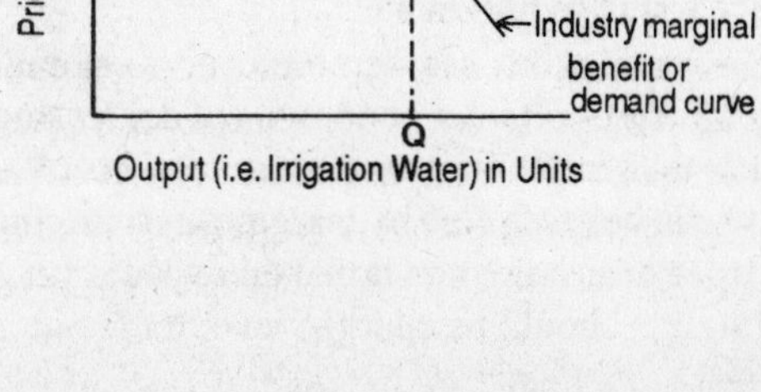

Fig. 1 Showing Fixation of Water Charges Under Pure Competition

Further, in case of increasing average cost (Fig. 2 at the market-determined level of production), a charge fixed by the economic requirement more than satisfies the *financial requirement*, whereas in case of decreasing average cost, there is a dilemma. Marginal cost pricing P_1 does not raise enough revenue and average-cost pricing P_2 restricts economic use. However, some adjustment between the conflicting requirements is required.

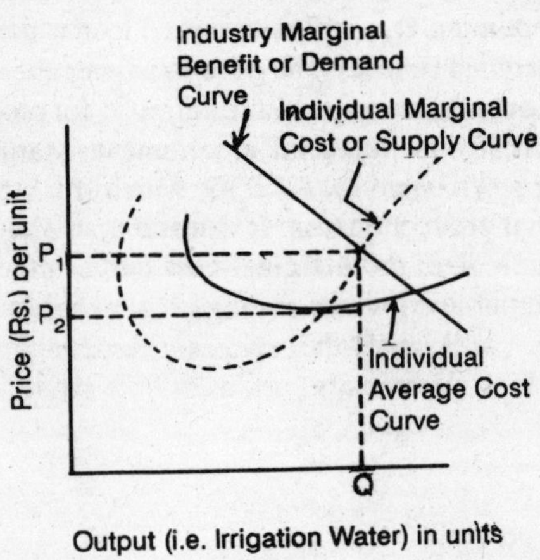

Fig. 2 Showing the Fixation of Price for large Optimum Production Unit (Increasing Average Cost)

FINANCIAL AND ECONOMIC REQUIREMENT*

There are three available alternative approaches to reconcile between financial and economic requirements:

(i) Price Discrimination can be employed to capture some of the consumer's surplus under conditions of decreasing average cost, and the total benefit may exceed the total cost P_2Q even though only P_1Q can be recovered by marginal cost pricing. The primary goal in price discrimination is that those benefitting by an amount exceeding P_1, should be charged an extra fee in order to satisfy

*Source: Economics of Water Resources Planning, L. Douglas James and Robert R. Lee, pp. 541-550, Tata McGraw-Hill Publishing Co., Ltd., New Delhi.

the revenue requirement, which could result in a marginal cost fee plus a surplus fee. Surplus fee varies with the value the consumer derives from use of the output. However, in practice, it is difficult to discriminate among individual users. A typical example of price discrimination is that industrial users are charged higher charges for water than agricultural users. The application of price discrimination requires division of the users into the groups, as resorted by marketers by adopting 'Market Segmentation'.

(ii) Benefactor – an outside benefactor is found who should be willing to subsidize the project by the amount $(P_1-P_2)Q$. In water resources planning, the benefactor is usually Union Govt. while this approach satisfies the revenue requirement. However, it distorts economic resource allocation by divertiing to the project, tax funds which have greater value in other uses. It redistributes income from those paying the taxes to those receiving the subsidies.

(iii) Non-Marginal Charge or Tax – it is used to raise the revenue (P_1-P_2) Q. While maintaining marginal-cost pricing is to levy a non-marginal charge or tax on those using the output. Thus, each user would pay a flat fee independent of the quantity used plus a charge per unit of use. The unit charge would equal the marginal cost, while the flat fee would be set to raise the balance of the required revenue. The non-marginal levy may be assessed in various ways. In case of irrigation water, an equal sum could be charged to each user. A charge could be made proportional to farm size, or a charge could be made proportional to farm value.

Of the three approaches the non-marginal charge or tax, is the fairest because it considers both the size of the farm and the quality of the land. Use of a non-marginal charge requires both user benefit and ability to pay to exceed the levy. If more benefits accrue to output users, price discrimination works best where users can be grouped by unit benefit received and a non-marginal charge works best where users receive approximately equal unit benefits. A combination of the above mentioned approaches may be used for a large project producing diverse kinds of output.

Using either of the criteria, it is essential that the investments in irrigation should be evaluated like investment in any other sector.*

---

*Apart from this, 'It is now established that Indian farmers do respond to price stimuli. Therefore, price mechanism could also be used by the Government to achieve desired targets'. (Prof. Manmohan Singh, the then Dy. Chairman, Planning Commission, 'Vijnana Parichaya' Indian Institute of Science, Bangalore, March, 1986, p-4).

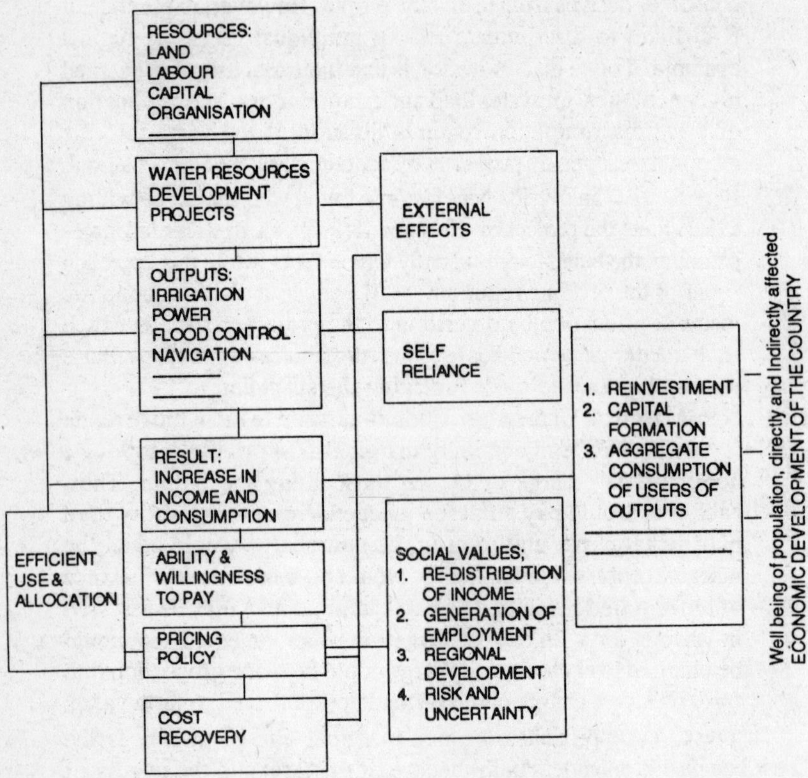

FLOW CHART1 WATER RESOURCES–PROJECT OUTPUT PRICING

ECONOMIC CRITERIA FOR PRICING OF WATER

Pricing of output is essential for evaluating a project by finding out (1) whether the cost of the project can be recovered in due course of time, and (2) also to some extent to save for investment in future projects. Pricing affects many economic and non-economic activities on the one hand, and on the other hand, price is determined due to the pressure exerted by these activities on the price fixing criterion.

Flow Chart 1 indicates the various steps involved in planning and implementation of a Water Resources Project, and also the forces acting upon the output pricing, The inter-dependent factors/forces have also been indicated.

The purpose of building a Water Resources Project is to suitably change the availability of water in a stream both in space and time, so that the available water is put to its most beneficial use. Such projects employ factors of production like land, labour, capital and organisation. The primary output of a project could be irrigation water and/or hydroelectric energy, flood control, navigation, conservation etc. The output (intermediate goods) help in producing marketable consumer goods which would in turn increase the income and consumption of the people directly benefitted by the project.

With the increase in income, the 'ability to pay' and 'willingness to pay' a higher price for the output (here water) also goes up, as also consumption of goods and services. But just because there is increase in income, it is not possible to raise the price of the output – say irrigation water–proportionately. This increase is restrained by many social, economic and political factors.

Hence, a pricing policy, has to take into consideration the following aspects:

(a) An efficient use and allocation of the factor of production, the Water Resources Project as a whole, each one of the output of W.R. Project, and finally the increased income and consumption capacity.

(b) Recovery of cost involved on the Water Resources Project which in turn is affected by (i) need for self-reliance or self-dependency, and (ii) external effects of diverting the resources to competitive channels, etc.

(c) Maintaining of social values by (i) covering risk involved, (ii) encouraging equitable distribution of income, and (iii) helping the development of under-developed regions.

The ultimate aim of such a pricing of water resources project's output is in the interest of the 'National Economic Development' through re-investment, capital formation and increased aggregate consumption of output by users.

The general principles concerned to overall Water Resources Project, and the fixation of price of water in particular has the following objectives:

(i) to maximise the efficiency in the use of irrigation water,

(ii) to achieve equitable sharing of the benefits, between the direct beneficiaries of irrigation and rest of the country-man,

(iii) to accelerate overall income distribution and achievement of social equity, and

(iv) to speed up economic growth of the country and regional development.

PRODUCTION FUNCTION APPROACH FOR PRICING OF IRRIGATION WATER

Calculation of the potential output of a particualr crop is an extremely complex function of climatic, nutritional and management inputs. Therefore, to develop a model for output calculation, the uncontrolable variables have to be considered as constraint. This yield response of crops to various inputs could be expressed as:

$$Y = f(X_1, X_2, X_3, X_4 \ldots. X_n)$$

where, Y = output of the crop

$X_1, X_2, X_3, X_4 \ldots. X_n$ = levels of various inputs

However, for developing water-crop-yield relationship, water alone is considered as the variable input and all other inputs are held constant *i.e*. kept at fixed levels, *i.e.*

$$Y = f(X_w/X_1, X_2 \ldots. X_{n-1})$$

Price Fixation

Apart from the above consideration production function of a given crop, the other two main factors which have to be taken into account for price fixation are (a) the demand for irrigation water, and (b) capacity to pay and willingness to pay for the water used.

(a) Demand for Irrigation Water

When the water requirement of crops is wholly met by irrigation, the amount of water that a rational farmer would use is guided by:

(i) the shape of production function,
(ii) the price of the product *i.e.* yield, and
(iii) the price or cost of irrigation water.

One of the simplest models suggested by Dr. G.N. Padhi is given below:

Objective function, Max Z = Increase in net farm income
Subject to Y = f(X), the production function
or Max Z = $Y.P_y - X.P_x - C$ subject to
Y = f(X)

where,

P_y = Unit price of crop
P_x = Unit price of water
C = Cost of cultivation (excluding water)
(C is considered constant, since all other inputs are kept at fixed levels)

The Lagrangian function

$$L = Y, P_y - X.P_x - C + \lambda\,[Y\text{-}F(X)]$$

where, λ is the Lagrangian Multipler
differentiating

$$\frac{\delta L}{Y} = P_y + \lambda$$

$$\frac{\delta L}{X} = P_x + \lambda \frac{\delta F(X)}{\delta X} \quad \text{and} \quad \frac{\delta L}{\delta X} = Y - F(X)$$

Equating each expression to zero, it follows that

$$\frac{\delta F(X)}{\delta X} = -P_x/P_y$$

Since the price of crop is known, it is generally possible to determine the various values of X for different levels of water application, corresponding to different values of P_x *i.e.* price of water. This relationship is the demand function of water. As the price of water increases, the demand may decrease and *vice versa*, with the usual negative slope of the demand function. Such a demand curve is known as the static factor demand curve, because the level of other inputs are assumed to be unchanged with variation in quantity of water demanded.

This static factor demand curve has some specific characteristics. While calculating the marginal value product, the incremental yield is fully attributed to water. But the fact is that the user not only has to pay for the marginal unit of water but has also to pay for the full quantum of water. From the total value, if the cost of all other inputs are deducted, the residual may not be sufficient to meet the water charges. As such, the 'price' as obtained from the static factor demand curve does not represent the 'willingness to pay' – which needs also to be taken into account for obtaining a real basis for pricing.

(b) Capacity and Willingness to pay

When there is some balance left over, out of the total produce, after paying for all the inputs, the farmers would be willing to pay for the irrigation water they use. This procedure has, however, to be adopted for each level of water use. The method of calculation of the capacity to pay could be adopted as:

$$\frac{\text{Residual or Net value product}}{\text{Quantity of water demanded}} = \text{Capacity to pay}$$

'Capacity or ability to pay' is not necessarily equal to 'willingness to pay'. However, if there are no outside forces (socio, economic or political) working on the mind of the farmer, and when he has a real need or demand for a particular amount (at a particular time) of water, his ability normally becomes his willingness to pay.

Model Applied

Fig. 3 shows the ability to pay (ATP) for various levels of water application. The maximum ability to pay is at the point (Q), where it intersects the demand curve. This (PQ) could be called the equilibrium price per unit of water. The AVP and ATP curves are almost flat beyond the intersection point, because of the low marginal productivity. The relevant range of applicability is quite small. On account of this, when this Model is applied, the quantity of water demanded is not sensitive to pricing.

The most desirable situation for price fixation is obtained at the stage of 'OP' Cm. of water application at the 'equilibrium' price of Rs. 'OR' per Cm. *i.e.*, where the marginal product equals the ability to pay.

From the point of view of ability to pay, the quantity of water demanded is almost equal to the Xmax. This illustration is also applicable in most of the cases (as shown in Table 1) since the shape of production for different crops are not very different.

But due to other uncertainties *viz*. technological and weather conditions inherent in crop production, it may not be worthwhile to determine the optimum quantity of water from production function, which approaches the maximum. Further, the production functions are derived under laboratory (*i.e*. experimental farm) conditions and their use for decisions at farm levels in general may lead to erroneous results. On the basis of this limitation and realising fully that the price to be obtained with the use of different models may not be realistic. The Irrigation Department is charging only a fraction of the price (Table 2) derived according to the Production Function Model. This practice needs a lot of improvement. It is not proper to discard a scientific method of production function analysis branding it as unreliable and defective. Pricing of water has to be based on scientific methods (No one would disagree on this point) and hence the best method available now is the production function analysis which should be improved, so as to give a more realistic calculation. Based on this, and taking into consideration the other socio-economic and even political aspects (at times) a more accurate water charges should be levied. In any case, the present method of paying only nominal charges (based on unscientific assumptions or calculations) is totally defective and needs earliest substitution by a better method.

An increase in water charges would be in the interest of the nation, and that would also provide an opportunity for the neo-rich farmers to contribute their share for national development.

Prevailing Water Rates in the States

To make a comparison, the prevailing water rates in different parts of the country are shown in Table 3. There is a large variation in the prices charged from State to State, as can be seen from the following:

Crop	Lowest per Ha State		Highest per Ha	
1. Paddy	Rs. 3.71	Tamil Nadu	Rs. 123.55	Gujarat
2. Wheat	Rs. 13.59	Punjab	Rs. 150.00	Maharashtra
3. Cotton	Rs. 3.71	Tamil Nadu	Rs. 250.00	Maharashtra
4. Sugarcane	Rs. 11.12	Tamil Nadu	Rs. 850.00	Gujarat
5. Garden Orchard	Rs. 14.38	Uttar Pradesh	Rs. 239.45	West Bengal
			(Summer rate, for any crop)	

In general, the water rates in Tamil Nadu are found to be the lowest, whereas highest are in Gujarat and Maharashtra. This may probably be due to the fact that in Tamil Nadu, farmers generally grow such crops except paddy which require less amount of water. The farmers' ability to pay is also comparatively low.

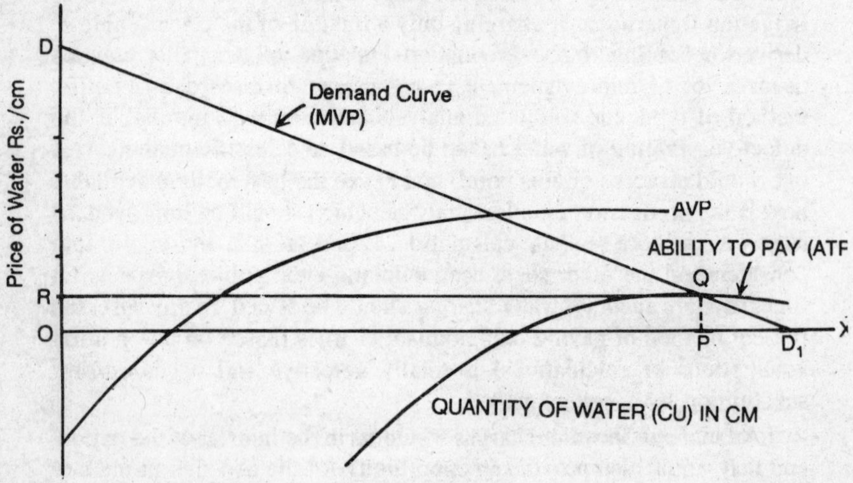

Fig. 2: Pricing of Water-Production Function Approach

TABLE 1

Price of Water

Sl. No.	Name of crop	Net income from irrigated crop	Ability to pay	Price to be charged		
				Large farmers	Medium farmers	Small farmers
1.	Wheat	1210	337	368.70	292.30	207.60
2.	Oilseeds	885	147	160.80	136.40	92.40
3.	Pulses	935	188	216.60	183.70	122.50
4.	Potato	1950	610	667.30	529.00	378.00
5.	Gram	1050	290	317.30	251.50	179.90
6.	Sugarcane	1805	419	458.40	363.80	259.70

Source: Ph.D. thesis – Padhi G.N. (earlier cited), p. 167.

TABLE 2

Water Rates for and Income from, Principal Crops in U.P. (for flow irrigation)

Sl. No.	Crop	Water rate per ha.	Income
1.	Rice	41.83 to 98.84	1035
2.	Wheat	44.48 to 99.84	1210
3.	Cotton	9.80 to 39.54	885
4.	Sugarcane	34.69 to 197.69	1805
5.	Garden Orchards	14.38 to 74.13	N.A.
6.	Oil Seeds	N.A.	885
7.	Pulses	N.A.	935
8.	Potato	N.A.	1950
9.	Gram	N.A.	1050

Source: Ph.D. thesis – Padhi G.N. (earlier cited), extract from pp. 433-40 (duly modified).

TABLE 3

Water Rates for Principal Crops in Various States of India for Flow Irrigation (Rs. per hectare)

Sl. No.	Name of State	Rice	Wheat	Cotton	Sugarcane	Garden Orchards
1.	Andhra Pradesh	74.13	49.42	49.42	74.13	-
2.	Bihar	40.76 to 77.80	33.45 to 44.46	-	122.27 to 211.19	25.92 to 40.76
3.	Gujarat	74.13 to 123.55	74.13 to 103.78	-	585.65 to 850.05	-
4.	Haryana	49.42 to 74.13	19.77 to 61.78	29.65 to 61.78	49.42 to 98.84	61.78
5.	Karnataka	49.42 to 74.13	44.48	44.48	197.69 to 296.53	88.96
6.	Madhya Pradesh	39.54 to 59.31	37.06 to 49.42	39.54	98.80 to 148.20	98.84
7.	Maharashtra	50.00 to 100.00	75.00 to 150.00	250.00	750.00	-
8.	Orissa	59.31	22.23	37.06	66.69	44.46
9.	Punjab	48.19 to 48.83	13.59 to 29.13	32.54 to 38.92	66.72 to 81.55	15.86 to 51.40
10.	Rajasthan	34.60 to 51.78	29.65 to 37.06	49.42 to 61.78	74.13 to 86.49	83.93
11.	Tamil Nadu	3.71 to 60.78	9.98 to 61.78	3.71 to 49.42	11.12 to 74.13	7.41 to 74.13
12.	U.P.	41.83 to 98.84	44.48 to 99.84	9.88 to 39.54	34.69 to 197.69	14.38 to 99.84
13.	West Bengal	49.42 Kharif	0.930 Rabi			239.45

Note: Water rates have since been revised in some States.

For details, See (1) Padhi, G.N. 'Pricing Policy for Irrigation Water unpublished Ph.D. thesis (Aug. 83), University of Roorkee, Roorkee (2) Padhi, G.N. 'Pricing of Irrigation Water: Production Function Approach', Journal of Indian Water Resources Society, Roorkee, Vol. 4, No. 1, p. 39.

REFERENCES

1. Padhi, G.N., Pricing Policy for Irrigation Water unpublished Ph.D. thesis, W.R.D.T.C., University of Roorkee, Roorkee, 1983.
2. James L. Douglas and Lee, R. Robert, Economics of Water Resources Planning, Tata McGraw Hill Publishing Company Ltd., New Delhi, 1971.
3. Padhi, G.N., Pricing of Irrigation Water: Water Production Function Approach, Journal of Indian Water Resources Society, Roorkee, Vol. 4, No. 1, p. 39.
4. Pandey, S.N. (1981), 'Effect of Price on Fertilizer Consumption, Fertiliser News, Vol. 26, No. 12, pp. 12-15.
5. Dwivedi, R.C. (1972), 'New Strategy of Agricultural Development in India', Layal Book Depot, Ludhiana.
6. Hall, Warren A. and Dracup, John, A., Water Resources Systems Engineering, McGraw Hill Book Company, New York, 1970.
7. Report of the National Commission on Agriculture, Govt. of India, 1976.
8. Heady, Earl O., Economics of Agricultural Production and Resource Use, Prentice Hall, New Delhi, India, 1968.
9. Mande, O.D., Evaluation of Social Benefits and Costs of Conjunctive Use of Surface and Ground Waters in Gomti Kalyani Doab, unpublished M.E. Dissertation, WRDTC, University of Roorkee, 1980.
10. Indian Journal of Agricultural Economics, Conf. Number, Oct.-Dec. 78, Vol. XXXIII, No. 4, Indian Society of Agricultural Economics, Mahatma Gandhi Road, Fort, Bombay.
11. Report of the Irrigation Commission, Govt. of India, 1972.
12. Indian Journal of Agricultural Economics, July-September, 1984, Vol. XXXIX, No. 3, Indian Society of Agricultural Economics, Mahatma Gandhi Road, Fort, Bombay.
13. Indian Journal of Agricultural Economics, Oct.-Dec. 1985, Vol. XI, No. 4 Indian Society of Agricultural Economics, Mahatma Gandhi Road, Fort, Bombay.
14. Institutional Framework on Improved On-Farm Water Management in Pakistan, Special Report Prepared by Water Management Research Project Staff, Colorado, State University, U.S.A.
15. Pradhan, B.B. (1987), "Pricing of Energy: An Analytical Study of Jaldhaka Hydro Electric Project", unpublished M.E. Dissertation, WRDTC, University of Roorkee, U.P.
16. Mishra, S.N. and Beyer, John (1976), "Cost-Benefit Analysis — A Case Study of the Ratnagiri Fisheries Project", Hindustan Publishing Corporation (India), Delhi.